New Yeats Papers XIII

Liam Miller

The Noble Drama
of W. B. Yeats

DUBLIN : The Dolmen Press   NORTH AMERICA : Humanities Press Inc.

Set in Pilgrim type
and printed and published in the Republic of Ireland
at the Dolmen Press,
North Richmond Industrial Estate, North Richmond Street, Dublin 1

Published in the United States of America and in Canada by
Humanities Press Inc.,
171 First Avenue, Atlantic Highlands, N.J. 07716

First published 1977

ISBN 0 85105 301 7 THE DOLMEN PRESS
ISBN 0 391 00633 9 HUMANITIES PRESS INC.

Library of Congress Cataloging in Publication Data
Miller, Liam.
  The noble drama of W. B. Yeats.
  (New Yeats papers; 13)
    1. Yeats, William Butler 1865-1939. 2. Theater ——
Great Britain. I. Title. II. Series.
PR5906.M48 1976   822'.8   76-18813

Contents

The Noble Drama of W. B. Yeats

'When our political passions have died out in the fulfillment
of their aims shall we, I wonder, have a fine native drama of
our own? It is likely.'   *United Ireland*, 11 July 1891

Early dramatic poems
The Land of Heart's Desire

'It will take a generation, and perhaps generations, to restore
the theatre of Art; for one must get one's actors, and perhaps
one's scenery, from the theatre of commerce, until new actors
and new painters have come to help one.'   *Beltaine*, 1899

The Irish Literary Theatre 1899-1901

The Countess Cathleen
Diarmid and Grania

Beltaine
Samhain

'Our movement is a return to the people, like the Russian
movement of the early seventies, and the drama of society
could but magnify a condition of life which the countryman
and the artisan could but copy to their hurt.'   *Samhain* 1902

The National Theatre Society 1902-1904

Cathleen Ni Houlihan
Where There is Nothing
The Pot of Broth
The Hour-Glass
The King's Threshold
The Shadowy Waters (first version)

'It will be necessary to create a household of living art in
Dublin, and principles that have become habits, and a public
that has learnt to care for a play because it is a play and not
serviceable to some cause.'   *Samhain 1904*

The Abbey Theatre 1904-1909
On Baile's Strand
Deirdre

'It was only by watching my own plays that I came to understand that this reverie, this twilight between sleep and waking, this bout of fencing, alike on the stage and in the mind, between man and phantom, this perilous path as on the edge of a sword, is the condition of tragic pleasure, and to understand why it is so rare and so brief.'

'The Tragic Theatre': *The Mask*, 1910

'Perhaps some day a play in the form I am adapting for European purposes shall awake once more, whether in Gaelic or in English, under the slope of Slieve-na-Mon or Croagh Patrick ancient memories; for this form has no need of scenery that runs away with money nor of a theatre building.'

Certain Noble Plays of Japan, 1916

'I want so much — an audience of fifty, a room worthy of it (some great dining-room or drawing-room), half a dozen young men and women who can dance or speak verse or play drum and flute and zither, and all the while, instead of a profession, I but offer them "an accomplishment." '

'A People's Theatre': *The Irish Statesman*, 1919

'When I remember the great honour that you have conferred upon me, I cannot forget many known and unknown persons. Perhaps the English committees would never have sent you my name if I had written no plays, no dramatic criticism, if my lyric poetry had not a quality of speech practised upon

the stage, perhaps even — though this could be no portion of their deliberate thought — if it were not in some degree the symbol of a movement.'
    'The Irish Dramatic Movement' (Nobel Prize address) 1923
        1923-1929
        Sophocles' King Oedipus
        Sophocles' Oedipus at Colonus
        The Resurrection (first version)
        Vrouwe Emer's Groote Strijd
        Fighting the Waves

    'I must speak of things that come out of the common consciousness, where every thought is like a bell with many echoes.' *Wheels and Butterflies*, 1934
        1930-1938
        The Words Upon the Window Pane
        The Resurrection (final version)
        The King of the Great Clock Tower
        A Full Moon in March
        The Herne's Egg
        Purgatory

    'I have had greater luck than any other modern English-speaking dramatist; I have aimed at tragic ecstasy and here and there in my own work and in the work of my friends I have seen it greatly played.' *On the Boiler*, 1939
        1939
        The Death of Cuchulain

        On the Boiler

*

Illustrations

Plates

Illustrations in the text

Introduction

This book has grown out of an obsession with Yeats's plays which has lasted for over a quarter of a century, and expresses a desire to see the plays and to have them seen in the context for which they were created — the stage. While several excellent books treat of the plays as literature, I felt that there was a need to view Yeats as a man of theatre and to look behind that one of the many 'masks' which make up his long creative life. This facet of Yeats's life and work is reflected in the statement he made in his last year that he had given so much of his life to the expression of other men's genius. So my study must, while it treats mainly of Yeats's own development as a playwright, take into account his position as a catalyst and consider the great deal of his life which was concerned with the development and organisation of the Irish National Theatre.

Our National Theatre, later more popularly known by the name of its playhouse, the Abbey, must be acknowledged as largely Yeats's creation — a creation which had its origin in his contact with the national traditions of Ireland through John O'Leary and Standish O'Grady in the 1880s. For over fifty years, Yeats nurtured his creation and watched it develop along lines which seemed at times to run contrary to his concerns about Ireland. By 1891 he pondered in a review whether his countrymen should ever have a fine native drama of their own. Three years later, the first play of his to be performed was presented on a London stage and, in 1899, before the century was out, Dublin saw, in the first season of the Irish Literary Theatre, the first manifestation of the movement from which our National Theatre developed.

While Yeats's career in theatre, and its extent and involvement, would represent a magnificent lifetime's achievement for any man, it is only one part, and not necessarily the largest, of an extraordinarily creative life, and thus must be looked at in the context of the other parts of that life. As a man of theatre he concerned himself with every aspect of the processes which end in the realisation of the play before its audience — the formation of a company of players, finding directors, designers, scene-painters, musicians and choreographers and, on occasion, designing and directing plays himself.

Yeats's own plays, written at first for the 'public' theatre, with a few exceptions gradually developed into pieces to be played in intimate surroundings. But, for whatever scale of theatre they were written, all his plays are informed by an instinct for theatre practice which, I feel, has not been equalled by any other great dramatic poet for centuries past. His development as a playwright was extraordinary, from his early experiments inspired by Shelley and the other Romantics to the development of his own unique form of drama which derived from the Nō, the aristocratic theatre of Japan. Much of his own work was, perhaps, before its time and I feel that only now have we developed a theatre which can present the Noble Drama of W. B. Yeats to its deserved audience.

My own interest in staging Yeats goes back about thirty years, when Kevin O'Carroll and the Company of the Green Circle in London allowed me to present several of the plays in their little basement theatre. Much later, work at the Lantern Theatre in Dublin enabled me to experiment further and extend my knowledge. In July 1967 the directors of the Abbey Theatre invited me to mount an exhibition, 'Stage Design at the Abbey Theatre,' and to contribute my thoughts on the Noble Drama of W. B. Yeats as a lecture illustrated by excerpts performed by the younger members of the company during the seminar that accompanied the exhibition. The principal encouragement which led to writing this book came from Mrs. W. B. Yeats who showed me the notebook in which Yeats recorded his experiments with the Gordon Craig screens, letters from Craig to Yeats, designs by Robert Gregory and other documents which opened my eyes to Yeats's wide knowledge of theatre practice. Miss Anne Yeats and Senator Michael B. Yeats have continued to express an interest in the work. The late T. R. Henn invited me to speculate further in a lecture at Sligo and a performance there of the later ballads. Many friends on both sides of the Atlantic have looked at and discussed sections of the work in progress. Here I am especially indebted to David R. Clark, Robin Skelton, Robert Hogan, and Robert O'Driscoll. Kathleen Raine provided the interpretation of Miss Horniman's letter offering the Abbey Theatre to Yeats. Mrs. Croese of the Stadsschouwburg, Amsterdam, was indefatigable in providing details and programmes of the Dutch productions in the 1920's. Herman Chessid led me to Mrs. Antheil, and located Elgar's score for *Diarmid and Grania*. Michael Scott advised on the architectural details of the original Abbey and Peacock Theatres.

My wife, Jo, has borne patiently with my interminable experiments and discussions and has even sewn costumes for some of my productions. I have leaned heavily on the indulgence of my own Press during the two years the book has been in production, and feel especially indebted to Eileen Power who has typed the entire work, verified the quotations and made possible the assembly of the text which I present below.

LIAM MILLER   1964-1977

Acknowledgements

Grateful acknowledgement is made to the holders of copyright for all matter quoted in this book, and to the sources of text illustrations and plates. If I have committed any involuntary infringement of copyright, I apologise for my apparent negligence.

Acknowledgement is made :

To Miss Anne Yeats, Senator Michael B. Yeats, A. P. Watt & Son, Macmillan Publishers Limited and the Macmillan Company of New York for permission to quote from the work of W. B. Yeats; to Miss Anne Yeats and Senator Michael B. Yeats for permission to transcribe and reproduce sections from the scene notebook of W. B. Yeats; to Miss Anne Yeats, Senator Michael B. Yeats and the Directors of the Cuala Press for permission to reproduce pages and texts from Cuala Press editions.

To the Administrators of the Estate of Edward Gordon Craig for quotations from Craig's works.

To Colin Smythe Limited for quotations from *Our Irish Theatre* by Lady Gregory, edited by Roger McHugh, and from *Hail & Farewell* by George Moore, edited by Richard Cave.

To Proscenium Press and Professor Robert Hogan for quotations from *Joseph Holloway's Irish Theatre*, edited by Robert Hogan and Michael O'Neill.

To Southern Illinois University Press for quotations from *Joseph Holloway's Abbey Theatre*, edited by Robert Hogan and Michael O'Neill.

To Miss Riette Sturge Moore for permission to quote from her father's letters in *W. B. Yeats and T. Sturge Moore. Their Correspondence 1901-1937* edited by Ursula Bridge.

To New Directions Publishing Corporation for quotations from *The Classic Noh Theatre of Japan* by Ernest Fenollosa and Ezra Pound.

To the Society of Authors on behalf of the Estate of George Bernard Shaw for quotations from Shaw's letters to Florence Farr.

To the Society of Authors as the literary representative of the Estate of James Joyce, and to the Viking Press, Inc., for a passage from *The Day of the Rabblement*.

To Faber and Faber Limited and Farrar, Straus & Giroux, Inc., for a passage from T. S. Eliot's memorial lecture on Yeats, published in *On Poetry and Poets*, © 1957 by T. S. Eliot.

To Professor David R. Clark for a passage from *W. B. Yeats and the Theatre of Desolate Reality*.

To Professor Donald Keene and Kodansha International for a quotation from *Nō, the Classical Theatre of Japan*.

To Mrs. Eileen O'Casey and Macmillan Publishers Limited for a passage from *Inishfallen, Fare Thee Well* by Sean O'Casey.

To Novello & Company Limited for permission to reproduce the title page of, and a lyric from, Edward Elgar's Opus 42.

To Mrs. Boski E. Antheil for a fragment of George Antheil's unpublished score to *Fighting the Waves* and for a passage from *Bad Boy of Music* by George Antheil.

To Miss Anne Yeats for permission to reproduce from her collection, designs by Edward Gordon Craig, Robert Gregory and Charles Ricketts.

To Senator Michael B. Yeats for permission to reproduce Edmund Dulac's mask for Cuchulain and John B. Yeats's drawings of Miss Horniman and Frank Fay.

To D. Travers Smith (Mrs. D. Robinson) for the use of photographs of her designs for *Fighting the Waves*.

To the Stadsschouwburg, Amsterdam, for the use of photographs of Hildo Krop's masks for *Vrouwe Emer's Groote Strijd*.

To Miss Norah McGuinness for permission to reproduce a costume design for *The Only Jealousy of Emer*.

To the Directors of the Abbey Theatre and to its Press Officer, Miss Deirdre McQuillan, for access to their programme collection and for permission to reproduce the portrait of Joseph Holloway by Lilian Davidson, the photographs of F. J. McCormick and Dulac's cartoon of W. B. Yeats.

To the Governors and Guardians of the National Gallery of Ireland and to its Director, Mr. James White.

To the National Library of Ireland and its Director, Mr. Alf MacLochlainn.

This book is for Oliver, and in memory of Kevin

1 *a fine native drama of our own*

'I was in all things Pre-Raphaelite,'[1] W. B. Yeats recalled in the second volume of his *Autobiographies, Four Years*, printed at his sister's Cuala Press in 1921. He was describing his fifteen- or sixteen-year-old self, a student at the art school in Kildare Street, Dublin, friend and contemporary of George W. Russell (1867-1935) who as 'Æ', the poet, playwright, and mystic, was to play a large part in the early development of Ireland's National Theatre movement, and of Oliver Sheppard (1864-1941), the sculptor whose 'Death of Cuchulain' in bronze stands in Dublin's General Post Office to commemorate the Easter Rising of 1916.

The discipline of the art school was not that sought by Yeats who

carried into the school some knowledge of English poetry, especially of Browning, who had begun to move me by his air of wisdom,[2]

and 'longed for pattern, for Pre-Raphaelitism, for an art allied to poetry.'[3] He felt in his heart that 'only ancient things and the stuff of dreams were beautiful'[4] and, looking back on those days, felt that he

had as many ideas as I have now, only I did not know how to choose from among them those that belonged to my life.[5]

His father's influence upon his thoughts was then at its height and, at breakfast time every morning, he listened to the parental voice

read passages from the poets, and always from the play or poem at its most passionate moment. He never read me a passage because of its speculative interest, and indeed did not care at all for poetry where there was general-isation or abstraction however impassioned.[6]

His father, the painter John Butler Yeats, was a member of a minor tributary of the main Pre-Raphaelite stream, 'The Brotherhood,' which consisted of himself, John Trivett Nettleship, a watercolourist who later achieved fame as an animal painter, George Wilson, a painter of symbolic women, and Edwin J. Ellis (1848-1915), with whom W. B. Yeats was to collaborate in editing the first collected Blake, published in 1893, and to whom, in his collected *Poems* of 1895, Yeats dedicated 'The Wanderings of Oisin.' Nettleship was a friend of Browning's and had published *Essays on Browning's Poetry* in 1868. He drew the frontispiece to *The Countess Kathleen and Various Legends and Lyrics* by W. B. Yeats in 1892 with, as subject, 'Cuchullin Fighting the Waves,' illustrating the long poem, 'The Death of Cuchullin.' Yeats grew to dislike this first graphic mani-festation of his epic hero and wrote, in a copy sent to John Quinn in 1904,

Nettleship who made this rather disappointing picture might have been a great imaginative artist. Browning once in a fit of enthusiasm said a design of his of "God creating Evil" was "the most sublime conception of ancient or modern art." [7]

In the late 1870's John Butler Yeats, perhaps influenced by Nettleship's *Essays* as well as his own delight in the poetry, was producing pictures based on Browning's writings, including the dramatic poem *Pippa Passes*. This was during the family's first period of residence in Bedford Park, the London suburban development designed by Norman Shaw as an extension into domestic architecture of the Pre-Raphaelite aesthetic defined by William Morris. J.B.Y. described Bedford Park to his family as 'a little city protected by walls against newspapers and the infections of commercial progress.' [8] One of the earliest residents of Bedford Park was J.B.Y.'s friend from his years in Trinity College Dublin, John Todhunter, then a wealthy doctor who devoted his leisure to writing poetry and verse drama and who was the principal patron of the artist's work. Browning, who was pleased with the design for *Pippa Passes*, called on J.B.Y. at his home, but the artist was out. [9] Both the painting, 'Pippa Passes,' in mixed media on board, and a study in chalk for the picture are now in the National Gallery of Ireland.

Despite the patronage of Todhunter and other friends, London proved too expensive and the Yeats family moved back to Dublin in 1880. A cottage in Howth was made available as a family home and John Butler Yeats rented a studio at York Street in the centre of the city. He enrolled W.B. in the art school and travelled into the city before breakfast every morning with his son. Over breakfast at the York Street studio W.B. would listen to his father

read out the first speeches of the *Prometheus Unbound*, but never the ecstatic lyricism of that famous fourth act; and another day the scene where Coriolanus comes to the house of Aufidius and tells the impudent servants that his home is under the canopy. I have seen *Coriolanus* played a number of times since then, and read it more than once, but that scene is more vivid than the rest, and it is my father's voice that I hear and not Irving's or Benson's. [10]

In *Reveries Over Childhood and Youth*, Yeats acknowledges his father's influence in laying the foundations of his career in poetic drama, an influence which points with great precision to the course that his development in that form was to take. 'All must be an idealisation of speech, and at some moment of passionate action or somnambulistic reverie,' [11] he wrote before 1915, when he discovered his formula in the classic drama of Japan.

From Browning, whose *Dramatis Personae*, 1864, collected his psychological monologues and might have suggested the title for that part of W.B.Y.'s autobiographical writings which deals most closely with theatre affairs, the lineage instilled by his father's readings carried the novice poet backward, through Leigh Hunt, who linked Browning with Shelley, to the English Romantic poets and thence to Blake and, further back, to the seventeenth century and to Spenser. The young W. B. Yeats had, early in the 1880's,

begun to write poetry in imitation of Shelley and of Edmund Spenser, play after play — for my father exalted dramatic poetry above all other kinds — and I invented fantastic and incoherent plots. My lines but seldom scanned, for I could not understand the prosody in the books, although there were many lines that taken by themselves had music.[12]

Another college friend of his father's, Edward Dowden, encouraged Yeats in his enthusiasm for Shelley, entertaining father and son to a series of breakfasts and reading to them some chapters of his unpublished *Life of Shelley* and, as W.B.Y. recalled, 'I who had made the *Prometheus Unbound* my sacred book was delighted with all he read.'[13]

But as the young poet began to study psychical research and mystical philosophy he gradually broke away from his father's influence and felt that, with the formation of 'the Hermetic Society that met near the roof in York Street,'[14] he had found new allies with whom to share his secret thoughts. The urge towards dramatic expression, however, remained:

I had, when we first made our Society, proposed for our consideration that whatever the great poets had affirmed in their finest moments was the nearest we could come to an authoritative religion, and that their mythology, their spirits of water and wind were but literal truth. I had read *Prometheus Unbound* with this thought in mind and wanted help to carry my study through all literature. I was soon to vex my father by defining truth as "the dramatically appropriate utterance of the highest man." And if I had been asked to define the "highest man," I would have said perhaps, "We can but find him as Homer found Odysseus when he was looking for a theme."[15]

'It all came upon me when I was close upon seventeen like the bursting of a shell.'[16] So Yeats described his awakening to sex, an awakening which was accompanied by a heightened awareness and a curiosity about the natural world. He thought that 'having conquered bodily desire and the inclination of [his] mind towards women and love, [he] should live, as Thoreau lived, seeking wisdom.'[17] He

wanted to find what sea-birds began to stir before dawn . . . for the poem that became fifteen years afterwards *The Shadowy Waters*, and it had been full of observation had [he] been able to write it when [he] first planned it.[18]

And he began to write plays :

I was writing a long play on a fable suggested by one of my father's early designs. A king's daughter loves a god seen in the luminous sky above her garden in childhood, and to be worthy of him and put away mortality, becomes without pity and commits crimes, and at last, having made her way to the throne by murder, awaits his coming among her courtiers. One by one they become chilly and drop dead, for, unseen by all but her, her god is in the hall. At last he is at her throne's foot and she, her mind in the garden once again, dies babbling like a child.[19]

His early love for a cousin, Laura Armstrong, spurred Yeats to complete his early dramatic poems. He pictured her, 'a wild creature, a fine mimic, and given to bursts of religion,'[20] as his heroine. He secretly referred to her as 'Vivien,' and her single surviving letter to him is so signed. (She addressed him as 'Clarin.')[21] And, in a letter to Katharine Tynan, written in 1899 when there was a possibility that his 'Countess O'Shea,' the piece which finally became *The Countess Cathleen*, might be acted in Dublin by amateur players with Miss Gonne in the title role, he invoked his memories of Laura in his assessment of the prospect :

she [Maud Gonne] had a borrowed interest, reminding me of Laura Armstrong without Laura's wild dash of half-insane genius. Laura is to me always a pleasant memory. She woke me from the metallic sleep of science and set me writing my first play.

Do not mistake me, she is only as a myth and a symbol. Will you forgive me for having talked of her? She interests me far more than Miss Gonne does and yet is only as a myth and a symbol. I heard from her about two years ago and am trying to find out where she is now in order to send her *Oisin*. "Time and the Witch Vivien" was written for her to act. The "Island of Statues" was begun with the same notion, though it soon grew beyond the scope of drawing-room acting. The part of the enchantress in both poems was written for her. She used to sign her letters Vivien.[22]

Yeats published four of his early dramatic poems during the 1880's. The first printed was *The Island of Statues*, which was read 'to a gathering of critics who were to decide whether it was worthy of publication in the College magazine'[23] early in 1885 and, with the subtitle 'An Arcadian Play in Imitation of Edmund Spenser,' it was serialised in *The Dublin University Review* between April and July of that year. *The Seeker* appeared in the September issue of the same journal. In the following year, *Mosada*, which was to become Yeats's first separately published book, appeared in the June issue of the *Review*. *Mosada*, the text offprinted from the type set for the *Review* with a special cover and a frontispiece portrait from a drawing by his father, was separately issued in Autumn 1886 in an edition which

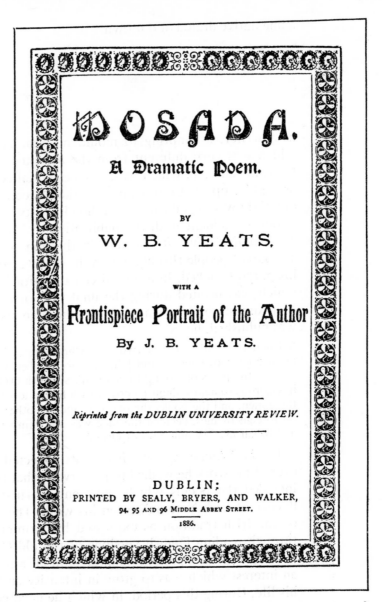

1. *Mosada*. Dublin, 1886. Yeats's first separately published work.
Front cover (reduced). Original 8½ × 5¼".

probably consisted of less than one hundred copies. The fourth of the
early dramatic poems, *Time and the Witch Vivien*, although it may
have been among the earliest in conception, was not printed until it
was included in the contents of Yeats's first collection of poetry,
The Wanderings of Oisin and other poems, which was published in
London in January 1889.

*

Although all four of Yeats's early dramatic pieces appeared either
entire or in part among the contents of *The Wanderings of Oisin*,
none of them was specifically Irish in theme or style, nor were they
in any way informed by a practical knowledge of the theatre. Nevertheless, they reveal that Yeats was, even at the outset of his career

as a writer, attempting to mould his dramatic writings in a style which was very different from the accepted conventional forms of the time, and one which was, in its essential concepts of imagination and philosophy, to remain remarkably consistent throughout his dramatic writings during the following fifty years.

But, coincident with the publication of his first dramatic piece in *The Dublin University Review*, in the summer of 1885, he did meet a group of people through whom he discovered the dimension which his purpose lacked. In a reminiscence, entitled 'I Became an Author,' which was printed during the final year of his life, in *The Listener* of 4 August 1938, he stated that at the time his first dramatic writing was published, he

fell under the influence of two men who were to influence deeply the Irish intellectual movement — old John O'Leary the Fenian leader, in whose library I found the poets of Young Ireland; and Standish O'Grady, who had rewritten in vigorous romantic English certain Irish heroic legends. Because of the talk of these men, and the books the one lent and the other wrote, I turned my back on foreign themes, decided the race was more important than the individual, and began my "Wanderings of Oisin." [24]

In *The Wanderings of Oisin* Yeats collected and rearranged whatever of his work he wished to preserve at that time, and this selection included the poems which represent the first flowering of the influence of Irish Nationalism on his work. The result of his discovery of the Irish tradition as expressed by writers in English, and later through reading English versions of the old Gaelic writers, was the development of a passionate interest in all aspects of Irish culture — an interest which was to grow in intensity and endure to the end of his life. During this period, in which he devoted much time to intensive reading of Irish literature, he edited a number of successful Irish anthologies, among them *Fairy and Folk Tales of the Irish Peasantry*, 1888, *Stories from Carleton*, 1889, *Representative Irish Tales*, 1891, and *Irish Fairy Tales*, 1892. At the same time, the direction and character of his own writing changed radically and the Irish influence of 'Davis, Mangan, Ferguson' replaced that of Shelley and the English Romantic poets, under which his early dramatic pieces, inspired by a search for an ideal and passionate love, had been composed.

*

The title, *Four Years 1887-1891*, which Yeats chose for the second volume of his *Autobiographies* indicates the significance to him of these years in his discovery of the directions that his work, in its various forms, was to take. He does not recount the events of his life during 1887, which he spent in London, in any detail in that book but that he did not like the change from Ireland is evident from passages in his letters to his Dublin friend Katharine Tynan, such as this, written on 1 July 1887:

I do not think I shall ever find London very tolerable. It can give me nothing; I am not fond of the theatre, literary society bores me, I loathe crowds and was very content in Dublin, though even that was a little too populous.[25]

Yeats's pessimism at that time may have been partly due to separation from his family and to his life in a boarding-house while his father sought a permanent London residence. He returned to spend the late summer and autumn with relatives at Sligo, where he finished the long poem which gave *The Wanderings of Oisin* its title. After he returned to London, life was made tolerable by contact with William Morris, whose Socialist play, *The Tables Turned, or Nupkins Awakened* was produced at the Hall of the Socialist League on 15 October 1887. Morris's playwriting was, however, to influence Yeats much less than his poetry, particularly his retelling of saga literature, which may have prompted Yeats to think that similar themes might possibly be evolved from Irish heroic sources, continuing a process which had already begun with 'The Wanderings of Oisin.'

A new concept of the drama was revealed to him after his family moved in March 1888 to the house described in the first paragraph of *Four Years*, 3 Blenheim Road in Bedford Park. John Todhunter, again a near neighbour and family friend, introduced Yeats to the practical elements of stagecraft. This 'stirring of his imagination' was described in section IV of *Four Years*:

Bedford Park had a red-brick clubhouse with a little theatre that began to stir my imagination. I persuaded Todhunter to write a pastoral play and have it performed there.

A couple of years before, while we were still in Dublin, he had given at Hengler's Circus, remodelled as a Greek Theatre, a most expensive performance of his *Helena of Troas*, an oratorical Swinburnian play which I had thought as unactable as it was unreadable. Since I was seventeen I had constantly tested my own ambition with Keats's praise of him who left "great verse unto a little clan", so it was but natural that I should persuade him that we had nothing to do with the great public, that it should be a point of honour to be content with our own little public, that he should write of shepherds and shepherdesses because people would expect them to talk poetry and move without melodrama. He wrote his *Sicilian Idyll*, which I have not looked at for thirty years, and never rated very high as poetry, and had the one unmistakable success of his life.[26]

The building alterations, scenic design, properties and costumes of the production of *Helena in Troas*, given for six performances at Hengler's Cirque in Argyll Street, London, in May 1886, was one of the last works undertaken by the architect and designer Edward William Godwin, who died later in the same year. Godwin was the father of Gordon Craig, who was to have a great and abiding influence on Yeats's own theatrical development both in theory and practice after he met Craig in 1900. The production was reported in the *Graphic* of 5 June 1886 with illustrations by another Bedford Park neighbour, H. M. Paget, who designed the production of *A Sicilian Idyll* at the Bedford Park theatre and was later to design London productions of *The Land of Heart's Desire* and *The Shadowy Waters* for Yeats.

But the most important contact Yeats made through the little theatre in Bedford Park was 'a discovery that was to influence [his] life,' his meeting Florence Farr. With Florence Farr he was to work out his theories of the delivery of verse to an audience. She

lived in lodgings some twenty minutes' walk away at Brook Green, and I was soon a constant caller, talking over plays that I would some day write her. She had three great gifts, a tranquil beauty like that of Demeter's image near the British Museum Reading-Room door, and an incomparable sense of rhythm and a beautiful voice, the seeming natural expression of the image.[27]

Bernard Shaw, introducing his letters to Florence Farr many years later, gave the following picture of the actress:

Florence was the daughter of Dr. William Farr, famous as a sanitary reformer in the mid-nineteenth century when he and Sir Edwin Chadwick were forcing us to realize that England was dying of dirt.

Florence had been born unexpectedly long after her mother had apparently ceased childbearing: she was possibly indulged as a welcome surprise on that account. Though Dr. Farr survived his wits and lost most of his means by senile speculations before his death in 1883, he left enough to enable Florence to live modestly without having to sell herself in any fashion, or do anything that was distasteful to her.

She went on the stage and married a clever actor who was a member of the well-known Emery family. There was some trouble (not domestic) that ended in his emigrating to America and passing out of Florence's life. She attached so little importance to the incident, being apparently quite content to forget him, that I had some difficulty in persuading her to divorce him for desertion by pointing out that as long as their marriage remained undissolved, he might turn up any moment with very serious legal claims on her.

Whatever the trouble was that took him out of the country Florence gave up the stage for the moment, and set herself to learn the art of embroidery under Morris's daughter May. She acted in an entertainment at the house on the Mall; and on this occasion I made her acquaintance, and had no difficulty in considerably improving it. She set no bounds to her relations with men whom she liked, and already had a sort of Leporello list of a dozen adventures, none of which, however, had led to anything serious. She was in violent reaction against Victorian morals; especially sexual and domestic morals; and when the impact of Ibsen was felt in this country, and I wrote somewhere that "home is the girl's prison and the woman's workhouse" I became *persona grata* with her; and for some years we saw a great deal of one another. . . .

She played the heroine in my first play in 1892. In 1894 the late Miss Horniman gave her money to produce modern plays at the old Avenue Theatre, now replaced by The Playhouse. The first production, inadequately cast and acted, failed; and Florence was about to replace it by my first play, when I wrote *Arms and the Man* for her instead, selecting the cast myself. With Yeats's *Land of Heart's Desire* as an exquisite curtain raiser it had a startling first night success, and kept the theatre open (average receipts £17) until Miss Horniman's money was exhausted.[28]

Seeing 'the little theatre' in Bedford Park must have confirmed Yeats's feeling that his instinct about the form of theatre he sought was right and that his ideal might, some day, be realised. He

discovered for the first time that in the performance of all drama that depends for its effect upon beauty of language, poetical culture may be more important than professional experience.[29]

His notice of *A Sicilian Idyll*, which was first presented on 5 May 1890, appeared in *The Boston Pilot* of 14 June. Later, when *A Sicilian Idyll* achieved a London production at the Vaudeville Theatre, he contributed a longer notice of the play to *United Ireland* in which he predicted his future work for an Irish theatre, a prediction that should be considered in relation to a passage in *Four Years*, written thirty years later, in which he summarised what he had then perceived.

Yeats's review of Todhunter's play in *United Ireland*, 11 July 1891, ends:

When our political passions have died out in the fulfillment of their aims shall we, I wonder, have a fine native drama of our own? It is very likely. A very great number of the best playwrights who have written for the English stage, from Sheridan and Goldsmith to our own day, have been Irishmen. We are a young country, and still care, I think, for the high thoughts and the high feelings of poetry, if in a somewhat uncultivated fashion. We love the dramatic side of events and have too much imagination to think plays which advertise "a real locomotive engine" or "a real fire engine" as the chief attraction to be a better form of drama than the heroic passions and noble diction of the great ages of the theatre. We have never yet been fairly tested. Our playwrights have been poor men who were forced to write for an English public in the very last stages of dramatic decadence. I should very much like to see what Dr. Todhunter could do with an Irish theme written for and acted before an Irish audience. Surely, they would not find it being poetry the very great difficulty English audiences seem to find it. We have had the only popular ballad literature of recent days. Does not that prove the poetic capacities of our uneducated masses? Or has English influence and "the union of hearts" made us as prosaic as our neighbours? [30]

In section XXIII of *Four Years* he restated these thoughts of 1891 on the possibility of using native Irish sources in the development of his life's work:

I could not endure, however, an international art, picking stories and symbols where it pleased. Might I not, with health and good luck to aid me, create some new *Prometheus Unbound*; Patrick or Columcille, Oisin or Finn, in Prometheus' stead; and instead of Caucasus, Cro-Patrick or Ben Bulben? Have not all races had their first unity from a mythology that marries them to rock and hill? We had in Ireland imaginative stories, which the uneducated classes knew and even sang, and might we not make those stories current among the educated classes, rediscovering for the work's sake what I have called "the applied arts of literature," the association of literature, that is, with music, speech, and dance; and at last, it might be, so deepen the political passion of the nation that all, artist and poet, craftsman and day-labourer would accept a common design? [31]

In Bedford Park he had seen the possibility of defining, in terms of his own talent in the theatre, the ideals which John O'Leary and his other Irish friends had preached. His next move would be towards the realisation of this dream.

*

The Wanderings of Oisin was well received on publication and in a letter dated 1 February 1889 Yeats announced to John O'Leary that Dowden had urged him 'to write a poetic drama with a view to the stage.' This was to be 'one founded on the tale of "Countess Kathleen O'Shea" in the folk lore book.' [32] On 8 February he wrote to George Russell that he was 'starting a new drama founded on an Irish folk-tale. The best plot I ever worked on.' [33] By the end of the month he could inform Katharine Tynan that

This new poem of mine promises to be my most interesting poem and in all ways quite dramatic, I think. I shall try and get it acted by amateurs (if possible in Dublin) and afterwards try it perhaps on some stage manager or actor. It is in five scenes and full of action and very Irish.[34]

The choice of subject for his first truly Irish play may have been prompted by his meeting Maud Gonne, an event which had occurred on 30 January, coincident with Dowden's suggestion that he should attempt a stage play. It is evident that he visualised Maud Gonne in the title role of the piece and, in its first printed version in *The Countess Kathleen and Various Legends and Lyrics*, 1892, the play is dedicated 'To my friend, Miss Maud Gonne, at whose suggestion it was planned out and begun some three years ago.' The play, although it was to undergo many revisions and rewritings over a period of twenty years and was not to be staged until the Irish Literary Theatre was formed in Dublin in 1899, represents the real beginning of Yeats's career as a writer for the stage.

Yeats's letters written during 1889 and the first half of 1890 indicate that he was constantly at work on *The Countess Kathleen*. But he was also thinking about other dramatic subjects, perhaps with Todhunter's theatre club in mind, and in his letter of 1 July 1890 he told Katharine Tynan that he was planning a Mystery Play on the subject of the Adoration of the Magi. Although this project did not materialise as a play, Yeats developed the plot into a short story which was published in 1897.

The Countess Kathleen was granted the statutory Lord Chamberlain's licence for public performance on 5 May 1892 and a copyright 'performance' was given at the Athenaeum Theatre, Shepherd's Bush, on the following day. This was a staged reading of the piece given to fulfil the requirements of the copyright act and could not in any way have given Yeats insight into the complexities of stagecraft.

In 1891 Yeats was instrumental in organising the preliminary discussions which led to the foundation of the Irish Literary Society in London, which Society was officially inaugurated in May 1892. Later in that year a Society of the same name was founded in Dublin, another offshoot of his enthusiasm. Although both these organisations were primarily devoted to disseminating Irish national ideas, and to encouraging publication of the work of Irish writers, they were important milestones in the road which led, at the end of the decade, to the foundation of an Irish National Theatre. In the summer of 1892 Yeats wrote from Dublin to Edward Garnett that the National Literary Society was 'growing under our hands into what promises to be a work of very great importance.'[35] This was to be achieved by founding reading rooms throughout the country which could later be developed as distribution centres for the publication programme planned under the aegis of the Society. Meetings, lectures and concerts were planned, of which the inaugural meeting took place in the Antient Concert Rooms, in Great Brunswick Street (now Pearse Street), Dublin, where, almost seven years later, the first productions of the Irish Literary Theatre were staged.

Yeats's interest in Irish epic literature is also reflected by the inclusion in *The Countess Kathleen and Various Legends and Lyrics* of his long narrative poem, 'The Death of Cuchullin.' The frontispiece of the book, showing 'Cuchulain Fighting the Waves' was by J. T. Nettleship, R.A. Although Yeats later came to dislike this picture, the choice of this particular subject as frontispiece precedes by over ten years his dramatic use of the epic material surrounding the ancient Irish hero and foreshadows the final scene of *On Baile's Strand*, the first tale from the Cuchulain epic that he chose to treat in dramatic form.

Even though *The Countess Kathleen* was rewritten several times before its production in the first season of the Irish Literary Theatre in 1899, the publication of what might be regarded as his first stage-worthy drama, a piece which in concept and construction was very unlike the average stage play of the period, must have been a great encouragement to Yeats who, as T. S. Eliot, giving the first Yeats memorial lecture at the Abbey Theatre, Dublin, in June 1940, observed

started writing plays at a time when the prose-play of contemporary life seemed triumphant, with an indefinite future stretching before it; when the comedy of light farce dealt only with certain privileged strata of metropolitan life; and when the serious play tended to be an ephemeral tract on some transient social problem. We can begin to see now that even the imperfect early attempts he made are probably more permanent literature than the plays of Ibsen or of Shaw; and that his dramatic work as a whole may prove a stronger defence against the successful Shaftesbury Avenue vulgarity which he opposed as strongly as they. Just as, from the beginning, he made and thought his poetry in terms of speech and not in terms of print, so in the drama he always meant to write plays to be played and not merely to be read. He cared, I think, more for the theatre as an organ for the expression of the consciousness of a people, than as a means to his own fame and achievement; and I am convinced that it is only if you serve it in this spirit that you can hope to accomplish anything worth doing with it. Of course, he had some great advantages, the recital of which does not rob him of any of his glory : his colleagues, a people with a natural and unspoilt gift for speech and for acting; and this theatre — it is impossible to disentangle what he did for the Irish theatre from what the Irish theatre did for him. From this point of advantage, the idea of the poetic drama was kept alive when everywhere else it had been driven underground. I do not know where our debt to him as a dramatist ends — and in time, it will not end until that drama itself ends.[36]

*

In the spring of 1894, the first public production of a play by Yeats was heralded by the appearance on the London billboards of the famous poster designed by Aubrey Beardsley which announced the opening, at the Avenue Theatre on 29 March, of *The Land of Heart's Desire*, as a curtain-raiser to *A Comedy of Sighs* by John Todhunter. The design inspired the satirical genius of Owen Seaman who published in *Punch* some verses entitled 'Ars Postera' which strangely prophesied the two main influences that were to direct Yeats's theatrical development. The first stanza reads :

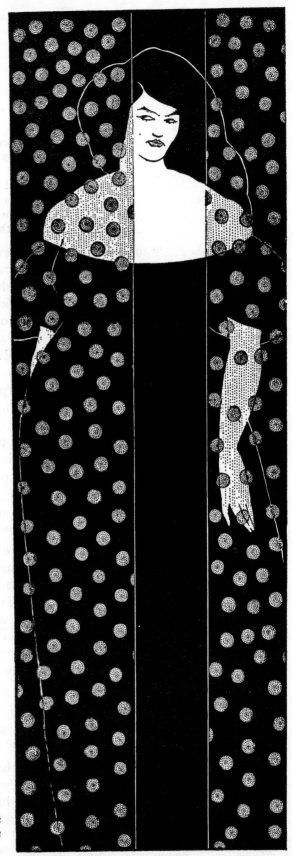

2. The 'Japanee-Rosetti' Girl. Detail of Aubrey Beardsley's poster for the Avenue Theatre season, London, March 1894. The original is printed in blue and yellow-green.

> Mr. Aubrey Beer de Beers,
>   You're getting quite a high renown;
> Your Comedy of Leers, you know,
>   Is posted all about the town;
> This sort of stuff I cannot puff,
>   As Boston says, it makes me "tired";
> Your Japanee-Rossetti girl
>   Is not a thing to be desired.[37]

Seaman's ironic verses revealed that Yeats's reputation in London had become allied to the new 'Nineties' movement in the theatre and in the arts generally. Beardsley's poster design symbolised the attempt to break through the barriers of convention and at the same time reflected the romantic approach which informed almost all of Yeats's writing at the time. It was adapted for the cover design of the published version of the play which T. Fisher Unwin issued in the following month. Beardsley's design is recognised today as one of his finest works and a masterpiece in its genre — the figure of a girl emerging through diaphanous drapes, executed in the unlikely colour combination of a cerulean blue with a yellow-green, finely realised by two-colour lithographic printing.

The 'Japanee-Rossetti' girl must have seemed to Yeats a symbolic reflection of the faery folk of his play:

> . . . we who will ride the winds, run on the waves
> And dance upon the mountains are more light
> Than dewdrops on the banner of the dawn.

The Land of Heart's Desire is a simple, lyrical one-act play which Yeats derived from the same body of Western Irish folklore and legend as the stories and articles he wrote at the same period and collected in The Celtic Twilight, published by A. H. Bullen in December 1893. The plot, a simple one, is his first use in his play-writing of the folk theme of the changeling — the mortal tempted from the natural world into that of the People of the Sidhe, the underworld folk who supposedly inhabit the ancient raths and ring-forts of prehistoric Ireland. The action occurs on the old pagan festival of Bealtaine, or May-Eve, when the Sidhe

> . . . may steal new-married brides
> After the fall of twilight.

The faery child, who is the envoy of the Sidhe, foils the priest's attempt to avert the tragedy by persuading him to remove the crucifix from the cottage room in which the action takes place and then, symbolising some of her movements in a dance sequence, possesses the spirit of the young bride, Mary Bruin, leaving her lifeless body, over which the priest can but pronounce the helpless lamentation that ancient sorceries are still about in the world.

A programme note which was also included in the early printings of the play stated that the place and time of the play was the Barony of Kilmacowen in the County of Sligo at the end of the eighteenth century and that 'the characters are supposed to speak in Gaelic,' indicating the hesitations in Yeats's mind when faced with the problems of producing a practical text for a stage presentation. Nevertheless, he completed the play at the request of Florence Farr, who had asked him for a short play which would have a part for her niece, Dorothy Paget, for a season under her management which she was planning at the Avenue Theatre with the financial backing of Miss A. E. F. Horniman. The text of *The Land of Heart's Desire* was completed early in 1894, as indicated by Yeats's letter, written to John O'Leary on 7 February, which stated that the effort had tired him out and that now that it was done and 'gone to the typewriter for the actors I shall rest till rehearsals begin.' [38]

But Beardsley's mysterious girl-figure is also the starting point of one of the elements which characterise Yeats's approach to the image of woman which he presented all through his plays. She represents the first pictorial embodiment of his 'Woman of the Sidhe' who, in her manifestation in human shape, is only fully realised in the later plays such as *The Only Jealousy of Emer*, *The King of the Great Clock Tower*, and *A Full Moon in March* — the woman-type which is the embodiment of an unearthly beauty which, over a quarter of a century later in his life, Yeats was to fit into the system he embodied in *A Vision*. I see, in the face depicted by Beardsley, the first graphic representation of Yeats's concept of the mask — a concept which he could not define for himself in 1894 because he lacked a pointer towards the knowledge of the form of theatre which his instinct dictated, but which he was only to begin to develop after his contact with Gordon Craig in the following decade — and the face from the poster might be used as a model for one of the archetypal masks in the later plays, and be seen as the first realisation of one detail of an approach to the stage which was to be developed, with modifications and adjustments, all through Yeats's career as a playwright.

Before the rehearsals of *The Land of Heart's Desire* began — rehearsals to which Yeats, without any practical knowledge of theatre practice, can have had little to contribute — he made a journey to Paris which led to his experiencing a further and most significant dimension of his search for a dramatic form. Arthur Symons, his fellow member of the Rhymers' Club, had read to Yeats some of his metrical translations from Villiers de l'Isle Adam's symbolist drama, *Axel*, and apparently suggested that Yeats should see the Paris production of the play. At the same time, he gave Yeats introductions to Verlaine and Mallarmé. On 26 February 1894, accompanied by Maud Gonne, Yeats attended the production of *Axel* and was so profoundly impressed by the event that this visit to the theatre probably marks the turning point in his decision to pursue a career in drama. *Axel*, as a Rosicrucian writing, influenced Yeats in his philosophical thinking, but also, as a symbolist drama, disclosed to the novice playwright the possibilities of developing a non-realistic form of theatre and became one of the principal models for the symbolism built into his dramatic writings after 1894.

On his return to London, Yeats wrote a long and enthusiastic review of *Axel* for *The Bookman*, which appeared in the April 1894 issue under the title 'A Symbolical Drama in Paris,' and which may be regarded as the most significant of his early pronouncements on his theatrical theories. His review opens:

The scientific movement which has swept away so many religious and philosophical misunderstandings of ancient truth has entered the English theatres in the shape of realism and Ibsenism, and is now busy playing ducks and drakes with the old theatrical conventions. We no longer believe that the world was made five thousand years ago, and are beginning to suspect that Eve's apple was not the kind of apple you buy at the greengrocer's for a penny, but we have still a little faith in the virtuous hero and the wicked villain of the theatre, and in the world of tricks and puppets which is all that remains of the old romance in its decadence.

Later in the review he states that

The final test of the value of any work of art to our particular needs, is when we place it in the hierarchy of those recollections which are our standards and our beacons. At the head of mine are a certain night scene long ago, when I heard the wind blowing in a bed of reeds by the border of a little lake, a Japanese picture of cranes flying through a blue sky, and a line or two out of Homer.

Although in this review he found occasion to criticise certain elements in the play and its construction, he ended with a bold claim that

The imaginative drama must inevitably make many mistakes before it is in possession of the stage again, for it is so essentially different to the old melodrama and the new realism, that it must learn its powers and limitations for itself. It must also fail many times before it wins the day, for though we cannot hope to ever again see the public as interested in sheer poetry, as the audiences were who tolerated so great a poet, so poor a dramatist as Chapman, it must make its hearers learn to understand eloquent and beautiful dialogues, and to admire them for their own sake and not as a mere pendent to the action. For this reason its very mistakes when they are of the kind made by the promoters of "Axel" help to change the public mind in the right direction, by reminding it forcibly that the actor should also be a reverent reciter of majestic words.[39]

Thirty years later Yeats contributed a preface to H. P. R. Finberg's prose translation of *Axel* which was published in an edition of 500 copies with decorations by T. Sturge Moore in May 1925. The preface, which drew largely on his *Bookman* review of 1894 for its content, however, included the fact that, after his visit to Paris

On my return to London I tried to arrange a performance there, and Miss Florence Farr, who was producing *Arms and the Man* and my *Land of Heart's Desire*, offered her theatre for nothing, but the London public was thought unprepared, being in its first enthusiasm for Jones and Pinero.[40]

The Avenue Theatre season in London which opened on 29 March 1894 may well be regarded as the beginning of the Irish Literary Theatre. The season was financially guaranteed by Miss A. E. F. Horniman who later became the 'fairy godmother' of the Irish National Theatre. The principal piece in the opening programme of the season, *A Comedy of Sighs* by John Todhunter, was a failure, but the curtain-raiser, *The Land of Heart's Desire** by Yeats had a moderately favourable reception and was kept on the bill with Bernard Shaw's *Arms and the Man*, which replaced the Todhunter play after it was taken off on 14 April. The theatre closed for a week during rehearsals of *Arms and the Man*, which opened on 21 April and played with the Yeats play in the bill until 12 May, after which another curtain-raiser was substituted. Yeats summarised the public reaction in a letter of 15 April to John O'Leary:

Todhunter's play *The Comedy of Sighs* was taken off last night. My little play *The Land of Heart's Desire* is however considered a fair success and is to be put on again with the play by Shaw which goes on next week. It is being printed by Unwin and will be sold in the theatre with the programmes. The whole venture has had to face the most amazing denunciations from the old

---

*The cast of *The Land of Heart's Desire*, as given in the first edition of the play was:

THE LAND OF HEART'S DESIRE
Produced at the Avenue Theatre, London, 29 March 1894

Maurteen Bruin	James Welch
Shawn Bruin	A. E. W. Mason
Father Hart	G. R. Foss
Bridget Bruin	Charlotte Morland
Maire Bruin	Winifred Fraser
A Faery Child	Dorothy Paget

(Directed by Florence Farr)

type of critics. They have however been so abusive that a reaction has set in which has brought a rather artistic public to the theatre. The takings at the door rose steadily but not rapidly enough to make it safe to hold on with Todhunter's play which was really a brilliant piece of work. If Shaw's play does well a new play of mine will be put on — a much more ambitious play than anything I have yet done. It will give you some notion of the row that is going on when I tell you "chuckers out" have been hired for the first night of Shaw. They are to be distributed over the theatre and are to put out all people who make a row. The whole venture will be history anyway for it is the first contest between the old commercial school of theatrical folk and the new artistic school.[41]

Yeats attended many of the performances during the six weeks that his play ran at the Avenue Theatre, 'noting,' as his biographer Joseph Hone records, 'the changes he might make in the monosyllabic verse, in which his interpreters were ill at ease.'[42]

Bernard Shaw, however, disapproved of Florence Farr's style of speaking the verse which he described as 'cantillation' and, as late as 1902, wrote to her, refusing to enter into what he called 'cantillatory politics,'

The fact is, there is no new art in the business at all : Yeats thinks so only because he does not go to church. Half the curates in the kingdom cantilate like mad all the time. Toastmasters cantilate. Public speakers who have nothing to say cantilate. And it is intolerable except in the one obvious and complete instance — the street cry. Sarah Bernhardt's abominable "golden voice," which has always made me sick, is cantilation, or, to use the custom- ary word, intoning. It is no use for Yeats to try to make a distinction : there is no distinction, no novelty, no nothing but nonsense.[43]

Although *The Land of Heart's Desire* is considered by many critical writers as one of the slightest of Yeats's dramatic works, it was the work through which he served his apprenticeship to theatre practice and he continued to revise both the spoken text and the details of the action of the play for almost thirty years until he published what might be considered the definitive version in *Plays and Controversies*, 1923. Several separate editions and reprints were issued and the variations in text and stage directions in these reveal his increasing aptitude in stage techniques and his growing realisation of the need to adapt to meet circumstances. In the note on the version revised in 1911, after its presentation on the Abbey stage, where it was first performed on 16 February 1911,* under the direction of Lennox Robinson and in which the part of the Faery Child, originally written for a child actress, was described on the programme as 'A Faery' and played by Máire O'Neill, he wrote :

Till lately it was not part of the repertory of the Abbey Theatre, for I had grown to dislike it without knowing what I disliked in it. This winter, however, I have made many revisions and now it plays well enough to give me pleasure. It is printed in this book in the new form, which was acted for the first time on 22 February 1912, at the Abbey Theatre, Dublin.

At the Abbey Theatre, where the platform of the stage comes out in front of the curtain, the curtain falls before the priest's last words. He remains outside the curtain and the words are spoken to the audience like an epilogue.[44]

Yeats's preface to his final version of *The Land of Heart's Desire*, published in *Plays and Controversies*, 1923, goes further in showing his realisation of the practicalities of performance by companies of various kinds, professional or amateur, but at the same time reveals that this, his first performed play, was still dear to him :

This play contains more of my first experiments in blank verse than any other in my books, for *The Countess Cathleen*, though published before it, was all rewritten for later editions. Many passages that pleased me when I wrote them, and some that please me still, are mere ornament without dramatic value. A revival of the play but a few days ago at the Abbey Theatre enabled me to leave out these and other passages and to test the play without them. I think that it gained greatly, became indeed for the first time tolerable drama; certainly for the first time for many years gave its author pleasure. Amateurs perform it more often than any other play of mine, and I urge them to omit all lines that I have enclosed in brackets. It should sound simple and natural if played with the text I recommend, and it may be that it would read better too, being a more perfect action, but I hesitate to leave out altogether what many people like, what, it may be, I can no longer judge. Somebody, Dr. Todhunter, the dramatic poet, I think, had said in my hearing that dramatic poetry must be oratorical, and I think that I wrote partly to prove that false; but every now and then I lost courage, as it seems, and remembering that I had some reputation as a lyric poet wrote for the reader of lyrics. When I saw it played with all needless and all mere lyrical passages cut away, I recalled the kind of pleasure that I had sought to create, and at last listened with the hope that this pleasure had reached those about me. Mr. Lennox Robinson, the producer, had kept all the players except the fairy child as still and statuesque as possible, so that the blank verse where there is so little animation seemed their natural utterance.[45]

---

*First production by The Irish National Theatre Society Limited
at the Abbey Theatre, Dublin,
on 16 February 1911

THE LAND OF HEART'S DESIRE
a play in one act, by W. B. Yeats

Bridget Bruin	Eileen O'Doherty
Shawn Bruin	Fred O'Donovan
Maurteen Bruin	J. M. Kerrigan
Father Hart	Arthur Sinclair
Maire Bruin	Sara Allgood
A Faery	Maire O'Neill

(Produced by S. L. Robinson)

Even in this, his first play to be realised in performance, as Una
Ellis-Fermor pointed out in her book, *The Irish Dramatic Movement*,
1939, Yeats

communicated his experience of certain aspects of beauty. Neither then nor
at any other time did he allow influences which were not part of his artistic
experience to affect his poetry or his drama. This is not, of course, to say that
he did not accept all aesthetic experience that offered itself, even to the
exploration of some of the stranger territories of metaphysical speculation, as
in *Where there is Nothing* at the beginning of his career or *The Words upon
the Window Pane* some thirty years later. But, strict as was his discipline in
such matters as theatrical technique, he never allowed even the technique of
the theatre so to interfere at the moment of conception as to modify the
resulting material and its inevitable choice of form.[46]

His total approach to a theatrical form for expression was a continuing quest for a technique, a dramatic language by which he might
communicate with his audiences, small or large, and this approach
was, as time went on, modified by the other explorations he conducted in his creative life. The 'Mythologies' of his early writings
were later qualified by concerns other than those prompted by the
course of Irish history during his lifetime. But even in *The Land of
Heart's Desire*, where the triumph of the People of the Sidhe is
commemorated by the dance of the Faery Child for which the stage
directions ask, one can see the beginning of the pathway leading to
the discoveries which were eventually to cause him to cast his dramatic writing in a form modelled on the classical drama of the East and
to realise, in the Woman of the Sidhe as presented in *The Only
Jealousy of Emer*, the mystery and the mask prefigured by the face in
Beardsley's drawing.

*

3. The 'mask' in Beardsley's poster. Detail.

The 'much more ambitious play' which Yeats hoped might succeed *The Land of Heart's Desire* in the Avenue Theatre bill after 12 May 1894 was not ready, but he continued to work at the text of this play, which was *The Shadowy Waters*, the theme of which had been on his mind since he first conceived the idea of writing dramatic verse. He was always hopeful that he would resolve the dramatic poem centred on the old Irish concept of a sea-quest, which had obsessed him ever since his first essays in dramatic verse. On 26 June he wrote to John O'Leary that he hoped for the performance of his new play in the autumn,[47] after spending the summer in the West of Ireland, but on 5 November he was still at Sligo and wrote to his father that the play

... is however giving me a devil of a job. More than anything I have done for years. In my struggle to keep it concrete I fear I shall so overload it with legendary detail that it will be unfit for any theatrical purposes — at least as such are carried out at present.[48]

Five days later he wrote to John O'Leary that he hoped to dispatch *The Shadowy Waters*, which he described as a poem, to Elkin Mathews,[49] but later letters indicate that he had put aside the project for the time being to concentrate on work which would provide a more immediate source of income, such as *A Book of Irish Verse*, which he edited for Methuen & Co. Ltd., and which was published in March 1895. He also worked on the collected edition of his own work up to this time which included an extensive revision of *The Countess Kathleen*, in which the spelling of the heroine's name was altered to its final form, 'Cathleen.'

Early in the summer of 1895 he returned to London, and busied himself with earning what he could by literary journalism, and with seeing through the press his volume, *Poems*, which included both *The Land of Heart's Desire* and the revised version of *The Countess Cathleen*. The book was published in October 1895, by T. Fisher Unwin, with a binding designed by H. Granville Fell, which Yeats found very admirable at first but grew to dislike so intensely that when a second, revised, edition of the book was issued in 1899, he insisted that a new binding design be made by Althea Gyles, which was retained on the subsequent editions and reprints of this book until 1924.

During the autumn of 1895 he moved from Blenheim Road to share chambers with his friend Arthur Symons at Fountain Court in the Temple in London and resumed frequent meetings with the members of the magical Order of the Golden Dawn, especially Florence Farr with whom he worked on her method of speaking or chanting his poetry. *Poems* achieved a considerable success and with the addition to his income and the prospects of his new book, *The Secret Rose*, a collection of stories which he was preparing for publication by Lawrence and Bullen, he felt sufficiently confident to find rooms for himself at 18 Woburn Buildings, near Euston, into which he moved on 25 March 1896.

He resumed work on *The Shadowy Waters* and by the summer he had become a contributor to *The Savoy*, a journal founded by Leonard Smithers, a new publisher, who planned also to produce a number of finely illustrated books, with Aubrey Beardsley as his principal artist. Yeats contributed poems, fiction, reminiscences and essays to the January, April, July, August, September and November issues of *The Savoy*, and resumed his work on *The Shadowy Waters* with the prospect, offered by Smithers, that he would produce a fine edition of the dramatic poem with six drawings by Aubrey Beardsley, similar in style to the edition of *Salomé* by Oscar Wilde which Beardsley had illustrated for John Lane in 1894.

The early versions of *The Shadowy Waters* are collated by David R. Clark and George P. Mayhew in *A Tower of Polished Black Stones*,[50] and in greater detail by the same editors with Michael J. Sidnell in *Druid Craft*,[51] and both these volumes contain the materials which Yeats, in October 1896, sent to Smithers and to Beardsley as briefing for the proposed edition. A notebook, now in the Henry Huntingdon Library in California, contains several sketches by Yeats which accompany a scenario consisting of eleven typewritten leaves with corrections in Yeats's hand, 'sent to Leonard Smithers that Beardsley might make designs for it.'[52] The seven Yeats sketches reveal how rapidly his visualisation of stage presentation had developed in the two years since the Avenue Theatre season. Beardsley, who was in the final year of his life, completed only one drawing for the book, which has not been located. His letters to Smithers during 1896 indicate his admiration for Yeats and his willingness to make the drawings: 'I'll take on Yeats play as soon as you like, am in working form.' (29 October 1896); 'When will Yeats be ready?' (18 November); 'Yeats play will well stand 6 prs. I am now doing a double page picture for it of the young man on horseback following the young woman on horseback.' (27 November). This last letter refers to the only drawing completed by Beardsley which, from the description quoted, is as remote in its conception of any incident in the finished play as were some of the designs in other books he illustrated. Beardsley's final reference to the project in a letter to Smithers on 29 November reads: 'The Yeats pictures will be amusing. The young

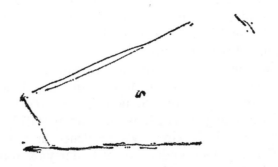

4. *The Shadowy Waters.* A sketch sent by Yeats to Beardsley, October 1896.

man on horseback is vastly beau, & the young woman vastly belle.
I am drinking beaune.'[53]

In the synopsis of *The Shadowy Waters* which Yeats sent to
Smithers, and which was sent on to Beardsley, there is a passage
which probably formed the inspiration for Beardsley's design. On
folio 4 the speech delivered by the Seabar on the poop, describing
Forgael's druid power, refers to his

visions of unavailing and eternal desire : a hound with one red ear following
a doe over the waters, a youth following on horseback a girl who rode over
the sea tossing a golden apple. He knew these were images of doom, images
out of the old days.[54]

In mid-December Beardsley had a vast haemorrhage which left
him very weak and although he lived in deteriorating health until
16 March 1898 there is no further reference to the Yeats project in
his correspondence. The project may also have been deferred by
Smithers due to his continuing lack of funds, and the collapse of
The Savoy at the end of 1896 after only eight numbers had appeared
may have made the planned edition impossible. Beardsley's drawing
cannot be traced today but it may possibly have been acquired by
Edward Martyn, who was a collector of the artist's work.

Nevertheless, Yeats continued to work on his dramatic poem,
always seeking an adequate solution to the problems he had posed in
his drafts and early versions, but he did not yet have the stage
experience, which he only gained after his 'discovery' of the Nō,
that would have allowed him to visualise the presentation of his
dramatic poem in a series of nearly static tableaux with dance movement to point significant moments in the action. A stage production
proved impossible at the time and the play had to wait for its
presentation until the Irish National Theatre was established. However, the piece was printed, first in *The North American Review* in
May 1900, and in book form by Hodder and Stoughton in London in
December of the same year.

During his work on the drafts and scenario of *The Shadowy
Waters* in 1896, Yeats spent part of August and September on a
walking tour with Arthur Symons in the West of Ireland where they
were for a time guests of Edward Martyn at Tulyra Castle in County
Galway, near Lady Gregory's residence at Coole Park. Yeats and
Lady Gregory met under Edward Martyn's roof, and later, after
Symons' return to London, Yeats spent a few days as her guest. He
and Symons also visited the Aran Islands, so that Yeats could acquire
local colour for his proposed novel which he had promised to Bullen
and on which he had received an advance. Their Irish visit also took

them to Sligo. In December of the same year the two poets visited Paris, where Yeats met J. M. Synge for the first time. The *Dramatis Personae* of the Irish National Theatre were coming together.

*

Much of Yeats's thinking in Paris during the end of 1896 and January 1897 was devoted to developing his urge towards poetic drama. On 10 January he wrote to Robert Bridges

> I was and indeed am sunk in work about which I am very much in earnest. When I wrote I was more or less desperate about a dramatic poem which refused to go faster than my average of some eight or nine lines a day, despite material necessities that it should, and am still in a tempered desperation. I am trying for a more remote wisdom, or peace, for they are much the same, and find it hard not to lose grip on the necessary harvest of mere exterior beauty, in seeking for this visionary harvest. I am doing my best work or my worst and do not well know which.[55]

At about the same time he wrote to 'Fiona MacLeod' (William Sharp), whose book, *From the Hills of Dream*, he had reviewed in the December 1896 issue of *The Bookman*, a letter which indicated that his thoughts were moving towards a Celtic movement in drama, which would not necessarily be confined to Ireland in its influence:

> Our Irish Literary and Political literary organisations are pretty complete (I am trying to start a Young Ireland Society, among the Irish here in Paris at the moment) and I think it would be very possible to get up Celtic plays through these Societies. They would be far more effective than lectures and might do more than anything else we can do to make the Irish, Scotch and other Celts recognise their solidarity. My own plays are too elaborate, I think, for a start, and have also the disadvantage that I cannot urge my own work in committee. If we have one or two short direct prose plays, of (say) a mythological and folklore kind, by you and by some writer (I may be able to move O'Grady, I have already spoken to him about it urgently) I feel sure we could get the Irish Literary Society to make a start. They have indeed for some time talked of doing my *Land of Heart's Desire*.
>
> My own theory of poetical or legendary drama is that it should have no realistic, or elaborate, but only a symbolic and decorative setting. A forest, for instance, should be represented by a forest pattern and not by a forest painting. One should design a scene which would be an accompaniment not a reflection of the text. This method would have the further advantage of being fairly cheap, and altogether novel. The acting should have an equivalent distance to that of the play from common realities. The plays might be almost, in some cases, modern mystery plays.[56]

This long letter goes on to discuss possibilities of deriving plays from 'Fiona MacLeod' whom Yeats had not yet identified as the pseudonym used by William Sharp to sign his 'Celtic' writings, and it also discusses the ever-present difficulties in the revisions to *The Shadowy Waters*. He suggests, too: 'I shall try my own hand possibly at some short prose plays also, but not yet.' [57]

His dialogue with Robert Bridges continued after his return to Woburn Buildings, and he published an essay on Bridges' *The Return of Ulysses* in *The Bookman* for June which he retained, dated 1896, as part of his book, *Ideas of Good and Evil*, in which he stated

Some day the few among us who care for poetry more than any temporal thing, and who believe that its delights cannot be perfect when we read it alone in our rooms and long for one to share its delights, but that they might be perfect in the theatre, when we share them friend with friend, lover with beloved, will persuade a few idealists to seek out the lost art of speaking, and seek out ourselves the lost art, that is perhaps nearest of all arts to eternity, the subtle art of listening.[58]

In the same essay he revealed, too, his own desire to see a school of epic drama develop.

There is one play especially, *The Return of Ulysses*, which we will praise for perfect after its kind, the kind of our new drama of wisdom, for it moulds into dramatic shape, and with as much as possible of literal translation, those closing books of the *Odyssey* which are perhaps the most perfect poetry of the world, and compels that great tide of song to flow through delicate dramatic verse, with little abatement of its own leaping and clamorous speed.[59]

This, taken with a further passage from the letter to 'Fiona MacLeod' quoted above, indicates that the path along which his own dramatic career was to develop was already apparent to Yeats. He wrote that, after his revision of *The Shadowy Waters* and the writing of his projected novel, *The Speckled Bird*, on which Bullen had paid him an advance, he intended to

start a long-cherished project — a poetical version of the great Celtic epic tale, Deirdre, Cuchullin at the Ford, and Cuchullin's death, and Dermot and Grainne. I have some hopes that Mr. Sharp will come to Paris on his way back to England. I have much to talk over with him. I am feeling more and more every day that our Celtic movement is approaching a new phase. Our instrument is sufficiently prepared as far as Ireland is concerned, but the people are less so, and they can only be stirred by the imagination of a very few acting on all.[60]

Even at this early date in his theatrical career, Yeats saw himself as a leading spirit in a movement which, using symbolism rather than 'realism,' could revitalise and bring the poetic spirit back into the theatre. This is very much evident in his general approach to artistic principles which he expressed in such writings as his essay on the symbolist artist, Althea Gyles, which he contributed to *The Dome* in its Christmas issue for 1898, and in which he stated that there are tides in the imagination of the world and a motion in one or two minds may show a change in tide.[61]

*

By May 1897 Yeats was back in Sligo, writing book reviews and continuing to work on his novel, *The Speckled Bird*, which proved a difficult task. He was planning a further visit to Edward Martyn at Tulyra and to Lady Gregory at Coole, a visit which occurred in July and during which the first discussions of an Irish theatre which had taken place during his visit in the previous year, and had developed further in meetings with Lady Gregory and in his exchanges of letters with such people as Robert Bridges and 'Fiona MacLeod' during the months between, turned towards the formulation of a definite plan.

Lady Gregory, in *Our Irish Theatre*, recalls the meeting at which the foundation of the Irish Literary Theatre took place, at the home of her friend 'the old Count de Basterot, at Duras, that is beyond Kinvara and beside the sea':

On one of those days at Duras in 1898 [actually 1897] Mr. Edward Martyn, my neighbour, came to see the Count, bringing with him Mr. Yeats, whom I did not then know very well, though I cared for his work very much and had already, through his directions, been gathering folk-lore. They had lunch with us, but it was a wet day, and we could not go out. After a while I thought that the Count wanted to talk to Mr. Martyn alone; so I took Mr. Yeats to the office where the steward used to come to talk, — less about business I think than of the Land War or the state of the country, or the last year's deaths and marriages from Kinvara to the headland of Aughanish. We sat there through that wet afternoon, and though I had never been at all interested in theatres, our talk turned on plays. Mr. Martyn had written two, *The Heather Field* and *Maeve*. They had been offered to London managers, and now he thought of trying to have them produced in Germany, where there seemed to be more room for new drama than in England. I said it was a pity we had no Irish theatre where such plays could be given. Mr. Yeats said that had always been a dream of his, but he had of late thought it an impossible one, for it could not at first pay its way, and there was no money to be found for such a thing in Ireland.

We went on talking about it, and things seemed to grow possible as we talked, and before the end of the afternoon we had made our plan. We said we would collect money, or rather ask to have a certain sum of money guaranteed. We would then take a Dublin theatre and give a performance of Mr. Martyn's *Heather Field* and one of Mr. Yeats's own plays, *The Countess Cathleen*. I offered the first guarantee of £25.[62]

The event is commemorated today by a plaque in the room in which this historic conversation took place, which, as its dating is taken from Lady Gregory's book, is inaccurate by a year, but which forcefully reminds the visitor to that country house, now a youth hostel on the Atlantic coast of the West of Ireland, of the statement made by Yeats in the penultimate paragraph of that part of his *Autobiographies* which he called 'The Stirring of the Bones' in which he asked: 'where, but for that conversation at Florimond de Basterot's, had been the genius of Synge?'[63]

A letter seeking the needed funds was drafted, and typed out by Lady Gregory to enlist support for the project, and requesting a guarantee fund of £300 which was to make the work of the Irish Literary Theatre possible for a three-year period. It began:

We propose to have performed in Dublin, in the spring of every year certain Celtic and Irish plays, which whatever be their degree of excellence will be written with a high ambition, and so build up a Celtic and Irish school of dramatic literature. We hope to find in Ireland an uncorrupted and imaginative audience trained to listen by its passion for oratory, and believe that our desire to bring upon the stage the deeper thoughts and emotions of Ireland will ensure for us a tolerant welcome, and that freedom to experiment which is not found in theatres of England, and without which no new movement in art or literature can succeed. We will show that Ireland is not the home of buffoonery and of easy sentiment, as it has been represented, but the home of an ancient idealism. We are confident of the support of all Irish people who are weary of misrepresentation, in carrying out a work that is outside all the political questions that divide us.[64]

Much of the autumn and winter of 1897 was devoted by Yeats to fund-raising and to finding solutions to the practical difficulties that the organisation of the theatre project involved. These included the changing of the law regarding the licensing of halls for the projected performances, lobbying persons influential in Parliament and in the Dublin Corporation, pleading the non-commercial nature of the production. This business of creating a theatre free of the British patent regulations occupied much of Yeats's time during the first half of 1898, while, at the same time, he was planning the practical details of casting and presentation of the plays. As he wrote in *Samhain 1901*,

We thought that three years would show whether the country desired to take up the project, and make it a part of the national life, and that we, at any rate, could return to our proper work, in which we did not include theatrical management, at the end of that time. A little later, Mr. George Moore joined us; and, looking back now upon our work, I doubt if it could have been done at all without his great knowledge of the stage; and certainly if the performances of this present year bring our adventure to a successful close, a chief part of the credit will be his.[65]

Due to the efforts of Yeats and Lady Gregory to persuade members of parliament to take up their cause, a clause was added to the Act regulating theatre patents which allowed the Lord Lieutenant to issue, on application by the county or city council of Dublin, an occasional licence for performances of 'stage plays or other dramatic entertainments' in any theatre, room or building where the profits arising therefrom were to be applied for charitable purposes or in aid of funds of any society instituted for the purpose of science, literature or the fine arts exclusively. While the immediate result of this amendment of the law made the pursuit of the aims of the Irish Literary Theatre possible, its enduring effect was the benefit which, for many years following, it gave to many other amateur and experimental societies involved in the arts of the theatre in Dublin and district.

*

'It was now that George Moore came into our affairs,'[66] wrote Yeats in *Dramatis Personae*, introducing the only member of the original group who had any practical experience of dealing with theatrical managements and with theatrical affairs, into his account of the genesis of the Irish Literary Theatre. This, however, was not Yeats's first confrontation with Moore, who attended *The Land of Heart's Desire* at the Avenue Theatre in 1894 and wrote of the play as 'an inoffensive trifle.'[67] At the time both Moore and Edward Martyn had rooms in the Temple, where they 'used to talk literature and drama until two or three in the morning,'[68] as Moore recounted in the 'Overture' to *Ave*, the first of the three volumes of his reminiscences of the Irish Literary Revival. The strange friendship of Moore and Martyn is described by Yeats later in the same section of *Dramatis Personae*, where he states that Martyn had invited Moore to help him cast *The Heather Field*. As Yeats put it

They were cousins and inseparable friends, bound one to the other by mutual contempt. When I told Martyn that Moore had good points, he replied : "I know Moore a good deal longer than you do. He has no good points." And a week or two later Moore said : "That man Martyn is the most selfish man alive. He thinks that I am damned and he doesn't care." I have described their friendship in a little play called *The Cat and the Moon*; the speaker is a blind beggar-man, and Laban is a townland where Edward Martyn went to chapel : . . . "Did you ever know a holy man but had a wicked man for his comrade and his heart's darling? There is not a more holy man in the barony than the man who has the big house at Laban, and he goes knocking about the roads day and night with that old lecher from the county of Mayo, and he a woman-hater from the day of his birth."[69]

Although Yeats saw the pair as 'in certain characteristics typical peasants, the peasant sinner, the peasant saint,'[70] each played a vital part in the achievement of the Irish Literary Theatre during the three

years of its existence and the work they produced inspired much of
the idiom which made the Irish Theatre movement unique in its time
and contributed certain elements which, for over half a century,
remained identifiable with the 'Abbey' style of play.

Moore described Yeats and Martyn coming to him with their plan:

W. B. Yeats, the Irish poet, came to see me in my flat in Victoria Street,
followed by Edward. My surprise was great at seeing them arrive together, not
knowing that they even knew each other; and while staring at them I remembered they had met in my rooms in the King's Bench Walk. But how often had
Edward met my friends and liked them, in a way, yet not enough to compel
him to hook himself on to them by a letter or a visit? . . . it was this
knowledge of the indolence of his character that caused me to wonder at
seeing him arrive with Yeats. Perhaps seeing them together stirred some
fugitive jealousy in me, which passed away when the servant brought in the
lamp, for, with the light behind them, my visitors appeared a twain as fantastic as anything ever seen in Japanese prints — Edward great in girth as an
owl (he is nearly as neckless), blinking behind his glasses, and Yeats lank as a
rook, a-dream in black silhouette on the flowered wall-paper.
But owls and rooks do not roost together, nor have they a habit or an
instinct in common.[71]

Later, having observed that 'the drama brings strange fowls to
roost,' Moore went on to 'pity their forlorn project':

A forlorn thing it was surely to bring literary plays to Dublin! . . . Dublin of
all cities in the world !
It is Yeats, I said, who has persuaded dear Edward, and looking from one to
the other, I thought how the cunning rook had enticed the profound owl
from his belfry — an owl that has stayed out too late, and is nervous lest he
should not be able to find his way back; perplexed, too, by other considerations, lest the Dean and Chapter, having heard of the strange company he is
keeping, may have, during his absence, bricked up the entrance to his roost.[72]

However, agreement was reached that Moore should help with his
advice and with finding a cast for Martyn's play and, in his individual
way, he managed to involve himself also with the preparations for
The Countess Cathleen, although Yeats had invited Florence Farr to
find actors for his play. Florence Farr had originally chosen for the
title role Dorothy Paget who, five years before, had played the Faery
Child in *The Land of Heart's Desire*, but, as Yeats described in
Dramatis Personae:

Moore descended upon my rehearsals. I was relieved, for I was rehearsing in
the part of Countess Cathleen a young girl who had made a great success
some years before as the Faery Child in my *Land of Heart's Desire*. She had a
beautiful speaking voice but lacked experience. I describe the result: "Moore
has put a Miss Whitty to act Countess Cathleen. She acts admirably, and has
no sense of rhythm whatever. . . . She enrages me every moment, but will

make the part a success. Mrs Emery (Florence Farr) alone satisfies my ear." Perhaps I should have insisted upon the young girl, for after Miss Whitty's dress rehearsal somebody said: "Miss Whitty brought tears into my eyes because she had them in her voice, but that young girl brought them into my eyes with beauty." [73]

While the rehearsals for the first performances of the Irish Literary Theatre proceeded in London where, as Yeats expressed again when he came to change the style of his dramatic writing to one modelled on the Japanese Nō theatre seventeen years later, he had to go in quest of the skills he sought, the prospect of the Theatre was continuing to arouse interest in Dublin, and, as both plays had appeared in print, *The Heather Field* in 1890, and *The Countess Cathleen* in its various versions in the successive editions of Yeats's books, the texts were looked at by Irish critics, both clerical and lay, before the performances took place.

And here it is perhaps proper to introduce the 'ordinary man,' the chronicler of the Dublin theatre from 1896 until his death at the age of eighty-four, in 1944 — Joseph Holloway, who recorded in an invaluable series of Diaries, now in the National Library of Ireland, his 'Impressions of a Dublin Playgoer.' Holloway wrote a preface to the first volume of his journals in which he confessed:

I have no prejudices nor fads; all performers appeal to me only on their merits as performers, whether they pose as comedians, tragedians, vocalists, elocutionists, music-hall artistes or lecturers. To see whether the mirror has been held up to Nature is the object I always keep before my mind in writing. . . . It is as an ordinary play-goer, and not in the capacity of a professional critic, that I have given expression to my thoughts. [74]

Holloway was a man of some means and, by profession, a successful Dublin architect, who was, in 1904, commissioned by Miss Horniman to design the conversion of part of the old Mechanics' Institute and the old city morgue into the Abbey Theatre, the National Theatre's permanent home. He recorded in his journal the 'Conversazione' on 9 January 1899 at which W. B. Yeats announced the ideals and the plans for the first season of the Irish Literary Theatre, and concluded his entry on a hopeful note:

That the scheme may be a success is my ardent wish. If enthusiasm can command success, then it is assured, as nothing could be more enthusiastic than the manner in which Mr. Yeats has taken up the idea. [75]

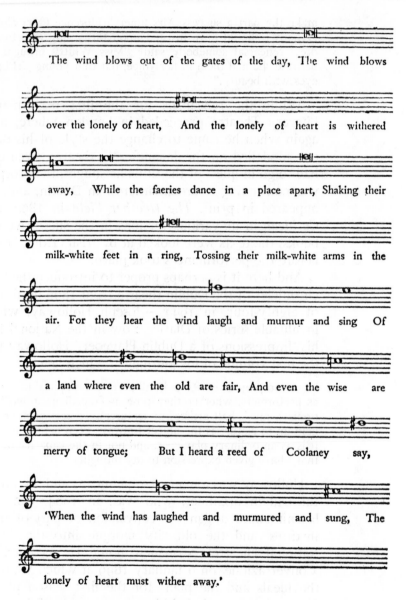

The wind blows out of the gates of the day, The wind blows

over the lonely of heart,   And the lonely of heart is withered

away,   While the faeries dance in a place apart, Shaking their

milk-white feet in a ring, Tossing their milk-white arms in the

air. For they hear the wind laugh and murmur and sing   Of

a land where even the old are fair, And even the wise   are

merry of tongue;   But I heard a reed of   Coolaney   say,

'When the wind has laughed   and   murmured   and   sung,   The

lonely of heart must wither away.'

¹ The music as written suits my speaking voice if played an octave lower than the notation.—F. F.

5. Florence Farr's musical setting for the lyric in
The Land of Heart's Desire, 1894.

The Antient Concert Rooms, usually hired out for musical events and occasional dramatic performances, in Great Brunswick Street, Dublin, was the venue for the first season of the Irish Literary Theatre on 8, 9, 10, 12 and 13 May 1899. The performances were presented under the auspices of the Irish Literary Society and were thus an extension of the work of the Literary Societies founded by Yeats in London and in Dublin in 1892. The Antient Concert Rooms was built in 1824 as the Dublin Oil Gas Station and, about the middle of the century, became a concert auditorium. Later, James Joyce and John McCormick were to make their Dublin debuts in the same auditorium and, later again, Great Brunswick Street was to be renamed Pearse Street in memory of the brothers Patrick and Willie Pearse, leaders of the 1916 Rising, who had lived there. The building became a cinema in the 1920's, originally named the Palace and is now the Academy Cinema. There is no plaque or other marking to commemorate the importance of the building as the birthplace of Ireland's National Theatre.

6. The Antient Concert Rooms in Great Brunswick Street, now Pearse Street, Dublin — a reconstruction of the nineteenth-century façade.

Two plays were presented during this first season, *The Heather Field* by Edward Martyn and *The Countess Cathleen* by W. B. Yeats, which had four performances to three of Martyn's play. The company was hired and rehearsed in London and the scenery and costumes were supplied by London contractors, probably out of stock. Yeats was, however, moving towards a realisation of what his theatrical objectives should be and was aware of the limitations of the presentation. Early in 1899 he entered the controversy which developed from William Archer's review of the published text of

The Heather Field and wrote, in a letter published in *The Daily Chronicle* on 27 January:

I see in my imagination a stage where there shall be both scenery and costumes, but scenery and costumes which will draw little attention to themselves and cost little money. I have noticed at a rehearsal how the modern coats and the litter on the stage draw one's attention, and baffle the evocation, which needs all one's thought that it may call before one's eyes lovers escaping through a forest, or men in armour upon a mountain side. I have noticed, too, how elaborate costumes and scenery silence the evocation completely, and substitute the cheap effects of a dressmaker and of a meretricious painter for an imaginative glory. . . . Such scenery might come, when its makers had mastered its mysteries, to have a severe beauty, such as one finds in Egyptian wall-paintings, and it would be more beautiful, even at the beginning, than the expensive scenery of the modern theatre, even when Mr. Tree has put into the boughs in the forest those memorable birds that sing by machinery.

This long letter embodied Yeats's first important definition of his ideal theatre and, today, can be recognised as the fundamental statement of a *Credo* from which the whole development of his work in the theatre sprang. The letter continues:

We have forgotten that the Drama began in the chanted ode, and that whenever it has been great it has been written certainly to delight our eyes, but to delight our ears more than our eyes. Greek actors with masks upon their faces, and their stature increased by artifice, must have been content to delight the eyes with but an austere and monotonous beauty, and Elizabethan actors who had to speak so much that would seem irrelevant poetry to modern audiences must have thought oratory a principal part of acting. I believe that the reason why the men of letters of this century have failed to master the technique of the modern theatre, while the men of letters of past times mastered the technique of the theatre of their times without difficulty, is that the modern theatre has discovered that you can move many thousands, who have no imagination for beautiful words to awaken, by filling the stage with landscapes, which are at best like the landscapes of Mr. Leader, and with handsome men and women in expensive dresses, who pose when happily inspired like persons in popular German pictures. The accepted theory is that men of letters have suddenly lost the dramatic faculty, but it is easier to believe that times and seasons change than that imagination and intellect change; for imagination and intellect are that which is eternal in man crying out against that which is temporal and perishing.

And, having defined his position, he went on to predict how his ideals might be realised in the creation of a National Theatre for his own country, a theatre which could accommodate itself to the needs of a concerned audience:

The theatre can only escape by working for that small public which cares for literature and the arts without losing all hope of the theatre; and how small it is is shown by the impossibility of making a play of Ibsen's run for more than a few afternoons. If we are to have an endowed theatre, it should work for this public, which will grow a little larger in time; for compromise is as impossible in literature as in matters of faith. We will work for it in Dublin, producing our plays at the same time every year, that persons who have ceased to read theatrical news may come to know about us; and we will produce them inexpensively and for but a few days, that we may be independent of popular taste, and, as I hope, with austere and grave costumes and scenery, that we may appeal to the imagination alone.[1]

In January 1899 some scenes from *The Countess Cathleen* were presented as *tableaux vivants* at the Viceregal Lodge in Dublin, a performance to which Yeats consented with reluctance but allowed because he realised that any publicity for the coming season of the Irish Literary Theatre was valuable. His talent as manager of theatre affairs was developing rapidly and during the spring of 1899 while he was preparing the Dublin public for the season he was, at the same time, seeing to rehearsals of the plays in London where, as he wrote to George Russell on 6 March, George Moore was constantly present, 'looking, as some friend of Miss Farr's said, like a "boiled ghost." . . . He is quite the most exacting critic I know.'[2]

Moore was probably behind the decision to use a fully professional cast except for walk-on parts and the high standard achieved in the first productions was, to a large extent, due to his uncompromising attitude in matters of style. He overcame Martyn's doubts and hesitations after Martyn had consulted a theologian as to the propriety of Yeats's play and succeeded in maintaining an uneasy peace between the players and the management until he could describe, as he put it, 'the departure of the mummers from Euston':

Yeats and the lady in green had started some days before — Yeats to work up the Press, and the lady to discover the necessary properties that would be required in Dublin for both plays. Noggins were wanted for *The Countess Cathleen*, and noggins could not be procured in London. Yeats and the lady in green were our agents in advance, Edward with universal approbation casting himself for the part of baggage-man. He was splendid in it, with a lady's bag on his arm, running up and down the station at Euston, shepherding his flock, shouting that all the luggage was now in the van, and crying : The boy, who is to look after him? I will be back with the tickets in a moment. Away he fled and at the ticket-office he was impassive, monumental, muttering fiercely to impatient bystanders that he must count his money, that he had no intention of leaving till he was sure he had been given the right change.

Now, are you not coming with us? he cried to me, and would have pulled me into the train if I had not disengaged myself, saying :

No, no; I will not travel without clothes. Loose me. The very words do I remember, and the telegram two days after : The sceptre of intelligence has passed from London to Dublin. Again and again I read Edward's telegram. If it be true, if art be winging her way westward? And a vision rose up before me of argosies floating up the Liffey, laden with merchandise from all the ports of Phoenicia, and poets singing in all the bowers of Merrion Square; and all in a new language that the poets had learned, the English language having been discovered by them, as it had been discovered by me, to be a declining language, a language that was losing its verbs.[3]

*

THREEPENCE—INCLUDING PROGRAMME.

BELTAINE

An Occasional Publication. Number One. May 1899.

THE ORGAN OF THE IRISH LITERARY THEATRE

LONDON: AT THE SIGN OF THE UNICORN.

DUBLIN: AT THE "DAILY EXPRESS" OFFICE.

7. *Beltaine*, No. 1, 1899. Front cover (reduced). Original 8½ × 6¾″.

Beltaine, subtitled 'The Organ of the Irish Literary Theatre,' was first published to coincide with the Irish Literary Theatre's season in May 1899, and included in its contents the programme of the performances. Yeats, although not named as such in the first issue, was editor of the journal, and used its pages to set out the theories on which his approach to theatre was based. The first of the three numbers issued contained an article on the Scandinavian dramatists by C. H. Hereford, reprinted from *The Daily Express*, introductions to the two plays in the season, the prologue written by Lionel Johnson for the opening performance and two contributions by Yeats in which he developed the theories on which his approach to stage performance was based. In the unsigned section headed 'Plans and Methods' he wrote, 'The chief endeavour with Mr. Yeats's play has been to get it spoken with some sense of rhythm,' and went on to define the approach to verse speaking which had grown out of his experiments with Florence Farr:

The two lyrics, which we print on a later page, are not sung, but spoken, or rather chanted, to music, as the old poems were probably chanted by bards and rhapsodists. Even when the words of a song, sung in the ordinary way, are heard at all, their own proper rhythm and emphasis are lost, or partly lost, in the rhythm and emphasis of the music. A lyric which is spoken or chanted to music should, upon the other hand, reveal its meaning, and its rhythm so become indissoluble in the memory. The speaking of words, whether to music or not, is, however, so perfectly among the lost arts that it will take a long time before our actors, no matter how willing, will be able to forget the ordinary methods of the stage or to perfect a new method.[4]

This approach to verse speaking was defined in the essay, 'Speaking to the Psaltery,' which, with the assistance of Florence Farr, Yeats wrote in 1902. This contains examples of the settings made for the psaltery which Arnold Dolmetsch had constructed for them,

a beautiful instrument, half psaltery, half lyre, which contains, I understand, all the chromatic intervals within the range of the speaking voice; and he taught us to regulate our speech by the ordinary musical notes.[5]

In her book, *The Music of Speech*, printed in 1909, Florence Farr describes the psaltery as having thirteen open strings, with a compass from G below the middle C of the piano to G above. As her speaking voice was low this range suited it, but when a similar psaltery was made for Mrs. Patrick Campbell, the compass of that instrument was pitched from B flat to B flat. And, in her footnote to the Faery Child's song from *The Land of Heart's Desire*, printed in Yeats's essay, Florence Farr said that the music as written would suit her speaking voice if played an octave lower than the notation.

The musical examples in 'Speaking to the Psaltery' include two settings of lyrics from Yeats's plays, the Faery Child's song from *The Land of Heart's Desire* and Aleel's song from the first act of *The Countess Cathleen*. Yeats added a note to the latter setting:

> It is written in the old C clef, which is, I am told, the most reasonable way to write it, for it would be "below the stave on the treble clef or above it on the bass clef." The central line of the stave "corresponds to the middle C of the piano; the first note of the poem is therefore D." The marks of long and short over the syllables are not marks of scansion, but show the syllables one makes the voice hurry or linger over.

But the most important statement in the 1899 *Beltaine* was Yeats's essay, 'The Theatre' which he had first published in the April issue of *The Dome* and in which he continued his definition of the theatre he sought:

> Even if poetry were spoken as poetry, it would still seem out of place in many of its highest moments upon a stage, where the superficial appearances of nature are so closely copied; for poetry is founded upon convention, and becomes incredible the moment painting or gesture remind us that people do not speak verse when they meet upon the highway. The theatre of Art, when it comes to exist, must therefore discover grave and decorative gestures, such as delighted Rossetti and Madox Brown, and grave and decorative scenery, that will be forgotten the moment an actor has said "It is dawn," or "It is raining," or "The wind is shaking the trees"; and dresses of so little irrelevant magnificence that the mortal actors and actresses may change without much labour into the immortal people of romance. The theatre began in ritual, and it cannot come to its greatness again without recalling words to their ancient sovereignty.
>
> It will take a generation, and perhaps generations, to restore the theatre of Art; for one must get one's actors, and perhaps one's scenery, from the theatre of commerce, until new actors and new painters have come to help one; and until many failures and imperfect successes have made a new tradition, and perfected in detail the ideal that is beginning to float before our eyes. If one could call one's painters and one's actors from where one would, how easy it would be. I know some painters,* who have never painted scenery, who could paint the scenery I want, but they have their own work to do; and in Ireland I have heard a red-haired orator repeat some bad political verses with a voice that went through one like flame, and made them seem the most beautiful verses in the world; but he has no practical knowledge of the stage, and probably despises it.[6]

*

---

*This essay was reprinted in *Ideas of Good and Evil*, 1903, and in later editions Yeats added a footnote, dated 1924, stating that he had Charles Ricketts in mind when writing this passage.

Antient Concert Rooms
BRUNSWICK STREET, DUBLIN.

THE

IRISH LITERARY THEATRE
Under the auspices of the National Literary Society.

May 8th	. .	THE COUNTESS CATHLEEN: 8.30.
„ 9th	. .	THE HEATHER FIELD: 8.30.
„ 10th	. .	THE COUNTESS CATHLEEN: 3.0.
		THE HEATHER FIELD: 8.30.
„ 12th	. .	THE COUNTESS CATHLEEN: 8.30.
„ 13th	. .	THE HEATHER FIELD: 3.0.
		THE COUNTESS CATHLÉEN: 8.30.

A Prologue by Mr. Lionel Johnson will be spoken at the First Performance.

General Manager	MISS FLORENCE FARR.
Treasurer	MR. EDWARD MARTYN.
Secretary	MRS. GEORGE COFFEY.
Stage Manager	MR. BEN WEBSTER.
Assistant Stage Manager	MR. BRENDON STEWERT.

Dresses and Wigs by NATHAN and CLARKSON.

*Herr Bast's ' Suite on Irish Airs' (for String Quartet in 4 Movements) will be
played before and between the acts each evening.
Violin and harp for incidental music.
Artistes: Mr. P. Delany, M. Ivors Cree, M. Grisard, Herr Bast,
Miss Phyllis Paul (Harp).*

8. Programme of performances in *Beltaine*, No. 1, 1899.

The ancient Irish pagan festival of *Bealtaine*, in May, was the chosen occasion for the first performances of the Irish Literary Theatre, and the journal of the same name opened with the programme of performances reproduced here. Lionel Johnson's Prologue, spoken on the first evening of the season, ended:

Now, at this opening of the gentle May,
Watch warring passions at their storm and play;
Wrought with the flaming ecstasy of art,
Sprung from the dreaming of an Irish heart.[7]

The 'warring passions' were not confined to the actors on the stage, but also affected the audience of between four and five hundred in the Antient Concert Rooms, as Joseph Holloway recorded:

Monday, May 8. At last the Irish Literary Theatre is become an actuality, and the red letter occurrence in the annals of the Irish Literary movement took place in the Antient Concert Rooms where a large and most fashionable audience filled the hall. There a pretty little miniature stage, perfectly appointed, had been erected. W. B. Yeats's miracle play in four acts, *The Countess Cathleen*, was the work selected to inaugurate the Theatre,* and from one cause or another the event was looked forward to with considerable excitement and interest, owing to the hostility exhibited in certain quarters to the author.[8]

George Moore, who made his way from his hotel 'with quick, irritable steps,' formed a different impression of the Antient Concert Rooms,

whither the hall-porter had directed me, and finding them by a stone-cutter's yard. Angels and crosses ! A truly suitable place for a play by Edward Martyn, I said. The long passage leading to the rooms seemed to be bringing me into a tomb. Nothing very renascent about this, I said, pushing my way through the spring doors into a lofty hall with a balcony and benches down the middle, and there were seats along the walls placed so that those who sat on them

---

*   THE COUNTESS CATHLEEN

Presented by the Irish Literary Theatre
at the Antient Concert Rooms, Brunswick Street, Dublin
on Monday 8 May 1899

The Countess Cathleen	Miss May Whitty
First Demon	Mr. Marcus StJohn
Second Demon	Mr. Trevor Lowe
Shemus Rua	Mr. Valentine Grace
Teig Rua	Master Charles Sefton
Maire Rua	Madame San Carolo
Aleel	Miss Florence Farr
Oona	Miss Anna Mather
Herdsman	Mr. Claude Holmes
Gardener	Mr. Jack Wilcox
First Peasant	Mr. Walford
Sheogue	Miss Dorothy Paget
Peasant Woman	Miss M. Kelly
Servant	Mr. F. E. Wilkinson

Directed by Florence Farr, assisted by W. B. Yeats
Lyrics set by Florence Farr

would have to turn their heads to see the stage, a stage that had been con-structed hurriedly by advancing some rudely painted wings and improvising a drop-curtain.[9]

The epigraph quoted from Saint Paul on the programme of *The Countess Cathleen*, 'I wished to be anathema for my brethren,' might have provided the text for the protestors in the audience. Even in this, its very first production in Dublin, the Irish Literary Theatre was beset by disturbances and protests, setting a pattern that was to be repeated over the years whenever controversial plays were presented, and occasionally, too, when the Dublin audience was not satisfied with the standards of presentation in the theatre. On this first occasion the protests were caused by the issue of a pamphlet, *Souls for Gold*, by F. Hugh O'Donnell,* which attacked the play on theo-logical grounds and caused such an outcry in the press that Cardinal Logue felt compelled to contribute an ambiguous letter. 'The Celtic Muse of W. B. Yeats,' wrote F. Hugh O'Donnell,

is tireless in its flattering appreciations of the Irish nation. Its men, apostate cowards; its women — such as this; its priests, the prey of demon swine; its shrines, kicked to pieces by its Celtic peasantry; the awful majesty of the Christian God flouted and mocked by spirits from the pit! What is the meaning of this rubbish? How is it to help the national cause? How is it to help any cause at all? Mysticism? Nonsense! This is not Mysticism. The great mystics are intellectual and moral glories of Christian civilisation. This is only silly stuff, and sillier, unutterable profanity.

Where can you find actors, amateur or professional, for such offensiveness? Where can you get an audience? Not among Catholics. Not among Protestants. Not among Nationalists of any manly race or nation.[10]

Yeats consulted two theologians, Father Finlay and Father William Barry, author of *The New Antigone*, both of whom approved of the play and, in his letter to Yeats, Father Barry quoted the line from Saint Paul. Nevertheless, as Yeats related in *Dramatis Personae*,

Before the first performance, to the charge of heresy was added that of representing Irish men and women as selling their souls, whereas "their refusal to change their religion, even when starving, proved that they would not." On the night of the performance, there was a friendly house drawn from the general public, but many interrupters in the gallery. I had asked for police protection and found twenty or thirty police awaiting my arrival. A sergeant explained that they could not act unless called upon. I turned to a friend, once Secretary to the Land League, and said: "Stay with me, I have no experience." All the police smiled, and I remembered a lying rumour that I had organised the Jubilee riots.[11]

---

*The full text of this pamphlet is reprinted as Appendix VIII in *Our Irish Theatre* by Lady Gregory with a foreword by Roger McHugh. Colin Smythe, Gerards Cross, 1972.

Souls for Gold!

Pseudo=Celtic Drama in Dublin.

"There soon will be no man or woman's soul
Unbargained for in five-score baronies."

Mr. W. B. Yates on "Celtic Ireland."

LONDON MDCCCXCIX.

9. The front cover of *Souls for Gold*, London 1899.

Yeats did not want his play turned into an occasion for an anti-clerical demonstration, but,

In using what I considered traditional symbols I forgot that in Ireland they are not symbols but realities. But the attacks in the main, like those upon Synge and O'Casey, came from the public ignorance of literary method. The play itself was ill-constructed, the dialogue turning aside at the lure of word or metaphor, very different, I hope, from the play as it is to-day after many alterations, every alteration tested by performance. It was not, nor is it now, more than a piece of tapestry. The Countess sells her soul, but she is not transformed.[12]

Yeats counted Florence Farr's performance as Aleel among his 'unforgettable memories,' [13] but found May Whitty as the Countess, 'effective and commonplace.' [14] Holloway liked both actresses, but thought the general effect of the verse speaking indistinct. However, the event proved a triumph for the Irish Literary Theatre and was acclaimed by the critics, among them Max Beerbohm, who came to Dublin to write about the occasion for *The Saturday Review*, and said:

In writing *The Countess Cathleen*, and in starting The Irish Literary Theatre, Mr. Yeats's aim has been to see whether beauty be not after all possible on the stage. Every one who cares about the stage ought to be grateful to him, whatever the outcome of his experiment. . . . Despite the little cramped stage, and the scenery which was as tawdry as it should have been dim, I was, from first to last, conscious that a beautiful play was being enacted, and I felt that I had not made a journey in vain.[15]

*

The Countess Cathleen is a morality in which Yeats presents a basically simple struggle between the forces of good and evil, but with significant departures from the accepted ideas of such a confrontation. By the time the first staged version had developed, elements of the philosophies of the magical Order of the Golden Dawn had become entwined with the plot, and an obsession with Pre-Raphaelite imagery is evident in the stage directions. And, all the time, beneath the apparently Christian surface motifs of the play, the older traditions of Pagan Ireland are stirring, creating tensions which are ever present in the highly decorative 'poetic language' of the text.

The Countess, who sells her soul to relieve the sufferings of her serfs, belongs more to Oisin's world than to Patrick's, and her attendant poet, Aleel, seems also to belong to the older order. The glimpse of heaven at the end of the play, with 'vapour full of storm and ever changing light,' angels in ancient battered armour looking sternly downward on the mortals, and the far-off horns which seem to sound from the heart of the heavenly light, is remote from Christian imagery, but approaches that of Wagner's *Gotterdammerung*. Even the *dramatis personae* of the earlier versions of the play bear this out as the crowd is made up of 'Angelical Beings, Spirits and Faeries,' while, in the first production, the fairy child of *The Land of Heart's Desire* is reflected by the presence in the cast list of 'Sheogue,' (a young fairy, or a fairy child) which was played by Dorothy Paget.

10. Detail from a woodcut by Sir Edward Burne-Jones in the Kelmscott Press *Chaucer*, printed by William Morris, 1896. This figure suggests to me Aleel, the poet.

Yeats's stage directions to *The Countess Cathleen* suggest that the action takes place within a wood, such as might be seen in a medieval illumination. Perhaps, in the transformation scene at the end of the play, we reach the edge of this wood, and the new life, where light has triumphed over dark, is a resumption of the same order of things, of castle and demons removed. But Yeats's vision of this medieval world is tempered by a Pre-Raphaelite view, and a parallel approach might be sought in the illustrations made by Sir Edward Burne-Jones to the *Chaucer* which William Morris finished printing at the Kelmscott Press in 1896. In scene one Yeats asks for

a door into the open air, through which one sees, perhaps, the trees of a wood and these trees should be painted in flat colour upon a gold or diapered sky. The walls are of one colour. The scene should have the effect of missal painting.

11. Detail from the Kelmscott *Chaucer*, 1896. Compare with
the stage directions in *The Countess Cathleen*.

The directions for scene two ask that the scenery be

A wood with perhaps a distant view of a turret house at one side but all in
flat colour, without light and shade against a diapered or gold background,

and so on. The variants in these directions can be found in Russell
K. Alspach's *Variorum Edition of the Plays* and show, throughout the
many re-writings of the text of the play, a remarkable consistency in
the visual approach.

The influence of the *Chaucer* woodcuts on Yeats is reflected in a
letter written to John Quinn on 29 June 1905, thanking him for sub-
scribing to the copy of the book, by then a rare one, which, at the
instigation of Lady Gregory, was presented to Yeats by a group of
friends to mark his fortieth birthday.

The book is a very great pleasure, coming as it does just when I am setting
out to read Chaucer. I have always thought it the most beautiful of all printed
books. The pictures have already raised images of stage scenery, and one of
them has made an important change in the setting of the Deirdre play.[16]

And, in *Pages from a Diary Written in Nineteen Hundred and
Thirty*, Yeats gave a further possible source for the angelic visitors at
the end of the play:

When I was in my twenties I saw a drawing or etching by some French artist
of an angel standing against a midnight sky. The angel was old, wingless and

12. An armed angel. Detail from the Kelmscott *Chaucer*, 1896.

armed like a knight, as impossibly tall as one of those figures at Chartres Cathedral, and its face was worn by time and by innumerable battles.[17]

After the 1899 production, the play was not performed by the Irish National Theatre until December 1911 and in the following year the seventh edition of the text appeared with an alternative ending, written to overcome the difficulties of the stage in the Abbey, accompanied by a note which indicates how Yeats's developing knowledge of stagecraft had given him confidence to deal with problems of production :

After the performance in 1899 I added the love scene between Aleel and the Countess, and in this new form the play was revived in New York by Miss Wycherley, as well as being played a good deal in England and America by amateurs. Now at last I have made a complete revision to make it suitable for performance at the Abbey Theatre. The first two scenes are almost wholly new, and throughout the play I have added or left out such passages as a stage experience of some years showed me encumbered the action; the play in its first form having been written before I knew anything of the theatre. I have left the old end, however, in the version printed in the body of this book, because the change for dramatic purposes has been made for no better reason than that audiences—even at the Abbey Theatre—are almost ignorant of Irish mythology — or because a shallow stage made the elaborate vision of armed angels upon a mountainside impossible. The new end is particularly suited to the Abbey stage, where the stage platform can be brought out in front of the proscenium and have a flight of steps at one side up which the Angel comes, crossing towards the back of the stage at the opposite side. The principal lighting is from two arc lights in the balcony which throw their lights into the faces of the players, making footlights unnecessary. The room at Shemus Rua's house is suggested by a great grey curtain — a colour which becomes full of rich tints under a stream of light from the arcs. The short front scene before the last is just long enough when played with incidental music to allow the scene set behind it to be changed.[18]

Not only does this passage show how Yeats's practical knowledge of stagecraft increased in the period between the two editions, but it also reveals how much he gained by meeting Gordon Craig in 1901 and from his subsequent 'apprenticeship' to Craig's theories of theatre, which was to culminate in the introduction of Craig's system of stage scenery at the Abbey Theatre in 1911.

*

The second season of the Irish Literary Theatre opened at the Gaiety Theatre, Dublin, on 19 February 1900. As in the previous year, the company consisted of actors hired and rehearsed in London, principally under the watchful eye of George Moore, whose play, *The Bending of the Bough*, opened on 20 February. The other plays performed were the two-act *Maeve* by Edward Martyn and Alice Milligan's one-act, *The Last Feast of the Fianna*, which were played together as a double-bill which opened the season.

Moore's play derived from a play by Edward Martyn, *The Tale of a Town*. His offer to help Martyn had ended in his taking over the plot and persuading Yeats to collaborate on the dialogue, a process which ended in a severe rift between Moore and Martyn. Yeats's part in the piece was minimal, nor did he have any deep involvement with this second season of the Irish Literary Theatre. He did, however, edit the second and third issues of *Beltaine*, which were published in February and April respectively.

In *Beltaine*, number two, Yeats wrote the editorial, 'Plans and Methods,' in which he stated that he was inclined

to agree with Renan and to set store by a certain native tradition of thought that is passed on in the conversations of father and son, and in the institutions of life, and in literature, and in the examples of history. It is these that make nations and that mould the foreign settler after the national type in a few years; and it is these, whether they were made by men of foreign or of Celtic blood, that our theatre would express.[19]

Yeats also contributed an essay to *Beltaine*, number two, 'The Irish Literary Theatre, 1900,' which first appeared in the January issue of *The Dome*, in which he moved further towards his definition of a National Theatre for Ireland:

Scandinavia is, as it seems, passing from her moments of miracle; and some of us think that Ireland is passing to hers. She may not produce any important literature, but because her moral nature has been aroused by political sacrifices, and her imagination by a political pre-occupation with her own destiny, she is ready to be moved by profound thoughts that are a part of the unfolding of herself.[20]

The third and final issue of *Beltaine*, published in April 1900, contained only a survey of the season, written by Yeats, in which he made the claim that, 'We have brought the "literary drama" to Ireland, and it has become a reality.' [21]

*

Yeats returned to London after the second Irish Literary Theatre season and worked with Moore on the text of *Diarmid and Grania*, which they had planned to write together for presentation in the third season. He recognised Moore as much more accomplished in dramatic construction, and realised that he had much to learn from him. That the partnership was an uneasy one is reflected in Yeats's correspondence with Lady Gregory and with Moore, to whom he wrote in January 1901, when the play was in final draft,

You say both should make concessions. I think so too, but so far I have made them. I have recognised that you have a knowledge of the stage, a power of construction, a power of inventing a dramatic climax far beyond me, and I have given way again and again. I have continually given up motives and ideas that I preferred to yours, because I admitted your authority to be greater than mine. On the question of style however I will make no concessions. Here you need give way to me. Remember that our original compact was that the final words were to be mine. I would never have begun the play at all, but for this compact. It is no use going on with the work at all if we are not clear on this point. I send you what seems to me a sufficient version of Act I. I will listen to any suggestions you make, or consider any emendations of language as I have always done, but the final version must be in my words or in such words of yours as I may accept. [22]

The play was offered and read to various famous English actors and actresses, among them Forbes-Robertson and Mrs. Patrick Campbell, but always with the stipulation that the first performance be in Dublin or that the play open simultaneously in Dublin and London. Eventually Yeats and Moore withdrew these offers and decided that the Irish Literary Theatre should commission F. R. Benson's Shakespearean repertory company to perform the play in Dublin.

The difficulties of collaborating with Moore were, however, to a large degree offset by other events in Yeats's life. These included the publication, in December 1900, of *The Shadowy Waters*, with an introductory poem on the seven woods of Coole; meetings with London friends such as Arthur Symons, whose services were invoked as a referee between Moore and Yeats ('I will accept any form of words of yours that Symons approves of' [23]); and his discovery of Gordon Craig.

*

13. Edward Gordon Craig.
Woodcut self-portrait, c. 1907.

Edward Gordon Craig, the son of Ellen Terry and Edward Godwin, the architect who had designed for John Todhunter at the Bedford Park little theatre, was born on 16 January 1872. As a boy he was taken on tour by his mother and became a member of Henry Irving's company, in which he played many parts between 1889 and 1897. (Beardsley made a caricature of him in Tennyson's *Becket*, which Irving produced at the Lyceum Theatre, London, on 6 February 1893.) He became enthusiastic about wood engraving and began publishing *The Page* in 1898.

In 1900 Craig began to design stage scenery and, with his composer friend, Martin Shaw, produced and designed *Dido and Aeneas* by Henry Purcell for the Purcell Operatic Society at the Hampstead Conservatoire of Music on 17, 18 and 19 March. The production was enthusiastically received and Craig and Shaw began preparing and rehearsing the Masque from Purcell's opera *Diocletian* which, under the title *The Masque of Love*, was presented in a double-bill with a revival of *Dido and Aeneas* at the Coronet Theatre, Notting Hill Gate, for six performances commencing on 26 March 1901. Craig prepared a Souvenir Programme for the production, for which he engraved fourteen designs on wood.

Yeats was among the audience at the revival of *Dido and Aeneas* and was so impressed by the presentation that he wrote to Craig from 18 Woburn Buildings on 2 April:

Dear Mr. Craig: I thought your scenery to "Aeneas and Dido" the only good scenery I ever saw. You have created a new art. I have written to Frank Harris to ask him to let me do an article on the subject in his new paper "The Saturday Review."

I would like to talk the thing over with you. Could you dine with me here Monday next if you do not mind a not very excellent dinner? Seven o'clock and of course not dress. I am just behind New Street, St. Pancras Church. Ring the top bell.

If you are not free on Monday I would like some other opportunity of talking things over.
Yours sincerely, W. B. Yeats.

Although Craig commented on this letter in his autobiography, 'If it had not been a poet, and Yeats the poet, one would have murmured, "And is it only scenery you saw?"'[24] he formed a friendship with Yeats which was to last until Yeats died. Ideas and experiments developed out of this friendship which were of first importance in the growth of Yeats's approach to theatre practice, an approach which, in turn, was, in 1911 at the Abbey Theatre, to provide Craig with the first theatre to adopt his methods of scenic presentation. The Abbey, too, was the only theatre where Craig's scenery had an extended period of use.

14. Backdrop in *Dido and Aeneas*. Woodcut by Gordon Craig, 1900.

Craig's approach to staging *Dido and Aeneas* was, in the theatre of 1900, revolutionary. He avoided all the conventional trappings of the stage, abolished borders which served to conceal the overhead lighting and stage machinery, and relied on simple areas of colour on which he directed coloured lighting to create atmospheric effects. His woodcuts which relate to the production indicate the mood he sought, but in these the mood is realised in a different medium. The total effect created aroused the enthusiasm of such perceptive critics as Arthur Symons, who devoted an essay, 'A New Art of the Stage,' to Craig's work, in which he wrote,

The aim of modern staging is to intensify the reality of things, to give you the illusion of an actual room, or meadow, or mountain. We have arrived at a great skill by giving this crude illusion of reality. Our stage painters can imitate anything, but what they cannot give us is the emotion which the playwright, if he is an artist, wishes to indicate by means of his scene. It is the very closeness of the imitation which makes our minds unable to accept it. The eye rebounds, so to speak, from this canvas as real as wood, this wood as real as water, this water which is actual water. Mr. Craig aims at taking us beyond reality; he replaces the pattern of the thing itself by the pattern which that thing evokes in his mind, the symbol of the thing. As, in conventional art, the artist unpicks the structure of the rose to build up a mental image of the rose in some formal pattern which his brain makes over again, like a new creation from the beginning, a new organism, so, in this new convention of the stage, a plain cloth, modulated by light, may be the tight walls of a tent or the sky and the clouds. The eye loses itself among these severe, precise, and yet mysterious lines and surfaces; the mind is easily at home in them; it accepts them as readily as it accepts the convention by which, in a poetical play, men speak in verse rather than in prose.[25]

Details of the staging of *Dido and Aeneas* are revealed in an essay by Haldane MacFall on the stagecraft of Gordon Craig which appeared in *The Studio* in September 1901:

In the performance of *Dido and Aeneas* there was no attempt at presenting a series of realistic pictures, done from photographs taken upon the spot. The authorities on Carthage had been left in undisturbed dust, long-winded and ineffectual, upon the shelves of museums and libraries. At the rising of the curtain a very different Carthage was discovered. The spirit of each scene in the opera was carried out in a colour-scheme that essayed to convey the emotion of that scene as deliberately to the eye as the music essayed to convey it to the ears. A broad simple tone of the violet of night was given on a back-cloth — the stage being kept free from all petty and distracting detail. The players at once took on their full size, dignity and individuality. The result was a haunting impression of glowing colour, used with the sombre restraint of a great painter — an impression in which, all unwittingly, the eye helped the ear in grasping the intention of the scene. The note of tragedy was sustained throughout the piece with consummate mastery in the colour as in the music. The stage, for all its simplicity, was always filled. No posturing actor took the limelight in order to show off his personality or advertise his necessity. The main scheme of the play was the main thing — it was never anything but the main thing.[26]

Craig's production proved to Yeats that the realisation of his 'theatre of Art' need not take the 'generation and perhaps generations' which he had predicted in his statement in *Beltaine* only two years before, and it opened his eyes to what might have been possible, instead of 'the little cramped stage and the scenery which was as tawdry as it should have been dim'[27] which Max Beerbohm had experienced at the Antient Concert Rooms in Dublin.

Craig had taken a concert hall in London, the Hampstead Conservatoire, and adapted its existing features to the mounting of his
production, using his massive backcloths to focus the attention of the
audience on the stage action. As he wrote in his autobiography,

We used no wings, and no sky-borders. It never occurred to me that I had to
push in wings and borders and footlights and so on, to oblige the "Trade."
But then I regret to say I wasn't thinking of the Trade, and so I forgot wings
and borders and floats. In all four scenes my great sky-cloths, blue or grey,
went far out of sight, so that one felt (people said "for the first time") a sense
of space on a stage. In Greece and Rome, in 400 B.C. or A.D. 400, space and
sky were available. And our dresses were not made so as to create a sense of
variety — they were to create a sense of unity.[28]

MacFall summed up Craig's achievement,

To attain such perfection of stage craft, the stage-manager must be an artist.
Here is an art which is completely national — which contains that great virile
forcefulness, wedded to subtle taste, that has made our literature what it is.
Our notion of mending is always to go spending. So vulgarity succeeds to
vulgarity. If we had a few stage managers who were artists and men of large
artistic gifts such as this, the expenses of producing plays and operas would
not be the paralysing disease of the dramatic world. Here is no extravagant or
tawdry waste of monies to produce garish stupidities, in order that the ground-
lings may stare open-mouthed in primitive wonder at the thousands of guineas
spent. These stage-pictures are equally suited to large or small stages; they are
fitted to reasonable cost; they are consummately artistic; they are altogether
beautiful.[29]

*

Towards the end of April Yeats visited Stratford on Avon to see F. R.
Benson's company perform in the Shakespeare Memorial Theatre and
to make arrangements with them for the third season of the Irish
Literary Theatre in December, in which the play he had written with
George Moore, *Diarmid and Grania* was to be performed. He saw
the six historical plays, *King John, Richard II, Henry IV*, part two,
Henry V, Henry VI, part two and *Richard III*

played in their right order with all the links that bind play to play unbroken;
and partly because of a spirit in the place, and partly because of the way play
supports play, the theatre has moved me as it has never done before.[30]

Sir Frank Robert Benson (1858-1939), after an apprenticeship to
Irving, founded a touring Shakespearean repertory company in 1883
in which he and his wife were for many years the leading players.
Many notable British actors and actresses commenced their careers
in Benson's company, which carried on the 'antique' tradition of
Shakespearean acting in a declamatory and highly mannered style.

Benson played many seasons at Stratford on Avon, where he was eventually made a Governor of the Memorial Theatre. He was noted for his noble appearance and handsome aquiline features. He was knighted by King George V in recognition of his services to English drama.

At Stratford on Avon Yeats began to add up his experiences in the theatre into something like a systematic approach. He speculated on the form of theatres, and, with Gordon Craig in mind, on stage presentation, seeing that in Shakespeare's

art, as in all the older art of the world, there was much make-believe, and our scenery, too, should remember the time when, as my nurse used to tell me, herons built their nests in old men's beards! Mr. Benson did not venture to play the scene in *Richard III* where the ghosts walk as Shakespeare wrote it, but had his scenery been as simple as Mr. Gordon Craig's purple back-cloth that made Dido and Aeneas seem wandering on the edge of eternity, he would have found nothing absurd in pitching the tents of Richard and Richmond side by side. Goethe has said, "Art is art, because it is not nature!" It brings us near to the archetypal ideas themselves, and away from nature, which is but their looking-glass.[31]

This season also prompted him to think of the epic nature of the six plays played in sequence, perhaps forming the germ of the idea behind his later attempt to create a cycle of dramas based on the old Irish epic, the *Táin*.

The six plays, that are but one play, have, when played one after another, something extravagant and superhuman, something almost mythological. These nobles with their indifference to death and their immense energy seem at times no nearer the common stature of men than do the gods and the heroes of Greek plays. Had there been no Renaissance and no Italian influence to bring in the stories of other lands, English history would, it may be, have become as important to the English imagination as the Greek myths to the Greek imagination; and many plays by many poets would have woven it into a single story whose contours, vast as those of Greek myth, would have made living men and women seem like swallows building their nests under the architrave of some Temple of the Giants.[32]

*

Yeats spent the summer of 1901 partly with his relatives at Sligo and partly as Lady Gregory's guest at Coole. He continued to plan for his Irish theatre. He proposed a Gaelic dramatic touring company to Moore, who thought the idea a good one, and he began to prepare a further number of *Beltaine* to be published during the next Irish Literary Theatre season. This, he felt, 'should be a Gaelic propaganda paper this time.'[33] An echo of Craig's *Dido and Aeneas* programme is evident in a letter about this to Lady Gregory:

SAMHAIN

Edited for the Irish Literary Theatre by W. B. Yeats and containing a Play in Irish by Douglas Hyde with English translation by Lady Gregory and Articles by George Moore and by Edward Martyn. Published in October 1901 by Sealy Bryers & Walker in Dublin and by T. Fisher Unwin in London and sold at Sixpence.

15. *Samhain*, No. 1, 1901. Front cover (reduced). Original 8¾ × 7″.

Yes, we should offer *Beltaine* to Dublin publishers, but insist on its being done as well as possible — I certainly like the woodcut idea — and then if the publishers refuse send it to Watt and write a note in *Beltaine* on those publishers. I don't know which would do the most good, publication in Dublin or the note on publishers. I certainly agree to give profits to the Gaelic League. The only thing I really care about is the get up of the thing. I have always felt that my mission in Ireland is to serve taste rather than any definite propaganda.[34]

In July he wrote to Arthur Griffith suggesting that Griffith might include something about the American success of *The Land of Heart's Desire* in his paper, *The United Irishman*, and informed him that he had commenced a play about Cuchullin and Conchubar, the first mention of the series of Cuchulain plays which he was to write at intervals during the rest of his life. The piece in *The United Irishman* was written by Frank Fay, who was at the time the dramatic critic for the paper. Yeats wrote to thank Fay for his piece and promised to see him and his brother William perform at the Antient Concert Rooms, a meeting from which the next phase of the evolution of the Irish National Theatre emerged.

By October Yeats was in Dublin for rehearsals of *Diarmid and Grania* and his disillusionment at the progress of the production is indicated by a fragment of a letter written at the time,

Yesterday we were rehearsing at the Gaiety. The kid Benson is to carry in his arms was wandering in and out among the artificial ivy. I was saying to myself, "Here are we a lot of intelligent people, who might have been doing some sort of work that leads to some fun. Yet here we are going through all sorts of trouble and annoyance for a mob that knows neither literature nor art." [35]

Nevertheless, he continued to pursue the ideal. A Dublin publishing firm, Sealy, Bryers and Walker, agreed to issue the journal of the Theatre which was renamed *Samhain* because of the time of the year in which the season occurred, *Samhain* being the old Irish autumn festival as *Bealtaine* was the spring festival. The design of the journal reflected Craig's typography, large black type on coarse brown paper. Yeats, as editor, contributed a series of paragraphs headed 'Windle-straws' and there were articles by Lady Gregory and George Moore. Douglas Hyde's one-act play in Irish, *Casadh an tSugáin*, was printed with an English translation by Lady Gregory, but the most important feature in *Samhain 1901* was a manifesto, signed by Edward Martyn, setting down the aims and ideals of the Irish National Theatre.

A PLEA FOR

A NATIONAL THEATRE IN IRELAND

There are many movements now for the encouragement of Irish manufacture in all its branches and for preventing the scandalous outpouring of Irish money into the pockets of Englishmen and other foreigners. Quite recently a movement has been started to turn the enormous demand for church art from the workshop of the foreign *tradesman* and to get it supplied by the native Irish *artist*. It is impossible to calculate the sum of money that this will save the country. It will be enormous. Two such able and practical men as Mr. Horace Plunkett and Mr. T. P. Gill are so convinced of this that they have decided to form a school for teaching the making of stained glass as a branch of the School of Art in Dublin, and have procured a teacher from probably the greatest master of the art in modern times. We shall thus have stained glass of the highest excellence executed by Irishmen in Ireland.

But there is another form of art besides church art in Ireland which needs reform, and for which there is an equally large demand, supplied, as usual, by the foreigner, and, as usual, badly supplied, almost invariably. I refer to the plays supplied to our theatres by strolling English companies of actors. It would be interesting to know how much money yearly those companies take out of Ireland as a reward for Anglicising and corrupting the taste of the Irish people. It must be as enormous even as the sum we pay the foreign purveyor of church art for disfiguring our churches. We have grappled with and, I think, solved the problem of nationalising church art. Is it not time that our dramatic art also should be placed on a national basis? Are we so degenerate that we cannot meet this demand also by a supply of national art? The first requisite is to provide a stock company of native artists because the foreign strollers are too wedded to the debased art of England to fall in with the change. This can only be done by instituting a school for the training of actors and actresses, a most important branch of which should be devoted to teaching them to act plays in the Irish language. Now it is quite legal and feasible to obtain a grant from the Department of Technical Instruction for this purpose which is the same in principle as the teaching of stained glass manufacture. It is a home industry in the best sense, and means a vast economic saving to the country, besides being a most refining educational influence upon the artistic and moral character of the nation. I think it will not be difficult to make the enlightened Vice-President and Secretary of the Department understand this.

With a company of artists such as I have described we might put before the people of Ireland native works, also translations of the dramatic masterworks of all lands, for it is only by accustoming a public to the highest art that it can be led to appreciate art, and that dramatists may be inspired to work in the great art tradition.

Edward Martyn[36]

Even though Martyn's wording of the 'Plea' was verbose and his comparisons irrelevant, he did manage to express the basic aims of the Theatre, aims which were much better and more forcefully put by Yeats in his editorial paragraphs:

. . . we have for good and all taken over the intellectual government of our country, and if the degeneration of England goes on as quickly as it has these last years, we shall take over for certain generations the intellectual government of that country also whether we will or no; and because we believe, when others have ceased to believe, we have, I think, taken up the wheel of life in our hands that we may set it to whirl upon a new axle tree.

.   .   .   .   .   .

The stock company would perform in Dublin perhaps three weeks in spring, and three weeks in autumn, and go on tour the rest of the time through Ireland, and through the English towns where there is a large Irish population. It would perform plays in Irish and English, and also, it is proposed, the masterpieces of the world, making a point of performing Spanish and Scandinavian, and French, and perhaps Greek masterpieces rather more than Shakespeare, for Shakespeare one sees, not well done indeed, but not unendurably ill done in the Theatre of Commerce. It would do its best to give Ireland a hardy and shapely national character by opening the doors to the four winds of the world, instead of leaving the door that is towards the east wind open alone. Certainly, the national character, which is so essentially different from the English that Spanish and French influences may well be most healthy, is at present like one of those miserable thorn bushes one sees twisted towards one side by some prevailing wind.[37]

*

In *Salve*, Moore described the process by which *Diarmid and Grania* was written as 'literary brewing'. Yeats, he said,

came every morning to edit the dialogue I had written for *Diarmuid and Grania*, and to regret that I had not persevered with the French version, which Lady Gregory was to translate into English, Taidgh O'Donoghue into Irish, Lady Gregory back into English, and Yeats was to put style upon.[38]

Although the actual process was not so extreme, the play suffered from the collaboration of its joint authors and is to be seen more as a curiosity of literature than as an addition to Yeats's development as a dramatist.

Moore felt that Yeats's alterations seemed to drain the text of all vitality and that they should have been working together at an opera, 'for we are always agreed about the construction, and the musician would be free from his criticism.'[39] The question of music for the play came up and Moore, remembering some music he had heard by Edward Elgar, wrote to the composer:

Mr. Benson is going to produce *Diarmuid and Grania*, a drama written by Mr. Yeats and myself on the great Irish legend. Finn's horn is heard in the second act, and all my pleasure in the performance will be spoilt if a cornet-player tootles out whatever comes into his head, perhaps some vulgar phrase the audience has heard already in the streets. Beautiful phrases come into the mind while one is doing odd jobs, and if you do not look upon my request as an impertinence, and if you will provide yourself with a sheet of music-paper before you shave in the morning, and if you do not forget the pencil, you will be able to write down a horn-call, before you turn from the right to the left cheek, that will save my play from a moment of vulgarity.[40]

Edward Elgar (1857-1934), who was then at the beginning of his career as a composer and had just completed his oratorio, *The Dream of Gerontius*, sent six horn-calls to choose from and Moore replied by asking him to compose a further piece, a setting of the funeral march in the third act. This, too, Elgar sent and, at rehearsal, it seemed to Moore that

Elgar must have seen the primeval forest as he wrote, and the tribe moving among the falling leaves — oak-leaves, hazel-leaves, for the world began with oak and hazel.[41]

This was followed by a setting for a lyric in the first act. The original lyric in the first act was Laban's spell, beginning, 'Do all that I bid you.' Yeats replaced this with a lyrical invocation, beginning, 'There are seven that pull the thread' which, entitled 'Spinning Song', was printed in *A Broad Sheet* in January 1902. Elgar's setting of this song was issued in June or July 1902 by Novello and Company, who also published, in the same year, an edition of Elgar's full score for the play, including the horn calls, the funeral march and the song. This work, Elgar's Opus 42, was dedicated to his friend Henry J. Wood.

The new lyric which Elgar set does not appear in any edition of the play, but can be found in the *Variorum Poems* as a 'Poem not in the Definitive Edition.' The text, with Elgar's air, is given here.[42]

There are se-ven that pull the thread There is one un-der the waves, There is one where the winds are wove, There is one in the old grey house Where the dew, where the dew is made be-fore dawn One lives in the house of the sun, And one in the house of the moon, And one lies un-der the boughs Of the gol-den ap - ple tree, And one spin-ner is lost. Ho - li - est, ho - li - est seven Put all your pow'r on the thread That I've spun in the house to - night.

16. 'There are seven that pull the thread.'
Edward Elgar's setting of the lyric in *Diarmid and Grania*, 1901.

*

The third, and final, season of the Irish Literary Theatre opened at the Gaiety Theatre, Dublin, on Monday 21 October 1901, with *Diarmid and Grania* by George Moore and W. B. Yeats, followed, at evening performances only, by *Casadh an tSugáin* (*The Twisting of the Rope*) by Douglas Hyde, performed by the members of the Gaelic Amateur Dramatic Society. The Moore-Yeats play was produced by F. R. Benson's Shakespearean company at the request of the Irish Literary Theatre.*

The productions were received warmly by the Dublin press and public. *The Freeman's Journal* found Douglas Hyde's play in Irish the most satisfying and successful effort of the Irish Literary Theatre but thought that *Diarmid and Grania* had

lost a little of the simplicity, the inevitableness, the elemental character which seems to belong to these figures of a mythical age and have become characters which it is easy to fancy in modern garments. So far has the process been carried out that Grania recalls recent heroines of the novel and the stage.[43]

The reviewer found Mrs. Benson's Grania 'an excellent imitation of the manner of Mrs. Patrick Campbell,' a remark which may have caused Yeats to regret that his first choice had not played the part.

---

*   DIARMID AND GRANIA
            A New and Romantic Play in Three Acts
                 by George Moore and W. B. Yeats

Produced by Mr. F. R. Benson
by request of the Irish Literary Theatre
at the Gaiety Theatre, Dublin, on Monday 21 October 1901

King Cormac	Mr. Alfred Brydone
Finn MacCoole	Mr. Frank Rodney
Diarmid	Mr. F. R. Benson
Goll	Mr. Charles Bibby
Usheen	Mr. Henry Ainley
Caoelte	Mr. E. Harcourt Williams
Fergus	Mr. G. Wallace Johnstone
Fathna	Mr. Walter Hampden
Griffan	Mr. Stuart Edgar
Niall	Mr. Matheson Lang
Conan the Bald	Mr. Arthur Whitby
An Old Man	Mr. H. O. Nicholson
A Shepherd	Mr. Owen
A Boy	Miss Ella Tarrant
A Young Man	Miss Jean Mackinlay
Grania	Mrs. F. R. Benson
Laban	Miss Lucy Franklein

Special Music written by Dr. Edward Elgar

The *Evening Herald* critic, M.A.M., comparing her with Mrs. Patrick Campbell, found Mrs. Benson's Grania 'an embryo Mrs. Tanqueray, B.C.' and King Cormac 'a mild precursor of Polonius.' He noted that the scenery was 'appropriate, if the first set — a dingy stock scene — be excepted.'[44] Joseph Holloway pronounced his general verdict as 'favourable if not enthusiastic' but thought that 'the lackadaisical manner and eternal attitudinising of Mrs. Benson' nearly wrecked the play. He admired Elgar's music, but said of the stage presentation,

The last scene — the wooded slopes of Ben Bulben — was picturesque, but the others I thought only so-so, while the lighting of the stage was very erratic at all times.[45]

The most violent and longest remembered attack on the production came from James Joyce, then a student at University College Dublin. He had attended the earlier seasons of the Irish Literary Theatre and had written his play, *A Brilliant Career*, with the intention of submitting it for production to the company. The Gaiety production, however, roused his indignation and he wrote 'The Day of the Rabblement' to express this. The article was rejected by the College magazine, *St. Stephen's*, and Joyce, with his friend Francis Sheehy Skeffington, who also had an article rejected by the paper, issued the two essays as a pamphlet in November. The piece opens,

No man, said the Nolan, can be a lover of the true or the good unless he abhors the multitude; and the artist, though he may employ the crowd, is very careful to isolate himself. This radical principle of artistic economy applies specially to a time of crisis, and today when the highest form of art has just been preserved by desperate sacrifices, it is strange to see the artist making terms with the rabblement. The Irish Literary Theatre is the latest movement of protest against the sterility and falsehood of the modern stage. Half a century ago the note of protest was uttered in Norway, and since then long and disheartening battles have been fought against the hosts of prejudice and misinterpretation and ridicule. What triumph there has been here and there is due to stubborn conviction, and every movement that has set out heroically has achieved a little. The Irish Literary Theatre gave out that it was the champion of progress, and proclaimed war against commercialism and vulgarity. It had partly made good its word and was expelling the old devil, when after the first encounter it surrendered to the popular will. Now, your popular devil is more dangerous than your vulgar devil. Bulk and lungs count for something, and he can gild his speech aptly. He has prevailed once more, and the Irish Literary Theatre must now be considered the property of the rabblement of the most belated race in Europe.[46]

The most perceptive supporter of Yeats's purpose was Frank Fay, writing in *The United Irishman*. His experience in trying to mould a company of Irish players with his brother William gave him an

Two Essays.

"A Forgotten Aspect of the University Question"

BY

F. J. C. SKEFFINGTON

AND

"The Day of the Rabblement"

BY

JAMES A. JOYCE.

PRICE TWOPENCE.

Printed by
GERRARD BROS.,
37 STEPHEN'S GREEN,
DUBLIN.

17. Title page of 'The Day of the Rabblement.' Dublin, 1900.

Gaiety Theatre, Dublin.

Lessees ... ... MICHAEL GUNN, Ltd
Manager ... ... MR. C. HYLAND
Telegrams—"GAIETY, DUBLIN." *Telephone*, 592.

PROGRAMME .... ONE PENNY

FOR FIVE NIGHTS AND
MATINEES—

WEDNESDAY, AT 2.30 P.M. ... ... DIARMID AND GRANIA
SATURDAY, AT 2.30 P.M. - - - KING LEAR

THIS (TUESDAY), and WEDNESDAY EVENINGS, OCTOBER 22nd and 23rd, 1901, at 8,
BY REQUEST OF THE IRISH LITERARY THEATRE,

⊰ MR. F. R. BENSON ⊱
WILL PRODUCE

A New and Romantic Play in Three Acts, entitled :

DIARMID AND GRANIA.

BY GEORGE MOORE AND W. B. YEATS.

King Cormac	the High King	...	Mr. ALFRED BRYDONE
Finn MacCoole, the Chief of the Fianna		...	Mr. FRANK RODNEY
Diarmid		...	Mr. F. R. BENSON
Goll	} his Chief {	...	Mr. CHARLES BIBBY
Usheen	Men	...	Mr. HENRY AINLEY
Caoelte		...	Mr. E. HARCOURT WILLIAMS
Fergus		...	Mr. G. WALLACE JONNSTONE
Fathna	} Spearmen {	...	Mr. WALTER HAMPDEN
Griffan		...	Mr. STUART EDGAR
Niall		...	Mr. MATHESON LANG
Conan the Bald	a Head Servant	...	Mr. ARTHUR WHITBY
An Old Man	one of the Fianna	...	Mr. H. O. NICHOLSON
A Shepherd		...	Mr. OWEN
A Boy		...	Miss ELLA TARRANT
A Young Man		...	Miss JEAN MACKINLAY
Grania	the King's Daughter	...	Mrs. F. R. BENSON
Laban	an old Druidess	...	Miss LUCY FRANKLEIN

Serving Men, Troops of the Fianna, &c.

Act 1 .. .. THE BANQUETING HALL IN TARA
Act 2 .. .. DIARMID'S HOUSE
Act 3 .. .. .. THE WOODED SLOPES OF BEN BULBEN

Special Music Written by Dr. EDWARD ELGAR.

Acting Manager	...	Mr. A. SMYTH-PIGOTT
Stage Manager	For	Mr. LEONARD BUTTRESS
Assistant Stage Manager	Mr. F. R. BENSON.	Mr. EDWARD BROADLEY
Advance Representative		Mr. JAMES FOX

To be Followed on Monday, Tuesday, and Wednesday Evenings by

'THE TWISTING OF THE ROPE.'
By DOUGLAS HYDE, LL.D.
Cast filled by Members of the Gaelic Amateur Dramatic Society.

Thursday, Friday, and Saturday, and Saturday Matinee - **KING LEAR.**

ORCHESTRA.

Overture ...	Shakesperian	...	*Jules Guilton*
Selection ...	The Lily of Killarney	...	*Arr. by G. R. Chapman*
Excerpt ...	Songs without Words	...	*Mendelssohn*
Funeral March	Diarmid and Grania	...	*Dr. E. Elgar*

BOX OFFICES at Messrs. Cramer, Wood & Co., 4 & 5 Westmoreland-street, open from 10 a.m. to 5.30 p.m. Saturdays, from 10 a.m. to 2 p.m. Also at Shelbourne Hotel, and in the evenings at Theatre, from 5.45 p.m. to 9 p.m. Saturdays, from 2.15 p.m. to 9 p.m. All Letters and Telegrams to Box Office, Cramer's, 4 and 5 Westmoreland-street.

PRICES—Balcony Stalls (Dress), **5s.** Balcony (bonnets allowed), **4s.** Pit Stalls **3s** Upper Circle, **2s.**; Pit, **1s.**; Gallery, **6d.** Private Boxes, **20s.**, **30s.**, and **40s.** Children under twelve years of age half-price to Balcony Stalls, Balcony and Upper Circle. **Early Doors** to Upper Circle, Pit and Gallery, **6d.** Extra—Open at 7 o'clock. Matinee at 1.30 o'clock. **ORDINARY DOORS**—Evening at 7.30. Commence at 8. Matinee at 2. Commence at 2.30.

MONDAY NEXT—
THE LATEST LONDON SUCCESS,
⊱ THE WEDDING GUEST ⊰
By J. M. BARRIE, Author of "The Little Minister,' &c.
From the GARRICK THEATRE, LONDON.

This Theatre is Disinfected with "Jeye's" Sanitary Compounds.

QUIRK, PRINTER, WICKLOW STREET, DUBLIN

18. Original Gaiety Theatre, Dublin, programme for *Diarmid and Grania*, 1901.

insight into the difficulties which Yeats had encountered and understood. He doubted whether 'two authors of such opposite literary temperaments as Mr. W. B. Yeats and Mr. George Moore benefit by collaboration,'[47] and, in a later piece he detailed his dissatisfaction with the acting:

I cannot help thinking that much of the disappointment I have heard expressed about the play is really the result of the execrable — I can use no milder word — acting it received at the hands of Mr. Benson and his company.

He went on to explain that the realisation of the play was impossible to actors trained in the English tradition, defended the company against Joyce's attack, and concluded,

Those who write and talk so glibly about what the Irish Literary Theatre ought to do and ought not to do are people who have no idea of the difficulties such an institution has to contend with.[48]

Yeats's appeals for an imaginative and non-realistic approach to stage presentation were also echoed in *The Freeman's Journal*,

As usual, the attempt at realistic production has not been a success, and Fionn's striped trews, the material and colouring of which is so obviously and aggressively modern, can hardly be said to be convincing. Had a more subdued and suggestive method been employed both with regard to costumes and scenery — had a little more been left to the imagination of the audience — the effect would have been infinitely better.[49]

Elgar's music, his first for the stage, came off best. His biographer, Percy M. Young, wrote enthusiastically about the score in 1955, and the experience of having fine music which was an integral part of the production must have revealed to Yeats an element of dramatic completeness which was reflected throughout his subsequent career in the concern with which he sought out composers for his plays.

The curtain speech given by Yeats on the first night of *Diarmid and Grania* showed that he realised that the three-year experiment of the Irish Literary Theatre was ended and that he must seek further developments in using Irish talents. He repeated the remarks he had made in *Samhain*, much to the embarrassment of the English company that had been commissioned to present the play. As Benson described it in his *Memoirs*, published in 1930,

The enthusiastic poet, W. B. Yeats, in front of the curtain at the end of the first night's performance, seized the opportunity to indulge in invective against English actors, English companies and all their works. His eloquent periods were abruptly cut short by Mrs. Benson grasping his coat-tails and dragging him back onto the stage.[50]

Yeats agreed to modify his remarks and made amends to the company. Thirty-five years later, in *Dramatis Personae*, he wrote,

What was it like? York Powell, Scandinavian scholar, historian, an impressionable man, preferred it to Ibsen's *Vikings at Helgeland*. I do not know. I have but a draft of some unfinished scenes, and of the performance I can but recall Benson's athletic dignity in one scene and the notes of the horn in Elgar's dirge over the dead Diarmuid.[51]

*

19. Title page of Elgar's score for *Diarmid and Grania*. London, 1902.

Frank J. Fay's articles in *The United Irishman* during 1901 reveal a growing respect for Yeats's work in the theatre and at the same time offer advice on how best a truly Irish theatre might develop from these efforts. 'Plays dealing with Ireland should be played by Irish actors,' he wrote, 'they are available if sought for.'[1] He could see that the Irish Literary Theatre seasons did not fill Ireland's need for a theatre.

In Ireland we are at present only too anxious to shun reality. Our drama ought to teach us to face it. Let Mr. Yeats give us a play in verse or prose that will rouse this sleeping land. There is a herd of Saxon and other swine fattening on us. They must be swept into the sea along with the pestilent breed of West-Britons with which we are troubled, or they will sweep us there. This land is ours, but we have ceased to realise the fact. We want a drama that will make us realise it. We have closed our ears to the piercing wail that rises from the past; we want a drama that will open them, and in no uncertain words point out the reason for our failure in the past and the road to success in the future.[2]

But, at the same time, he realised that the ideals of Yeats and his fellow directors of the Literary Theatre provided a foundation on which a National movement could be built, if they could be persuaded to abandon their practice of hiring English actors and companies for their plays.

It is manifestly the duty of those who will benefit by the Irish Literary Theatre plays to train up a company of Irish actors to do the work they want. Antoine did it in Paris and trained himself as well, for he was originally a clerk, and had been refused admission to the Conservatoire where the majority of French actors learn their business. Lugné-Poë, although a successful Conservatoire student, and although his company consists of several other successful Conservatoire students, had to do the same, and the Elizabethan Stage Society followed the same course.

And he stated the need for a permanent home for the theatre.

Cannot the committee of the Irish Literary Theatre build a hall of their own with a stage about the size of the stage of the Queen's Theatre? There they could act their plays with the certain knowledge that so long as they appeal to Irish sympathies they will get the support of the immense and delightful audiences who are supporting the movement which is reviving our music. During the off-months of the year they could let it to the Gaelic League for their monthly sgoruidheacht and to the other societies who are working so hard and so successfully to recreate an Irish Ireland.[3]

During the summer of 1901, while *Diarmid and Grania* was in preparation, Yeats began a correspondence with Frank Fay and on 26 August he attended the performance given for Inghínidhe na hEireann (The Daughters of Erin), a republican Society which included Maud Gonne among its leaders, by W. G. Fay's Ormonde Dramatic Society. He recalled the occasion in *Dramatis Personae*,

I saw William Fay's amateur company play Miss Milligan's *Red Hugh*, an historical play in two scenes in the style of Walter Scott. "Yonder battlements," all the old rattle-traps acquired modernity, reality, spoken by those voices. I came away with my head on fire. I wanted to hear my own unfinished *On Baile's Strand*, to hear Greek tragedy, spoken with a Dublin accent.[4]

His enthusiasm was reflected in *Samhain 1901* in which he made several references to the work of the Fays, condemning the construction of the plays and praising the playing. And, after seeking the advice of Lady Gregory, he offered his new play, *Cathleen Ni Houlihan*, to Willie Fay for production, 'the first play where dialect was not used with an exclusively comic intention.'[5] And as the Irish Literary Theatre ended to the notes of Elgar's dirge for Diarmuid, a new combination of talents was formed under the title of W. G. Fay's Irish National Dramatic Company.

*

The Fay brothers were born in Dublin, into a family which was originally named O'Fahey in County Galway. Francis John (Frank J.) was born in 1870 and William George (W.G.) in 1872. Both brothers attended the Model School in Marlborough Street, Dublin, a couple of minutes' walk from the Mechanics' Institute which was later converted into the Abbey Theatre. Frank became a clerk stenographer with the accountants Craig Gardner and Company and developed through his reading a wide knowledge of theatre. He was an ardent nationalist and his study of theatre in Europe led to a belief in the importance to Ireland of the formation of a national dramatic movement which would have an immense influence on the preservation of the Irish language. He was particularly influenced by the new naturalistic drama of the 1880's and by the work of Ole Bull, founder of the Norwegian National Theatre.

Until Ole Bull founded the Norwegian National Theatre, his countrymen had thought "Norwegian," which I understand is practically a dialect of Danish, unfit to be spoken on the stage. In the same way we thought it was time to make the Irish accent and idiom, in speaking English, a vehicle for the expression of Irish character on the stage and not for the sole purpose of provoking laughter.[6]

But perhaps the greatest influence in the development of Frank Fay's dramatic theories was the work of the founder of the Théâtre Libre in Paris, André Antoine (1858-1943). Like Fay, Antoine commenced his theatrical career as a dedicated amateur and, in 1887, he founded the Théâtre Libre with the purpose of introducing to the French public the works of the new naturalistic school of drama, particularly

that of such dramatists as Ibsen, Strindberg and Brieux. Though the
Théâtre Libre only lasted seven years, its continuing influence on the
development of dramatic practice in France was very great, and his
reforms affected not only acting style but also the approach to stage
presentation. Antoine's later involvements were with the work of
new dramatists in his Théâtre Antoine, founded in 1897. He later
became director of the Odéon in Paris and influenced, among many
others, Jacques Copeau, founder of the Vieux-Colombier in Paris
where, in recent times, many of Samuel Beckett's plays have been
first presented.

Thus, Frank Fay, when he met Yeats, had formulated, from an Irish
Nationalist viewpoint, a plan for an ideal Irish Theatre which was in
many aspects parallel to Yeats's dream. And it is not in any way
surprising that Yeats, soured by his three-season-long experience of
English 'Professionals,' should turn to the Fay brothers and their
amateur group to guide the Irish Theatre through its next stage of
development.

Frank's brother, William, had more experience of the rough and
tumble of the theatre. After leaving school he went as advance agent
for Lloyd's Mexican Circus and later played with obscure touring
stock companies in England and Ireland. He also became a trained
electrician and worked at this in Dublin while he and Frank were
developing their dramatic societies during the 1890's. He was thus
the only Irish member of the national theatre company to have
'professional' stage experience and it was under his name that they
played, at first pseudonymously as 'W. G. Ormonde's Combination,'
which presented a 'Screaming Sketch' at the Father Matthew Centenary Hall in Dublin in 1891, and as the 'Ormonde Dramatic Society'
between then and 1899, playing farce in coffee palaces and finally as
either 'Mr. W. G. Fay's Celebrated Variety Co.' or 'Mr. W. G. Fay's
Comedy Combination' until, under the sponsorship of Inghínidhe na
hEireann and as 'W. G. Fay's Ormonde Dramatic Society,' the company presented Alice Milligan's *Red Hugh* at the Antient Concert
Rooms in the presence of Yeats and Lady Gregory on 26 August 1901,
which inspired Yeats to offer the company his *Cathleen Ni Houlihan*.

*

Yeats's offer of his play, and Russell's offer of his *Deirdre* led to
another change in the name of the company which, though it retained the family name, came near to expressing the ideal aim.
'W. G. Fay's National Dramatic Society' presented the double bill
at Saint Teresa's Hall in Clarendon Street, Dublin, on 2 April 1902

with a company drawn from the members of Fay's players and of Inghínidhe na hEireann, including one of their prominent members, Maud Gonne, who took the leading part in Yeats's play.*

The play was rehearsed at the Coffee Palace Theatre and a later Abbey dramatist, J. H. Cousins, recalled the first reading of the piece.

The Fay Company's rehearsals of the full-size *Deirdre* in the Coffee Palace theatre proceeded with growing mastery and enthusiasm. Everybody learned everybody else's part for sheer love of the thing. The lack of a suitable curtain-raiser worried the management. But their worry disappeared when it was whispered that Yeats had had a dream, and had put it into a one-act play, and that Maud Gonne would have the central part. The play *Cathleen ni Houlihan* was read to the company. I shall not in this life forget the thrill of patriotic realisation that went through me at the final lines, after the departure of the "poor old woman" (symbol of Ireland at the end of the eighteenth century, in which the play was set, and not less symbolical in 1902) when an unsuspecting lad put prophecy into his reply to a question : Did you see an old woman going down the path?
I did not, but I saw a young girl, and she had the walk of a queen.[7]

Frank Fay wrote to Yeats :

Your little play has reached us safely through Mr. Russell, and it is now in rehearsal. We are all delighted that Miss Gonne is to act Kathleen and I look for a great success for all of us. If we achieve it, I think it will result in our endeavouring to give more frequent performances of such plays by Irish authors as we can get. I may mention that our company for *Deirdre* includes two poets† and that one of these has written several little plays and we hope to produce one for him when he is a little stronger in technique.[8]

He also asked Yeats for sketches for the costumes (Æ had designed his own *Deirdre*) and enquired whether he wished anything special

---

*   CATHLEEN NI HOULIHAN

Presented by W. G. Fay's National Dramatic Society
at Saint Teresa's Hall, Clarendon Street, Dublin
on 2 April 1902

Cathleen Ni Houlihan	Maud Gonne
Delia Cahel	Maire Nic Shiubhlaigh
Bridget Gillan	Maire T. Quinn
Patrick Gillan	C. Caulfield
Michael Gillan	J. Dudley Digges
Peter Gillan	W. G. Fay

Directed by W. G. and Frank J. Fay

†The two poets were James H. Cousins, who appeared under the stage name H. Sproule, and Padraic Colum, whose three-act play, *Broken Soil*, was produced by the company on 3 December 1903. Cousins' *The Sleep of the King* was produced on 29 October 1902.

done with the play and if there was any special music for the songs which Maud Gonne was to sing. Yeats does not seem to have responded to the request for designs and the play was set by W. G. Fay. However, in his writing about the occasion, Yeats appears to have learned a lesson from the staging of Æ's play and refers to the scenery and costumes several times. From the first production of *Cathleen Ni Houlihan* he learned that

its one defect was that the mild humour of the part before Kathleen came in kept the house in such delighted laughter, that it took them some little while to realise the tragic meaning of Kathleen's part, though Maude Gonne played it magnificently, and with weird power. I expect that I should have struck a tragic note at the start — I have an idea of revising it before I put it in a book and of making Kathleen pass the door at the start. They can call her over and ask her some question and she can say she is going to old "so and so's" and pass on (they might ask her to come in and she might not have time). When she came in the second time she might say that old so and so was shearing his sheep or the like and would not attend to her.[9]

So his theatre apprenticeship continued. Lady Gregory, the recipient of the letter quoted above, helped with the construction and the dialogue of the 'patriotic realistic' play which had such an inspiring effect on its audience that late in his life, recalling this, Yeats could ask

Did that play of mine send out
Certain men the English shot?[10]

The play deals with the seven-centuries-long struggle for Irish independence and in it Yeats stated a theme which he would restate with growing power in *The Dreaming of the Bones* and in *The Death of Cuchulain*. *Cathleen Ni Houlihan* is placed in 1798, during the Rebellion, while military aid from France is expected in a landing on the western seaboard. The symbolic 'Old Woman' enters an Irish household and exacts patriotic tribute from the son of the house so that he leaves his family and his betrothed to follow her cause. As Yeats expressed it in his dedication of the play to Lady Gregory,

She was Ireland herself, that Cathleen Ni Houlihan for whom so many songs have been sung and for whose sake so many have gone to their death. I thought if I could write this out as a little play I could make others see my dream as I had seen it.

This sense of historic awareness, almost of myth, is reflected in the final lines chanted by the Old Woman as she leaves the stage :

They shall be remembered for ever;
They shall be alive for ever;
They shall be speaking for ever;
The people shall hear them for ever.

As Yeats put it in an interview printed in *The United Irishman* on
5 May 1902,

I have written the whole play in the English of the West of Ireland, the
English of people who think in Irish. My play, *The Land of Heart's Desire*
was, in a sense, the call of the heart, the heart seeking its own dream; this
play is the call of country, and I have a plan of following it up with a little
play about the call of religion,* and printing the three plays together some
day.[11]

Some of the impact of the piece on its first audience, an audience
conditioned to patriotic utterance, was captured by Joseph Holloway,
who defines Maud Gonne's performance as one of 'creepy realism'
instead of the 'weird power' used by Yeats.

. . . to the cottage comes a mysterious old lady — Cathleen ni Houlihan —
who so plays on the feelings of the coming bridegroom that he gives up his
bride and follows her to strike a blow for ould Ireland, whom she symbolises.
The matter-of-fact ways of the household and the weird, uncanny conduct of
the strange visitor make a very agreeable concoction. And as the piece was
admirably played, it made a deep impression. Most of the sayings of the
mysterious "Cathleen" (a part realised with creepy realism by the tall and
willowy Miss Maud Gonne, who chanted her lines with rare musical effect,
and crooned fascinatingly, if somewhat indistinctly, some lyrics) found ready
and apt interpretation from the audience who understood that Erin spoke in
"Cathleen," and they applauded each red-hot patriotic sentiment right heartily,
and enthusiastically called for the author at the end, and had their wish
gratified.[12]

Cathleen Ni Houlihan proved the qualities of the Fay brothers'
company and did much to establish the characteristic acting style of
the Irish national theatre. Yeats had given the company a play which,
based as it was on popular 'rebel' sentiment, was elevated by its
treatment of plot and language into being a fine minor work by a
great craftsman. It signposted the path which Synge, and later
O'Casey, were to take in creating a unique idiom for the Irish theatre
and it enabled the company, under Frank Fay's direction, to develop
a style of acting which became famous on both sides of the Atlantic.
In a note on the play, dated 1907, Yeats wrote:

This was the first play of our Irish school of folk-drama, and in it that way of
quiet movement and careful speech which has given our players some little
fame first showed itself, arising partly out of deliberate opinion and partly
out of the ignorance of the players. Does art owe most to ignorance or to
knowledge? Certainly it comes to its deathbed full of knowledge. I cannot
imagine this play, or any folk-play of our school, acted by players with no
knowledge of the peasant, and of the awkwardness and stillness of bodies
that have followed the plough, or too lacking in humility to copy these
things without convention or caricature.[13]

*The Hour-Glass. These three plays were, in fact, never printed together.

In his preface to *The Unicorn from the Stars and other plays* by William B. Yeats and Lady Gregory, published in New York in 1908, Yeats acknowledged his debt to her in constructing the play:

I had dreamed the subject of *Cathleen ni Houlihan*, but found when I looked for words that I could not create peasant dialogue that would go nearer to peasant life than the dialogue in *The Land of Heart's Desire* or *The Countess Cathleen*. Every artistic form has its own ancestry, and the more elaborate it is, the more is the writer constrained to symbolise rather than to represent life, until perhaps his ladies of fashion are shepherds and shepherdesses, as when Colin Clout came home again. I could not get away, no matter how closely I watched the country life, from images and dreams which had all too royal blood, for they were descended like the thought of every poet from all the conquering dreams of Europe, and I wished to make that high life mix into some rough contemporary life without ceasing to be itself, as so many old books and Plays have mixed it and so few modern, and to do this I added another knowledge to my own. Lady Gregory had written no Plays, but had, I discovered, a greater knowledge of the country mind and country speech than anybody I had ever met with, and nothing but a burden of knowledge could keep *Cathleen ni Houlihan* from the clouds.[14]

As with the dialogue, Yeats realised that the music used in folk-drama must develop from a native tradition and, in the 1904 London printing of *Cathleen Ni Houlihan*, in the second volume of his *Plays for an Irish Theatre*, he printed the traditional airs for the three songs in the play, prefaced by a 'Note on the Music.' He elaborated this note in the Collected Edition of his work, published in 1908, and revised it further for the 1922 edition, *Plays in Prose and Verse*, in which he wrote:

All the music that is printed here is of that kind which I have described in *Samhain* and in *Ideas of Good and Evil*. Some of it is old Irish music made when all songs were but heightened speech, and some of it, composed by modern musicians, is none the less to be associated with words that must never lose the intonation of passionate speech. No vowel must ever be prolonged unnaturally, no word of mine must ever change into a mere musical note, no singer of my words must ever cease to be a man and become an instrument.
    The degree of approach to ordinary singing depends on the context, for one desires a greater or lesser amount of contrast between the lyrics and the dialogue according to situation and emotion and the qualities of players. The words of Cathleen ni Houlihan about the "white-scarfed riders" must be little more than regulated declamation; upon the other hand, Cathleen's verses by the fire, and those of the pupils in the *Hour-Glass*, and those of the beggars in the *Unicorn*, are sung as the country people understand song. Modern singing would spoil them for dramatic purposes by taking the keenness and the salt out of the words.[15]

20. Traditional Irish airs as arranged for *Cathleen Ni Houlihan*.
Plays in Prose and Verse, 1922.

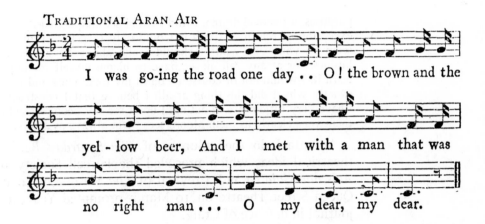

TRADITIONAL ARAN AIR

I was go-ing the road one day .. O! the brown and the

yel-low beer, And I met with a man that was

no right man ... O my dear, my dear.

21. Traditional Irish air as arranged for *The Hour-Glass.*
Plays in Prose and Verse, 1922.

Edward Martyn did not approve of the new departure towards peasant drama and criticised the production in *The United Irishman.* Yeats replied to this article in the 1902 issue of *Samhain*, which appeared in October to coincide with the company's next season during which *Cathleen Ni Houlihan* was revived.

Mr. Martyn argued in the *United Irishman* some months ago that our actors should try to train themselves for the modern drama of society. The acting of plays like *Deirdre*, and of *Cathleen Ni Houlihan*, with its speech of the country people, did not seem to him a preparation. It is not, but that is as it should be. Our movement is a return to the people, like the Russian movement of the early seventies, and the drama of society could but magnify a condition of life which the countryman and the artisan could but copy to their hurt. The play that is to give them a quite natural pleasure should either tell them of their own life, or of that life of poetry where every man can see his own image, because there alone does human nature escape from arbitrary conditions.[16]

*

While the Fays were preparing for the Dublin season, Yeats spent February and March of 1902 in London, where he began to write his first Cuchulain play. In March he went to Stratford on Avon to see another 'Shakespeare cycle.' And he conceived the notion that he might himself take up acting, as he wrote to Lady Gregory on 22 March:

I am going to surprise you by an idea that has been in my head lately. I never until yesterday spoke of it to anybody. I have an idea of going on the stage in small parts next autumn for a few months that I may master the stage for purposes of poetical drama. I find I could get on quite easily, and that with the exception of rehearsal times it would only take my evenings. Does the idea seem to you very wild? I should make about £2 a week, and learn my business, or at any rate never have to blame myself for not having tried to learn it. I would not of course go on in my own name and I would tell people exactly why I did the thing at all. I believe that I construct all right — but I have very little sense of acting. I don't see my people as actors though I see them very clearly as men. Moore sees them always as actors.[17]

An attack in the columns of *The Saturday Review* on Craig's theatrical ideas which preceded the Purcell Society production of *Acis and Galatea* and a revival of *The Masque of Love* at the Great Queen Street Theatre on 10 March prompted Yeats to write to the journal in defence of Craig.

Sir, J.F.R. in last week's *Saturday Review* condemned the Purcell Society and practically told his readers that the performances, which are to be given in Great Queen Street next week, will not be worth going to. I know nothing of music. I do not even know one note from another. I am afraid I even dislike music and yet I venture to contradict him. Last year I saw *Dido and Aeneas* and *The Masque of Love*, which is to be given again this year, and they gave me more perfect pleasure than I have met with in any theatre this ten years. I saw the only admirable stage scenery of our time, for Mr. Gordon Craig has discovered how to decorate a play with severe, beautiful, simple, effects of colour, that leave the imagination free to follow all the suggestions of the play. Realistic scenery takes the imagination captive and is at best but bad landscape painting, but Mr. Gordon Craig's scenery is a new and distinct art. It is something that can only exist in the theatre. It cannot even be separated from the figures that move before it. The staging of *Dido and Aeneas* and of *The Masque of Love* will some day, I am persuaded, be remembered among the important events of our time.[18]

After Yeats had seen the production he wrote again to Craig to express his admiration of the work.

I have been trying to find time to write to you. I was delighted with "The Masque of Love" in all its details, as delighted as ever, and with certain scenes of the "Acis and Galatea." Surely that second Polyphemus scene, the scene where he kills Acis, belongs to an art which has lain hid under the roots of the Pyramids for ten thousand years, so solemn it is. . . .[19]

This led to a renewal of the friendship formed in the previous year and to an exchange of views about stagecraft from which Yeats benefitted greatly. He returned to London about 10 April, after the Dublin production, elated by the qualities he perceived in the acting of the Fays and their company, and wrote to Frank Fay on 21 April that he had 'learnt a great deal from Gordon Craig.'[20] Methods of verse speaking continued to obsess him and he worked with Arnold Dolmetsch and Florence Farr on speaking his verses to the psaltery, writing his poem, 'The Players Ask For a Blessing on the Psalteries and Themselves' which he originally conceived as a 'Prayer to the Seven Archangels to bless the Seven Notes'[21] and which was printed in *In the Seven Woods* in the following year.

THE PLAYERS ASK FOR A BLESSING ON THE PSALTERIES AND THEMSELVES

Three Voices together

> Hurry to bless the hands that play,
> The mouths that speak, the notes and strings,
> O masters of the glittering town!
> O! lay the shrilly trumpet down,
> Though drunken with the flags that sway
> Over the ramparts and the towers,
> And with the waving of your wings. . . .[22]

By the middle of June Yeats had, on Craig's advice, acquired a model stage and he wrote to Lady Gregory that he proposed bringing it with him to Coole later in the month. He had planned two lectures for the autumn — 'one on a simpler theatre, and one on the speaking of verse to notes,'[23] which Florence Farr might illustrate. He had finished drafting *The Hour-Glass* and hoped it might be performed in the autumn season. The scenario of the play was read to Craig who was 'greatly delighted' and

wants to show the play to Irving but my belief in the commercial theatre liking such a thing is but slight. What is more to the point is that he is very anxious to stage some of my things himself, and so far as I can make out there is a possibility of his mother taking part in the venture.[24]

At the same time he was pursuing his idea of a cycle of plays based on Cuchulain, not all of them to be written by himself, and had asked Wilfrid Scawen Blunt to choose a theme from the epic. Blunt chose to take 'The Only Jealousy of Emer' as the plot for his play which, under the title *Fand*, was eventually produced at the Abbey Theatre in 1907.

During the summer months, spent as Lady Gregory's guest at Coole, Yeats worked at further collaborations with his hostess. *The Pot of Broth*, originally titled *The Beggarman*, was sent to Frank Fay for his next season and Lady Gregory was 'trying to get the air of "There's broth in the Pot." '[25] His letter of 7 September to Frank Fay reveals how much confidence he had gained in giving instructions about theatre practice.

Your brother must get some common air for "The Spouse of Naoise," and sing it as much as possible as traditional singing. I adapted the words from "Ben-Eirinn i" in Walsh's *Popular Songs*.

I will send sketches of costume for *The Hour Glass* and will have the skins in time. And we will get a few bits of crockery for cottage scenes.

I send you some Latin words which will do for the wise man's prayer, these are the Latin words, broken for the actor : "Confiteor Deo omnipotenti— how does it go on? — Omnipotenti beatae Mariae — I cannot remember."

I think it would be a mistake to have verses for the opening of the Theatre. Such things are never done well and give the air of a penny reading enter- tainment.

Digges should not make up too old. The wise man is a man in the full vigour of life. I hear from Mr. Quinn that he read the part very finely and you yourself I hear played very excellently. Quinn was very much struck. I should like, however, to hear how *The Pot of Broth* goes.

Let the fool's wig, if you can, be red and matted.[26]

The success of the productions in April led to the formation of the Irish National Dramatic Society and a small hall at 34 Camden Street, Dublin, was taken on a twelve-month lease as a permanent home for the company. W. B. Yeats was unanimously elected President of the Society in August, and Æ Vice-President. The Secretary of the Society was Frank Ryan, and its purpose was to carry on, on a more per- manent basis, the work of the company organised by Frank and Willie Fay. Lady Gregory's first play, *Twenty-Five*, was rejected in September 1902 while the autumn productions were being planned, but *The Pot of Broth* was put into rehearsal for the coming season.

In September Yeats returned to London, where he completed a further play, *Where There is Nothing*. This was originally planned as a collaboration with George Moore, but Yeats withdrew the play and finished it himself. Moore threatened to prevent Yeats publishing the play and said he was using the theme for a story, but Yeats sent the play to Griffith, who published it as a special supplement to *The United Irishman* on 1 November 1902.

Where There is Nothing is Yeats's only attempt at a drama which might be considered as part of the contemporary theatre of its time, in the line of the European masters such as Ibsen. On the one hand, the play is a realistic piece with a message of protest from its central character, Paul Ruttledge, against conventional life, but this changes in the last two acts, set in a monastery, where the protest is made in terms of the mystical system Yeats pursued, and the text reflects this change of thought to the detriment of the play. *Where There is Nothing* also suffers from the lingering effect of the Pre-Raphaelite Brotherhood on Yeats's ideas and Paul Ruttledge seems to have in- herited some of the characteristics of William Morris.

This play was not offered to the Irish company but was shown by Yeats to Craig and his sister Edy in London. It aroused some enthus- iasm and a brief hope that Craig might produce it. In November, through Edy Craig's efforts on his behalf, Yeats had an offer of a production from the Stage Society in London, and they eventually presented the play at the Royal Court Theatre for three performances on 26, 27 and 28 June 1904.* The play was admired by Bernard Shaw, who felt the Irish company should come to act the play in London, and by his wife, and the designs were made by Edith Craig and Pamela Coleman Smith, as Yeats wrote to Lady Gregory on 4 December 1902, describing the designs and also the construction of the play:

Last Monday evening Pamela Smith brought round a big sketch book full of designs for the play made by herself and Edith Craig. They were particularly pleased because they know Gordon Craig's little stage dodges and are using them rather to his annoyance. He is rather disgusted at the chief part being offered to Harry Irving instead of himself. I thought the design for the Monastery scene extremely impressive. The design for Act I was a little humdrum. To some extent that was my own fault, for that croquet lawn and garden path has been the opening of so many plays. Suddenly while I was looking at it, it occurred to me that it could all be made fantastic by there being a number of bushes shaped Dutch fashion into cocks and hens, ducks, peacocks

---

*   WHERE THERE IS NOTHING

Presented by the Stage Society, London
at the Royal Court Theatre
on 26, 27 and 28 June 1904

Paul Ruttledge	E. Lyall Swete
Thomas Ruttledge	James Gelderd
Mrs. Thomas Ruttledge	Miss Dora Barton
Magistrates : Mr. Dowler	Fewlass Llewelyn
Mr. Algie	Athol Stewart
Col. Lawley	Ean Macdonald
Mr. Joyce	Lewis Casson
Mr. Green	A. S. Homewood
Sabina Silver	Miss Thyrza Norman
Mollie, the Scold	Miss Freda Bramleigh
Tinkers : Charlie Ward	Blake Adams
Paddy Cockfight	Trent Adams
Tommy, the Song	J. Cooke Beresford
Johneen	Philip Tonge
A Child	Miss Marion Plarr
Friars : Father Jerome	Harcourt Williams
Father Aloysius	Lewis Casson
Father Coleman	Fewlass Llewelyn
Father Bartley	James Gelderd
The Superior	A. E. Drinkwater
Other Friars and Countrymen	Ean Macdonald, Athol Stewart, Fred Foss, Warburton Gamble, C. Warren, Alfred Wareham

Directed by H. Granville Barker
Designed by Edith Craig and Pamela Coleman Smith

etc. Pamela began sketching them at once. It can be supposed that these fowl have been the occupation of Paul Ruttledge's ironical leisure for years past. I never did know before what he had been doing all that time.

The changes I am thinking of, the opening of the Monastery scene, in no way touched the vitals of the scene. They are all before the entrance of the Superior. I think that some comedy there will help the balance of the play. Every other act of the play has comedy. I wouldn't mind if one of the early acts was quite serious. They would balance then.[27]

In 1907, under the title *The Unicorn from the Stars*, Yeats rewrote the play with Lady Gregory's assistance and it was produced at the Abbey Theatre in November of that year. In his preface to the text Yeats acknowledged the hand of Lady Gregory in the new version:

of the first version of "The Unicorn," "Where There is Nothing," a five-act play written in a fortnight to save it from a plagiarist . . . her share grew more and more considerable.[28]

New ideas and ways in which the Irish company might develop continued to emerge and Yeats continued to learn from Craig. Edy Craig took him backstage to the rehearsals of *Bethlehem* by Laurence Houseman which Craig was preparing for production at the Imperial Institute in South Kensington, where it was performed in December. On 26 September Yeats wrote to Lady Gregory,

I have suggested that they play foreign masterpieces. I find I can get through Miss Horniman a translation of a fine play of the heroic age of Sudermann's. I have not spoken of this yet but have suggested the last act of *Faustus* to F. Fay. I have learned a great deal about the staging of plays from "the nativity," indeed I have learned more than Craig likes. His sister has helped me, bringing me to where I could see the way the lights were worked. He was indignant — there was quite an amusing scene. I have seen all the costumes too, and hope to get patterns. He costumed the whole play — 30 or 40 people I should say — for £25.[29]

In October Yeats returned to Dublin for the rehearsals of the newly-styled Irish National Dramatic Company's season which included *The Pot of Broth** and which opened at the Antient Concert Rooms on 30 October. The second issue of *Samhain* was published to coincide with the season and *Cathleen Ni Houlihan* was first printed in its pages. The editorial paragraphs, headed 'Notes,' reviewed the end of

---

* THE POT OF BROTH

Presented by the Irish National Dramatic Company
at the Antient Concert Rooms, Dublin
on 30 October 1902

A Beggarman	W. G. Fay
Sibby	Maire T. Quinn
John, her husband	P. J. Kelly

Directed by Frank J. Fay

the Irish Literary Theatre and the productions done by the Fay company in the previous April. The announcement that the season's plays would be repeated at the little hall in Camden Street, the company's 'permanent' home, in November led to the statement that

If they could afford it they would have hired some bigger house, but, after all, M. Antoine founded his *Théâtre Libre* with a company of amateurs in a hall that only held three hundred people.[30]

(The Camden Street hall held fifty!)

The Pot of Broth is a slight one-act folk drama in which Yeats adapted a West of Ireland tale and, with Lady Gregory's help, cast it into a simple fable about a tramp who tricks a couple of country folk out of their food. Yeats did not pursue this line of playwriting further, even though the piece was very popular with Irish audiences. In December he handed the draft of his play, *The Country of the Young*, over to Lady Gregory who rewrote the piece as one of her short plays, entitled *The Travelling Man*.

As new plays and new playwrights emerged to extend the theatre movement in Ireland, Yeats returned to his own preoccupation with verse drama and with the principles by which his ideal theatre should be developed. On 1 November he lectured on 'Speaking to Musical Notes' in Dublin, with illustrations given by Florence Farr.

After the Dublin season Yeats returned to London and does not seem to have come to Dublin for the repeat performances in December at the company's own Camden Street hall. He brought to London with him Robert Gregory's sketch for the setting of *The Hour-Glass* which was planned for an early production by Frank Fay, and had a commission to prepare a lecture in which he would lay down the principles on which the Irish company would operate. Theatre management had been added to his concern with playwriting and, as 1902 came to an end, he entered into a period of intense activity in the various aspects of his theatre life.

*

The Hour-Glass was inspired by a folk-tale printed by Speranza, Lady Wilde, in her *Ancient Legends of Ireland*, 1887. It is a morality, in which the structural idea was based on the medieval drama and the characters are presented as types — Wise Man, Fool, Angel, etc. The simple plot concerns the Wise Man, who is a Teacher, and denies the existence of the 'invisible country' with such eloquence that his Pupils are led into erroneous beliefs. The Fool, however, does not accept the Wise Man's teachings and, when the Angel appears and points out the doom that will overtake the Wise Man because of his error, it is to the Fool that he appeals for affirmation of the older beliefs before the sand in the hour-glass runs out. Thus the Wise Man assures the salvation of his soul.

This is the 'little play about the call of religion' that Yeats mentioned in his interview in *The United Irishman* of 5 May 1902, as forming a trilogy with *The Land of Heart's Desire* (the call of the heart) and *Cathleen Ni Houlihan* (the call of country). It is the most accomplished of the early plays and the 1903 version shows how much he had learned of theatre technique in the two years since his first meeting with Craig.

By early January 1903 he had found 'a wonderful "angel"'[31] in London and was planning to produce the play there with the help of T. Sturge Moore (1870-1944), the writer and artist. More hoped that Ricketts would raise about £600 which should be used to finance a London production by Gordon Craig of *The Countess Cathleen* in which Yeats and Sturge Moore would supervise the verse speaking, but this project did not materialise. Yeats did ask Sturge Moore if he would translate Robert Gregory's scene design for *The Hour-Glass* into practical terms. Robert Gregory's sketch was vague, but did in general follow the stage directions, which read,

A large room with a door at the back and another at the side opening to an inner room. A desk and a chair in the middle. An hour-glass on a bracket near the door. A creepy stool near it. Some benches. An astronomical globe perhaps. Perhaps a large ancient map of the world on the wall or some musical instruments. Floor may be strewed with rushes.

Moore's response to the request was to make a detailed black and white drawing with notes on practical properties which he enclosed with a letter to Yeats in November 1902.

I have done the best I could for you. It was no use attempting a coloured sketch as I had neither the colours of the dresses nor of the background. I think a raw undyed material would be best for the walls and ceiling. If it is not hung on the blind principle it might be stretched on canvas stretchers but this would be more expensive. The floor should be covered with the stuff they use to reddle sheep with, which is very cheap. Mrs. Morton, the housekeeper at 20 Fitzroy Street, could tell you where to get it in case Fay did not know. She uses it for doing in behind the stoves. The angel ought not to wear wings or she could not get through the door, and no one must lean against the walls etc.

There is no need for doors, which are expensive if workable, and as long as there are doorways all that is needed is there.

Hoping this will be in time and answer its purpose.   Yours sincerely
                                                                                              T. S. Moore

The master's desk is to stand bang in the centre of the stage but near the back wall, leaving only room for his stool behind it.[32]

The letter was accompanied by a drawing of the setting, with written instructions on both sides of the sheet. Above the drawing Moore wrote :

Any dull grey or buff colour will do for walls and ceiling. The floor should be done over with dull red. Then as long as the costumes are dark and rich they will harmonise.

22. T. Sturge Moore. Setting for *The Hour-Glass*, 1902, after a sketch by Robert Gregory.

and, below the drawing :

Design to scale for scene on stage height, depth, and width all alike 12 feet. Distance from front of curtain representing back wall. A.A. from 8 to 9 feet. Doorway 32 inches wide to be cut or left between widths of stuff, in latter case shorter strip with opening for bell to be hung down so as to leave doorway seven feet high.
Doorway in left wall nearer to front than to curtain.

Behind doorway right against wall of theatre a back cloth of a dark material grey or dark blue or green best.

Curtains representing side walls to be 8 or 9 ft. wide back wall curtain to continue at least six inches behind them on either side.

Curtains to be made of widths of stuff not sewed together but hung so as to overlap 2 or 3 inches from curtain pole at top with heavy rods in seams at bottom like blinds so that they may hang straight.

If ceiling cannot be made of same material stretched tight draw curtain up to pencil line and leave it.

The effect of the scene will depend on keeping lines straight, the proportions between the measurements exact and on adding no superfluous items.

For furniture see over.

On the back of the sheet, the directions for the stage properties, called 'furniture' above, were given:

Bell to hang outside from roof so as to be visible through opening in the centre when at rest.

In order that it may ring it must have some such lever as this. A.A. to which at one end is attached the cord to ring it by at the other the handle of the bell with a fisell spindle C crossing between the bell and A.A. The spindle to rest in holes in a horse shoe piece D tied on to rope E by which it hangs.

Desk to be made of two uprights 5 ft six inches high and two 4 ft high. These uprights to be 2½ inches square and joined by battens 2½ inches wide nailed on the outside one foot from ground and one foot from top of 5 ft uprights though only 2 inches from top of 4 ft uprights. The top to be boarded for leaning on and covered down to beneath battens with same cloth as is used for backcloth outside door. The Master's stool must be a very high office stool so that his feet are well off the floor. The other stools to be as low and as rustic and as like one another as possible.

Hourglass on a solid simple bracket right in front on the right its top being 6 ft above floor.[33]

Yeats wrote to Lady Gregory about Moore's design on 9 December:

Moore has done me some designs for *The Hour-Glass* working out Robert's sketch into practical detail. He is emphatic, however, about the great difficulty of getting a green that will go well with purple and wants me to have the curtains made of some undyed material. I have written to Fay for some patterns of the purple and to ask if there was to be any green in the costumes. I think the Moore design looks very impressive.[34]

It is evident that this scheme was adhered to from the note on the play in the 1908 Collected Edition,

We always play it in front of an olive-green curtain, and dress the Wise Man and his Pupils in various shades of purple. Because in all these decorative schemes one needs, as I think, a third colour subordinate to the other two, we have partly dressed the Fool in red-brown, which is repeated in the furniture. There is some green in his dress and in that of the Wife of the Wise Man who is dressed mainly in purple.[35]

This also suggests that the furniture in the play may have been toned down in colour after the first performance, as, in a letter to Sturge Moore Yeats wrote,

I found that the brown back of a chair during the performance of *The Hour-Glass* annoyed me beyond words. Further, the black, brown and white effect is just one of those effects which we like in London because we have begun to grow weary with the more obvious and beautiful effects. But it is precisely those obvious and beautiful effects that we want here.[36]

For the Pupils' song in the play Yeats adapted an old Irish ballad with the refrain, 'O the brown and the yellow beer!' and he selected an Aran Island air to accompany the words. This was used to introduce the Pupils at their second entrance in the play, as the Wise Man dies.

The Hour-Glass* was presented by the Irish National Theatre Society on 14 March 1903, in a double bill with Lady Gregory's first produced play, *Twenty-Five*, which the Society had rejected in the previous autumn. Yeats delivered his lecture, 'The Reform of the Theatre' between the plays. The Camden Street premises had proved unsuitable for the production and the Molesworth Hall was rented. This hall seated an audience of three hundred and had a sixteen-foot proscenium opening with a twelve-foot stage depth. With this production, which played to full capacity audiences, the sincerity of

---

*   THE HOUR-GLASS

Presented by the Irish National Theatre Society
at the Molesworth Hall, Dublin
on Saturday 14 March 1903

The Wise Man	J. Dudley Digges
Bridget (his wife)	Maire T. Quinn
His children	Eithne and Padragan Nic Shiubhlaigh
His pupils	P. J. Kelly
	Seamus O'Sullivan
	P. Columb
	P. Mac Siubhlaigh
The Angel	Maire Nic Shiubhlaigh
The Fool	F. J. Fay

Directed by W. G. Fay
Setting and costumes designed by Robert Gregory
Setting realised from drawing by T. Sturge Moore

purpose of the Irish National Theatre was made evident. Joseph
Holloway concluded that 'the evening was the turning point in the
career of the Irish National Theatre Company, and has placed them
on the wave of success.' [37] His admiration for the presentation of *The
Hour-Glass* shows that Yeats's concern with stage presentation and
the knowledge he had acquired from Craig and Sturge Moore were
necessary and valuable additions to the expertise of the company.

The stage setting was simplicity itself — a background of green unrelieved by
any colour with entrances of the same shade; a rude desk with a ponderous
tome thereon, a bell pull (that refused to convey its message to the bell on
occasion when pulled), and a tiny bracket supporting an hour glass were all
the properties, while the costumes of the players were composed of materials
that worked in harmony with the said background — "The Angel" and "The
Fool" alone being clad in tints with a little warmth in them. The effect of this
scheme, in such a piece, I think, heightened the effect and enchained the
interest. . . . The result was profoundly impressive !
    The acting was in keeping with the subject. Mr. J. Dudley Digges, if one
forgot his over-facial expression (he looked like "Richard III" during most of
the time) ably and powerfully enacted the role of "The Wise Man". He spoke
well and acted finely for the most part. Miss Mary Walker [Miss Maire nic
Shiubhlaigh] impersonated "The Angel" in a way that Dante Gabriel Rossetti
or Burne-Jones would have loved to limn. Her pose as she stood immoveable
at the door was very beautiful and quite after the pre-Raphaelite manner of
her measured delivery, most telling and effective. No member of the company
has improved so much since I first heard her last year in *Deirdre* at St. Teresa's
Hall as the heroine's foster-mother. She seems to me to be a most earnest
student and enters the spirit of each part she plays. Enthusiasm and earnest-
ness are bound to come out on top in the end. Mr. F. J. Fay's conception of
"The Fool" was A-1, and he scored a big success in the part as the play proceeded. He is another enthusiast who is reaching the top of his ambition also
by legitimate hard work. . . . [38]

This production, described by Lady Gregory as 'our first attempt
at the decorative staging long demanded by Mr. Yeats,' [39] introduced
to the stage the archetypal Fool, a character which recurs in later
plays from *On Baile's Strand* onward. In 1911, after the revival of the
play designed by Gordon Craig, Yeats wrote of this character,

The same Fool and mask, the Fat Fool of folklore who is as wide and wild as
a hill and not the Thin Fool of modern romance, may go with a masked blind
man into *On Baile's Strand*. [40]

The impact of this medieval dramatic form restated, remote from
real life in its formality, was reinforced by Yeats's lecture on 'The
Reform of the Theatre,' which he published in the third issue of
Samhain later in the year. This lecture shows the confidence Yeats
had gained as his practical knowledge of theatre had developed and,
at the same time, set a high standard for the young company.

THE REFORM OF THE THEATRE

I think the theatre must be reformed in its plays, its speaking, its acting, and its scenery. That is to say, I think there is nothing good about it at present.

1st. We have to write or find plays that will make the theatre a place of intellectual excitement — a place where the mind goes to be liberated as it was liberated by the theatres of Greece and England and France at certain great moments of their history, and as it is liberated in Scandinavia to-day. If we are to do this we must learn that beauty and truth are always justified of themselves, and that their creation is a greater service to our country than writing that compromises either in the seeming service of a cause. . . .

If one does not know how to construct, if one cannot arrange much complicated life into a single action, one's work will not hold the attention or linger in the memory, but if one is not in love with words it will lack the delicate moment of living speech that is the chief garment of life; and because of this lack the great realists seem to the lovers of beautiful art to be wise in this generation, and for the next generation, perhaps, but not for all generations that are to come.

2nd. But if we are to restore words to their sovereignty we must make speech even more important than gesture upon the stage.

I have been told that I desire a monotonous chant, but that is not true, for though a monotonous chant may be a safer beginning for an actor than the broken and prosaic speech of ordinary recitation, it puts one to sleep none the less. The sing-song in which a child says a verse is a right beginning, though the child grows out of it. An actor should understand how to so discriminate cadence from cadence, and to so cherish the musical lineaments of verse or prose that he delights the ear with a continually varied music. Certain passages of lyrical feeling, or where one wishes, as in the Angel's part in *The Hour Glass*, to make a voice sound like the voice of an immortal, may be spoken upon pure notes which are carefully recorded and learned as if they were the notes of a song. Whatever method one adopts one must always be certain that the work of art, as a whole, is masculine and intellectual, in its sound as in its form.

3rd. We must simplify acting, especially in poetical drama, and in prose drama that is remote from real life like my *Hour Glass*. We must get rid of everything that is restless, everything that draws the attention away from the sound of the voice, or from the few moments of intense expression, whether that expression is through the voice or through the hands; we must from time to time substitute for the movements that the eye sees the nobler movements that the heart sees, the rhythmical movements that seem to flow up into the imagination from some deeper life than that of the individual soul.

4th. Just as it is necessary to simplify gesture that it may accompany speech without being its rival, it is necessary to simplify both the form and colour of scenery and costume. As a rule the background should be but a single colour, so that the persons in the play wherever they stand, may harmonize with it, and preoccupy our attention. In other words it should be thought out not as one thinks out a landscape, but as if it were the background of a portrait, and this is especially necessary on a small stage where the moment the stage is filled the painted forms of the background are broken up and lost. Even when one has to represent trees or hills they should be treated in most cases decoratively, they should be little more than an un-obtrusive pattern. There must be nothing unnecessary, nothing that will distract the attention from speech and movement. An art is always at its greatest when it is most human. Greek acting was great because it did everything with the voice, and modern acting may be great when it does everything with voice and movement. But an art which smothers these things with bad painting, with innumerable garish colours, with continual restless mimicries of the surface of life, is an art of fading humanity, a decaying art.[41]

*

The Irish National Theatre Society had established itself in Dublin with the Spring 1903 season and felt confident enough to issue a statement of its objects which, in saying that it was formed 'to continue — if possible on a more permanent basis — the work begun by the Irish Literary Theatre,' affirmed the continuity of its President's authority. The company toured to the West of Ireland in April with a bill that included *The Pot of Broth* and Æ's *Deirdre*. The performance must have seemed strange to the country audiences and, when Yeats included *The Pot of Broth* in the 1922 edition of his plays, he recalled,

In some country village an audience of farmers once received it in stony silence, and at the fall of the curtain a farmer stood up and said nobody there had ever seen a play. Then Mr. William Fay explained what a play was, and the farmer asked that it might be performed again, and at the second performance there was much laughter and cheers.[42]

A very different audience saw the company at work when, in response to an invitation to Yeats from Stephen Gwynn, the company went to London on 2 May to give two performances at the Queen's Gate Hall, sponsored by the Irish Literary Society. On 8 May, A. B. Walkley, in *The Times*, wrote enthusiastically about the plays and the performance. His article announced the creation of the Irish National Theatre to the world,

It is part of a national movement, it is designed to express the spirit of the race, the "virtue" of it, in the medium of acted drama. That is an excellent design. If the peculiarities of Irish thought and feeling can be brought home to us through drama we shall all be the better for the knowledge; and the art of drama, too, cannot but gain by a change of air, a new outlook, a fresh current of ideas. . . .

First and foremost, there is the pleasure of the ear. This, of course, is an accidental pleasure; we mean that it has nothing to do with the aesthetic aims of the Society, nothing to do with the dramatic theories or poetic gifts of its President, Mr. W. B. Yeats, nothing to do with art at all; it results from the nature of things, from the simple fact that Irish speakers are addressing English listeners. It is none the less a very exquisite pleasure. We had never realized the musical possibilities of our language until we had heard these Irish people speak it. . . . We are listening to English spoken with watchful care and slightly timorous hesitation, as though it were a learned language. That at once ennobles our mother-tongue, brings it into relief, gives it a daintiness and distinction of which, in our rough workaday use of it, we had never dreamed. . . .

The next pleasure is for the eye. These Irish gentlemen and ladies are good to look at; the men are lithe, graceful, bright-eyed, and one at least of the maidens, with the stage name of Maire Nic Shiubhlaigh, is of a strange, wan, "disquieting" beauty. . . . As a rule they stand stock-still. The speaker of the moment is the only one who is allowed a little gesture—just as in the familiar convention of the Italian marionette theatre the figure supposed to be speaking is distinguished from the others by a slight vibration. The listeners do not distract one's attention by fussy "stage business," they just stay where they are and listen. When they do move it is without premeditation, at haphazard, even with a little natural clumsiness, as of people who are not conscious of being stared at in public. Hence a delightful effect of spontaneity. And in their demeanour generally they have the artless impulsiveness of children — the very thing which one found so enjoyable in another exotic affair, the performance of Sada Yacco and her Japanese company. Add that the scenery is of Elizabethan simplicity — sometimes no more than a mere backcloth — and you will begin to see why this performance is a sight good for sore eyes— eyes made sore by the perpetual movement and glitter of the ordinary stage.

But it is time to say something of the vital part of our pleasure, the pleasure of mind and mood. That, too, is largely a pleasure of rest — and resignation. The mind is steeped in seriousness; the mood is uniformly sad . . . the Irish theatre is really of its own kind and of none other. Its sustained note of sub-dued gravity, with here and there faint harmonies of weird elfish freakishness ("harps in the air", Hilda Wangel would have called them) is entirely Irish and entirely delightful. Take Mr. Yeats' "morality," *The Hour Glass*. An angel gives a man a few moments wherein to try and find means of salvation before he dies with the last running out of the sand. Imagine how the ordinary dramatist would treat this, how largely the hour-glass would bulk in the foreground, how the man would writhe and shriek in the frenzied horror of imminent death. . . . The whole tone of the thing, as we have said, is grave and subdued, its whole texture such stuff as dreams are made of. . . .

No doubt there is a touch of affectation in their methods; they have some-thing of the self-importance of children surpliced for service at the altar, or "dressed-up" for a grand domestic occasion. A style "deliberately adopted" is the harmless little boast of their prospectus. Well, that is a matter of course. All new movements in art are self-conscious, abound in little exaggerations and affectations. Is there not an Irish precept, "Be aisy; and if ye can't be aisy, be as aisy as ye can"? We may commend that to the Irish National Theatre Society. And for ourselves we are quite "aisy"; for the "deliberate" methods of these enthusiasts will surely lose their stiffness in due course of time.[43]

Walkley's article was a great encouragement to the endeavours of the company, but also must have confirmed to the Fays that Yeats was right in his approach to the theatre. To Yeats it must have meant an endorsement of his ideals, while the comparison with the Japanese company sounded a note heralding developments in his dramatic work which were yet some thirteen years ahead.

An invitation from Lady Aberdeen to play in America for six months at the Saint Louis Exhibition followed the London success and although the company were eager to go, Yeats felt that they were not yet ready for such an exposure. The players, still amateurs, returned to their daily labours in Dublin and set to planning the autumn season. Yeats remained in London, pursuing the various threads of a career that was becoming rapidly more diverse and was soon further involved by the entry of the 'fairy godmother,' Miss Horniman.

*

Annie Elizabeth Fredericka Horniman (1860-1937) whose father was Chairman of the family firm of tea merchants was interested in the theatre from an early age. She was an art student at the Slade School in London and through friendships made there she became an early member of the mystical Order of the Golden Dawn and thus met Florence Farr and Yeats. She was the backer of Florence Farr's Avenue Theatre season in 1894, during which *The Land of Heart's Desire* was first produced and she later helped Yeats with his secretarial work in London. She was probably the 'wealthy friend' to whom Yeats had spoken in April 1902 and whom he had quoted in a letter to Frank Fay as saying

"Work on as best you can for a year, let us say, you should be able to persuade people during that time that you are something of a dramatist and Mr. Fay should be able to have got a little practice for his company." [44]

By September 1902 she was advising Yeats on foreign plays which the Dublin company might attempt. Her letters to Yeats, which are phrased in the cryptic terminology of the Order of the Golden Dawn, use Tarot card readings to predict the developments of the theatrical enterprise of 'the Prince of S'.

When the company visited London in May 1902 Miss Horniman wrote to Yeats that she had consulted the Tarot as to 'How will the result of tomorrow's performance of his plays affect the Prince of S?' [45] and informed him that the Tarot answered that he would enjoy 'the materialisation of his ideas' and 'a gain of authority about his dramatic affairs', [46] which oracle was accompanied by a warning that Fay and Yeats were incompatible characters. In September she wrote predicting 'new energy leading to fame and power' but with the warning of a 'disappointment in friendship.' [47] By this time she had designed the costumes for *The King's Threshold*, which was produced with the first play of J. M. Synge's to reach the stage, *In the Shadow of the Glen* and a revival of *Cathleen Ni Houlihan* in which Sara Allgood played with the company for the first time, on 8 October.*

Yeats sent the text of *The King's Threshold* to William Fay in August and wrote to Frank about the play, which was at that time named *Seanchan*, after the principal character. His letter is specific about his requirements from the producer and indicates his hopes for the play,

I am sending your brother Seanchan to-day. (If you are reading it, pronounce "Shanahan.") If I can get them done I shall send at the same time the maps of the more important positions. I think it will play about an hour and a half. It is quite a long elaborate play, and is constructed rather like a Greek play. I think it the best thing I have ever done, and with the beautiful costumes that are being made for it I should make something of a stir. I am afraid you will have an exhausting part in Seanchan, but you will find plenty to act and the best dramatic verse I have written to speak. Your brother told me that he meant to cast you as Seanchan, and I am very glad of it. I have long wanted to see you with some part which would give you the highest opportunities. Your playing of the Fool in *The Hour-Glass* was beautiful, wise and subtle, but such a part can never express anyone's whole nature. It has to be created more or less from without. Your performance of Seanchan will,

---

*   THE KING'S THRESHOLD

Presented by the Irish National Theatre Society
at the Molesworth Hall, Dublin
on 8 October 1903

Seanchan, Chief Poet of Ireland	F. J. Fay
King Guaire	P. J. Kelly
The Lord High Chamberlain	Seumas O'Sullivan
Soldier	William Conroy
Monk	S. Sheridan-Neill
The Mayor of Kinvara	W. G. Fay
A Cripple	P. Columb
Another Cripple	E. Davis
Aileen, a Court Lady	Honor Lavelle
Essa, Another Court Lady	Dora Melville
Princess Buan	Sara Allgood
Princess Finnhua, her Sister	Doreen Gunning
Fedelm, Seanchan's Sweetheart	Maire Nic Siubhlaigh
Servants of Seanchan :	
Cian	P. MacSiubhlaigh
Brian	P. Josephs
Pupils of Seanchan :	
Senias	George Roberts
Arias	Caitia Nic Chormac

Directed by W. G. Fay
Costumes designed and made by Miss A. E. F. Horniman

I believe, establish all our fames. I wish very much you could send me the right measurements for a curtain, such a curtain as we can use when our fortunes have improved and our stage grown bigger. I want to get it embroidered if I can. I look upon it as part of the staging of Seanchan, for there is to be a prologue spoken by Mr. Russell in the Wise Man's dress. I want the dark dress and the dark curtain to fix themselves on the minds of the audience before the almost white stage is disclosed. If I cannot get the measurements by Monday it may be too late, as the designer who is now here is going away.[48]

Like the theme of *The Hour-Glass*, the folk-tale from which Yeats derived the plot of *The King's Threshold*, 'Seanchan the Bard and the King of the Cats,' may be found in Lady Wilde's *Ancient Legends of Ireland*, 1887, and, although some critics have suggested other versions of the same tale as the source material for the play, it seems likely that Yeats would have used the same book as a common source for two plays composed within so short a time. Another source which Yeats acknowledged is *Sancan the Bard*, a verse play by his friend Edwin J. Ellis. 'I have borrowed some ideas for the arrangement of my subject in *The King's Threshold* from *Sancan the Bard*, a play published by Mr. Edwin Ellis some ten years ago.'[49] This acknowledgement to Ellis indicates the very deep impression the folk tale had made on Yeats and, although he acknowledged Lady Gregory's help with the construction of the plot, *The King's Threshold* remains a powerful and convincing reflection of Yeats's belief in the individuality of the poet and an affirmation of the essential freedom of the creative spirit, despite the restrictions which society may impose on that freedom.

Seanchan the poet, at the court of King Guaire at Gort, is ousted by the conniving courtiers and clerics from his position of privilege at the King's table. His protest against this indignity takes the form of a 'hunger-strike,' which he mounts at the palace gates, on 'the King's threshold,' where he states his intention of starving to death to make public the wrongs he has suffered at the hands of the court. In his notes on the revised text of the play in *Plays in Prose and Verse*, 1922, Yeats wrote,

When I wrote this play neither suffragette nor patriot had adopted the hunger strike, nor had the hunger strike been used anywhere, so far as I know, as a political weapon.[50]

All attempts to divert Seanchan from his avowed course of action fail until, at last, King Guaire himself approaches and, in appeasement of the wrong done to Seanchan, offers him his crown. Seanchan, in accepting the proffered crown, shows his belief in the validity of the poet's position and the right of his protest. The mind (the poet) can command a greater authority than material things (the king).

Another important quality in *The King's Threshold* is the play's affirmation of the 'spirit of place' which is an important quality also of the Japanese Nō plays on which Yeats was to model his later work in the theatre. While its general theme is universal, the play is closely associated with the folklore of Gort, the nearest town to Lady Gregory's home at Coole, and it draws its locale and its language from the indigenous lore and tradition of that specific place in the West of Ireland.

The play, which amply justifies Miss Horniman's prediction to Yeats of 'a gain of authority about his dramatic affairs,' is the most skilfully wrought of the early plays. It was conceived with a specific company, the Irish National Theatre Society, in mind, and the leading role of Seanchan the poet was written for Frank Fay. When the play was included in the contents of *Poems 1899-1905*, published in 1906, it was dedicated 'To Frank Fay because of his beautiful speaking in the part of Seanchan.'

Rehearsals of *The Shadowy Waters* were suspended while *The King's Threshold* was prepared for production. Joseph Holloway, who had by then become a constant presence at rehearsals as well as at performances, recorded the difficulties under which the play was produced as the carpenters were also at work in the confined space of the Camden Street Hall, hammering and sawing away while the actors wrestled with their lines,

Friday, August 21. . . . Visited the Camden Street "Theatre" where I saw Mr. Synge's curious play, *In the Shadow of the Glen*, rehearsed, and also W. B. Yeats's new play in verse, entitled *Seanchan*. I followed the first play with much interest, but as a carpenter was busy sawing, sandpapering, and hammering some "cages" for lights, etc., all the while just behind me, I heard little of the latter work. It certainly was rehearsing under difficulties . . .[51]

but, on 4 September, the carpenters were apparently absent and Holloway could comment on the rehearsal.

Seanchan is one of those poetic fancies of Yeats which the National Theatre knows how to interpret so lovingly and poetically. Mr. Frank Fay, as the discarded poet who resolves to starve himself to death on the doorstep of his late master, speaks Yeats's verse extremely musically, and enters the spirit of the poet's thoughts with inspired effectiveness. Mr. W. G. Fay's attempts at the sing-song chanting as "The Mayor" were very crude to my mind, and much resembled the sounds produced by an infant class repeating lessons aloud. He is a born impersonator of tramps and quick-witted beggars. Poetic drama is out of his line. The others are shaping well in their respective roles.[52]

Miss Horniman designed and made the costumes for *The King's Threshold* and the staging of the play was an attempt to realise

Craig's doctrine as relayed by Yeats to the company. A stepped stage with a draped surround was used, lighted without using footlights and, although Holloway considered the stage grouping and the lighting successful, he saw that such a change from conventional methods needed more preparation than had been given to the piece.

On future occasions we should recommend the Irish National Theatre Society to hold at least one dress-rehearsal of their productions with the view of definitely arranging their lighting effects. Neglect to do this led to some amusing incidents on Thursday night. To a large extent the lighting methods of Mr. Gordon Craig were followed, no footlights being used. Adequate illumination was given for the most part by a powerful projector placed at the back of the audience. The turning of this on immediately before the rising of the curtain rendered the flimsy green draperies transparent, with the result that shadow pantomimes were enacted which by their unexpectedness sent the audience into fits of laughter.[53]

Although Miss Horniman's costumes were praised in such Press notices as this, by T. M. Kettle from *New Ireland*,

the costumes of King Guaire and his Court were of a richness almost barbaric. The cut and colour of each garment was adjusted, I understand, to a scheme marvellous in its emotional and symbolic value, and beyond the capacity of any but a society journal to record,[54]

Yeats, writing to Frank Fay about future plans, expressed some reservations. He went to New York at the end of October on an extended lecture tour, and devoted much thought to the future development of the Irish National Theatre, while he worked at completing his first Cuchulain play. The practical side of stagecraft was now always present in his approach to play construction, and the adaptation of Craig's techniques to his own requirements is evident.

Now about scenery. I think you will find that the persons in *Cuchullain** will stand out clearly against the plain sacking. It is not necessary to do this by contrasting colour always — light and dark will do it. *The Shadowy Waters* I thought an exception to rule and thought one should lose the persons in the general picture. I had a different feeling about [the] stage when I wrote it — I would not now do anything so remote, so impersonal. It is legitimate art however though a kind that may I should think by this time prove itself the worst sort possible for our theatre. The whole picture as it were moves together — sky and sea and cloud are as it were actors. It is almost religious, it is more a ritual than a human story. It is deliberately without human characters. *Cuchullain* or *The King's Threshold* are the other side of the halfpenny. I do not think the greys kept the people in the latter from standing out, though there were other defects — too many colours and so on. Miss Horniman has to learn her work however and must have freedom to experiment. I think her *Baile's Strand* will prove much better. I had told her that

*On Baile's Strand.

old stages permitted elaborate dress though not elaborate scenes, and this combined with [the] fact of its being a Court misled her into overdoing colour and the like in certain parts. Surely the people of heroic age wore trews? I have heard that the bare legs and kilts of the highlanders come from the Romans, that the Celts had both kinds. Anyway Miss Horniman has Joyce's *Social Ireland* and was deep in it when I saw her.[55]

This letter develops the ideas which Yeats expressed in his essay, 'The Reform of the Theatre,' which was printed in *Samhain 1903*, published to coincide with the Molesworth Hall season. *Samhain* also had a frontispiece after John Butler Yeats's portrait of W. G. Fay, about whom Yeats wrote in his editorial Notes,

We owe our National Theatre Society to him and his brother, and we have always owed to his playing our chief successes.[56]

*

In *The United Irishman* of 9 September 1903 Yeats published a Prologue to *The King's Threshold* but this was not spoken in the production because 'owing to the smallness of the company, nobody could be spared to speak it.' [57] In his letter to Frank Fay on 8 August, Yeats had mentioned this Prologue as 'to be spoken by Mr. Russell in the Wise Man's dress,' but the piece does not seem to have ever been attempted in performance. Nevertheless, it forms one of Yeats's most important theatrical statements and is an attempt to create a bridge between the 'Theatre of Art' and the reality of the Irish Theatre founded on the Fays' company. It is also the first of a series of attempts at this kind of exposition which Yeats was to repeat in draft form for *On Baile's Strand* and *The Shadowy Waters* and which he was not to realise fully until he wrote his last play in the final months of his life, when he composed the magnificent speech with which *The Death of Cuchulain* opens.

The Prologue to *The King's Threshold* reads,

A PROLOGUE

An old man with a red dressing-gown, red slippers and red nightcap, holding a brass candlestick with a guttering candle in it, comes on, in front of curtain.

OLD MAN — "I've got to speak the prologue. (*He shuffles on a few steps.*) My nephew, that's one of the players, came to me and I in my bed, and my prayers said, and the candle put out, and he told me there were so many characters in this new play, that all the company were in it, whether they had been long or short at the business, and that there wasn't one left to speak the prologue. Wait a bit, there's a draught here. (*He pulls the curtain close together.*) That's better. And that's why I'm here, and maybe I'm a fool for my pains.

"And my nephew said, there are a good many plays to be played for you, some to-night and some on other nights through the winter, and the most of them are simple enough, and tell out their story to the end. But as to the big play you are to see to-night, my nephew taught me to say what the poet had taught him to say about it. (*Puts down candlestick and puts right finger on left thumb.*) First, he who told the story of Seanchan on King Guaire's threshold long ago in the old books told it wrongly, for he was a friend of the king, or maybe afraid of the king, and so put the king in the right. But he that tells the story now, being a poet, has put the poet in the right.

"And then (*touches other finger*) I am to say : Some think it would be a finer tale if Seanchan had died at the end of it, and the king had the guilt at his door, for that might have served the poet's cause better in the end. But that is not true, for if he that is in the story but a shadow and an image of poetry had not risen up from the death that threatened him, the ending would not have been true and joyful enough to be put into the voices of players and proclaimed in the mouths of trumpets, and poetry would have been badly served. (*He takes up the candlestick again.*)

"And as to what happened Seanchan after, my nephew told me he didn't know, and the poet didn't know, and it's likely there's nobody that knows. But my nephew thinks he never sat down at the king's table again, after the way he had been treated, but that he went to some quiet green place in the hills with Fedelm, his sweetheart, where the poor people made much of him because he was wise, and where he made songs and poems, and it's likely enough he made some of the old songs and the old poems the poor people on the hillsides are saying and singing to-day. (*A trumpet-blast.*)

"Well, it's time for me to be going. That trumpet means that the curtain is going to rise, and after a while the stage there will be filled up with great ladies and great gentlemen, and poets, and a king with a crown on him, and all of them as high up in themselves with the pride of their youth and their strength and their fine clothes as if there was no such thing in the world as cold in the shoulders, and speckled shins, and the pains in the bones and the stiffness in the joints that make an old man that has the whole load of the world on him ready for bed.

"And it would be better for me, that nephew of mine to be thinking less of his play-acting, and to have remembered to boil down the knapweed with a bit of threepenny sugar, for me to be wetting my throat with now and again through the night, and drinking a sup to ease the pains in my bones." [58]

*

The Shadowy Waters, the play which had occupied much of Yeats's creative thought from the middle of the 1880's onwards, did not appear in print until 1900. In the final form of the play the lovers, Forgael and Dectora, are surrounded by spirits in the guise of sea-birds, and in the earlier drafts these spirits appear on stage alternately with the sailors, so that Lady Gregory was troubled by the problems of staging the piece because, as she said : 'Half his characters have eagles' faces.' [59]

The manuscripts of the play reveal the many changes in text during this long period of composition. The 'characters with eagles' faces,' the *Seabar*, had been written out of the piece before its first printing in 1900, in the form of a dramatic poem. A production of the play was planned by the Irish National Theatre Society in 1903, but it was postponed in favour of *The King's Threshold*, which was staged during the Society's autumn season. *The Shadowy Waters* was finally staged on 14 January 1904 at the Molesworth Hall, during Yeats's absence in America.* After the production of *The Hour-Glass* Yeats had asked T. Sturge Moore to advise on the realisation of the stage setting which had been designed by Robert Gregory. His letter shows an increased concern for the practical details of the stage presentation and reveals a concept of the cyclorama which, for its time, was very advanced.

I don't like the colour scheme at all. I know the effect of gauze very well and it will not pull this scheme together. The white sail will throw the hounds into such distinctness that they will become an irritation. I found that the brown back of a chair during the performance of *The Hour-Glass* annoyed me beyond words. Further, the black, brown and white effect is just one of those effects which we like in London because we have begun to grow weary with the more obvious and beautiful effects. But it is precisely those obvious and beautiful effects that we want here. The fault is very largely mine, for you had, as you thought, to bring in the red, black and white hounds. Now that I have had to think things out I have come to the conclusion that the hounds must be all in some one colour and be almost lost in the main colour of the sail. Your scheme would upset all my criticism here. I have been explaining on these principles : —

1. A background which does not insist on itself and which is so homogeneous in colour that it is always a good background to an actor wherever he stand. Your background is the contrary of all this.
2. Two predominant colours in remote fanciful plays. One colour predominant in actors, one in backcloth. This principle for the present at any rate until we have got our people to understand simplicity. *The Hour-Glass* as you remember was staged in this way and it delighted everybody.

Now what do you mean by backcloth to be continued? The wings of a theatre are ordinarily about this proportion to whole stage.

---

*   THE SHADOWY WATERS (first version)

Presented by the Irish National Theatre Society
at the Molesworth Hall, Dublin
on Thursday, 14 January 1904

Forgael	F. J. Fay
Aibric	P. J. Kelly
Helmsman	Seumas O'Sullivan
Sailors	G. Roberts, P. MacSiubhlaigh, U. Wright
Dectora	Maire Nic Shiubhlaigh

The Prologue spoken by Honor Lavelle

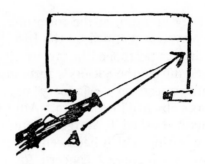

If we continue your bulwark or sail in a straight line a man at A will see into the machinery. If we arrange our stage with enormous wings we will not fit into some of the halls we may have to play in.

We shall have to bring the scene round like this

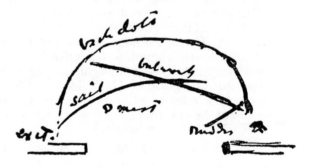

I have been working this out on a model and it has been a rather troublesome thing. The sail had better slope like this when seen from front, as that will hide the view into wings best and enable sailors at end to fight half hidden by the sail as they are meant to.

I have written to Fay for the exact measure of his stage, which is now a little larger than it used to be, the size of wings, etc.

Now as to colour scheme. The play is dreamy and dim and the colours should be the same — (say) a blue-green sail against an indigo-blue backcloth, and the mast and bulwark indigo blue. The persons in blue and green with some copper ornaments. By making one colour predominate only slightly in backcloth and one only slightly in persons the whole will be kept dim and mysterious, like the waters themselves. What do you think?

Now as to costumes. Nothing later than (illegible)th century, Wagner's period more or less, though a more modern touch no harm. We want to keep to a vague period that our costumes may be combined and re-combined in various plays.

Have I worried you too much over the thing? I can carry it out myself but I would far sooner that you did. If you were over here five minutes' conversation would put all right and you could work as many hours a day as you like with your Shakespeare.

If I have not disgusted you and put you out of patience I can send you the exact measurements after I have got all right on my model and in consultation with Fay.[60]

The Prologue which was spoken at the production was that printed in the 1900 edition of the play, the poem beginning, 'I walked among the seven woods of Coole.' A draft in manuscript exists for a Prologue similar to that written for *The King's Threshold*, which may date from later in the year when Yeats asked Charles Ricketts to design a costume for the actor who speaks the Prologue, a Black Jester. He fills the same function as the Old Man of the earlier Prologue, namely that of being a spokesman for Yeats, both as poet-playwright and as stage manager in the sense that Yeats understood this function as defined by Craig. This relates the theme of the play to 'Edain and Midhir,' the Irish tale from which it derives, and explains the symbolic or heraldic implications of the hound design on the sail which is mentioned in the letter to Sturge Moore quoted above. The Black Jester is arguing with the 'Stage Manager,' who is offstage,

No. I wont listen any more. Go away. What is that you are saying? (*Goes R.I.E. & speaks as if talking to somebody*) No. I'll have my own way. I told you from the first I was go[ing] to. Yes I'm quite ready to take the consequences (*Goes C*) He's always interfering. As if one could make any kind of enchantment worth looking at, if one had always to be thinking of him (*at C, facing audience*) The Stage Manager says I've got to juggle for you. That I'm to cause a vision to come before your eyes, but he doesn't want to let me please myself. He says it must be simple, easy to understand, all about real human beings but I am going to please myself this time (*going halfway to side*). It's no use shaking your hand at me there. I am going to do just as I like. What is the use of getting the black jester out of the waste places if he is not to do what he like (*returns to C*). These are my friends that I have here hung round my neck. Some of them I picked up on the wayside, some of them I made with a jack knife. I am going to make you dream about them & about me. I am going to wave my fingers & you will begin to dream. These two are Aengus & Edaine. They are spirits & whenever I am in love it is not I that am in love but Aengus who is always looking for Edaine through somebody's eyes. You will find all about them in the old Irish books. She was the wife of Midher another spirit in the hill but he grew jealous of her & he put her out of doors, & Aengus hid her in a tower of glass. That is why I carry the two of them in a glass bottle. (*holds bottle in front of me* [*him?*]) O Aengus ! O Edaine ! be kind to me when I am in love & to everybody in this audience when they are in love & make us all believe that it is not you but us ourselves that love. These others — the black dog, the red dog & the white dog. — I am always afraid of them. Sometimes the black dog gets on my back, though I have not been juggling but I will not talk about him for he was very wicked. I do not know the red dog from myself whenever I am angry or excited or running about. And it is only when I escape from him & [?] the black dog that the pale dog leads me where I would go. go to everything impossible & lasting To the place where these poor flowers that I have round my head can never die because they are made out of precious stones. They too are myself but that is a great mystery. The dogs & the little king & queen in the bottle & the flowers, they are all going to be in the dream that you are going to dream presently, but they will be great & terrible & my birds will be there too (*takes out birds*). These sea birds that I shall be like when I get out of the body & this eagle that carries me messages from beyond the body & this jewsharp that I play on when my birds & my beasts wont talk to me & I too shall be there, there in the dream & that I did long ago or that I would like to do.[61]

The stage directions to the 1900 version describe the symbolism pictured by Yeats, which he omitted in writing directions to the later revisions of the play.

The deck of a galley. The steering-oar, which comes through the bulwark, is to the left hand. One looks along the deck toward the high forecastle, which is partly hidden by a great square sail. The sail is drawn in toward the stern at the left side, and is high enough above the deck at the right side to show a little of the deck beyond and of the forecastle. Three rows of hounds, the first dark, the second red, and the third white with red ears make a conventional pattern upon the sail. The sea is hidden in mist, and there is no light except where the moon makes a brightness in the mist.
Forgael is sleeping upon skins a few yards forward of the steering-oar. He has a silver lily embroidered over his breast. A small harp lies beside him. Aibric and two sailors stand about the steering-oar. One of the sailors is steering.[62]

The Prologue devised for the Black Jester was not completed, but a letter of 26 July 1904 to Charles Ricketts shows that Ricketts had made a design for the character and that Yeats had in mind to use the character, perhaps again as Prologue to the play he was then preparing for production, *On Baile's Strand*.

I have been a long time in writing to thank you for having sent me such admirable designs for the Black Jester. I showed them to Frank Fay in Dublin, and he was delighted with them. And as soon as I can make some little progress with the poems I have in my mind for recitation, I will have the costume made. The Black Jester is one of the characters in a play I am now writing, and for that too the design will serve.[63]

On his return from America, Yeats set about making a 'stage version' of *The Shadowy Waters* which was produced at the Court Theatre in London on 8 July 1905, with Florence Farr as Dectora, in a setting designed by H. M. Paget. The production was favourably noticed and Yeats immediately set to further revising the play, with the practical demands of the staging in mind, and with a view to a possible Abbey Theatre revival. He wrote to Florence Farr in great detail about the performance,

I am making a new play of *The Shadowy Waters*. It is strong simple drama now, and has actually more poetical passages. Aibric is jealous of Forgael's absorption in his dream at the outset and ends by being jealous of Dectora. Instead of the sailors coming back drunk at the end, Aibric comes to appeal to Forgael to go back to his own land, but on finding that he is taken up with Dectora bursts out in jealousy. Forgael bids Dectora choose whether she will go back to her own land or not, and she chooses to go on with him — then Aibric cuts the rope and leaves them. This gives me a strong scene at the end. I wish you could get a good verse speaker who is a man. I wish I could persuade you that you are mistaken over Farquharson. I have been taken in in the same way more than once myself. When a young man has even a slight vulgar element — and it is not slight in Farquharson — one thinks it will leave him as he grows older. I thought that about Le Gallienne — who had what seemed like genius. It never leaves them, but when the enthusiasm of youth is over it gets much stronger till finally all else has left them. I have never known an exception. Apart from all else Farquharson is a man who always requires to be explained. Mrs. Shakespear for instance thought his manner was personally very offensive to you off the stage. He is really impossible as an artist. I had to use the greatest self control over myself all through those rehearsals. Only my fear of making things difficult for you kept me quiet.
I want you to try and get me Paget's model for the *Shadowy Waters* scene. I will probably work out a scene for Dublin, which could be used by you if necessary. Our stage is nearly as big as the Court. I can probably get that harp made too — we have carpenters and so on of our own now. We are in all likelihood to have a large scene dock next door this winter and will be able to work things out very perfectly. You must come over sometime and see our scenery, when the show comes off. You will I think prefer it to Craig. It is more noble and simple.[64]

After this rewriting the play was retained by Yeats in two versions, the 'poetic version' which continued to appear, with still further revisions, among his poems, and the 'acting version' which was printed in the successive editions of the plays. The definitive stage version was first played at the Abbey Theatre on 8 December 1906, with Frank Fay repeating the part of Forgael, Miss Darragh as Dectora and Arthur Sinclair as Aibric. This was an edited version of

the revised 'poetic' text and a note on that text in *Poems 1899-1905*
written before the production reveals Yeats's concern with the play.

I hope I have set it to rights now, and that if it finds an audience familiar with
the longing of a lover for impossible things, and longings that are like his, it
will hold the attention and have some pleasure in it for the players. I have
not yet seen this new version played, but have rehearsed it, and Mr. Robert
Gregory has designed the boat and sail. The colours of all will be as at the
first performance, dark blue and dark green, but for Dectora a lighter green
against the darker tints in sky and boat, with some glimmer of copper here
and there, and the lighting a not very bright moonlight. The effect of this
monotony of colour was to my eyes beautiful, and made the players seem like
people in a dream. I have described these colours a little in the stage directions, not because I think of them as a necessary part of the play, but because
it is necessary for some remote and decorative picture of the action, to float
up into the mind's eye of the reader, who must imagine some sort of a stage
scenery. When we began to get together the properties in this new version,
the stage carpenter found it very difficult to make the crescent-shaped harp
that was to burn with fire; and besides, no matter how well he made the
frame, there was no way of making the strings take fire. I had, therefore, to
give up the harp for a sort of psaltery, a little like the psaltery Miss Farr
speaks to, where the strings could be slits covered with glass or gelatine on the
surface of a shallow and perhaps semi-transparent box; and besides, it amused
one to picture, in the centre of a myth, the instrument of our new art.[65]

Yeats wrote a programme note for the 1906 production* which
was printed in *The Arrow* and which reveals his obsessive concern
for the 'embodiment of every lover's dream' as expressed in the play:

I began "The Shadowy Waters" when I was a boy, and when I published a
version of it six or seven years ago, the plot had been so often re-arranged and
was so overgrown with symbolical ideas that the poem was obscure and vague.
It found its way on to the stage more or less by accident, for our people had
taken it as an exercise in the speaking of verse, and it pleased a few friends,
though it must have bewildered and bored the greater portion of the audience.
The present version is practically a new poem, and is, I believe, sufficiently
simple, appealing to no knowledge more esoteric than is necessary for the

---

*   THE SHADOWY WATERS ('acting version')

Presented by the Irish National Theatre Society
at the Abbey Theatre, Dublin
on Saturday 8 December 1906

Dectora	Miss Darragh
Forgael	F. J. Fay
Aibric	Arthur Sinclair
Sailors	U. Wright, A. Power,
	J. A. O'Rourke, J. M. Kerrigan

Music composed by Arthur Darley
Scenery designed by Robert Gregory

understanding of any of the more characteristic love poems of Shelley or of Petrarch. If the audience will understand it as a fairy-tale, and not look too anxiously for a meaning, all will be well.

Once upon a time, when herons built their nests in old men's beards, Forgael, a Sea-King of ancient Ireland, was promised by certain human-headed birds love of a supernatural intensity and happiness. These birds were the souls of the dead, and he followed them over seas towards the sunset, where their final rest is. By means of a magic harp, he could call them about him when he would and listen to their speech. His friend Aibric, and the sailors of his ship, thought him mad, or that this mysterious happiness could come after death only, and that he and they were being lured to destruction. Presently they captured a ship, and found a beautiful woman upon it, and Forgael subdued her and his own rebellious sailors by the sound of his harp. The sailors fled upon the other ship, and Forgael and the woman drifted on alone following the birds, awaiting death and what comes after, or some mysterious transformations of the flesh, an embodiment of every lover's dream.

The scenery and the lighting have been arranged by Mr. Robert Gregory.[66]

THE SHADOWY WATERS,

By W. B. YEATS.

ACTING VERSION,
As first played at the Abbey Theatre, December 8th, 1906.

A. H. BULLEN,
47 GREAT RUSSELL STREET, LONDON, W.C
1907.

23. *The Shadowy Waters* (Acting Version), 1907.
Title page (reduced). Original 7 × 5″.

The acting version was published separately in 1907 and, in this, the stage direction shows how closely Yeats had worked with the designer in realising the play.

The deck of an ancient ship. At the right of the stage is the mast, with a large square sail hiding a deal of the sky and sea on that side. The tiller is at the left of the stage; it is a long oar coming through an opening in the bulwark. The deck rises into a high poop behind the tiller, and the stern of the ship curves overhead. There is a stringed instrument upon the poop. All the wood-work is of dark green; and the sail is dark green, with a blue pattern upon it, having a little copper colour here and there. The sky and sea are dark blue. All the persons of the play are dressed in various tints of green and blue, the men with helmets and swords of copper, the woman with copper ornaments upon her dress.[67]

*

The staging of *The Shadowy Waters* in 1904 marked the end of the first phase of Yeats's dramatic development and even though his obsession with the play continued, the mainstream of his work in the theatre was channeled into new directions. As T. S. Eliot saw it, in his Yeats memorial address, delivered at the Abbey Theatre in 1940,

His longer narrative poems bear the mark of Morris. Indeed in his pre-Raphaelite phase, Yeats is by no means the least of the pre-Raphaelites. I may be mistaken, and I may seem impertinent, but the play, *The Shadowy Waters*, seems to me one of the most perfect expressions of the vague enchanted beauty of that school : yet it strikes me — and this is what may be an imper-tinence on my part — as the western seas descried through the back window of a house in Kensington; an Irish myth for the Kelmscott Press; and when I try to visualise the speakers in the play they have the great dim, dreary eyes of the Knights and ladies of Burne-Jones. I think that the phase in which he treated Irish legend in the manner of Rossetti or Morris is a phase of confusion. He did not master this legend until he made it a vehicle for his own creation of character — not really, until he began to write the Plays for Dancers. The point is, that in becoming more Irish, not in subject-matter but in expression, he became at the same time universal.[68]

The difficulty of playing in hired halls for the occasional seasons of a few performances, and the inadequacy of the Camden Street hall as a base for the Irish National Theatre Company was evident from the beginning of the collaboration of the Fay brothers with Yeats, and the provision of a suitable permanent home where both rehearsals and performances could take place became a constant topic of discussion at the company's meetings and rehearsals. Joseph Holloway, who had become a constant presence at rehearsals as well as the company's most diligent 'first-nighter,' was asked for his architectural advice and he recorded such a discussion in his journal for 21 August 1903, following a rehearsal of *The King's Threshold*:

I had a long chat with W. G. Fay re a "tin house" for a home for Irish drama and the probable cost of same. I told him I did not think such a structure as he described could be procured under £250 or thereabouts, and he suggested that some old Methodists' Hall might be picked up cheap on the other side and re-erected here. He also told me he intended making an offer of £50 per annum for three nights a week for the Molesworth Hall with the intention of giving three performances a month — these during the season. He had been speaking to the authorities re the Hall per night, and they told him they would let him have the use of it per night for £1.2.6, if he would guarantee not to play elsewhere during the season. £1.10.0 is the usual charged price per night for the hall. The Camden Street Hall was found impossible for public displays. It is right enough for rehearsing in. £20 a year is the rent they pay for it. It is strange that in a city like Dublin there is no public hall suitable for amateur theatricals.[1]

Yeats approached the problem of a playhouse from a different angle. His dialogue continued with the 'wealthy friend'[2] who had advised him in April 1902 to wait until he could persuade people that he was something of a dramatist and until Mr. Fay had got a little practice for his company; and the 'wealthy friend,' Miss Horniman, had designed and herself sewn the costumes for *The King's Threshold*, which opened on 8 October 1903. Their cryptic correspondence, in the language of the Golden Dawn, culminated in a letter written on 9 October, the day after the first production of *The King's Threshold*, in which she posed the question, 'What is the right thing for me to do in regard to the I.N.Th. now?'

This letter, in which the guidelines to the answer are given in a diagram based on a layout of Tarot cards, and in which she concluded that it might be propitious to support Yeats's plan for a National Theatre for Ireland, is one of the most significant documents in the history of that theatre.

What is the right thing for me to do in regard to the I.N.Th. now? Oct. 9th,/03? Some change is directed by the Highest Irresolution as to the course of action Anger in the mind.
Most solid materiality needed.

19 cards bad.
5 Trumps — within my own Will.

$$\left.\begin{array}{l} 5W \\ 2C \\ 3S \\ 4P \end{array}\right\} \text{Energy must prevail}$$

Three 3s — deceit — I think something now which is not fact.

I am in a happy friendly successful current, which will carry me on if I decide with a certain amount of self-assertion. That will restore peace & be well for a youngish man. All will change for the better & quarrels will pass away. Some gift will cause quarrels & anger but it will bring good fortune & gain whilst away from home — self-assertion is absolutely necessary.

---

24. Miss Horniman's letter offering to subsidise the Irish National Theatre.

Kathleen Raine has given me an interpretation of Miss Horniman's letter on the Tarot cards which is made in accordance with *The secret workings of the Golden Dawn Book 'T' : the Tarot* by S.R.M.D. *and others*. S.R.M.D. is MacGregor Mathers, and members of the Society would have followed his method and interpretation of the Keys. Although in manuscripts detailed descriptions of the symbols depicted on the cards are given, no pack corresponding to Mathers' descriptions was ever printed. The Waite pack was not available until 1907; and as Miss Horniman's consultation was made in 1903 it is likely that she used the Marseilles pack. Yeats himself used this pack, his copy being much worn and much annotated.

Miss Raine concludes that the outcome seems better for Yeats and for the Abbey Theatre — all Yeats's aspects are favourable — than for Miss Horniman herself. Miss Raine's full interpretation of the reading will be found as Appendix A.

As the omens seemed favourable, Miss Horniman decided to subsidise the theatre. Holloway recorded a discussion with Willie Fay on
7 January 1904 'about getting a playhouse for the Company that
would be their very own,' in which Fay 'hinted that £5,000 would
be forthcoming if necessary.'[4] Yeats returned from his American
lecture tour in the middle of March and on Thursday 24 March the
company travelled to London where they played a programme that
included *The King's Threshold* at the Royalty Theatre for a matinee
and an evening performance on Saturday. Miss Horniman seems to
have finally decided on the extent of her support during this London
visit and Willie Fay could inform the company on 6 April that Miss
Horniman was coming to Dublin later that week 'to sign the contract
to take over the Hibernian Theatre of Varieties, Abbey Street, and
turn it into a first class little theatre for them at her own expense.'[5]

Joseph Holloway was appointed architect for the conversion and
recorded his meetings with Miss Horniman and Yeats in his journal.

Sunday, April 10. Met Miss Horniman by appointment at her hotel (The
Standard, Harcourt Street) and had a chat about turning the Mechanics'
Institute and the Dublin City Morgue into a theatre chiefly for the Irish
National Theatre Society.

Monday, April 11. Met Miss Horniman and went through the Morgue with
her, but the irate manager in possession of the Mechanics' Institute Theatre
indignantly refused us permission to enter. Made appointment to return at
3:30 o'clock in the hopes of gaining an entrance, which we did. Mr. W. B.
Yeats came with Miss Horniman, and I was introduced to the poet who said
he had often heard of me. As we went over the building and had just reached
the stage, the manager came in by the door at the back of the stage, and
measuring us with a withering look, exclaimed, "You've got a cheek !" And
he ordered us out without further ado, which we accomplished without delay
amid a volley of "Land grabbers !" etc., at them, and a wink of the eye, by
way of a stage aside, to me. His parting shot — "May you and your morgue
have luck !" — was distinctly droll. I am just thinking how I can face him to
survey the place to-morrow or the next day. Miss Horniman and Mr. Yeats
then parted with me to go into the Hibernian Academy.

Friday, April 15. Called up with rough sketch plan of the Abbey Street Theatre
[The Mechanics] to Camden Street "Theatre" to have a chat over it with
Mr. W. G. Fay. Found W. B. Yeats, Stephen Gwynn, and George Russell
present. The former conducted a rehearsal of *The King's Threshold*. The new
"King" was Mr. Starkey (Seumas O'Sullivan). The great Yeats, by his inter-
ruptions every minute, proved himself an impossible man to rehearse before,
and if I were Starkey I would have been inclined to tell him to go to the "old
boy" more than once.[6]

The formal exchange of letters between Miss Horniman and the
company, which formed the agreement between them followed, and

these two letters were printed in that year's issue of *Samhain*, which was published to coincide with the opening of the theatre.

MISS HORNIMAN'S OFFER OF THEATRE
AND THE SOCIETY'S ACCEPTANCE

H 1 Montagu Mansions
London, W
April [1904]

Dear Mr. Yeats,

I have a great sympathy with the artistic and dramatic aims of the Irish National Theatre Company, as publicly explained by you on various occasions. I am glad to be able to offer you my assistance in your endeavours to establish a permanent Theatre in Dublin.

I am taking the Hall of the Mechanics' Institute in Abbey Street, and an adjoining building in Marlborough Street, which I propose to turn into a small Theatre, with a proper Entrance Hall, Green-room, and Dressing-rooms. As the Company will not require the Hall constantly, I propose to arrange to let it for lectures and entertainments at a rental proportionate to its seating capacity.

The Company can have the building rent free whenever they want it, for rehearsals and performances, except when it is let. The Green-room I hope to arrange to be kept for their sole use. They must pay for their own electric light and gas, as well as for the repair of damages done during their occupation. The building will be insured, and any additions to the lighting for special occasions or plays must be permitted by the Insurance Company, formally in writing.

If any President, Vice-President, or member of the Company wants the Hall for a lecture, concert, or entertainment, the rent must be paid to me as by an ordinary person. If a lecture be given on a dramatic or theatrical subject, and the gross receipts go to the Irish National Theatre, then the President, Vice-President, or member of the Company can have the Hall for nothing. But it must be advertised clearly as being for the sole benefit of the Irish National Theatre, pecuniarly, as well as in aid of its artistic objects.

The prices of the seats can be raised, of course, but not lowered, neither by the Irish National Theatre, nor by anyone who will hire the Hall.

This is to prevent cheap entertainments from being given, which would lower the letting value of the Hall. I hope to be able to arrange to number most of the seats and to sell the tickets beforehand, with a small fee for booking. The entrance to the more expensive seats will be from Marlborough Street, where there will be a Cloak Room.

The situation, being near to the Tramway Terminus, is convenient for people living in any part of Dublin. I shall take every possible means to insure the safety and convenience of the public. I can only afford to make a very little Theatre, and it must be quite simple. You all must do the rest to make a powerful and prosperous Theatre, with a high artistic ideal.

A copy of this letter will be sent to each Vice-President and another to the Stage Manager for the Company.

Yours sincerely,
A. E. F. Horniman

34 Lower Camden Street
Dublin
11 May 1904

Dear Miss Horniman,

We, the undersigned members of the Irish National Theatre Company, beg to thank you for the interest you have evinced in the work of the Society and for the aid you propose giving to our future work by securing a permanent Theatre in Abbey Street.

We undertake to abide by all the conditions laid down in your letter to the company, and to do our utmost to forward the objects of the Society.

W. B. Yeats.	Thomas G. Koehler.
F. J. Fay.	Harry F. Norman.
William G. Fay.	Helen S. Laird.
James G. Starkey.	George Russell.
Proinsias Mac Siúbhlaigh	Máire Nic Siúbhlaigh
(Frank Walker).	(Miss Walker).
Udolphus Wright.	J. M. Synge.
Márget Ní Ghárbhaigh	Sara Allgood.
(Miss Garvey).	Frederick Ryan.
Vera Esposito.	Pádraig MacCuilim
Dora L. Ainnesley.	(Patrick Colm).
George Roberts.	Stephen Gwynn.
An Craoibhín Aoibhín	Augusta Gregory.[7]
(Douglas Hyde).	

While Holloway prepared his plans for the conversion, Yeats and Miss Horniman set about getting a patent for the theatre which would licence it for public performances. Yeats recounted the proceedings of the statutory hearing to Lady Gregory in a letter dated 4 August, in which he described Miss Horniman and Willie Fay as impressive witnesses, and also recorded some of the legal objections raised at the hearing, including one barrister's attempt to prove that Maeterlinck and Ibsen were immoral writers. The fact that part of the Abbey Street premises had previously been used as a morgue occasioned some humour, both in Yeats's letters and in Holloway's chronicle, from which the following extracts describe the granting of the licence and the work of converting the building.

Saturday, August 20. Mr. Campbell, K.C. (Solicitor-General) gave judgment on the application for patents by Miss A. E. F. Horniman on behalf of the Irish National Theatre Society in respect to the hall attached to the Mechanics' Institute. . . . The following are the terms of the patent for the Irish National Theatre Society.

> The patent shall only empower the patentee to exhibit plays in the Irish and English languages, written by Irish writers on Irish subjects, or such dramatic works of foreign authors as would tend to interest the public in the higher works of dramatic art; all foregoing to be selected by the Irish National Theatre Society under the provisions of Part 6 of its rules

now existing and subject to the restrictions therein contained, a clause to be inserted against the assignment of any person or persons other than the trustee for Miss Horniman, her executors or assigns, the patent to cease if the Irish National Theatre Society is dissolved. No enlargement of the theatre is to be made, so as to provide for a greater number of spectators than it is capable of holding at present. No excise licence to be applied for or obtained.

*   *   *

Monday, October 31. Truly it was a strange coincidence that the merry little music-hall comedian Dan Leno should have shuffled off the mortal coil quite suddenly at his residence, Springfield, Clapham Park, from heart failure the same day that the Irish National Theatre Society held their first rehearsal on the stage of their new theatre in Abbey Street, where in the long ago Leno made his first separate appearance, when the hall was known as the Mechanics, and won his way into the favour of the Dublin public as an expert clog dancer.

*   *   *

Wednesday, November 16. . . . A few minutes after eight o'clock found me a-tapping at the stage door in old Abbey Street for admittance, and on it being opened I stepped to the right and descending a few steps found myself on the stage. A fireproof curtain was up, and the auditorium looked dim and mysterious with its few temporary electric lights here and there, as electricians fixed the electroliers round the balcony. A temporary sky border of electric lights lit the stage, and the yet unutilised grille looked strange and weird with hangman-like ropes suspended ominously therefrom. The drum lofts looked busy with carpenters' work scattered about, and a beautiful, unfinished landscape hung suspended at the back of the stage, where the artist, Mr. Bryer, had left it on knocking off work.

*   *   *

Thursday, November 24. An amusing incident — an echo of the past one might term it — occurred at the Abbey Theatre this afternoon during one of my professional visits. Hearing a ring at the stage door, I opened it as I was going out and found a man, accompanied by a little boy, there, who made this inquiry : "Is there an inquest going on here to-day?"

The inquiry took me aback at first, and then I explained to him that it was a theatre, not a dead house he was at, and he departed apologising. From this it would seem that its old fame clings to the transformed morgue still.[8]

The Dublin newspapers welcomed the new theatre and, in an editorial *The Irish Times* remarked that it would be 'the nearest approach that we have in these countries to an endowed theatre.'[9] Delays and difficulties caused the opening of the theatre to be postponed from the first week of December — the stage would not be finished in time to allow sufficient dress rehearsals, Miss Purser's stained glass windows for the vestibule were not ready — and, as the company were reluctant to open during Advent, the opening date was set for a few days after Christmas, on 27 December. The work was, however, sufficiently advanced to allow the Press to view the building at the end of November and the following description of the Abbey Theatre appeared in *The Freeman's Journal*.

25. The Abbey Theatre, Dublin. Reconstruction of the original façade.

As if by a wave of the harlequin's wand, an old and unsightly structure in Lower Abbey street and another in Marlborough street have all but disappeared, the stone front of the latter only having been utilized; and the two have been transformed into a stylish new theatre, capable of seating 562 persons. . . . The entrances are from Marlborough street, the central one being sheltered by a verandah. The visitor on going in finds himself in a large carpeted porch, the walls of which are hung with portraits, painted by Mr. W. B. Yeats [sic], of Mr. William Fay, the stage manager of the theatre; Mr. Frank Fay, Miss Maire Nic Shiubhlaigh, and Miss Horniman, proprietress of the theatre. In the green-room at one side are portraits of Dr. Douglas Hyde and Mr. George W. Russell, Vice-Presidents of the Irish National Theatre Society, also by Mr. Yeats, and a portrait of Mr. Yeats himself, painted by Madame Troncy, of Paris. Descending a carpeted stairway, one arrives at the stalls which seat 178 persons. Behind these are 186 pit seats. Both stalls and pit are ranged on an upward slope so that every occupant of a seat will be enabled to obtain a perfect view of the stage, and there will be no such thing as a bad seat. A large balcony extends round the interior above the lower seats, and this is fitted to accommodate 198 persons, the same care having been taken to construct the seating so that those occupying back seats can see the stage. Polished brass work separates each seat in every part of the house from those adjoining it on each side, and all the upholstering is in scarlet leather. There is no gallery over the balcony. All the passages within the interior, and also leading into it, are richly carpeted. Electric lighting prevails everywhere. A large light is in the centre of the ceiling of the interior, and round about the theatre are fourteen triple lamps. The walls are painted in colours, which harmonise well with the rest of the details, and on the walls are large medallions exhibiting the city arms, the Irish harp, and other devices appropriate to the national character of the entertainments to which the theatre is to be devoted. Room for a band, when that is required for any performance, will be augmented in front of the stage by the removal of the front row of stalls. All the requirements of the Corporation with respect to lighting, heating, ventilation and the safe ingress and egress of the audience have been strictly complied with; and there is, of course, a safety curtain, such as exists in all our other Dublin Theatres. All the materials used in the building and fitting up of the theatre are Irish, with a trifling exception. There is no bar; but at a buffet tea and coffee will be supplied.[10]

In *Samhain 1904*, Yeats wrote about the new theatre, 'the first endowed theatre in any English speaking country,' and restated the policy, particularly in relation to Gaelic-speaking and nationalist theatre. He saw that the policy of the theatre could not be fully implemented at the beginning and that,

Before this part of our work can be begun, it will be necessary to create a household of living art in Dublin, with principles that have become habits, and a public that has learnt to care for a play because it is a play and not because it is serviceable to some cause.[11]

And he reaffirmed his own approach to the theatre in a paragraph which, if read with an awareness of his later development, has prophetic overtones.

I would not be trying to form an Irish National Theatre, if I did not believe that there existed in Ireland, whether in the minds of a few people or of a great number I do not know, an energy of thought about life itself, a vivid sensitiveness as to the reality of things, powerful enough to overcome all those phantoms of the night. One thing calls up its contrary, unreality calls up reality, and besides, life here has been sufficiently perilous to make men think. I do not think it a national prejudice that makes me believe we are a harder, a more masterful race than the comfortable English of our time, and that this comes from an essential nearness to reality of those few scattered people who have the right to call themselves the Irish race. It is only in the exceptions, in the few minds, where the flame has burnt as it were pure, that one can see the permanent character of a race. If one remembers the men who have dominated Ireland for the last hundred and fifty years, one understands that it is strength of personality, the individualizing quality in a man, that stirs Irish imagination most deeply in the end. There is scarcely a man who has led the Irish people, at any time, who may not give some day to a great writer precisely that symbol he may require for the expression of himself.[12]

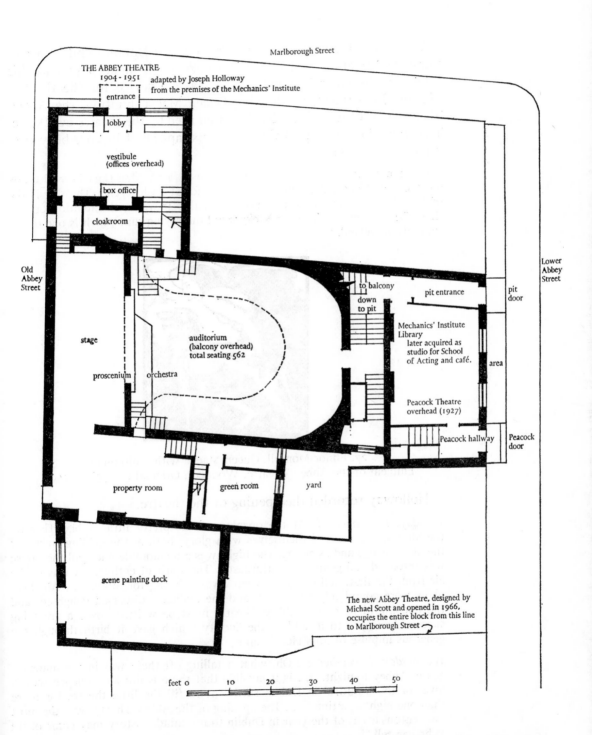

THE ABBEY THEATRE
1904 - 1951   adapted by Joseph Holloway
from the premises of the Mechanics' Institute

Marlborough Street

entrance

lobby

vestibule
(offices overhead)

box office

cloakroom

Old
Abbey
Street

stage

proscenium   orchestra

auditorium
(balcony overhead)
total seating 562

to balcony

down
to pit

pit entrance

pit
door

Lower
Abbey
Street

Mechanics' Institute
Library
    later acquired as
    studio for School
    of Acting and café.

area

Peacock Theatre
overhead (1927)

Peacock hallway

Peacock
door

property room   green room   yard

scene painting dock

The new Abbey Theatre, designed by
Michael Scott and opened in 1966,
occupies the entire block from this line
to Marlborough Street

feet 0   10   20   30   40   50

26. The Abbey Theatre, Dublin, 1904-1951. Ground plan of the conversion
and later additions.

Yeats saw the work of Elinor Monsell at a Dublin exhibition and found her treatment of epic themes so much in keeping with his ideas that he commissioned her to make a device for the theatre. The resulting woodcut, showing Queen Maeve hunting, the Abbey Theatre's 'Wolfhound' device, has been used by the theatre ever since. The following note, probably by Yeats, appeared in an Abbey programme in 1908:

It is the work of an Irish artist, Miss Monsell, now Mrs. Darwin, and represents Queen Maeve, the heroic queen of ancient Irish legend. The dog is the Irish wolf hound, and it is not known, whether it was with intention or not, that Miss Monsell put into the background the raying sun, which is one of the symbols of Ireland.[13]

27. Elinor Monsell. Queen Maeve with wolfhound.
Emblem of the Abbey Theatre. Woodcut. Original 6 × 5½". 1904.

Holloway recorded the opening of the theatre.

Tuesday, December 27. At the opening of the pretty little Abbey Theatre, the Messrs. Fay covered themselves with glory, both as the guiding spirits of the new theatre and as actors. The night was a memorable one, and the house was thronged and genuinely enthusiastic. The spirit of enthusiasm was in the air from the first, and everyone went away wishing for more. . . . All three plays were completely successful, and the audience dispersed delighted; and the opening night of the Abbey Theatre must be written down a great big success. Long life to it, and to the Society which gave it birth through the generous impulse of Miss Horniman !

Wednesday, December 28. Oh, what a falling off there was in the audience at the Abbey to-night. . . . Is it possible that there is not an audience with a love for the beautiful in Dublin sufficient to fill the little theatre for more than one night at a time? . . . The opening of the Abbey Theatre was the most momentous event of the year in Dublin to my mind. History may come of it ! Who can tell !!!![14]

*

Yeats's Preface to *Cuchulain of Muirthemne* by Lady Gregory is dated
March 1902, a month before the book was published. Lady Gregory's
re-telling of the old Irish epic, the *Táin Bó Cuailnge* and its subsidiary
tales, among these the story of Deirdre and the Sons of Uisnach,
provided Yeats with the material from which he derived six plays,
five dealing with the central hero figure in the epic, Cuchulain, of
which three were 'Plays for Dancers,' and *Deirdre*. Lady Gregory's
book was compiled from different versions of the tales, derived from
a variety of manuscript and printed sources, but, although its English
had a Kiltartan lilt, it did put together for the first time in a readable
and easily understood form the whole span of the epic. In the opening
paragraph of his Preface, Yeats stated

I think this book is the best that has come out of Ireland in my time. Perhaps
I should say that it is the best book that has ever come out of Ireland; for the
stories which it tells are a chief part of Ireland's gift to the imagination of
the world — and it tells them perfectly for the first time.

And his concluding paragraph echoed his hopes for the part an Irish
theatre would play in the Irish Renaissance.

If we will but tell these stories to our children the Land will begin again to
be a Holy Land, as it was before men gave their hearts to Greece and Rome
and Judea.[15]

The first fruit of Yeats's involvement with *Cuchulain of Muirthemne* was his play, *On Baile's Strand*, which was a dramatic development of the theme of his early epic poem, 'The Death of
Cuchullin' printed in *The Countess Kathleen and Various Legends
and Lyrics*, 1892, in which volume Nettleship's frontispiece depicted
Cuchullin fighting the waves. This play was the first of five he was to
base on the epic hero. His letters to Lady Gregory indicate that he
had begun to write the play in January 1902, with a view to its
production by the Fay brothers. By April he had gone over the play
with George Moore and found it

still in want of a little simplification which I am trying to get into it. I think
I shall get it simple enough for Fay in the end.[16]

The play reveals the concerns which occupied Yeats at the time
of its construction. His visit to Stratford on Avon in 1901 may have
suggested the Shakespearian verse-form of the play, and his return
visit to Stratford in March 1902 would seem to bear this out. At the
same time, he was very much concerned with the techniques of stage
presentation he had learned from Gordon Craig's 'new and distinct
art.' [17] By June he had conceived the idea that the Cuchulain cycle

might have a shared authorship and had asked Wilfrid Scawen Blunt
to contribute a play. Yeats reported to Lady Gregory,

Blunt is quite bent on the Cuchullin play and proposes to take "the only
jealousy of Emer" for his subject, which would fit into our plan very well.
I shall have to find out in Dublin however whether the young men will let an
Englishman write for them. I did not tell Blunt that I had any doubts on the
matter but told him that I would write precise dates etc. in a couple of
weeks.[18]

By December he was amending 'Cuchulain' for his sister Elizabeth,
who proposed to print the play as part of the first book from the Dun
Emer Press, which she had established in Dublin. By 3 January 1903
he could write to Lady Gregory that he hoped in a couple of days
'to have got *Cuchullain* finally right,'[19] and proposed to put it and
The Hour-Glass into the book after a sub-title, 'Plays for an Irish
Theatre.' On 15 January he wrote to Lady Gregory that *Cuchullain*
needed new passages here and there and that his work had got far
more masculine and had more salt in it.[20] During 1903 Yeats was
deeply involved in the Fay brothers' productions of *The Hour-Glass*
and *The King's Threshold* and with seeing through the press *In the
Seven Woods*, printed and published by his sister, and it appears that
he suspended work on the play beyond correcting it as printed by
his sister. However, during his American lecture-tour at the end of
the year, he did a great deal of revision on the play and wrote at
length, enclosing some revisions, to Frank Fay,

About Cuchullain. You have Lady Gregory's work I know. Remember however that epic and folk literature can ignore time as drama cannot — Helen
never ages, Cuchullain never ages. I have to recognise that he does, for he has
a son who is old enough to fight him. I have also to make the refusal of the
son's affection tragic by suggesting in Cuchullain's character a shadow of
something a little proud, barren and restless, as if out of sheer strength of
heart or from accident he had put affection away. He lives among young men
but has himself outlived the illusions of youth. He is probably about 40, not
less than 35 or 36 and not more than 45 or 46, certainly not an old man, and
one understands from his talk about women that he does not love like a
young man. Probably his very strength of character made him put off
illusions and dreams (that make young men a woman's servant) and made him
become quite early in life a deliberate lover, a man of pleasure who can never
really surrender himself. He is a little hard, and leaves the people about him
a little repelled — perhaps this young man's affection is what he had most
need of. Without this thought the play had not had any deep tragedy. I write
of him with difficulty, for when one creates a character one does it out of
instinct and may be wrong when one analyses the instinct afterwards. It is
as though the character embodied itself. The less one reasons the more living
the character. I felt for instance that his boasting was necessary, and yet I did
not reason it out. The touch of something hard, repellent yet alluring, self

assertive yet self immolating, is not all but it must be there. He is the fool —
wandering passive, houseless and almost loveless. Concobhar is reason that is
blind because it can only reason because it is cold. Are they not the cold
moon and the hot sun?[21]

The Fays were conducting preliminary rehearsals of *On Baile's
Strand* during Yeats's absence and, besides his preoccupation with
the text, Yeats also expressed himself concerned about the scenery
and costumes to be used. Miss Horniman was to design the costumes
and Yeats hoped that she would not repeat the over-colourful result
she had achieved for *The King's Threshold*. He advised Lady Gregory
that he had 'written to Miss Horniman suggesting as delicately as I
could that there ought not be gorgeousness of costume.'[22]

His delayed departure from America caused him to write on
31 January to Lady Gregory, asking her not to let *On Baile's Strand*
be played until his return, which did not occur until March, when
he was immediately involved in planning the acquisition, licensing
and opening of the Abbey Theatre, so that *On Baile's Strand* was first
performed on the opening night of the theatre.

Yeats revised his essay 'The Reform of the Theatre' which had
been printed in *Samhain 1903* and printed the revised and extended
version in *Samhain 1904* as 'The Play, the Player and the Scene.'
'The hour of convention and decoration and ceremony is coming
again,' he concluded, having set out the guiding principles by
which he felt the theatre should approach the problems of stage
presentation. The generalisations of the earlier version have become
definitions and the experiences of a further year's dedication are
embodied in the statement.

Having chosen the distance from naturalism, which will keep one's composition from competing with the illusion created by the actor, who belongs
to a world with depth as well as height and breadth, one must keep this
distance without flinching. The distance will vary according to the distance
the playwright has chosen, and especially in poetry, which is more remote
and idealistic than prose, one will insist on schemes of colour and simplicity
of form, for every sign of deliberate order gives remoteness and ideality. But,
whatever the distance be, one's treatment will always be more or less decorative. We can only find out the right decoration for the different types of play
by experiment, but it will probably range between, on the one hand, wood-
lands made out of recurring pattern, or painted like old religious pictures
upon gold background, and upon the other the comparative realism of a
Japanese print. This decoration will not only give us a scenic art that will be
a true art because peculiar to the stage, but it will give the imagination liberty,
and without returning to the bareness of the Elizabethan stage. The poet
cannot evoke a picture to the mind's eye if a second-rate painter has set his
imagination of it before the bodily eye; but decoration and suggestion will
accompany our moods, and turn our minds to meditation, and yet never

become obtrusive or wearisome. The actor and the words put into his mouth are always the one thing that matters, and the scene should never be complete of itself, should never mean anything to the imagination until the actor is in front of it.[23]

Yeats's widening experience allowed him to invoke the teachings of Adolphe Appia, as well as those of Craig. This was an independent discovery as Craig, in the Preface to the 1911 edition of *On the Art of the Theatre*, says that he did not see examples of Appia's work until 1908. Adolphe François Appia (1862-1928) was born in Geneva and studied musical composition. He became disillusioned with the standards of stage presentation aimed at 'realism' and, after 1888, devoted his life to the reform of theatrical production. During the 1890's he published several theoretical works and made his first designs for Wagner's operas which, in their use of multiple level platforms and massed simple shapes, foreshadowed Craig's later achievements in this field. In 1904 Yeats wrote,

I cannot understand what M. Appia is doing, from the little I have seen of his writing, excepting that the floor of the stage will be uneven like the ground, and that at moments the lights and shadows of green boughs will fall over the player that the stage may show a man wandering through a wood, and not a wood with a man in the middle of it.[24]

In November Yeats was in London, pursuing stage designers for the Abbey. He wrote to Lady Gregory on 7 November that Jack, his brother, was to do scenery for Synge's play, presumably *The Well of the Saints*, which was produced on 4 February 1905. Yeats went to see Charles Ricketts and Ricketts offered to do scenery for a play, and also to advise Robert Gregory who was designing the set for *On Baile's Strand*. Ricketts was to design costumes for several Abbey productions, among them a revival of *The Well of the Saints* by J. M. Synge in 1908. Towards the end of the month, Yeats was back in Dublin where his own play was in final rehearsal and he still found time to deal with management problems in the theatre and the question of scenery for the company. This is shown in his letter of 24 November, addressed from the Abbey Theatre to Lady Gregory.

On Baile's Strand is the best play I have written. It goes magnificently, and the end is particularly impressive. When I got here I found that Frank Fay seemed to have a curious incapacity to understand the part. He could do nothing with it and was in despair. It now promises to be his finest part. I think I shall be able to arrange the scenery for *Spreading the News* all right. I am waiting on Jack's designs for Synge's play, as it may be possible to use some bits of scenery which will afterwards come in useful for Synge. They should come to-day or to-morrow. Failing this I shall get Pixie Smith, who alone seems to understand what I want, to make a design. I am extremely anxious now that I am here, and for the moment at any rate master of the situation, to get designs of a decorative kind, which will set a standard and come in serviceable for different sorts of plays.

Don't be in any anxiety about the wings for your play. I shall get everything made under my own eyes, but the moment I am gone the old business will begin again. Robert's wing will be very good for a remote play like *The Shadowy Waters* but it is too far from realism to go with comedy or with any ordinary play. I am very glad to have it. I have found out that the exact thing I want is the sort of tree one finds in Japanese prints. If Robert could find time to look up some prints and to make me a wing of this sort in the next three or four days I would be very glad. I may probably use it in your play, certainly, in fact, if suitable, if not it will come in for something else. We are in great need of different types of design. The wings are 16 ft. high and 6 ft. wide at their greatest width. They must never be very narrow. *Spreading the News* is going magnificently.[25]

The staging of *On Baile's Strand*, described by Holloway as a boxed-in set of amber-coloured drapes, cannot have met the requirements of the stage direction with which Yeats prefaced his text,

SCENE : A great hall by the sea close to Dundalgan. There are two great chairs on either side of the hall, each raised a little from the ground, and on the back of the one chair is carved and painted a woman with a fish's tail, and on the back of the other a hound. There are smaller chairs and benches raised in tiers round the walls. There is a great ale vat at one side near a small door, & a large door at the back through which one can see the sea. Barach, a tall thin man with long ragged hair, dressed in skins, comes in at the side door. He is leading Fintain, a fat blind man, who is somewhat older,

nor can Miss Horniman's costumes have satisfied him either. Holloway recorded a scene at a dress rehearsal on 16 December.

On entering the stage door of the Abbey Theatre, I stepped down onto the stage and found it set for *On Baile's Strand* and with no one about — only the stage hands. The effect produced by the simple and novel setting, I thought, was very good and just the thing for rich costumed figures to disport themselves before.

Having viewed the scene from the front, I went up to the gentlemen's dressing room where I found all the actors in the confusion of dressing for their parts for the first time. The chaos of the whole thing was delightful to behold. I secured a corner out of the way and watched the transformation of the company into kings, warriors and beggars. One propped up a mirror against a barber's block as he built a whisker round his youthful face, transforming it into an aged countenance of a king; another wrestled with a tunic turning the wrong side forward; while others amid a din of "Where's my wig?" or "Where's my cloak?" or "Did anyone see my helmet?" kept going hither and thither in the large dressing room until things began to straighten themselves out and the actors presented a truly strange sight in their gorgeous, if strange, fantastical robes. Frequent tappings and inquiries at the door during the enactment of this scene told that the ladies in a neighbouring dressing room suffered the same confusion. Such questions as, "Did you see the Young

Kings' cloaks?" etc., were frequently heard, on the door being partly opened in answer to the gentle tapping of Mrs. Esposito, who kindly acted as wardrobe mistress to the company and played the part excellently.

The rehearsal proceeded smoothly, but many of the costumes, especially those of the old kings and the long, streaky hair worn by them, were found to border on the grotesque or eccentric, and at the conclusion of the play the entire company was recalled on the stage, and an exciting and amusing exchange of difference of opinion took place between author Yeats and designer Miss Horniman. He with his eye on the effect created as an author, and she as the designer of the colour scheme of the costumes. Yeats likened some of the kings to "extinguishers," their robes were so long and sloped so from the shoulders. Father Christmas was another of his comparisons. He wished the cloaks away, but the lady would have none of his suggestions. Then commenced a lively scene in which the actors played the part of lay figures, and Yeats and Miss Horniman treated them as such in discussing the costumes. The red-robed kings were told to take off their cloaks, which they did, and then the green-clad ones followed. After much putting on and taking off, and an abundance of plain speaking as to the figures or lack of them among the players, a compromise was arrived at, and the "grey fur" on the green costumes was "made fly," and the red-clad kings were allowed to carry their cloaks on their arms, though Miss Horniman was of opinion that the red unrelieved, somewhat marred the colour scheme she had intended. . . . Candidly I thought some of the costumes trying, though all of them were exceedingly rich in material and archaeologically correct. "Hang achaeology!" said the great W. B. Yeats. "It's effect we want on the stage!" And that settled it![26]

Music for the play was also a continuing concern with Yeats. Florence Farr set the two lyrics, the Fool's song in the first scene and the song for the three women, using the mode which she had used in her earlier settings for the psaltery. For the performance, however, Yeats had Herbert Hughes set the Fool's song, probably because Florence Farr's setting was outside Willie Fay's range. His note on the songs, printed with the revised text of the play in *Poems 1899-1905* (1906) indicates his concern.

These songs, like all other songs in our plays, are sung so as to preserve as far as possible the intonation and speed of ordinary passionate speech, for nothing can justify the degradation of an element of life even in the service of an art. Very little of the song of the three women can be heard, for they must be for the most part a mere murmur under the voices of the men. It seemed right to take some trouble over them, just as it is right to finish off the statue where it is turned to the wall, and besides there is always the reader and one's own pleasure.[27]

Florence Farr's setting of the Fool's Song in *On Baile's Strand*, as printed in *Plays in Prose and Verse, 1922*, reveals the demand made on the actor's vocal range and illustrates one of the frustrations that Yeats suffered in his work in the theatre.

THE FOOL'S SONG

FLORENCE FARR

Cuchulain has killed kings, Kings and sons of kings,

Dragons out of the water, and witches out of the air,

Banachas and Bonachas and people of the woods.

pp   *p*

Witches that steal the milk, Fomor that steal the children,

f

Hags that have heads like hares, Hares that have claws like witches,

All riding a cock-horse, Out of the very bottom of the bitter black north.

28. Florence Farr's setting of the Fool's Song in *On Baile's Strand*, 1904.[28]

On Baile's Strand derives closely from the tale, 'The Only Son of Aoife' as retold by Lady Gregory in *Cuchulain of Muirthemne*. In this, Cuchulain, vowing allegiance to Conchubar, King of Ulster, is confronted by a youth, and although attracted by the young warrior, is forced to challenge and fight him. He kills the youth and then discovers that the dead youth is his own son, by Aoife, the warrior queen of another province. In his remorse he is afflicted by an heroic madness and wades into the sea, striking at the waves with his sword, until he falls, apparently dead. Yeats added a subsidiary plot to the main action, involving the Fool and the Blind Man, his archetypal characters, who 'direct' the action and are the agents who reveal the awful truth to Cuchulain that he has killed his own son. The Fool is the Fool of *The Hour-Glass*, 'the Fat Fool of folklore who is "as wide and wild as a hill" and not the Thin Fool of modern Romance,'[29] and the Blind Man recurs in *The Death of Cuchulain* (1939) where he is the final instrument of Cuchulain's doom.

*

The Abbey Theatre opened on Tuesday 27 December 1904 with a bill made up of the first production of *On Baile's Strand*,* the first production of Lady Gregory's comedy, *Spreading the News*, and revivals of *Cathleen Ni Houlihan* and *In the Shadow of the Glen* by J. M. Synge. The programme printed for the occasion was the prototype of the Abbey programmes for over fifty years. A quarto, printed in black and red, its brown paper cover bore Elinor Monsell's emblem of the legendary Queen Maeve and the back cover proclaimed Miss Horniman as lessee of the theatre.

Yeats, in his curtain speech, paid tribute to Miss Horniman for her 'spirit and generosity' to which the Society owed its new home. The event was a success and the opening of the theatre was welcomed in the Press. Yeats's new play, however, was not as warmly received as the revival of his earlier work *Cathleen Ni Houlihan*, in which Maire Nic Shiubhlaigh played the title role. But the acting of the Fay brothers, Frank as Cuchulain and Willie as the Fool, Barach, received high acclaim. Willie earned from Yeats the dedication of the revised version of the play, when it was published in 1906,

TO

WILLIAM FAY

BECAUSE OF THE BEAUTIFUL PHANTASY OF HIS

PLAYING IN THE CHARACTER OF THE FOOL

*

---

*   ON BAILE'S STRAND

Produced by the Irish National Theatre Society
at the Abbey Theatre, Dublin
on Tuesday 27 December 1904

Cuchullain, the King of Muirthemne	F. J. Fay
Concobar, the High King of Ullad	George Roberts
Daire, a King	Arthur Sinclair
Fintain, a blind man	Seumas O'Sullivan
Barach, a fool	W. G. Fay
A Young Man	P. MacSiubhlaigh
Young Kings and Old Kings	Maire Ni Gharbhaigh, Emma Vernon, Sara Allgood, Doreen Gunning, R. Nash, N. Power, U. Wright, E. Keegan

Scenery by Robert Gregory
Costumes by Miss A. E. F. Horniman
Music by Herbert Hughes and Florence Farr

29. Programme cover. The Abbey Theatre, Dublin, 1904.
Reduced from 10 × 7".

Yeats spent much of 1905 on the organisation of the Abbey Theatre
company, its productions and its general policy. It proved difficult
to attract a sufficient regular audience to the theatre despite the
quality of the new works produced during the year — *The Well of
the Saints* by J. M. Synge on 4 February, *Kincora* by Lady Gregory
on 25 March, *The Building Fund* by William Boyle on 25 April,
The Land by Padraic Colum on 9 June and *The White Cockade* by
Lady Gregory on 9 December. In his review of the year in *Samhain
1905*, which he called 'Notes and Opinions,' he claimed that the first
year at the Abbey had been 'tolerably successful.' The company had
more than trebled its audiences of the Molesworth Hall days and,
helped considerably by the fact that the actors were unpaid, it could
'end the year with a little money.'

Perhaps the company's greatest gain was in its acquisition of a measure of professional discipline, and in developments in stage technique. Robert Gregory's staging of *Kincora*

was beautiful, with a high grave dignity and that strangeness which Ben Jonson thought to be a part of all excellent beauty, and the expense of scenery, dresses and all was hardly above £30.[30]

30. Back of a design by Robert Gregory for a stage wing in *Kincora*, annotated for painting. The bottom note seems to be in W. B. Yeats's hand.

Use 3 tones of green rather flat with dark blue-black outlines to the masses of foliage, indicate leaves lighter by patches of touches lighter than the ground. Trunks light with greenish shadows or stains or moss.
Light spots on trunks.
gray Use a little red in the light positions a sort of dirty flesh colour

Moss-green as much as possible

The policy that Yeats had pursued in publishing the texts of plays performed by the Irish National Theatre in *Beltaine* and *Samhain* was extended by the inauguration of the Abbey Theatre Series of Plays, at first published by the theatre and later taken over by the Dublin firm of Maunsel and Company. Fifteen plays were published in the first series between 1905 and 1911, and a further nine plays in the later series between 1911 and 1922. The series commenced with *The Well of the Saints* by J. M. Synge, issued in February 1905 to coincide with the first production of the play, and five further volumes appeared during that year. The first three volumes bore the Abbey Theatre imprint and were *The Well of the Saints*, *Kincora* by Lady Gregory and *The Land* by Padraic Colum. The next three titles were works by Yeats, three plays, *The Hour-Glass, Cathleen Ni Houlihan* and *The Pot of Broth* in volume four, *The King's Threshold* in volume five and *On Baile's Strand* in volume six. The series had a distinctive design which incorporated Elinor Monsell's emblem for the theatre and the books were priced at a shilling each. The Yeats plays were issued by arrangement with A. H. Bullen and consisted of sheets from his editions with special title pages and covers.

In May, Yeats visited Stratford on Avon again to meet Bullen. He arranged for the volume *Poems 1899-1905*, which was published in October 1906 and included three plays in revised versions, *The Shadowy Waters, On Baile's Strand* and *The King's Threshold*. This volume, which preceded the Collected Edition which Yeats was planning with Bullen, is of great importance in that the Notes to the plays reveal the development in his approach to theatre that resulted from his practical involvement with production. He wrote to Arthur Symons on 10 September,

You will hardly recognise not only *The Shadowy Waters* but *Baile's Strand* and a good deal of *The King's Threshold*. They have all been rewritten after rehearsal or actual performance, and *The King's Threshold* has been changed and rehearsed and then changed again and so on, till I have got it as I believe a perfectly articulate stage play. I have learned a great deal about poetry generally in the process, and one thing I am now quite sure of is that all the finest poetry comes logically out of the fundamental action, and that the error of late periods like this is to believe that some things are inherently poetical, and to try and pull them on to the scene at every moment. It is just these seeming inherently poetical things that wear out. My *Shadowy Waters* was full of them, and the fundamental thinking was nothing, and that gave the whole poem an impression of weakness. There was no internal life pressing for expression through the characters.[31]

He had discovered rhythm and movement as the great thing in drama, as he wrote to Frank Fay on 4 November, and he had learned from Symons' essay on Wagner that Wagner insisted that a play must not appeal to the intelligence but, by being 'a piece of self-consistent life directly to the emotions.'[32]

After the production of the revised *Hour-Glass* at the Abbey Theatre on 9 June, Yeats went to London for the rehearsals and production of the poetic version of *The Shadowy Waters* at the Royal Court Theatre on 8 July, with Florence Farr as Dectora. Her playing was the only part of the production that pleased him, but the occasion spurred him to spend much of the summer, when he was Lady Gregory's guest at Coole, in working at a stage version of the play.

The autumn was taken up with theatre management as it was decided to maintain control of the National Theatre Society by incorporating it as a Limited Liability Company with Yeats, Synge and Lady Gregory as Directors. There was some dissatisfaction in the company and some members left to form the Theatre of Ireland, among them Maire Nic Shiubhlaigh and her brother, Frank Walker. Some of the Abbey players, among them Frank Fay and Sara Allgood, were given salaried contracts and Yeats was at last confident of the survival of the National Theatre in Ireland.

The split in the company continued to discourage Yeats and his partners during the early months of 1906, nor did the additions to the theatre's repertoire during the first half of the year fulfil Yeats's hope for the Irish theatre. He spent a lot of his time at Coole, engaged in 'most unwilling industry,' [33] as he expressed it to Florence Farr. However, he did find time to pursue his own writings, revisions for Bullen's edition and a draft text for his heroic play, *Deirdre*. And he wrote in February to Florence Farr,

I have a sketch of a strange little play about the capture of a blind Unicorn. . . . The unicorn in the little play is a type of masterful and beautiful life, but I shall not trouble to make the meaning clear — a clear vivid story of a strange sort is enough. The meaning may be different with everyone.[34]

This probably refers to the first draft of the play which eventually became *The Player Queen*, which was not completed until 1918. But 1906 was, for Yeats, the year of *Deirdre*.

*

Yeats derived *Deirdre* from the same source book as the Cuchulain plays, Lady Gregory's *Cuchulain of Muirthemne*, her rendering of the *Táin Bó Cuailnge*. In the epic the tale, 'Fate of the Sons of Usnach' is one of the preliminary stories which reveal the motives behind the central plot of the *Táin*. The double betrayal of Deirdre — of her destined fate and of her love — attracted many dramatists. A play by Æ on the theme was presented in the 1902 season of the Irish National Theatre and Synge's version of the tragedy, all but finished at his death in 1909, was posthumously produced at the Abbey in January 1910. But, of all these, Yeats concentrates most powerfully on the final passages of the tale in deriving the plot for his play.

I feel that *Deirdre* is the play in which Yeats came near to realising, for the first time, the kind of dramatic structure which he had instinctively sought from the beginning of his playwriting career. The play might be seen as the bridge between the English blank verse model he had followed in the construction of *On Baile's Strand* in 1903 and the discipline he adapted from the classical Nō theatre of Japan in the composition of *The Only Jealousy of Emer* which he completed in 1918. His practical experience of theatre had allowed Yeats the freedom to cast *Deirdre* in a form very different from the 'theatre of naturalism' and one can see that from this experience he could, for the first time, conceive a unique dramatic form for his play.

Deirdre is a 'woman piece' designed for an intellectual sophistication in the actress who would portray the focal role of the foredoomed tragic queen. Yeats framed his central action within a chorus delivered by three musicians and here anticipated his later Nō-inspired work. And within this framework the tragic queen must convince her audience of the dramatic veracity of her fate — a fate predestined before her birth, its resolution decided by the ever-watching gods. Yeats summarised the plot in a note written for the first production of the play :

The legend on which "Deirdre" is founded is, perhaps, the most famous of all Irish legends. The best version is that in Lady Gregory's "Cuchulain of Muirthemne," and is made up out of more than a dozen old texts. All these texts differ more or less, sometimes in essential things, and in arranging the story for the bounds of a one-act play, I have had to leave out many details, even some important persons, that are in all the old versions. I have selected certain things which seem to be characteristic of the tale as well as in themselves dramatic, and I have separated these from much that needed an epic form or a more elaborate treatment. Deirdre was the Irish Helen, and Naisi her Paris, and Concobar her Menelaus, and the events took place, according to the conventional chronology of the Bards, about the time of the birth of Christ. Concobar was High King of Ulster, and Naisi King of one of the sub-kingdoms, and the scene of the play is laid in a guest-house among woods in the neighbourhood of Armagh, where Concobar had his palace.

Fergus, who in the old poems is a mixture of chivalry and folly, had been High King before Concobar, but had been tricked into abdicating in his favour. I have made no use of this abdication in my play, except that it helps to justify the popular influence I have attributed to him. I have introduced three wandering musicians, who are not in the legend, and Mr. Arthur Darley has written the music of their songs. The scenery has been designed by Mr. Robert Gregory.[35]

His search for the actress who would realise Deirdre is revealed in his letters during the year. Mrs. Patrick Campbell, who wanted to play the part, did not satisfy Yeats's requirements for his embodiment of the tragic queen. He wrote to his father about the quest — and about his discovery of the actress who created the part, Miss Darragh (Letitia Marion Dallas), who proved unpopular with the company at the Abbey, but who played Dectora in the revised version of *The Shadowy Waters* as well as playing Deirdre.

Mrs. Patrick Campbell has asked for my *Deirdre*, which she has seen though in somewhat incomplete form. She wants to produce it in the autumn and to take it on tour in America. I am not quite sure however whether I can let her have it, as my own theatre has first claims. And besides there is a new actress, a Miss Darragh, who may want it for England, and I am inclined to think that Miss Darragh has more intellectual tragedy in her. She is an Irish-woman, and played Leah in *The Walls of Jericho*. She gave a magnificent performance of Salome the other day. I am inclined to think, though I have not seen enough of her yet to be quite certain, that she is the finest tragedian on the English stage. I feel that a change is taking place in the nature of acting; Mrs. Campbell and her generation were trained in plays like *Mrs. Tanqueray*, where everything is done by a kind of magnificent hysteria (one understands that when one hears her hunting her monkey and her servant with an im-partial fury about the house). This school reduces everything to an emotional least common denominator. It finds the scullion in the queen, because there are scullions in the audience but no queens. It gives the scullion grace and beauty, but it must be the grace and beauty that the scullion dreams of. A new school of acting is now growing up under the influence of the various attempts to create an intellectual drama, and of changes deeper than that. The new school seizes upon what is distinguished, solitary, proud even. One always got a little of this in Mrs. Emery when she was good, and one gets a great deal of it in Miss Darragh. Both miss their climaxes as yet, for they are the reaction, and the old school missed everything else, at least in tragedy. Besides they are interested, the best of them anyway, in building up character bit by bit. I feel these things rather vaguely, as one feels new things; the problem with me just now is whether, as I am rather inclined to, to leap at the advertisement of a performance by Mrs. Pat, or to keep to my own people and my own generation till they have brought their art to perfection.[36]

Yeats hoped that Florence Farr would play the First Musician, as well as setting the lyrics in the play but she did not do either. He wrote to her in October, describing the difficulties in rehearsal with the company, and the company's difficulties with Miss Darragh, who was not popular with the other actors, nor with the backstage staff.

She is considered to lack tact and the finer feelings. At any rate she has got them into the right state to welcome you. I think she will be very useful to us in a number of parts, but there are a number of others that neither she or our own people can touch. I do believe I have made a great play out of *Deirdre* — "the authors are in eternity" etc. — most powerful and even sen-sational. I will get a copy made and send it to you I think, as it may be some time before it is printed. The first musician was written for you — I always saw your face as I wrote, very curiously your face even more than your voice, and built the character out of that.[37]

*

Deirdre was produced on 24 November 1906.* Some photographs of the production survive, but they fall far short in realisation of Robert Gregory's setting of a stage hung with draperies which was well ahead of the general theatrical standards of the time. Yeats was so delighted by this design that he dedicated the play jointly to Mrs. Patrick Campbell, who played in revivals of the play both in London and in Dublin, and to Robert Gregory, 'who designed the beautiful scene she played it in.' The watercolour design is an imaginative rendering of Yeats's direction.

A guest-house in a wood. It is a rough house of timber; through the doors and some of the windows one can see the great spaces of the wood, the sky dimming, night closing in. But a window to the left shows the thick leaves of a coppice; the landscape suggests silence and loneliness. There is a door to right and left, and through the side windows one can see anybody who approaches either door, a moment before he enters. In the centre a part of the house is curtained off; the curtains are drawn. . . .

David R. Clark, in his *W. B. Yeats and the Theatre of Desolate Reality*, examines the staging of *Deirdre* as implied in the directions in relation to the text of the play and shows how closely Yeats visualised the work in practical terms of stage technique during the construction of the piece. He concludes that

The whole play has been a tragic chess game in which each player followed the rules sacred to him : Conchubar sovereign pride, Fergus statesmanly good-faith, Naoise heroic honour and Deirdre the laws of love. In a sense the finish was determined before the start and all the action was like that of Lugaid Redstripe and his bride: "They moved the men and waited for the end."
Just as legitimately, however, one could say that the whole play has been

---

*   DEIRDRE

Presented by the Irish National Theatre Society Limited
at the Abbey Theatre, Dublin
on Saturday 24 November 1906

Concobar	J. M. Kerrigan
Fergus	Arthur Sinclair
Naisi	F. J. Fay
Messenger	U. Wright
Executioner	A. Power
First Musician	Sara Allgood
Second Musician	Maire O'Neill
Third Musician	Brigit O'Dempsey
Deirdre	Miss Darragh

Produced by W. B. Yeats
Scenery designed by Robert Gregory
The music to the lyrics composed by Arthur Darley

a rising fire of passion against the night sky of death. In terms of stage properties the fire spreads from the brazier, to the torches in the sconces, to the torches in the hands of Deirdre's belated defenders. All four chief characters show themselves in an intensity both of passion and of control in that last flaring scene.

The stage movement, like the psychological movement of the whole play, follows that of a pendulum. The early scenes show a great distance between Deirdre's passion and Naoise's honour and the action shifts obviously back and forth from one side to the other. These movements, both physical and psychological, become briefer and briefer as passion becomes honour and honour passion and as Deirdre and Naoise converge upon their place of death and triumph behind the central curtain.[38]

Joseph Holloway recorded some of the rehearsals for *Deirdre* in his Journal, and gave a vignette of Yeats directing, on 16 November.

Shortly after I was seated, Miss Sara Allgood and Mr. Kerrigan passed in, and also W. B. Yeats and Lady Gregory, and the rehearsal was under way. The Miss Allgoods as "Singing Women" open the play. W. B. Yeats takes up his stand at the footlights with his back to the auditorium. His attitudes during rehearsal were a sight to see, as he kept posing unconsciously all the time. The Miss Allgoods spoke in the measured tones dear to the heart of Yeats, and . . . Mr. Kerrigan, as the king, possesses a big voice which he uses too monotonously, and Mr. Arthur Sinclair declaims so loudly at times as to be quite out of the picture. A Yeats play is like a symphony in which the voices are the instruments employed, and if one or more is harsh or over-loudly employed the harmony is slain. . . .

Yeats's attitudes during rehearsal would have made a fortune for a comic artist had he been there to note them down. He is a strange, odd fish with little or no idea of acting, and the way he stares at the players from within a yard or two of them, as they act, would distract most people. You would think he had a subject under a microscope he stares so intently at them.[39]

The production was acclaimed, but did not attract audiences to the theatre and only the policy pursued by the company's new manager, W. A. Henderson, who insisted on popular successes, saved the theatre at this time. Miss Horniman was thinking of withdrawing from the venture as she was unhappy in her relationship with the Fays, and did not approve of Miss Darragh. Despite these difficulties, Yeats was pleased that *Deirdre* had been performed, and wrote to Katharine Tynan,

My play *Deirdre*, after leaving me doubtful for a little, is now certainly a success. It is my best play and the last half of it holds the audience in as strong a grip as does *Kathleen ni Houlihan*, which is prose and therefore a far easier thing to write. The difficulties of holding an audience with verse are ten times greater than with the prose play. Modern audience has lost the habit of careful listening. I think it is certainly my best dramatic poetry and for the first time a verse play of mine is well played all round. I think the Irish accent in blank verse is rather a shock to whatever ordinary theatregoers find their way to us, but they will get used to it. Miss Darragh, an Irish star on the English stage, who is playing for us, says our pit is a wonder; she never knew a pit to listen to tragedy with such silent attention.[40]

*

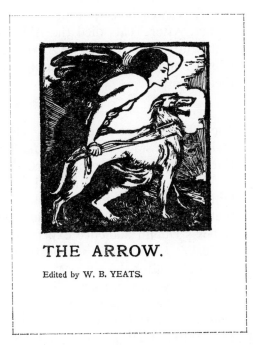

THE ARROW.

Edited by W. B. YEATS.

31. *The Arrow.* Cover. Reduced from 9¾ × 7¼".

The Arrow was conceived by Yeats as a more immediate vehicle to issue notes and comments about the theatre's work than *Samhain*, which had appeared annually since 1901. He planned the new periodical as a monthly paper and stated its purpose in the first number, issued on 20 October 1906,

I have been so busy finishing *Deirdre*, a play in verse, that I have put off *Samhain* for a month or so; but *The Arrow* is not meant as a substitute, for we hope that the queen with the wolf dog has one in her quiver for every month. It will interpret or comment on particular plays, make announcements, wrap up the programme and keep it from being lost, and leave general principles to *Samhain*.[41]

The heading of the first page bore a quotation from Wagner which reflected Yeats's purpose for the Theatre:

In the Theatre there lies the spiritual seed and kernel of all national poetic and national moral culture. No other branch of Art can ever truly flourish or ever aid in cultivating the people until the Theatre's all-powerful assistance has been completely recognised and guaranteed.

The hope of a monthly issue was not fulfilled, and only five issues appeared, on 20 October and 24 November 1906; on 23 February and 1 June 1907, both concerned with the 'Playboy riots,' and on 25 August 1909 when the topic was Shaw's The Shewing-up of Blanco Posnet. After Yeats died the Abbey directors issued a special commemorative number of The Arrow, edited by Lennox Robinson, with tributes and memories by people who had worked with him in the theatre.

*

The Abbey Theatre season in which Deirdre was first performed included the stage version of The Shadowy Waters, again with Miss Darragh in the leading part. (See above, p. 99). Joseph Holloway did not find the bill, which included the first production of The Canavans by Lady Gregory, 'very palatable' [12] and one can see from his Journal that the concentration of poetic drama presented was not what the Abbey's Dublin audience expected. Holloway goes on to report the critic W. J. Lawrence at a lecture at the National Literary Society two nights after the performance of The Shadowy Waters as saying, 'The Abbey was run according to the Gospel of Saint Yeats.' [13] The Abbey audience was, however, soon to have another object of concern. The Shadowy Waters was to have been followed by the first production of a new play by J. M. Synge, The Playboy of the Western World, originally announced for 29 December 1906, but the opening was deferred for a month during which the company staged several revivals, among them The Hour-Glass. The Playboy finally opened on Saturday 26 January 1907 to hooting and hissing, and was the detonator of the greatest 'riot' in the history of the Irish theatre. By the following Thursday, performances were being given with a guard of two hundred police in and around the Abbey.

The controversy about The Playboy continued with discussions in the theatre, statements and reports in the Press. Yeats saw the affair as an attack on the Freedom of the Theatre and organised a public discussion on that theme at the Abbey on Monday 5 February. As the author of Cathleen Ni Houlihan, he appealed for a hearing of Synge's play and saw the 'riots' as an attack on basic rights. In an interview printed in The Freeman's Journal he stated,

A serious issue . . . has been rising in Ireland for some time. When I was a lad, Irishmen obeyed a few leaders; but during the last ten years a change has taken place. Organised opinion of sections and coteries has been put in place of these leaders, one or two of whom were men of genius. Instead of a Parnell, or a Stephens, or a Butt, we must obey the demands of commonplace or ignorant people, who try to take on an appearance of strength by imposing some crude shibboleth on their own and others' necks. They do not persuade, for that is difficult; they do not expound, for that needs knowledge. There are some exceptions, as heretofore, but the mass only understand conversion by terror, threats, and abuse.[44]

The Nationalist press, however, saw a radical change in Yeats's attitude and construed his stand on *The Playboy* as an attack on the very freedom he was defending.

Mr. Yeats has struck a disastrous blow at the Freedom of the Theatre in Ireland. It was, perhaps, the last freedom left to us. Hitherto, as in Paris or Berlin to-day, or Athens two thousand years ago, the audience in Ireland was free to express its opinion on the play. Mr. Yeats has caused that freedom to be taken away. It is the Freedom of the Theatre for the playwright to produce what he pleases and for the audience to accept or reject as it pleases. Mr. Yeats has denied the audience in Ireland the right Victor Hugo admitted when he produced "Hernani" in Paris — the right the Greek audience always claimed and always exercised. He has wounded both art and his country. As to his country, Mr. Yeats claimed on Monday night that he had served it, and the claim is just. He served it unselfishly in the past. He has ceased to serve it now — to our regret. It is not the nation that has changed towards Mr. Yeats — it is Mr. Yeats who has changed towards the nation.
    There is a tendency in the Irish character to be distracted by minor and subordinate and often insignificant points from larger and more serious issues — and this tendency is likely to prove harmful to the national movement. The Abbey Theatre — which is a concern built and kept up by the money of an English lady, and boasts itself—"the fiddler calls the tune"—in no way more responsible to the Irish public than the police whose aid it enlists when the Irish public objects to being libelled on its stage, is in itself of small importance at all were it not that it labels itself the "National Theatre" of Ireland. That label has now been effectively torn from it, and it may be left to the adulation of a coterie — to substitute for criticism which it seeks — it may be left to the staging of squalor and the one-sided view of that which plays in the human economy the part that sewers may be held to play in the economy of the town.[45]

Yeats assembled an issue of *The Arrow*, dated 23 February, to reply to the controversy and included quotations from previous attacks on Irish playwrights. He reprinted the text of his speech at the debate held at the Abbey on 5 February to discuss *The Playboy*, and wrote in his editorial,

We have claimed for our writers the freedom to find in their own land every expression of good and evil necessary to their art, for Irish life contains, like all vigorous life, the seeds of all good and evil, and a writer must be free here as elsewhere to ripen weed or flower, as the fancy takes him. No one who knows the work of our Theatre as a whole can say we have neglected the flower; but the moment a writer is forbidden to show the weed without the flower, his art loses energy and abundance,

and he concluded,

The quarrel of our Theatre to-day is the quarrel of the Theatre in many lands; for the old Puritanism, the old bourgeois dislike of power and reality have not changed, even when they are called by some Gaelic name.[46]

32. *The Abbey Row.* Dublin, 1907. Cover. Reduced from 9¾ × 7¼".

By 15 March a parody of *The Arrow* had been issued by Maunsel and Company, with the title *The Abbey Row*. The cover lampooned the 'Queen Maeve' device of the Abbey with caricatures of Synge as the wolfhound being restrained by Mrs. Grundy (perhaps Lady Gregory) as the epic queen. The bottom line of the cover read 'NOT edited by W. B. Yeats.' The illustrations, by R. C. Orpen, included a caricature of Yeats addressing the audience during the 'riots' and this was reflected in the text,

. . . a herald in the shape of a gentleman arrived before the curtain and made as though to speak. Tall, slight, and pale as he was, and garbed with a careless affectation that could only mean one thing — connection with art or all the arts. His black hair hung gracefully across his brow till it came to the top left hand corner, where it sagged suddenly, and we feared every moment that it would blot out his right optic.

We enquired who he was, and were told that he was a poet, and, moreover, connected with the Abbey Theatre.

Not every theatre, we thought, could afford its own poet.[47]

33. 'The Poet addressed the Audience.'
Illustration from *The Abbey Row*, 1907.

Yeats's continuing concern, however disappointing the reception of his own plays may have proved, and despite the misunderstanding of his attitude towards the Dublin audience and critics, was to create, with Lady Gregory and his fellow directors of the Abbey, a fine national theatre for Ireland. To achieve this, it was also necessary to bear in mind the attitude of his patroness, Miss Horniman who at this time had more money to invest in her theatrical interests but was thinking of subsidising a Repertory Theatre in Manchester. She asked Yeats to place his poetic plays at her disposal but he refused, replying

I understand my own race and in all my work, lyric or dramatic, I have thought of it. If the theatre fails I may or may not write plays, there is always lyric poetry to return to, but I shall write for my own people, whether in

love or hate matters little, perhaps I shall not know which it is. Nor can I
make any permanent allocation of my plays while the Irish theatre may at
any moment need my help.[48]

Miss Horniman's money went to the Manchester Theatre which
opened in September. Her subsidy to the Irish National Theatre
Society was coming towards its end, and as she did not approve of
the Fays, nor of the general direction in which the Irish theatre was
moving she considered this as a lost cause and, in November, lamen-
ted to Yeats, 'But what are my words against the wooing of the
vampire Kathleen Ni Houlihan!' [49]

John O'Leary, Yeats's first mentor in Irish Nationalism, died in
Dublin on 16 March. Yeats could not bring himself to attend the
funeral, but during the summer he composed one of his finest essays,
'Poetry and Tradition,' dated August 1907, in O'Leary's memory. In
this he restated his concern that 'Ireland's great moment had passed,
and she had filled no roomy vessels with strong sweet wine,' [50] and

that, as belief in the possibility of armed insurrection withered, the old
romantic Nationalism would wither too, and that the young would become
less ready to find pleasure in whatever they believed to be literature. Poetical
tragedy, and indeed all the more intense forms of literature, had lost their
hold on the general mass of men in other countries as life grew safe, and the
sense of comedy which is the social bond in times of peace as tragic feeling
is in times of war, had become the inspiration of popular art. I always knew
this, but I believed that the memory of danger, and the reality of it seemed
near enough sometimes, would last long enough to give Ireland her imaginative
opportunity. I could not foresee that a new class, which had begun to rise
into power under the shadow of Parnell, would change the nature of the Irish
movement, which, needing no longer great sacrifices, nor bringing any great
risk to individuals, could do without exceptional men, and those activities of
the mind that are founded on the exceptional moment.[51]

And I feel that this time in handling the affairs of the theatre
prompted Yeats to draft his 'Advice to Playwrights who are sending
Plays to the Abbey, Dublin,' which was printed as a single sheet
issued by the Theatre.

ADVICE TO PLAYWRIGHTS WHO ARE SENDING
PLAYS TO THE ABBEY, DUBLIN

The Abbey Theatre is a subsidised theatre with an educational object. It will,
therefore, be useless, as a rule, to send it plays intended as popular entertainments, and that alone, or originally written for performance by some popular
actor at the popular theatres. A play to be suitable for performance at the
Abbey should contain some criticism of life founded on the experience or
personal observation of the writer, or some vision of life, of Irish life by
preference, important from its beauty or from some excellence of style; and

this intellectual quality is not more necessary to tragedy than to the gayest comedy.

We do not desire propagandist plays, nor plays written mainly to serve some obvious moral purpose; for art seldom concerns itself with those interests or opinions that can be defended by argument, but with realities of emotion and character that become self-evident when made vivid to the imagination.

The dramatist should also banish from his mind the thought that there are some ingredients, the love-making of the popular stage for instance, especially fitted to give dramatic pleasure; for any knot of events, where there is passionate emotion and clash of will, can be made the subject matter of a play, and the less like a play it is at the first sight the better play may come of it in the end. Young writers should remember that they must get all their effects from the logical expression of their subject, and not by the addition of extraneous incidents; and that a work of art can have but one subject. A work of art, though it must have the effect of nature, is art because it is not nature, as Goethe said; and it must possess a unity unlike the accidental profusion of nature.

The Abbey Theatre is continually sent plays which show that their writers have not understood that the attainment of this unity, by what is usually a long shaping and reshaping of the plot, is the principal labour of the dramatist, and not the writing of the dialogue.

Before sending plays of any length, writers would often save themselves some trouble by sending a "scenario," or scheme of the plot, together with one completely written act, and getting the opinion of the reading committee as to its suitability before writing the whole play.

We must also insist upon all plays being typewritten.

W.B.Y.[52]

*

Lady Gregory invited Yeats to join her and her son Robert on a tour of Italy in April, and afterwards he returned to spend the summer with them at Coole. He was revising and arranging his work for the *Collected Works* planned for publication by Bullen in London with a guarantee of £1,500 from Miss Horniman.

The work on the *Collected* edition provided Yeats with an opportunity to reconsider his earlier writings and he decided that *Where There is Nothing* should not be included in its original form. He asked Lady Gregory's help in recasting the play into a common idiom. He had a 'very full scenario'[53] ready by 4 July and, a week later, planned a place for the rewritten play, still under its old title, in the Bullen edition. The play was redesigned into three acts and was ready for rehearsal by October. Most of the dialogue in the rewritten play, *The Unicorn from the Stars*, was written by Lady Gregory who had taken Yeats's dictation of the play and Yeats acknowledged this in his Note to the play in *Plays in Prose and Verse*, 1922,

Since I had last worked with her, her mastery of the stage and her knowledge of dialect had so increased that my imagination could not go on neck and neck with hers. I found myself, too, stopped by an old difficulty, that my words never flow freely but when people speak in verse; and so after an attempt to work alone I gave up my scheme to her. The result is a play almost wholly hers in handiwork which is so much mine in thought that she does not wish to include it in her own works.[54]

*The Unicorn from the Stars,** billed as a collaboration between Yeats and Lady Gregory, was performed at the Abbey Theatre on 21 November 1907 but did not make any considerable impact on the audience. The attempt to marry Yeats's mystical philosophy with the actualities of theatre did not succeed as too many of the esoteric points in the earlier play had been omitted in the revision and the resulting piece was rather thin in plot, a failing which the enriched and enlivened dialogue could not remedy. Yeats contributed a programme note which may be compared with the plot of *Where There is Nothing*. (See above, p. 76.)

The Unicorn from the Stars is founded on *Where there is Nothing*, which was first printed as a Supplement to *The United Irishman* — now *Sinn Fein* — and was acted by the Stage Society in the Court Theatre. Last summer, while preparing for the collected edition of my writings which Mr. Bullen is bringing out, I decided that I could not include it in its old form, which was written too much from the point of view of the chief character for sanity, and had too much of heterogeneous life for artistic unity. I felt that the central idea of the play would seem vague and shadowy unless it were embedded in the circumstance of real life. I therefore asked Lady Gregory, the greater portion of whose work has been a study of the actual life of Ireland, to collaborate with me. Martin Hearne — the principal character, like many of the saints and of our own country people to-day, has been a visionary from childhood. He has become persuaded, through the partial remembrance of a vision, that he has been appointed to overthrow the modern organisation of life, that we may return to the more spontaneous life of ancient times, when the super-

---

*   THE UNICORN FROM THE STARS
     by W. B. Yeats and Lady Gregory

Produced by the Irish National Theatre Society
at the Abbey Theatre, Dublin
on Thursday 21 November 1907

Father John	Ernest Vaughan
Thomas Hearne, a coachbuilder	Arthur Sinclair
Andrew Hearne, brother of Thomas	J. A. O'Rourke
Martin Hearne, nephew of Thomas	F. J. Fay
Johnny Bacach, a beggar	W. G. Fay
Paudeen	J. M. Kerrigan
Biddy Lally	Maire O'Neill
Nanny	Brigit O'Dempsey

natural life was nearer than it is to-day. After one eventful night he comes to the conclusion that the natural order is itself the enemy, and that the battle was to have been fought out in his own mind.[55]

Yeats's programme note to *The Unicorn from the Stars* may, however, be read in a different light if one takes notice of the production of the German translation of the play, by Henry von Heiseler, which was first performed at Munich in 1940. Dr. Susanne Schaup has kindly given me the following notice of that production:

THE UNICORN FROM THE STARS (*Das Einhorn von den Sternen*) was performed at the *Kammerspiele* in Munich (still the most important Munich theatre), directed by Otto Falckenberg, on 9 March 1940. Falckenberg, one of the best-known theatre directors in Germany of the first half of this century, chose the play with much aesthetic, but hardly any political instinct. He was a lover of poetic, symbolic plays, and the fact that it deals with Irish rebellion against the British suppression (Germany was already at war with England at the time) seemed to him enough recommendation to satisfy the Nazi authorities. In those days no book could be published, no play produced that did not have the sanction of the regime.

Two things especially provoked the audience, amongst which there were many Brownshirts. Falckenberg had given the part of Martin Hearne, the hero, to a very gifted young actor, Heinz Thiele, who twisted the part somewhat by the irony and seeming insolence he gave to it. Secondly, Falckenberg had extended the second act by some songs in the Brechtian style, performed by the beggars, and so the audience — or, rather the Nazi spectators among them — began to smell "Communism."

I quote from a report written by Erna Fentsch-Wery, whose husband, Carl Wery, had the part of Thomas Hearne, and who witnessed the performance:

"The performance of the UNICORN had met with growing disapproval by the audience. Especially the Nazis among them were shocked by this difficult play, in which a mob of suspicious figures kept calling for a 'leader' (*Führer*). This word *Führer* slowly began to work like dynamite. Another cause for the misunderstanding of the play was the youthful leading man. It was played by an intellectual with a touch of the ironic and perfidious. The audience was not to blame. They were unable to distinguish between the part and the actor. When this 'perfidious' person kept calling for a *Führer*, the people of the Nazi party felt ridiculed.

"Up to the intermission there were no catcalls. When the curtain went down, hardly anybody clapped. Then arose a sharp dialogue in the audience whether or not the play was to be considered an insult of the Führer, and when the curtain went up again, there was aggressive laughter in the audience. This was caused by another external effect that had nothing to do with the play itself: Otto Brefin, who played the part of Father John, was dressed in a badly tattered cassock, and this looked very funny. Laughter. After the laughing had started, the actors were hardly able to make themselves heard. A gentleman in the front rows called in vain: 'Can't you pay respect to a dead poet!' Then it was my husband's turn to come on the stage. He stepped towards the edge of the stage and addressed the audience with those words he was supposed to say to his partner: 'It is very queer the world itself is.'

Then there was quiet, and the performance could be finished.

"After the curtain went down there was a turmoil in the audience that was continued in the street."

Otto Falckenberg was severely reprimanded by the authorities and had to cancel all subsequent performances.

The translation was by Henry von Heiseler, a German poet, who was among the first to discover Yeats and one of the first translators.

THE UNICORN FROM THE STARS was again performed in 1956 (Kammerspiele Köln) and in 1959 in Tübingen.

The music for *The Unicorn from the Stars*, printed in *Plays in Prose and Verse*, 1922, is derived from Irish traditional ballad tunes and shows a new direction in Yeats's approach to the use of music in his plays. The influence of Lady Gregory is very evident throughout the play — trying to shape a Yeatsian concept to the requirements of the popular stage and, perhaps, almost succeeding. It might have made a greater impact on the Dublin audience had some other writer collaborated with Yeats as the dialogue, which leans heavily on Lady Gregory's invented 'Kiltartan' dialect, seems stilted and artificial.

*

Earlier in the year, on 20 April 1907, the Abbey Theatre had presented *Fand* by Wilfrid Scawen Blunt, produced by Ben Iden Payne. This was the play which, in 1902, Yeats had invited Blunt to contribute to a Cuchulain Cycle which was to have multiple authorship. Described as *Fand, a Féerie*, Blunt's play, written in Alexandrines with lyric interludes set to music by Arthur Darley, must have proved a sharp contrast to the mood of Yeats's dramatic concepts after five years spent trying to shape the Irish dramatic movement and only three months after the *Playboy* affair had occasioned him to examine again his own role as dramatist.

During 1907, while *The Unicorn from the Stars* was in preparation, Yeats returned again to the old Irish epic for a theme, and wrote, in prose, his second play with Cuchulain as its central character, *The Golden Helmet*, derived from the old tale of 'The Feast of Bricriu' as printed in Lady Gregory's version in *Cuchulain of Muirthemne*. Cuchulain, in the play, is shown at the height of his powers, surrounded by Conall's household who have interminable dissentions and quarrels. Perhaps Yeats's stand during the *Playboy* riots and his vigorous defence of the old standards of life that he believed in are reflected in the play. But, by the time the play reached the Abbey stage, on 19 March 1908,* the Fays had left the company and Yeats had neither Frank's polished speaking nor Willie's comic gift to rely on to make a success of the piece.

The text of *The Golden Helmet* was printed in Volume IV of Bullen's collected edition, later in 1908, and Yeats appended a note to this text which displays his concern with the production:

In performance we left the black hands to the imagination, and probably when there is so much noise and movement on the stage they would always fail to produce any effect. Our stage is too small to try the experiment, for they would be hidden by the figures of the players. We staged the play with a very pronounced colour-scheme and I have noted that the more obviously decorative is the scheme and costuming of any play, the more it is lifted out of time and place, and the nearer to faeryland do we carry it. One gets also much more effort out of conceited movements — above all, if there are many players — when all the clothes are the same colour. No breadth of treatment gives monotony when there is movement and change of lighting. It concentrates attention on every new effect and makes every change of outline or of light and shadow surprising and delightful. Because of this one can use contrasts of colour, between clothes and background itself, the complimentary colours for instance, which would be too obvious to keep the attention in a painting. One wishes to make the movement of the action as important as possible, and the simplicity which gives depth to colour does this, just as, for precisely similar reasons, the lack of colour in a statue fixes the attention upon the form.[56]

The Golden Helmet was rewritten into ballad metre and retitled *The Green Helmet* between December 1909 and January 1910. In this version, while Yeats's verse resembled the Alexandrines used by Blunt in *Fand*, he described the version as 'a play in Ballad metre.' Many years later, in 'A General Introduction for my Work,' he wrote of this,

When I wrote in blank verse I was dissatisfied; my vaguely mediaeval *Countess Cathleen* fitted the measure, but our Heroic Age went better, or so

---

(see facing page)   THE GOLDEN HELMET
A HEROIC FARCE

Produced by the Irish National Theatre Society
at the Abbey Theatre, Dublin
on Friday 19 March 1908

Cuchulain	J. M. Kerrigan
Conal	Arthur Sinclair
Leagerie	Fred O'Donovan
Laeg, Cuchulain's Charioteer	Sydney Morgan
Emer, Wife of Cuchulain	Sara Allgood
Conal's Wife	Maire O'Neill
Leagerie's Wife	Eileen O'Doherty
Red Man	Ambrose Power
Scullions, Horseboys	S. Hamilton, T. J. Fox, U. Wright,
and Blackmen	D. Robinson, T. O'Neill,
	J. A. O'Rourke, P. Kearney

I fancied, in the ballad metre of *The Green Helmet*. There was something in what I felt about Deirdre, about Cuchulain, that rejected the Renaissance and its characteristic metres, and this was a principal reason why I created in dance plays the form that varies blank verse with lyric metres.[57]

The Green Helmet was produced on 10 February 1910.* The lyrics in the play were set to music by J. F. Larchet, and Yeats's stage direction to the play, which was first printed at the Cuala Press in the same year, reveals how closely he must have worked with the company on the production and his concern for its visual realisation,

SCENE : A house made of logs. There are two windows at the back door which cuts off one of the corners of the room. Through the door, one can see low rocks which make the ground outside higher than it is within, and beyond the rocks a misty moon-lit sea. Through the windows one can see nothing but the sea. There is a great chair at the opposite side to the door, and in front of it a table with cups and a flagon of ale. Here and there are stools.

At the Abbey Theatre the house is orange-red and the chairs and tables and flagons black, with a slight purple tinge which is not clearly distinguishable from the black. The rocks are black with a few green touches. The sea is green and luminous and all the characters except the Red Man and the Black Men are dressed in various shades of green, one or two with touches of purple which look nearly black. The Black Men all wear dark purple and have eared caps, and at the end their eyes should look green from the reflected light of the sea. The Red Man is altogether in red. He is very tall, and his height increased by horns on the Green Helmet. The effect is intentionally violent and startling.[58]

*

On 9 November 1908, Yeats's plans for *Deirdre* were fully realised when Mrs. Patrick Campbell came to play the part at the Abbey in Robert Gregory's setting. Yeats thought her performance 'magni-

---

* THE GREEN HELMET

Produced by the Irish National Theatre Society
at the Abbey Theatre, Dublin
on Thursday 10 February 1910

Cuchulain	J. M. Kerrigan
Conal	Arthur Sinclair
Leagerie	Fred O'Donovan
Laeg, Cuchulain's Charioteer	Sydney J. Morgan
Emer, Wife of Cuchulain	Sara Allgood
Conal's Wife	Maire O'Neill
Leagerie's Wife	Ethne Magee
Red Man	Ambrose Power
Scullions, Horseboys	Eric Gorman, J. A. O'Rourke,
and Blackmen	John Carrick, F. R. Harford,
	T. Moloney, T. Durkin, P. Byrne

ficent'[59] and eventually dedicated the published text jointly to her and to Robert Gregory. In announcing the performance in *Samhain 1908* he expressed the honour her playing the part was to the Abbey,

When we and all our players are with the dead players of Henley's rhyme, some historian of the Theatre, remembering her coming and giving more weight to the appreciation of a fellow artist than even to the words of fine critics, will understand that if our people were not good artists one of the three or four great actresses of Europe would never have come where the oldest player is but twenty-six. To the sincere artist the applause of those who have won greatness in his own craft is often his first appreciation, and always the last that he forgets.[60]

Mrs. Campbell's performance was one of the most significant in Yeats's experience of the theatre. For many years he hoped that he might, in *The Player Queen*, provide another vehicle for her talents, and, in his last year, in *On the Boiler*, among certain moments in the theatre that haunted him, he included 'Mrs. Patrick Campbell in my "Deirdre," passionate and solitary.'[61]

While *Deirdre* was in rehearsal, Yeats was engaged on the scenario of a new play — perhaps the play about the capture of a blind Unicorn about which he had written to Florence Farr in 1906. By the end of October he had drafted the prose version, named it *The Player Queen* and discussed the possibility that Mrs. Campbell might play in it. He worked on the play through the end of the year, but Synge's last illness and death on 24 March 1909 caused the deferment of the plan. Much more responsibility for the affairs of the Abbey now rested on Yeats, particularly as Miss Horniman's subsidy was coming to its end. But he continued to define his approach to his dramatic art, especially in the journals he kept at this period. His path was diverging from that of the theatre he founded, and he was, more and more, approaching the creation of a new form which he alone could control.

The artist grows more and more distinct, more and more a being in his own right as it were, but more and more loses grasp of the always more complex world. Some day setting out to find knowledge, like some pilgrim to the Holy Land, he will become the most romantic of characters. He will play with all masks. . . . The masks of tragedy contain neither character nor personal energy. They are allied to decoration and to the abstract figures of Egyptian temples. Before the mind can look out of their eyes the active will perishes, hence their sorrowful calm. Joy is of the will which labours, which overcomes obstacles, which knows triumph. The soul knows its changes of state alone, and I think the motives of tragedy are not related to action but to changes of state. I feel this but do not see clearly, for I am hunting truth into its thicket and it is my business to keep close to the impressions of sense, to common daily life. Yet is not ecstasy some fulfilment of the soul in itself, some slow or sudden expansion of it like an overflowing well? Is not this what is meant by beauty?[62]

*

Lady Gregory had visited Bernard Shaw at his home at Ayot St. Lawrence during the summer of 1909 and during this visit he gave her his play *The Shewing-up of Blanco Posnet* for production at the Abbey. The play had been refused a licence by the Lord Chamberlain's office and therefore could not be presented in public in England. Ireland, however, did not come under the jurisdiction of the English Censor and the play could be performed in Dublin. Yeats met Lady Gregory in London and they decided that the play could be accepted for the Abbey and that they should prepare it to open during the Dublin Horse Show in August. The Dublin Castle authorities tried to persuade the Abbey's directors to withdraw the production, but Yeats and Lady Gregory stood firmly by their principles and the play opened on 25 August. The directors issued a statement of their stand, signed by Yeats and Lady Gregory, which was printed in the fifth number of *The Arrow*, published with the programme of the play. This stand did much to gain popular support for the theatre in Ireland, especially from those who had protested about *The Playboy of the Western World*. To reinforce the argument, Yeats proposed that the Abbey should perform *Oedipus*, which was also banned by the English Censor, as he recorded in 1933 in a note published in New York, 'The Plain Man's Oedipus,'

When I first lectured in America thirty years ago, I heard at the University of Notre Dame that they had played *Oedipus the King*. That play was forbidden by the English censorship on the ground of its immorality; Oedipus commits incest; but if a Catholic university could perform it in America my own theatre could perform it in Ireland. Ireland had no censorship, and a successful performance might make her proud of her freedom, say even, perhaps, "I have an old historical religion moulded to the body of man like an old suit of clothes, and am therefore free." [63]

Yeats proceeded to prepare his version, with the idea that it would be played early in 1910 with Murray Carson in the lead, 'as a further precedent of our freedom from the Lord Chamberlain who has forbidden the play.' [64] Although Yeats worked at *Oedipus* into the early months of 1910, the play was not finished at the time and the thought of doing a version of the Greek tragedy was laid aside until almost twenty years later. Much of his energy during 1909 was directed towards completing the play he hoped would be a vehicle for the talents of Mrs. Patrick Campbell, *The Player Queen*.

He read *The Mask*, a new journal of the theatre, which Gordon Craig commenced to publish from his theatre school, the Arena Goldoni in Florence in March 1908. The twelfth number, issued in February 1909, contained the first instalment of 'Venetian Costume' translated by D. Nevile Lees from the book of Cesare Vecellio, which reprinted the woodcut designs of the original edition of 1590. Yeats wrote about these woodcuts in his journal for that year, eventually published as *The Death of Synge*,

34. Venetian costumes reproduced in *The Mask*, Vol. I, No. 12, February 1909.

I have been looking at Venetian costumes of the sixteenth century as pictured in *The Mask* — all fantastic; bodily form hidden or disguised; the women with long bodices, the men in stuffed doublets. Life had become so learned and courtly that men and women dressed with no thought of bodily activity. If they still fought and hunted, their imagination was not with these things. Does not the same happen to our passions when we grow contemplative and so liberate them from use? They also become fantastic and create the strange lives of poets and artists.[65]

In the first number of *The Mask* Craig had published the section of
Sebastiano Serlio's book on Architecture which dealt with stage
scenery and reproduced the classic woodcuts of 'The Comic Scene'
and 'The Tragic Scene.' I feel that Yeats's approach to *The Player
Queen* was influenced by these woodcuts and that he saw, in the
early drafts, a Renaissance tragedy, while his later treatment of the
play as a comedy has affinities with the *Commedia dell' Arte*, a style
which exerted a strong influence on Craig's theory of theatre and is
reflected both in Craig's own writings and in the earlier work he
chose to reprint in *The Mask*.

*

Yeats stayed at Coole Park from August until mid October 1909
working on *The Player Queen* in an attempt to have a text to show
to Mrs. Campbell in London. But, at the same time, he was planning
an edition of his plays which was to be published by Bullen, with
stage designs by Gordon Craig, and was writing 'an essay on "tragic
drama" ' [66] which was to form the introduction to the book,

> But of course nearly all my thoughts are on my long play, of which a great
> deal will be in rhyme. My theme is that the world being illusion, one must be
> deluded in some way if one is to triumph in it.[67]

In November he was in England, travelling to Oxford to see a performance of *The Wasps* 'with a view to *Oedipus*.' [68] He ordered Jebb's
translation and 'an edition used in a performance at Oxford.' [69] But
his main purpose was to interest Mrs. Campbell in *The Player Queen*.
He rejected her suggestion that Tree should be considered in writing
the piece. ('I have described his ideal of beauty as thrice vomited
flesh,' [70] he wrote to Lady Gregory.) At last Mrs. Campbell invited
him to lunch and to hear his play, but the occasion, although he
described it humorously in a letter to his father, must have been a
severe disappointment to Yeats.

> She wrote to me to come at 1.15, lunch and read it afterwards (this was
> yesterday week). I went and word was sent down with apologies she wasn't
> yet ready. On towards two she and lunch appeared. After lunch she listened,
> much interrupted by the parrot, to Act I with great enthusiasm. I was just
> starting Act II when a musician arrived, to play some incidental music she
> was to speak through in some forthcoming performance. She said : "This
> won't delay me long, not more than ten minutes," and then began an immense
> interminable quarrel with the musician about his music. After an hour and a
> half of this I said "I think I had better go and put off an invitation to dinner
> I had for to-night." She begged me to do so — full of apologies. I went away
> and returned at 6.30 just as the musician left. I then started Act II. A deaf
> man sat there whose mission was, it seemed, to say irrelevant enthusiastic

things to Mrs. Campbell. I got through Act II well. Mrs. Campbell still enthusiastic. Then there came in telephone messages and I was asked to stay to dinner and read it afterwards. At dinner there was young Campbell and his wife and two other relations of hers, probably poor ones. After dinner arrived Mrs. Campbell's dressmaker, this would also take only a few minutes. Presently there was a mighty stir upstairs and somebody sent down in an excited way, like a messenger in a Greek Tragedy, to say that the dress was 6 inches too short in front. At half past ten there was a consultation in the drawing room as to whether somebody shouldn't go up and knock at Mrs. Campbell's door. It was decided that somebody should but everybody refused to be the one. I wanted to go home but I was told on no account must I do that. At half past 11 Mrs. Campbell came down, full of apologies, it would only be a few minutes longer. At twelve young Campbell's wife, who is an American heiress, and therefore independent, announced that she was going home and did, taking her husband. I sat on with the relations, whose business it seems was to entertain me. We sighed together at the amount it would cost us in taxi cabs to get home. At half past twelve Mrs. Campbell came in so tired that she had to lean on her daughter to get into the room. I said: "This is absurd! You must go to your bed, and I must go home." She said: "No, I must hear the end of a play the same day as I hear the beginning." I began to read. She did not know one word I was saying. She started to quarrel with me, because she supposed I had given a long speech which she wanted to a minor character and because of certain remarks which I applied to my heroine which she thought applied to her. She said at intervals, in an exasperated sleepy voice: "No, I am not a slut and I do not like fools." Finally I went home and I'm trying to find a halcyon day on which to read her the play again. I've even had to assure her by letter that it was not she but my heroine who liked fools.[71]

Although he still hoped for some weeks that Mrs. Campbell might express an interest in the play, he gradually accepted that she was 'off it'[72] and by the end of the year he was 'working well again.'[73] He finished the new version of *The Golden Helmet* in verse, which was to appear as *The Green Helmet*. He also began to revise his first produced play, *The Land of Heart's Desire* which had never been played at the Abbey and, early in January 1910, he had a meeting with Gordon Craig in London which was to change his whole approach to stage presentation.

*

The Irish national theatre movement was ten years old in 1909 and the Abbey, the National Theatre, had been open for five years in December. Yeats and Lady Gregory issued a Statement of Affairs in November, printed as *Paragraphs written in Nov., 1909, with Supplement and Financial Statement* which listed the plays produced during the ten years and pointed out that Miss Horniman's subsidy would come to an end at the close of 1910. The theatre was operating on a modest profit margin but the company was still unpaid. Their principal achievement in establishing a national style both of play-writing and of acting had been recognised internationally as one of the vital influences in twentieth-century theatre. The wider aims of the founders had not, however, been fulfilled, but they still hoped for this, and expressed their determination in print,

The folk drama, for which our Theatre has given the opportunity, has a number of writers, and especially of late there have arisen young men of great promise whose future is probably bound up in the future of our Theatre. The creation of a folk drama was, however, but a part of the original scheme, and now that it has been accomplished we can enlarge our activities, bringing within our range more and more of the life of Ireland, and finding adequate expression for the acknowledged masterpieces of the world. A theatre, as we conceive it, should contain in its repertory plays from the principal dramatic schools. We have begun with three plays by Molière, as their affinities with folk drama have made them easy to our players. During our next season we shall add to them one of Goldoni's comedies. Our players have, however, given a good deal of their time to the speaking of verse, and we are about to produce "Œdipus the King." A French classical play, and one by Calderon, should come next; and when we apply for a new Patent we shall hope to remove the limitation of our present one, which prevents us from performing any Elizabethan work. We wish, in fact, while keeping the bulk of our work as Irish as possible, to enlarge gradually the experience of our players until the day has come when it will be possible to find in our repertory examples of the great schools, chosen as impartially as if they were pictures in some national gallery.

All the laborious building-up, the slow amassing of a large repertory of Irish plays, the training of actors, the making of a reputation with the general public, has been accomplished, or all but accomplished, and there is little needed to make the Abbey Theatre a permanent part of Irish life, the centre of a distinguished school of players, playwrights and translators. We ourselves are ready to accept much or little influence and any arrangement that will keep the Theatre intellectual and courageous. We would sooner it came to an end than see the tradition we have created give place to one less worthy.

W. B. YEATS
A. GREGORY[74]

Gordon Craig had gone to live in Florence in October 1906 and there he began to formulate the theories of stage presentation, or stage management as he preferred to term it, developed by him since his early productions in London, which had made a lasting impression on Yeats. Working from the second volume of the *Five Books of Architecture*, 1545, by Sebastiano Serlio, which dealt with architectural perspective in the theatre and from his experience of modern methods of staging and lighting in the theatre in Germany, Craig began to write and illustrate his own theory of a method of stage setting which would be both permanent and mobile, variable by the disposition of the shapes or forms which were used, and by the lighting employed.

35. Edward Gordon Craig. Design for stage scene. Wood engraving, 1907. This engraving is the genesis of the series of etchings eventually published as *Scene*, 1923.

In March 1908 he published from Florence the first number of *The Mask*, his journal of the Art of the Theatre, which had as motto 'After the Practice the Theory.' In the first number he printed Serlio's treatise on stage scenery as well as the first part of his own essay, 'The Artists of the Theatre of the Future.' Craig illustrated his writings with a series of engravings on wood, and a suite of etchings which were eventually published as *Scene*. He modified his ideas by working with a three-dimensional model, using figures cut on boxwood blocks to set the human scale in relation to the screens from which the 'scene' was arranged. The model also allowed movements to be blocked out and lighting effects to be determined.

Craig sent a copy of *The Mask* to Constantin Stanislavsky at the Moscow Art Theatre and Stanislavsky, who was searching for a new style to replace the absolute realism which the Moscow theatre sought in their presentations, persuaded his fellow directors that they should telegraph an invitation to Craig to direct a production for them. Craig immediately agreed to this and commenced planning *Hamlet*, to be staged in his screens, the 'thousand scenes in one scene.' Craig went to Moscow in October 1908 to discuss the projected *Hamlet* with Stanislavsky and returned for detailed discussions in the Spring of 1909. He spent the rest of that year preparing for *Hamlet*, writing for *The Mask* and engraving many designs. In December he returned to London to visit his mother and, early in January, met Yeats.

Craig had already begun to work on designs to illustrate Yeats's *Plays for an Irish Theatre* and these reflect Craig's view of stage design based on his 'screens.' When they met on 7 January 1910, his description of his system fired Yeats's enthusiasm. Yeats wrote to Lady Gregory,

5 January.
I enclose a letter of Craig's which explains itself. He is to dine here on Friday to meet Binyon. He wants to get the Print Room to take a series of designs (not plans but drawings and effects) of the new "invention" as a record. . . . If we are to get this design I may be anxious to put off *King's Threshold* till we can use it. . . . I am inclined to get his advice on all our scenic difficulties— perhaps to come to Dublin for the purpose. It would be a fine new start for us and put a new force in much that we do. It would not prevent Robert designing but would give us all the mechanism — a mountain to put our mountain on.[1]

8 January.
Craig dined with me last night and after Binyon had gone made drawings etc and explained further his "place" or whatever one should call his invention. I am to see his model on Monday at 5 — I think I shall, if it seems right, order one for us (this will cost he says about £2 for material and about £4 for the man's time). I asked if we would get his scene in time for *Oedipus* but he wants us to play about with his model first and master its effects. If we accept the invention I must agree, he says, to use it for all my poetical work in the future. I would gladly agree. I now think from what he told me that a certain modification will give us an entirely adequate open air scene. That we shall have a means of staging everything that is not naturalistic, and that out of his invention may grow a completely new method even for our naturalistic plays. I think we could get rid of side scenes even for naturalistic plays.[2]

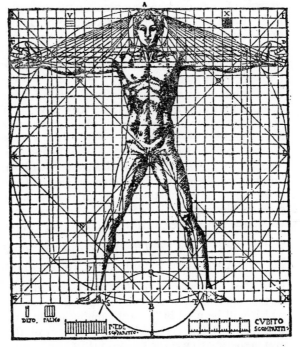

THE MASK

THE JOURNAL OF THE ART OF THE THEATRE. VOLUME ONE, NUMBER ONE MARCH 1908.

AFTER THE PRACTISE THE THEORY

THE CONTENTS OF THE FIRST NUMBER INCLUDE:
GEOMETRY. THE ARTISTS OF THE THEATRE OF THE FUTURE by GORDON CRAIG.
A NOTE UPON MASKS by JOHN BALANCE. SERLIO'S THEATRE IN ITALY; A TRANSLATION.
MADAME ELEONORA DUSE. THE REAL DRAMA IN SPAIN by EDWARD HUTTON.
BOOK REVIEWS. EDITORIAL NOTES. ANNOUNCEMENTS.
ILLUSTRATIONS. THREE SCENE DESIGNS AND TWO PLANS FOR A THEATRE FROM THE
TREATISE ON PERSPECTIVE OF SEBASTIANO SERLIO. A DESIGN FROM THE BOOK OF
VITRUVIO. THREE DESIGNS FOR MASKS by E. THESLEFF. VIGNETTES, ETC.

GEOMETRY. Beauty.... or Divine Demonstration, knows no confusion. It has the perfect balance. It remains true once and for ever.... needs no proof.... can reveal itself without words or arguments, and when we see I we again see Paradise. It is the dear Heaven. Science,... or Human Demonstration, t continually calling upon proof, trusting in many words, is as a restless Balance which continually rises and falls with the uncertainty of the centuries ... the restless Terror; has become the only Evil.

36. *The Mask*, edited by Gordon Craig. Vol. I, No. 1, Florence, March 1908.
Title page (reduced). Original 13 × 9".

Yeats gave Craig a version of the introductory essay he had written for *Plays for an Irish Theatre*, to be printed in *The Mask*, where it appeared under the title 'The Tragic Theatre' in the October issue (Volume 3, Number (4-6)). Craig printed an announcement that his scenery would be used at the Abbey in the January issue and Yeats had this announcement reprinted in the Abbey Theatre programme for 3 March 1910:

EXTRACT FROM "THE MASK."
A Quarterly Publication devoted to the Art of the Theatre.

Mr. Gordon Craig, having perfected a scene for the Poetic Drama, a scene capable of as much expression as the human voice or face, has determined to make use of this scene in the production of *Hamlet*, which he is preparing for the Moscow Art Theatre. Mr. Craig has been on a visit to England, and has shown a full size model of this scene to several artists.
Miss Ellen Terry has accepted it for a forthcoming revival, and the large scene itself has been made for her.
Mr. Craig's admiration for the work of the National Theatre of Ireland has induced him to present this scene to Mr. W. B. Yeats and Lady Gregory for use in their Dublin Theatre. We shall write more about this "scene" in our next number. "What a nice place," said a musician on being shown this "scene," and indeed that is the right name for it. . . . "a place," not a "scene." . . . It is indeed that strange and wonderful place called the land of imagination. It has not been seen before, and now that it has been brought upon earth (into the theatre of all places) it will to those of imagination prove a blessing. "Is it practical?" We know the question. "Yes, it is," now you know the answer. It is so practical that . . . but wait till the next number.[3]

The next issue of *The Mask* did not contain any further details, but the April 1910 issue had the following note:

In the last number of *The Mask* it was stated that this number would contain further information about Mr. Gordon Craig's Scene for the Poetic Drama which will be used in his forthcoming production of *Hamlet* in Moscow and which Miss Ellen Terry and the Directors of the Irish National Theatre are also preparing to use for various pieces.
The material relating to this Scene has, however, proved so abundant and so interesting that, rather than treat of it briefly and insufficiently in this number, we have wished to defer writing about it further until we can do so more fully. Indeed, a book upon this subject is now in preparation and further details of this will be given in an early number of *The Mask*.[4]

Craig's promised description of his Scene was not printed until July 1915 in *The Mask*, Volume 7, No. (2) which was largely devoted to his invention, but he submitted a specification for his Patent Application, dated 19 February 1910.

COMPLETE SPECIFICATION.
Improvements in Stage Scenery.

I, EDWARD GORDON CRAIG, Stage Manager, of Arena Goldoni, Florence, Italy, do hereby declare the nature of this invention and in what manner the same is to be performed, to be particularly described and ascertained in and by the following statement : —
My invention relates to apparatus for producing scenic effects on the stage and is particularly adapted for use in the representation of "poetic drama."
In the representation of such plays the producer has hitherto been obliged to choose between the alternatives of either employing scenery formed and

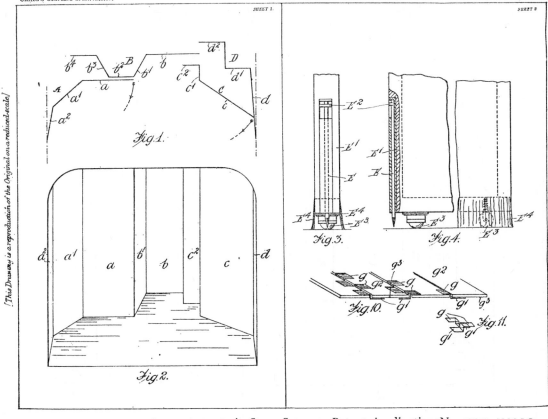

37. *Improvements in Stage Scenery*. Patent Application No. 1771. H.M.S.O.
1910 (reduced).

painted so as to produce the illusion of the actual scene intended by the playwright, or using plain curtains as a background. Many persons have come to
the conclusion that the latter method has certain æsthetic advantages and it
has the material advantage of cheapness and easy transport.

The object of my invention is to produce a device which shall present the
æsthetic advantages of the plain curtain but shall further be capable of a
multitude of effects which although not intended to produce an illusion shall
nevertheless assist the imagination of the spectator by suggestion.

My device is further intended to combine the artistic variety and mechanical
advantages of painted scenery with the portable nature of the curtain.

My invention consists in the use of a series of double jointed folding screens
standing on the stage and painted in monochrome — preferably white or pale
yellow. The screens may be used as background and in addition to this use
may be so arranged as to project into the foreground at various angles of perspective so as to suggest various physical conditions, such as, for example, the
corner of a street, or the interior of a building; by this means suggestion, not
representation, is relied upon and nevertheless variety is obtainable. The device
possesses the great advantage that the variety of effect is obtained from a very
simple apparatus which may be readily transported from place to place and
easily arranged and moved on the stage. Moreover this device is to all intents
and purposes self-supporting and, unlike scenery or curtains, does not require
to be suspended from above.

The screens may be mounted on any suitable arrangement of castors and
provided with struts or other suitable means for retaining the screens in their
arranged positions.

A.D. 1910. JAN. 24. N.º 1771.
CRAIG'S COMPLETE SPECIFICATION.

[4 SHEETS]

SHEET 3

SHEET 4.

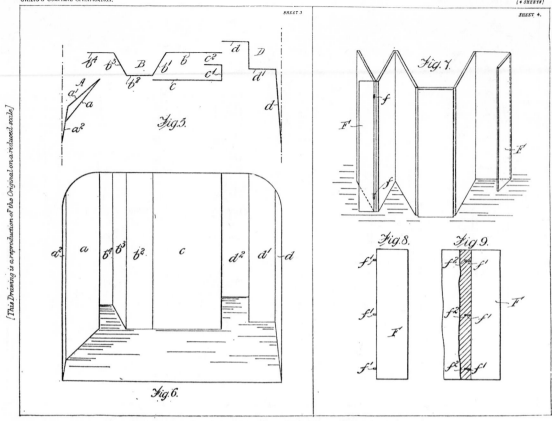

38. *Improvements in Stage Scenery.* Patent Application No. 1771. H.M.S.O.
1910 (reduced).

The accompanying drawings illustrate the way in which the invention is carried into effect.

A series of folding double jointed screens, indicated by A, B, C, D, as a whole, are arranged as shown diagrammatically in plan Figure 1 to convey by suggestion to the spectator the representation of the interior of a building, see Figure 2.

The screens may be formed with leaves of equal or varying widths as in Figures 1 and 5, and the end leaves provided with pointed struts E, Figures 3 and 4, arranged preferably within the frame E^1 of the leaf to be forced into the boards by means of the thumb or like piece E^2, and to hide the castors E^3 which may be of the ball or roller type and the space between the bottom of the leaves and the stage a valance E^4 carried by the lower part of the frame of the leaf may be employed and if desired an additional strut or struts F, Figure 7, may be used to assist in retaining the screens in their arranged position on the stage. These additional struts F, which may take the form of a leaf and be of the same or less dimensions as the leaves of a screen, may be permanently hinged as at f, Figure 7, to either end of a leaf or to the outer end of the end leaves, or said struts may be provided as in Figure 8 with pegs f^1 to take into holes f^2 in the framework E of the screen as in Figure 9.

The hinges between the leaves of a screen may best be formed in the manner indicated in Figures 10 and 11, that is to say, the hinges are formed of strips of webbing inserted between two adjacent leaves and the ends g of said strips fastened to the front face g^2 of the leaves, whilst the ends g^1 are fastened to the rear face g^3.

Should it be necessary in the course of the play to change the scene suggested in Figure 2 to an exterior view, then the leaf a of screen A, Figure 1, is swung round so as to hide leaf a^1 and practically leaf a^2, disclosing leaves b^4, b^3, b^2 of screen B. Screen C is then swung round, covering leaves c^1, c^2 of said screen C, disclosing leaves d, d^1, d^2 of screen D and hiding the leaves b, b^1 of screen B, the screens then being in the position shown diagrammatically in Figure 5, conveying by suggestion an exterior, as in Figure 6.

If desired the stage may be divided up by lines, or otherwise marked to facilitate the ready positioning of the screens according to a predetermined arrangement or chart.

From the above it will be obvious that by moving more than one leaf in each of the screens and by moving the screens themselves a multitude of suggested effects can be obtained.

After the performance the screens are readily folded, packed flat and transported to their fresh destination, taking up in packing and transport but little room.

Having now particularly described and ascertained the nature of my said invention and in what manner the same is to be performed, I declare that what I claim is : —

1. A device for producing scenic effects on the stage, consisting of a series of monochromatic folding double jointed screens standing on the stage and arranged so as to project at various angles of perspective to assist the imagination of the spectators by suggestion of various physical conditions such as the interior or exterior of a building substantially as herein described.

2. Monochromatic double jointed folding screens with leaves of equal or varying width provided with castors and struts substantially as and for the purposes set forth.[5]

*

During the Spring and Summer of 1910 Yeats experimented with Craig's model and found the 'Scene' an extremely flexible instrument. He found that he could plot the scenic arrangements in a notebook of squared paper and he wrote, in 'The Tragic Theatre':

All summer I have been playing with a little model, where there is a scene capable of endless transformation, of the expression of every mood that does not require a photographic reality. Mr. Craig — who has invented all this — has permitted me to set up upon the stage of the Abbey another scene that corresponds to this, in the scale of a foot for an inch, and henceforth I shall be able, by means so simple that one laughs, to lay the events of my plays amid a grandeur like that of Babylon; and where there is neither complexity nor compromise nothing need go wrong, no lamps become suddenly unmasked, no ill-painted corner come suddenly into sight. Henceforth I can all but "produce" my play while I write it, moving hither and thither little figures of cardboard through gay or solemn light and shade, allowing the scene to give the words and the words the scene. I am very grateful for he has banished a whole world that wearied me and was undignified and given me forms and lights upon which I can play as upon some stringed instrument.[6]

As he worked out his stage plans on the Craig model stage, Yeats discovered a new freedom in stage presentation and the further possibilities opened up to him by lighting the arrangements of the screens in different ways.

The primary value of Mr. Craig's invention is that it enables one to use light in a more natural and more beautiful way than ever before. We get rid of all the top hamper of the stage, all the hanging ropes and scenes which prevent the free play of light. It is now possible to substitute in the shading of one scene real light and shadow for painted light and shadow. Continually in the contemporary theatre, the painted shadow is out of relation to the direction of the light, and what is more to the point, one loses the extraordinary beauty of delicate light and shade. This means, however, an abolition of realism, for it makes scene painting which is, of course, a matter of painted light and shade impossible. One enters into a world of decorative effect which gives the actor a renewed importance. There is less to compete against him, for there is less detail, though there is more beauty.[7]

Yeats plotted the results of his experiments with the model stage and the screens in a small quarto notebook, its page 8¼ by 6½ inches in size and ruled in feint quarter-inch squares. The notebook originally consisted of forty-eight pages (twenty-four leaves) but one leaf is missing and its cognate leaf is now detached from the sequence. In my description of the notebook I have used the numbering 1 to 44 for the pages still in their original order. This document, which remains in the possession of the Yeats family,[8] reveals how intensely Yeats worked at the application of Craig's principles to the needs of the Abbey Theatre stage.

The notebook opens with a series of sketches and notes based on Lady Gregory's play *Mirandolina* which was first produced at the Abbey on 24 February 1910. Yeats arrived back in Dublin for the first production of *The Green Helmet* on 10 February and looked at the rehearsals of *Mirandolina*, full of enthusiasm for Craig's scenery. He revealed his new view of stage presentation in a note printed in the Abbey Theatre programme of the first performance.

The rather unsatisfactory scenic arrangements have been made necessary by the numerous little scenes, and the necessity of making the intervals between them as short as possible. We hope before very long to have a better convention for plays of the kind. — W.B.Y.[9]

I feel that *Mirandolina* provided Yeats with his first opportunity to relate Craig's screens to an actual production, giving him a standard against which to assess his own attempts at design. The *Mirandolina* notes occupy pages 1 to 11 of the notebook and begin with a blurred watercolour sketch, probably a front elevation, with the word 'Kitchen' at top left and, below the drawing, a note that seems to read 'spotty lemon yellow'. On the next opening (pp. 2-3) a pencil sketch develops the scheme of the first drawing but is cancelled or deleted. Facing this, on p. 2, some pencilled directions are written in two drafts, partly deleted, but these appear in a 'fair copy' written in ink on p. 5. This reads :

⌐might have stencil in
      blue
(1) 'In parlour' room with 3 doors. Used also in Act III scene II
                 also Act II scene II
                 ~~red stencil &~~
(2) Captain's room . design with ~~brown gold bands~~ . no door
                    pale blue bands & stencil.
(3) Another room . screening (?) lengthened room
                    blue curtained
          (or scene with ∧ door I R)
    Count's room
(4) Mirandolera room — Kitchen
          3 cloths to be painted

————

Colour all scene
~~X~~ New yellow — marked out with darker red.
    window frames pale blue — & curtain of door in 3
    pale blue.

These notes clearly relate to the list of scenes in the Abbey Theatre programme of 24 February 1910 (the first production of *Mirandolina*) which read,

Act 1, Scene 1 — An Inn Parlour.
      „   2 — The Captain's Room.
      „   3 — Another Room.
Act 2, Scene 1 — The Captain's Room.
      „   2 — The Count's Room.
Act 3, Scene 1 — An Inn Parlour.
      „   2 —   „   „ [10]

Mirandolina was not published until 1924 and in the printed text the stage directions give a simpler scheme :

Act   I scene (1). *Large room at an Inn, with rough furniture and three doors.*
       scene 2. *Captain's parlour*
Act II scene (1) *The Captain's room with a table laid for dinner*
Act III scene (1) *Room with three doors as in Act I, with a table, and linen*
             to be ironed.
       scene 2. *The same room.*[11]

The sketches for *Mirandolina* continue through to page 11 of the notebook, with further plans and elevations. Then Yeats turned to methods of staging his own plays and page 13 has the first plan which is specifically designed for the dimensions of the Abbey stage, with its twenty-one foot proscenium opening and fifteen foot depth. If an outline plan of the Abbey stage is divided into foot squares, the dimension to which Yeats applied the square rulings on the notebook pages, his intended plans can be easily related to the stage.

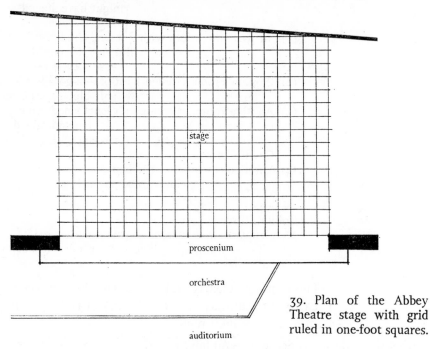

stage

proscenium

orchestra

auditorium

39. Plan of the Abbey Theatre stage with grid ruled in one-foot squares.

The plan on page 13 is a simple box set arrangement with its width marked as '20' (feet). There are two openings at the back and a wider opening or alcove in the centre of each side. There is a cloth to mask the upstage openings, inscribed 'blue or wood cloth.' The sketch is titled

Scene for Deirdre
or Baile's Strand (if doors taken out).

This is followed on the next opening by two sketches, play not specified, of which the first is headed

or this
but not so good I think

and deleted. Underneath, the arrangement of the two openings in the back of the set is repeated with the backing cloth specified as blue. The next sketch, on page 17, shows a development of the experiment, probably for *Deirdre*, although the play is not named,

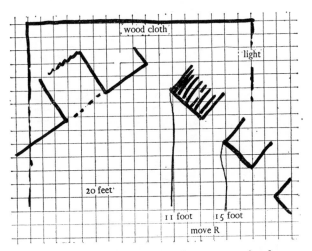

40. W. B. Yeats. Transcription of scene notebook, p. 17.

in which the arrangement of alcove and openings is set diagonally on the stage and the word 'light' appears for the first time.

The horizontal arrangement is used again on page 19, which is headed *Deirdre,* but with the large alcove, curtained at upstage centre and an opening at upstage left where the wood cloth is used as backing. Page 21 has a set for *The Land of Heart's Desire,* or *Deirdre,* with a nineteen foot proscenium opening.

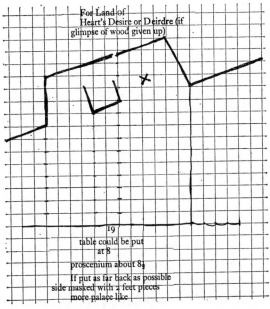

41. W. B. Yeats. Transcription of scene notebook, p. 21.

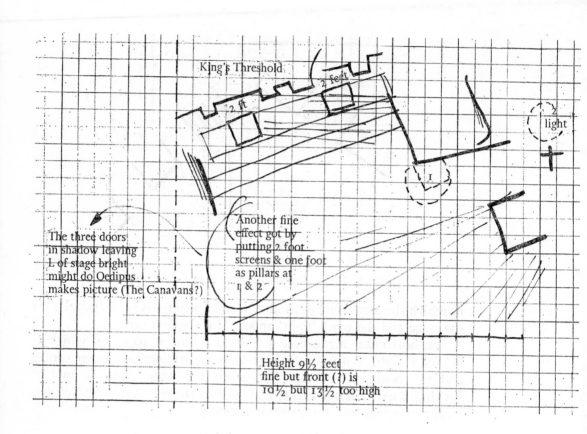

King's Threshold

2 feet

2 ft

light

2

I

Another fine
effect got by
putting 2 foot
screens & one foot
as pillars at
1 & 2

The three doors
in shadow leaving
L of stage bright
might do Oedipus
makes picture (The Canavans?)

Height 9½ feet
fine but front (?) is
10½ but 13½ too high

42. W. B. Yeats. Transcription of scene notebook, p. 23.

Here the setting of the height of the variable proscenium arch is given and this aspect of Craig's invention is explored further in the next drawing, for *The King's Threshold*, on pages 22-23. The elements of this are redisposed on page 25, to be set full depth on the stage, with a note that reads 'measurement nos (?) exact.'

A new arrangement appears on page 27, with three semicircular alcoves upstage and further notes on lighting effects.

Page 29 reverts to an arrangement for *The King's Threshold* which was also considered for *On Baile's Strand*.

A further arrangement, pillars set inside a curved back wall made up of one foot screens, appears in two versions on pages 30 and 31, and on the latter the use of footlights is suggested. This is followed by a study of the 'effects of narrow doors', page 32, and of directional lighting on pillars, page 33. Pages 34 to 37 contain draft arrangements for the first setting by Yeats which was to be executed on the

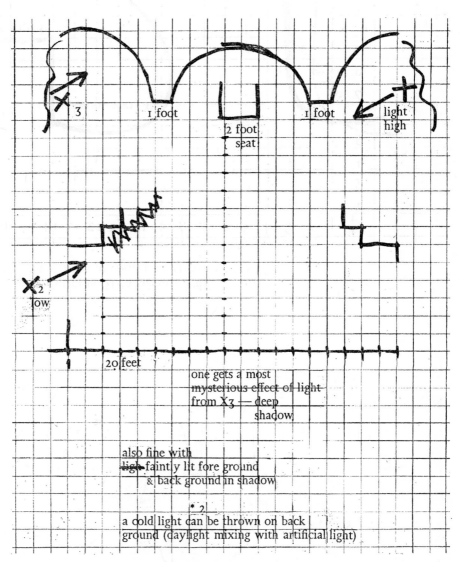

3 1 foot 2 foot seat 1 foot light high

X 2
ow

20 feet

one gets a most
mysterious effect of light
from X3 — deep
shadow

also fine with
light faintly lit fore ground
& back ground in shadow

* 2

a cold light can be thrown on back
ground (daylight mixing with artificial light)

43. W. B. Yeats. Transcription of scene notebook, p. 27.

stage, that for *The Deliverer* by Lady Gregory, which is drawn in
some detail on page 37 and followed by some tentative rearrange-
ments on pages 38 to 41. Pages 42 and 43 contain the plans of the
two plays first presented with the Craig screens at the Abbey, *The
Hour-Glass* by W. B. Yeats for which the arrangement of the screens
was designed by Craig, and Yeats's own arrangement for *The Deliverer*. This is reproduced overleaf. The remainder of the notebook
contains variations on these settings.

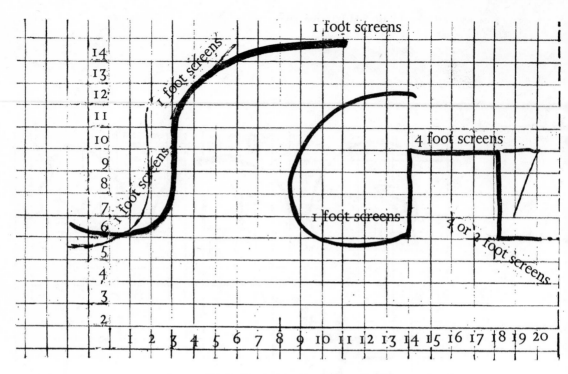

44. W. B. Yeats. Transcription of scene notebook, pp. 42-43.
(p. 42 above, p. 43 on facing page)

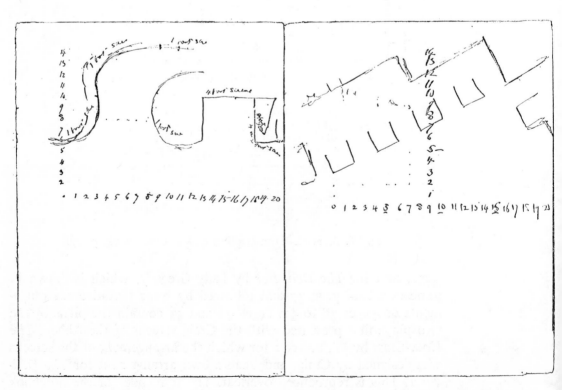

45. W. B. Yeats. Scene notebook, pp. 42-43 (reduced).

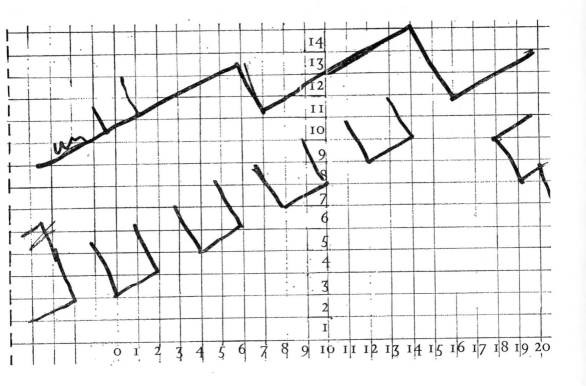

Craig's setting for *The Hour-Glass* can be seen in three versions—Yeats's plan of the stage arrangement, the watercolour reproduced as an illustration in *Plays for an Irish Theatre*, 1911, and in Craig's wood engraving dated 1913 from the same subject but reversed right to left, of which Craig later wrote,

I called it *The Hourglass* because it wasn't *unlike* — but strictly not *like*. Compare it with the drawing in Yeats's volume of *Plays for an Irish Theatre*. *That* is precise.[12]

*

46. Edward Gordon Craig. Setting for *The Hour-Glass*. Wood engraving, 1913.

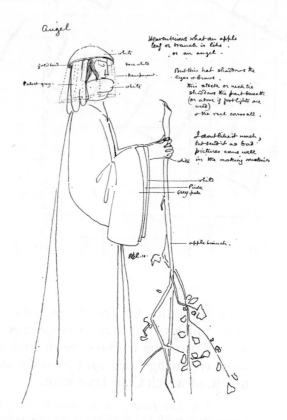

47. *The Hour-Glass.* Costume design for the Angel
by Edward Gordon Craig.

Gordon Craig also designed the costumes and masks to be used in *The Hour-Glass* and these must have seemed startling innovations to the Dublin audience. Craig's costumes did not draw on any period for their style but were devised by Craig from Yeats's text, with sometimes irreverent notes on the drawings. On the design for the Wise Man, Craig wrote,

No arms showing : only sleeves —
"wise" men do nothing
besides I can't draw hands.

But at the same time there are immensely practical directions about the cut and hang of the costumes. The drawing for 'A Scholar's Angel' is highly detailed and has two typical comments,

A scholar's eye I fear sees an angel in grey — & besides — his entrance is an imperceptible thing according to the drama — colour would hurt the mind there — — it might come later through light but —

and

So one thinks on paper — and when one comes to the stage one feels quite other — — I am a regular German to put it down so exactly — it is disgusting. But some pickings from it may serve you.

But Craig's greatest contribution to Yeats's idea of theatre was his lesson to Yeats in the significance of the mask in theatre. His drawing for the Fool in *The Hour-Glass* is for

Fool with a mask attached to a head dress.

The character is to have

A clear brow
clear eyes
great but not withered mouth

and should convey

a hint of clown
a hint of Death
and of sphinx
and of boy.[13]

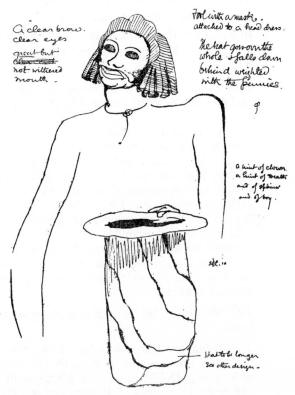

48. *The Hour-Glass.* Costume design for the Fool by Edward Gordon Craig.

49. *The Hour-Glass.* Woodcut of the Fool's mask
by Edward Gordon Craig, 1911.

The stage costume design was developed as an illustration for *Plays for an Irish Theatre* and Craig also made a woodcut of the Fool's mask. That the mask was not used in the 1911 production is shown by Yeats's Note to the revised play, printed in *Plays for an Irish Theatre*:

Up till the present year we always played it in front of an olive-green curtain, and dressed the Wise Man and his Pupils in various shades of purple (with a little green here and there); and because in all these decorative schemes, which are based on colour, one needs, I think, a third colour subordinate to the other two, we dressed the Fool in red-brown, and put touches of red-brown in the Wife's dress and painted the chair and desk the same colour. Last winter, however, we revived the play with costumes taken chiefly from designs by Mr. Gordon Craig, and with the screens he has shown us how to make and use, arranged as in the drawing in this book, and with effects that depend but little on colour, and greatly upon delicate changes of tone. The Fool was dressed as in Mr. Craig's drawing, but he advised us against using the mask till he was able to see to the making of it himself. The same Fool and mask, the Fat Fool of folklore who is "as wide and wild as a hill" and not the Thin Fool of modern romance, may go with a masked Blind Man into *On Baile's Strand.*[14]

This should be taken together with a comment in the Preface to the book:

The design for *The Hour-Glass* shows the scene as it was used in Dublin and "The Fool" — who belongs to *The Hour-Glass* and *On Baile's Strand* is as he was in Dublin in the first play, except that we have found no one who can make us a mask of leather, and we do not yet know how to make it ourselves.[15]

50. *On Baile's Strand*. Etching of the Blind Man's mask
by Edward Gordon Craig, 1911.

The mask design made such an impression on Yeats that he decided
that the Fool of *On Baile's Strand* should appear in the same mask
and he asked Craig to design a companion mask for the Blind Man in
that play. Craig complied with the request and made an etching for
the Blind Man, on which he commented in the catalogue of his
Dublin exhibition in 1913,

This is a design for a mask. It is rather more realistic than a mask should be,
but as a beginning I dare say it will do. The eyes are closed, they are still
cross, and I take it that the man sees with his nose. I imagine that he smells
his way in the dark, and he seems to keep up an eternal kind of windy
whistling with his pursed up lips. The advantage of a mask over a face is that
it is always repeating unerringly the poetic fancy, repeating on Monday in
1912 exactly what it said on Saturday in 1909 and what it will say on
Wednesday in 1999. Durability was the dominant idea in Egyptian art. The
theatre must learn that lesson. "But," you say, "the actor does not live for
ever, he is not immortal." Exactly, my friends, but his mask can live for ever.
Let us again cover his face with a mask in order that his expression — the
visualised expression of the Poetic spirit — shall be everlasting.[16]

Yeats's delight at Craig's designs was conveyed to his friends. He showed the costume designs to Robert Gregory and to Charles Ricketts, despite his earlier doubts about Ricketts' reaction to Craig's work. He wrote from London to ask Lady Gregory about her son's opinions:

What did Robert think of the designs? I am going to show them to Ricketts to-night. We were right about the pupils as you see. I am very much excited by the thought of putting the fool into a mask and rather amused at the idea of an angel in a golden domino. I should have to write some words into the play. "They fear to meet the eyes of men being too pure for mortal gaze" or the like. Craig evidently wants to keep what is supernatural from being inhuman. If the masks work right I would put the fool and the blind man in *Baile's Strand* into masks. It would give a wildness and extravagance that would be fine. I should also like the Abbey to be the first modern theatre to use the mask.[17]

In November, he wrote from Dublin to his father,

The Craig scenery will give us a very strange and beautiful stage. He has designed all the costumes and scene for a new production of *The Hour-Glass*. Given one of the characters a mask in the old Italian way. I shall get all my plays into the Craig scene and a new one of Lady Gregory's* which is a symbolical play ostensibly about Moses really about Parnell.[18]

But the practical work of installing Craig's scenery at the Abbey was not without its difficulties. As architect to the theatre, Joseph Holloway was consulted about the alterations to the stage structure which included relaying the stage floor to remove the traditional rake on which the screens with their castors would probably be unstable. On 14 July 1910, Holloway

Met W. B. Yeats at the Abbey about lowering of stage to level of footlights, and also discussed the Gordon Craig scheme for reducing the size of stage pictures by an arrangement that expands or contracts from sides and top automatically. But somehow to Mr. Barlow and me it did not seem very practical on a small stage like the Abbey. While waiting for the builder to come, Yeats spoke of Gordon Craig being so sensitive, and he foresaw the amount of correspondence he would draw down on his head if he could not carry out Craig's scheme intact.[19]

However, the difficulties were overcome somehow and the alterations were made and the screens built so that by 29 November Holloway could record that he had

called in at the Abbey and saw the stagehands setting Gordon Craig's new ideas of scenery — a series of square box-like pillars saffron-hued, with saffron background, wings, sky pieces, and everything. The entire setting struck me

The Deliverer.

as like as peas, only on a big scale, of the blocks I as a child built houses of. As Yeats never played with blocks in his youth, Gordon Craig's childish ideas give him keen delight now.[20]

*

But 1910 was not an entirely happy year in Yeats's theatre life. In February Miss Horniman agreed to pay her subsidy until the end of the year and then to transfer the ownership of the Abbey outright to the Directors for a payment of £1,000, an offer made by Yeats to secure the subsidy for the year, though Miss Horniman would have preferred to withdraw at the end of 1909. The already uneasy relationship between the Directors of the theatre and its patroness became a pitched battle in May when, inadvertently, the theatre did not close on the occasion of the death of King Edward VII. Miss Horniman took this as a deliberate insult conceived by the Irish nationalists who, she felt, were gaining control of the Abbey and she wrote a violent letter to the Dublin papers, which was printed on 14 May. In this she demanded an apology, saying that unless this was forthcoming her subsidy would be withdrawn immediately. Although an apology from the Directors and the Management of the theatre appeared in the same issue of the papers, this was not deemed sufficient and Miss Horniman reiterated her threat with the added warning that the renewal of the Patent would also be due in November. Yeats was away during the incident and after he returned he refused to add to the apology already published. Miss Horniman refused to pay the final two instalments of the subsidy and the Directors witheld the £1,000 purchase price for the theatre. Miss Horniman threatened legal action and the case finally went to an arbitrator who ruled, in April 1911, in favour of the Directors. On this bitter note, the link between the Abbey Theatre and its founding patroness ended.

In November Yeats and Lady Gregory applied for a renewal of the Theatre Patent for a period of twenty-one years and the Application was heard by the Solicitor-General at Dublin Castle. The lawyer representing the Directors, Mr. Day,

explained the assistance which Miss Horniman had given to the Abbey Theatre, but now that the Patent was on the point of expiring she thought the public ought to take their share of the responsibility. The Theatre had never paid, and Miss Horniman now proposed to hand over to the applicants her Patent on payment of £1000. That proposal had been accepted. Lady Gregory and Mr. Yeats proposed to raise £5000, and already £2000 had been subscribed. Three very well known gentlemen in Civil Service circles, Mr. W. F. Bailey, Mr. Bourke and Mr. Hanson, were prepared to act as Trustees of this fund.[21]

The Patent application was granted and Yeats and Lady Gregory could plan the next developments in their theatre. Yeats mentioned the Patent in a letter to his father on 27 November and reported that the theatre was getting good audiences and was even fashionable.[22] His essay, 'The Tragic Theatre,' was printed in the October issue of *The Mask* and the Abbey was preparing to stage its first presentation in Craig's screens.

On Thursday 12 January 1911 the curtain of the Abbey Theatre rose on the first plays staged in any country in Craig's screens, just a year before their use in *Hamlet* at the Moscow Art Theatre. The screens were used to stage two of the three pieces presented in the programme, the first production of *The Deliverer*, a tragic comedy by Lady Gregory and a revival of *The Hour-Glass* by Yeats. The third piece in the bill, which was played in conventional scenery, was another one-act play by Lady Gregory, *The Full Moon*. The programme carried a note which read:

THE NEW SCENERY AT THE ABBEY

The method of decoration in *The Deliverer* and *The Hour Glass* was invented by Mr. Gordon Craig for the famous Art Theatre of Moscow, where it will make possible a performance of the full *Hamlet*, with a different decoration for every little scene, so rapidly can the scenes be changed. Thursday night will, however, be its first public use. It does not aim at effects of realism, but at a decoration of the stage almost infinite in the variety of its expression and suggestion, and for the first time makes possible effects of lights and shadow various, powerful and delicate. Mr. Craig has given us the right to make use of his patent in Ireland, with the generosity of a great artist, and because he respects our work and ambition.[23]

The new method of stage presentation at the Abbey was generally thought to be a success. The reviewer in *The Irish Times* found,

in the first place a reduction of the stage furniture to its simplest elements, so that the figures of the players stand out more prominently against the primitive background and attention is concentrated on the human and truly expressive elements of the drama. There is next a careful design and adjustment of the simple elements of staging which still further tends to secure that effect. Lastly, there is a similar care in regard to the supplementary elements — lighting arrangements and costuming.[24]

While *The Hour-Glass*, fully designed by Craig, received generally favourable mention, *The Deliverer*, directed by its author and with the stage arrangement and lighting devised by Yeats and costumes after suggestions by Craig, fell far short of success, either as a play or in its presentation. The occasion gave Holloway an opportunity to carry his antipathy to Craig's whole concept a step further,

With a great flourish of egotistical trumpets on the part of the management and Yeats in dress clothes with crush opera hat in hand, the Gordon Craig freak scenery and lighting were tried at the Abbey in Lady Gregory's Hiberno-Egyptian one-act tragic comedy *The Deliverer*, and also in Yeats's morality *The Hour Glass*. And while most voted the innovation an affected failure with possibilities for effective stage pictures, none considered it in any way an improvement on the old methods. . . . The dresses designed or carried out from sketches supplied by Craig were most unsightly and ungainly, especially in *The Deliverer*. The ladies wore a sort of short hobble skirt that reached a little below the knees and brought to mind to Mr. Hughes *The Playboy's* description of "the twelve eastern maidens in their shifts." [25]

*

The Irish Theatre was once more Yeats's. Freed from the involvement with Miss Horniman, and even from the influence of the Fays, he was, for the time being, in command. He planned an American tour for the company, and to keep the theatre open while the principal players were away, he set about forming a second company. This would play his poetic drama in versions revised in the light of the knowledge of stage practice he had gleaned from Craig. And, indeed, the published versions of the revised plays, coming as they did after Abbey productions, seem to carry out the motto of *The Mask*, 'After the Practice the Theory.'

And he reflected his own practical knowledge of theatre, and the need to learn from experience the art of stagecraft, in his essay 'The Tragic Theatre,'

It was only by watching my own plays upon the stage that I came to understand that this reverie, this twilight between sleeping and waking, this bout of fencing, alike on the stage and in the mind, between man and phantoms, this perilous path as on the edge of a sword, is the condition of tragic pleasure, and to understand why it is so rare and so brief.[26]

After the 1911 production of *The Hour-Glass*, Yeats set about revising the play extensively and rewrote the dialogue in blank verse. This new text was printed in *The Mask* for April 1913 (Vol. 5, No. (4)). The stage directions reflect details of the Craig scenery and costumes. The opening scene was played on the forestage,

The stage is brought out into the orchestra so as to leave a wide space in front of the stage curtain. Pupils come in and stand before the stage curtain, which is still closed. . . .[27]

After the preliminary scene between the Pupils and the Fool,

one of the Pupils draws back the stage curtains showing the Master sitting at his desk. There is an hour-glass upon his desk or in a bracket on the wall. . . .[28]

and the Angel is Craig's,

An Angel has come in. It may be played by a man if a man can be found with
the right voice . . . , and may wear a little golden domino and a halo made of
metal. Or the whole face may be a beautiful mask.[29]

On 16 February 1911, *The Land of Heart's Desire* was played by
the Abbey Company for the first time (see pp. 18-19). Yeats disliked
it 'without knowing what (he) disliked in it,'[30] and set about revising
this, and others of his plays, with his new experience of the practice
of stagecraft to guide him. This practice, coming before the theory,
led to revivals of several of the plays and the consequent experience
is reflected in the later editions of the plays.

In September the Abbey players left for an American tour and
Yeats established a second company of younger actors to keep the
theatre open during the tour. He engaged Nugent Monck, an Anglo-
Irish actor who had made a reputation in producing medieval drama,
to direct this new company. Monck made use of the Craig scenery
at the Abbey, notably in a series of productions of medieval plays —
The Interlude of Youth on 16 November, *The Second Shepherd's Play*
a week later, *The Annunciation* and *The Flight into Egypt* on 4 January 1912 and, just before he left the company, *The Worlde and the
Chylde* on 29 February.

Yeats gave an interview to *The Irish Times* in September 1911,
before he left on a brief visit to launch the principal company's tour
in America, and described the formation of the second company:

. . . while our company is away the school of dramatic art, lately founded at
the Abbey Theatre, will carry on its work. We have placed at the head of it
for the autumn Mr. Nugent Monck, an Irishman of imagination and energy,
who has learnt his art of the stage under Mr. Poel, of the Elizabethan Stage
Society. We do not seek to form in Dublin a rival to Mr. Tree's school. Our
object is to train players to express the mind, and to copy the life of Ireland.
Mr. Monck, with the help of his pupils, and probably some professional
players, will give certain productions at the Abbey Theatre — perhaps a
classical play, probably some old interludes and mysteries, as well as reviving
a play or two from our repertory. We hope that in the course of time we
shall have trained in this way a second company which will play at the Abbey
when the main company is away, and we shall not greatly regret if we train
also some rivals to ourselves.[31]

Monck used the Craig screens to stage his production of the revised
text of *The Countess Cathleen* on 14 December 1911, a production
which is reflected in Yeats's new stage directions to the revised
version, published in London in 1912 as Volume I of 'Dublin Plays.'
His note in that edition gives an idea of the staging of Monck's
production:

Now at last I have made a complete revision to make it suitable for performance at the Abbey Theatre.* The first two scenes are almost wholly new, and throughout the play I have added or left out such passages as a stage experience of some years showed me encumbered the action; the play in its first form having been written before I knew anything of the theatre. . . . The new end is particularly suited to the Abbey stage, where the stage platform can be brought out in front of the proscenium and have a flight of steps at one side up which the Angel comes, crossing towards the back of the stage at the opposite side. The principal lighting is from two arc lights in the balcony which throw their lights into the faces of the players, making footlights unnecessary. The room at Shemus Rua's house is suggested by a great grey curtain — a colour which becomes full of rich tints under the stream of light from the arcs. The two or more arches in the third scene permit the use of a gauze. The short front scene before the last is just long enough when played with incidental music to allow the scene set behind it to be changed.[32]

---

*   THE COUNTESS CATHLEEN
(Revised Version)

Presented by the Irish National Theatre Society Limited (second company)
at the Abbey Theatre, Dublin
on Thursday 14 December 1911

Countess	Maire O'Neill
Oona	Oona Dara
Maire	Nell Byrne
Shemus	Patrick Murphy
Teig	Farrell Pelly
First Demon	Charles Power
Second Demon	W. J. Manser
Aleel	Nugent Monck
Steward	H. A. Browett
Old Woman	Sheila O'Sullivan
First Spirit	Maidha Tyrrell
Angel	Violet McCarthy
Miser	George St. John
Young Woman	Mildred Conway
Porter	Grenville Darling
Peasant Man	Ion Carter
Peasants	Mona Shiel, Eileen Cullen, Mona O'Beirne, Helen Slattery, Madge Slattery, N. Kelly, Eva Kelly, B. Mahony, D. Reddy, K. Reilly, J. Murray, Mæve O'Donnell, N. Clarke.

Dresses designed by Jeanie Moore
Forest Scene painted by J. F. Barlow
Produced by Nugent Monck

The revision of *The Countess Cathleen* at this time was possibly prompted by the proposal made by Messrs. Chappell, the London music publishers, that they should produce an operatic version of the play with a score by Leoni. Yeats felt that Craig should stage the opera but Chappell withdrew their interest and the project was abandoned.

On 22 February 1912, the finally revised *Land of Heart's Desire* was produced, and again Yeats reflected his close involvement with the theatre at this time in his Note on the published text of this version :

Till lately it was not part of the repertory of the Abbey Theatre, for I had grown to dislike it without knowing what I disliked in it. This winter, however, I have made many revisions and now it plays well enough to give me pleasure.[33]

The Countess Cathleen

By W. B. YEATS

Volume I. of Dublin Plays

PRICE ONE SHILLING NET

51. 'Dublin Plays' I. *The Countess Cathleen*, 1912. Front cover.

The 'theory' was reflected in Yeats's rewritten texts published at this period. During the year and a half after the introduction of screens at the Abbey, 'theatre editions' of several of the plays appeared. *The Countess Cathleen* and *The Land of Heart's Desire*

were issued as Volumes I and II of 'Dublin Plays' by T. Fisher Unwin
in 1912. Earlier, in June 1911, Bullen, under the imprint of his
Shakespeare Head Press, issued *Deirdre*. The back cover of *Deirdre*
announced the forthcoming *Plays for an Irish Theatre* as 'revised,
with new introductory Essay : illustrations by Norman (*sic*, later
corrected to Gordon) Craig.' Bullen also published similar editions of
The King's Threshold (November 1911), *Cathleen Ni Houlihan*, *The
Hour-Glass*, *On Baile's Strand*, *The Green Helmet* and *The Pot of
Broth*. A further revised edition of *Deirdre* appeared in 1914.

But the principal publication of this time in Yeats's theatre life
was *Plays for an Irish Theatre*, published in December 1911, which
contained seven plays, *Deirdre*, *The Green Helmet*, *On Baile's Strand*,
The King's Threshold, *The Shadowy Waters* in two versions, *The
Hour-Glass* and *Cathleen Ni Houlihan*. The essay 'The Tragic Theatre'
in an expanded form was the Preface to the book and there were new
notes to *Deirdre*, *The Green Helmet* and *The Hour-Glass*. The book
was illustrated with four designs by Gordon Craig, of which two
showed the setting and the Fool's costume from *The Hour-Glass* as
produced at the Abbey on 12 January 1911. The other two designs,
'The Heroic Age — Morning' and 'The Heroic Age — Evening' are
fine examples of Craig's 'scene' arrangement of figures in com-
positions of screens with atmospheric lighting. Of these, Yeats wrote
in his 'postscript' to the Preface :

Two of Mr. Craig's designs, "The Heroic Age — Morning," and "The Heroic
Age — Evening," are impressions worked out in Mr. Craig's scene, of the
world my people move in, rather than exact pictures of any moment of a
play. The one, however, suggests to me *On Baile's Strand*, and the other
Deirdre.[34]

And, in his note on *Deirdre*, he elaborated on the impact Craig's
'scene' had made on his approach to dramatic presentation,

Deirdre, like the other plays in this book, has been altered many times after
performance, till at last I had come to think I had put all my knowledge into
it and could not, apart from the always incalculable pleasure good playing
brings, look for greater pleasure than it had already given me. But now
because of Mr. Craig's scene which is fitted to so many moods and actions,
and makes possible natural and expressive light and shade, I have begun to
alter it again and to find in this a new excitement. Sooner or later it will be
tried at the Abbey Theatre with what is, I believe, a new stage effect. The
barbarous dark-faced men, who have not hitherto been all I imagined (perhaps
because our stage is shallow), will not show themselves directly to the eyes
when they pass the door, nor will the dark-faced messenger when he comes
and says that supper's ready, nor it may be Conchubar when he comes to spy
and not to fight. I will see passing shadows and standing shadows only.

Perhaps the light that casts them may grow blood-red as the sun sets, but of that I am not sure. I have tried these shadows upon the stage and thought them impressive, but as I have not tried them before an audience I leave the old directions for the present. Should these shadows become a permanent part of the representation I will have to abandon the windows and doors through which one sees at present a wood and evening sky. But, perhaps, shadows of leaves seen on the wall beside the door under a shifting light will accompany the Musician's long opening speech.[35]

*

One of the results of Nugent Monck's period at the Abbey was the founding of a School of Acting in which the company could train new actors who would, as Yeats saw, be more adaptable to his poetic drama than the older members of the company who had developed a very individual style which was superb in performing the folk and peasant drama on which the theatre's reputation was largely built. In March 1912, Yeats wrote to his father,

I've been very busy since I came back working at the Abbey Theatre School, we advertised for pupils last autumn, and got more than 60, out of these we have finally extracted, at the end of a long season of playing and being taught, a most excellent company of 17, plus a good many pupils we have not taken into it, some of whom promised to be good in time. We have produced a great number of plays and so kept the theatre open and we have now so many understudies that I think even Sara Allgood — if she comes back from America, as Jack says she will, "like Boadicea," will be much milder than ever before. The new people are better in tragic work of my sort than the old. Some we will bring to America next tour, and some we will leave here in Dublin as B Company to keep the theatre open and gradually, as we hope, to make a career for themselves as the old people have done. It is a moment of transition with us here. Nugent Monck — who has been the teacher of the School — has gone, and I am in charge until the Company arrives, which should be next week. I have done nothing but theatre for months now, and have hardly seen anyone outside it.[36]

Monck later founded the famous Maddermarket Theatre in Norwich and became one of the most influential figures in the development of style in the twentieth-century English theatre. His contribution to Yeats's development in theatre came at a most opportune time, when the theories of Craig were being put to the practical test. His work at the Abbey probably represented the nearest Yeats came to realising the ideal theatre he had projected in his essay, 'The Tragic Theatre' where he said that, given the freedom of Craig's method,

we shall have created a theatre that will please the poet and the player and the painter. An old quarrel will be ended, the stage will be beautifully decorated, every change will be full of meaning and yet never create a competing interest, or set bounds to the suggestions of speech and motion. At last liberated from the necessity of an always complete realisation, the producer, recovering caprice, will be as free as a modern painter, as Signor Mancini, let us say, to give himself up to an elliptical imagination. Gloster will be able to fall but from his own height and think that he has fallen from Dover Cliff, and Richard's and Richmond's tents can face one another again. We shall have made possible once more a noble, capricious, extravagant, resonant, fantastic art.[37]

*

On 16 July 1911 a dinner was given at the Café Royal in London to honour Craig. Yeats was on the organising committee, and the occasion was a brilliant success which did much to establish Craig's reputation in England. Yeats was to have been chairman but discovered he would have to propose the King's health and

that was impossible, as Lady Gregory and I have only held our movement together by insisting that nobody in England ever thinks of proposing such a toast at a gathering which has an exclusively artistic object.[38]

Although he was not chairman of the occasion, Yeats spoke at length in defence of artists. Craig remained in London to see to the assembly of an exhibition of his 'Drawings and models for *Macbeth* and other plays' which opened at the Leicester Galleries on 7 September. This was the first of a series of exhibitions of Craig's stage designs mounted in various English cities during 1911 and 1912.

Charles Ricketts visited the Leicester Galleries exhibition and wrote about it to Sydney Cockerell:

Should you have time — and I strongly advise you to find it — go and see the Craig Exhibition at the Leicester Gallery. It is well worth while. His designs are more "abstract" in character than mine, and in a sense more whimsical or inconsequent, but not always. The sketches are feeble in execution, they exaggerate also the possibilities of height and space obtainable in any London theatre. He does not realise that a figure is practically one-third of the height of the opening, therefore much of the element of surprise and originality might evaporate under execution. Nevertheless, one experiences an agreeable sense of novelty, a sense of an imaginative atmosphere which I have noticed only in my work upon the stage, and it is something like a disaster that his *Macbeth* setting was never realised. Tree's theatre would have made it possible.
p.s. If Craig had not attacked me in the Press I should like to write an article on his work.[39]

Yeats met Craig several times in London during 1912 and arranged a showing of Craig's exhibition in Dublin, to take place early in the following year.

The main Abbey company left for another American tour in December, but by then the second company was firmly established at the Abbey and could keep the theatre open. An interview, published in *The Daily News and Leader* in December allowed Yeats to plead for his ideal theatre and reveal the object of his quest:

... if we could create the drama of ideal life, with ecstasy for its object, we could use all the beauty of body and voice ever created. But it would not be the beauty of the popular imagination. It would be something more austere, more difficult for the ordinary man and woman to like. After all, perhaps, this theatre of ideal life is only possible in some moments of national crisis, some great epoch, when people are lifted above themselves.[40]

The new version of *The Hour-Glass* was presented at the Abbey before the American tour but as Craig had only licensed the use of the screens to the Abbey Theatre, Dublin, and this production formed part of the touring repertory, a different setting was used for Nugent Monck's production.* A programme note explained,

The Abbey Company has not the right to use in America Mr. Gordon Craig's screen decorations for "The Hour Glass." The old setting has, therefore, had to be abandoned for the moment, and it is hoped to use the present setting in America.

This note probably reflects Craig's reply to a letter from Yeats, 25 October 1911, now in the Bibliothèque Nationale in Paris in which he proposed to Craig an arrangement with George Tyler for the use of the screens to mount some of his plays during the American tour.

---

*   THE HOUR-GLASS
                              (New Version)

Presented by the Irish National Theatre Society Limited
at the Abbey Theatre, Dublin
on Thursday 21 November 1912

Fool	J. A. O'Rourke
First Pupil	Eric Gorman
Second Pupil	Charles Power
Third Pupil	Fred Harford
Fourth Pupil	Michael Dolan
Fifth Pupil	T. Barrett
Sixth Pupil	Desmond Fitzgerald
Pupils	Mr. Bowie, Mr. Power, Mr. Healy, Mr. Fisher
Wise Man	Nugent Monck
Angel	Mona Beirne
Wife	Eileen O'Doherty
Child	Kathleen Drago

Produced by Nugent Monck

This decision must have been disappointing to Yeats who was at this time Craig's most ardent disciple in every aspect of stage presentation — scenery, lighting, costumes and masks. The Notes to *Plays for an Irish Theatre* indicate that the revisions to *Deirdre* had been largely prompted by the possibilities of expressing so many moods and actions in the 'screens' and, in an interview in *Hearth and Home* which Craig quoted in *The Mask* for May 1915, Yeats acknowledged him as the greatest producer living. Despite the disappointment, however, he proceeded with the plan to mount a major exhibition of Craig's achievement in Dublin in March 1913.

In March, just before the Dublin opening of Craig's exhibition, Yeats discussed with him the possibility that they might both work on 'a big scheme of poetic drama'[41] in London. Miss Darragh, who had created the title role in *Deirdre* in 1906, had the idea of founding in London a theatre devoted to poetic drama with Yeats as literary adviser and Craig as producer and designer. A typewritten prospectus survives in the collection of the National Library of Ireland, and this document echoes so many of the statements and proposals drafted for the Irish National Theatre by Yeats that I feel it must be largely from his hand:

We propose to establish a theatre for plays which appeal to the sense of beauty and admit of beautiful staging. We propose that the production of these plays and the choice of players shall be made by Mr. Gordon Craig, and that Mr. W. B. Yeats be literary adviser. The work selected for production shall include, not only plays in the ordinary sense, but mime dramas, etc. A competent English musician to be associated with Mr. Yeats in the work of selection.

As it will take some time to create the theatre-going habit for work so unlike the routine work of the theatre, it is undesirable to begin upon a large scale. It is necessary to make whatever money we may be given, to last for as long as possible, that we may wait for our public.

We propose that there should be — let us say — 2 seasons (say) of a few weeks each; one perhaps in Spring, one perhaps in Autumn, and we do not wish to bind ourselves to any one place of performance. We might begin in London, or begin out of London. One advantage of this experimental beginning will be, that it will give time for Mr. Craig's School to train young players who will gradually take the place of players trained in a very different method.

We should not open before, at the earliest, the Spring or Autumn of 1914. It is important that Mr. Craig should have time to elaborate his plans; we think, however, that it is of importance that sufficient promises of money should be obtained to enable him to begin at once preparing designs, etc. We do not think that there will be a chance of success unless enough money is obtained to enable us to carry on our work in the way proposed, for, say, three years.[42]

This proposal did not come to realisation, probably because Craig was fully committed to his School, for which he had, at last, found financial backing, and to *The Mask* in Florence and Yeats was moving towards a different manifestation of his theatrical endeavours. Another scheme planned at this time which came to nothing was a revised edition of *Plays for an Irish Theatre* with two extra designs by Craig.

The Dublin Exhibition of Craig's designs organised by the United Arts Club opened at the Central Hall in Westmoreland Street on 16 March 1913. The catalogue, compiled by Craig, contained comments on the exhibits and some reproductions. The exhibition aroused much interest and there were several related lectures, including one, 'The Theatre of Beauty' given by Yeats on 18 March. On 19 March, *The Freeman's Journal* printed an interview he gave to 'E.C. O'B.' in which he paid tribute to Craig's influence on his own work in the theatre, which I reprint here:

STAGE SETTING

MR G. CRAIG'S EXHIBITION

Knowing the interest which Mr W B Yeats takes in the methods of stage production, which Dublin has now an opportunity of seeing in the exhibition of Mr Gordon Craig's work, I sought an opportunity of interviewing Mr Yeats for the benefit of the readers of the Freeman's Journal. Mr Yeats received the request with great kindness, and spoke with appreciation of the criticism which had appeared in the Freeman on the occasion of the first production, a couple of years ago, of Gordon Craig scenery in the Abbey Theatre. When I referred to the popular idea that Mr Craig had only quite recently undertaken the work of designing and producing stage settings, Mr Yeats pointed out that there were two erroneous ideas about his work in the public mind. Mr Craig had been, as a matter of fact, working for a long time at designs for a system of stage settings. His influence was obvious in the work of Rheinhardt — some of whose designs Mr Yeats thinks more commonplace than Craig's — as it was done in London under Mr Granville Barker's directions.

I asked Mr Yeats what was the other erroneous idea to which he referred.

"I was surprised," said Mr Yeats, "to read the other day that an American theatre-producer spoke of Mr Gordon Craig as if he had, while writing much on stage production, left the practice to others. Years ago, before anyone else had begun, he had already given the most beautiful production of plays seen in England in our time. Besides Purcell's operas he produced a year ago at Moscow a setting of 'HAMLET' of extraordinary interest, with the same system of screens as were used at the Abbey Theatre."

"Mr Craig's method," I suggested, "indicates a revolt against realism in stage production. What are your views on that revolt?"

"The theatre," answered Mr Yeats, "is changing over Europe. You cannot put on the stage, as a setting, a painting as good as a bad Academy picture. Take the best landscape of Sir Herbert Tree's Theatre, and it is merely a little less distinguished than a landscape by Leader. Realistic painting for the stage gives unreality, theatricality in the worst sense." Mr Yeats walked rapidly up and down the room, his hands clasped behind his back, as is his manner when he warms to his subject.

"The difference," said he, "is this. A fine easel painting reveals its beauty to you slowly; a fine stage setting must reveal its beauty in a few minutes. The stage decoration which men like Mr Craig desire is one which only wakes into its full significance when the players are in front of it. It must be closely associated with their moods and with the moods of the writer."

"Light and shade play a large part, do they not, in Mr Craig's system?"

EFFECT OF LIGHTING

"They play a very large part. The models at the Exhibition now in Dublin show the extraordinary effect of lighting. In these scenes Mr Craig makes the line of a wall, of a row of pillars, suggest in some mysterious way the mood of the scene itself."

Mr Yeats discussed what I consider one of the most beautiful models in the Exhibition — that in which Mr Craig sets the scene for the battlements of Elsinore in "HAMLET". "It is," said Mr Yeats, "no longer the Elsinore of history, but it may well be a symbol, as accurate as one mind can give of the mind of the author, of the imaginative mood in which Shakespeare wrote. Shakespeare had no photographs to tell him of Elsinore; he had never seen it. In so far as he put the events into any definite place, it must have been a vague land, getting its geography more from his mood than from his knowledge."

"Do you think that people will understand what Mr Craig is aiming at, or get into sympathy with his idea, when they see these settings?"

Mr Yeats said that he thought people might be startled. "All revelations in the visual sense," said he, "startle us at first. Those new to his work, and familiar with the traditional setting of 'HAMLET', will be as startled as they were, a few years ago, when they first saw the painting of John. But they will notice that in these scenes the first essential is light. The scene exists for the light. Light and shadow and the moving player — these are the three things which the producer of a play has, and which the painter of a picture has not. The producer, therefore, if he wishes for genuine art, and not an art which does badly what another art does well, must take the utmost care of these three. That is what Mr Craig is aiming at."

I reminded Mr Yeats that much criticism had been levelled at Mr Craig's settings, from the point of view of the player.

"Yes," said he, "I remember that a great actress, in criticising Mr Craig's designs to me, said she thought some splendid moments of chiaroscuro were over-used; that, splendid in themselves in the legitimate way of the stage, they would yet interfere with acting, which so often requires nothing but a clear full light. She would not have said this if she had seen enough of Mr Craig's work actually on the stage."

A PICTORIAL ARTIST

I suggested that in the exhibition some of Mr Craig's pictures for stage-setting, as distinct from the models, seemed, although extraordinarily beautiful, to be hardly adaptable to the stage.

"But one must remember," answered Mr Yeats, "in judging the exhibition that, in addition to being a stage producer, he is a pictorial artist of remarkable power. He seizes for the purpose of his drawing precisely those pictorial moments. When he produces a play he knows when he must subordinate his pictorial effects. The third act of the 'VIKINGS,' for example, produced by him for his mother, Ellen Terry, some years ago, was played without a single effect of chiaroscuro."

I reminded Mr Yeats of the productions, with Craig scenery, of "THE HOUR GLASS" and "THE DELIVERER," and "THE CANAVANS" at the Abbey Theatre, and asked him if Mr Craig had designed them.

"He designed the setting for 'THE HOUR GLASS' and the costumes also," said Mr Yeats; "but the other two designs were our own. 'THE DELIVERER' setting, my first experiment with screens, was a failure. I forgot the players. I made a scene which looked immensely impressive when the stage was empty. I put pillars of Egyptian vastness against a flat wall which looked to me like sun-baked stone. I forgot that on the little Abbey stage our pillars were only twelve feet high. When our players stood in front of them cyclopean Egypt had vanished !"

"But 'THE HOUR GLASS' setting was not to your mind a failure?"

"No, but when I saw the scene as designed by Craig I was so disappointed with it on the empty stage that I very nearly changed it. Then when the players moved in front of it, and the light began to move and shift about, it became like a faery palace carved out of the heart of a vast pearl. And I realised the value of the method and the design. Indeed I was so impressed with it that I could not recover my peace of mind till I had re-written the play, that I might get into the words of it something of that suggestion of wisdom and of mystery."

"Do you intend," I asked, "to use screens much at the Abbey?"

"I had intended to put all my work into that setting," said Mr Yeats, "but the necessity of having our plays in a shape ready for touring has compelled me to adopt another method. We have only the Dublin rights for Craig's invention."

I questioned Mr Yeats about the suitability of Mr Craig's system for producing modern plays. Mr Yeats agreed that the screens could not be used for every play, but he reminded me that Mr Craig worked in other methods as well. "And," said he, "like every great artist, he sometimes dreams impossible dreams."

E.C. O'B.[43]

The Post Office by Rabindranath Tagore was produced by Lennox Robinson at the Abbey on 17 May 1913. 'The scene, composed of Gordon Craig screens was arranged by J. F. Barlow.'[44] Although Yeats wrote to Craig,

Your work is always a great inspiration to me. Indeed I cannot imagine myself writing any play for the stage now, which I did not write for your screens,[45]

this was one of the few occasions of their use, except in revivals of Yeats's own plays. In October 1925 *The Hour-Glass* was revived at the Abbey with Craig's setting and costumes, and with the mask for the Fool used for the first time. Holloway still did not approve, but noted that

W B Yeats and his wife were present at the Abbey on the first night of the revival of his play. His raven locks are now silvered, but he still looks distinguished and with his thoughts in the clouds.[46]

In December 1926 Yeats's version of Sophocles' *King Oedipus* was staged in an arrangement of Craig screens. The screens were eventually cut down in size and used at the Peacock Theatre for verse and experimental drama, where they remained until the Abbey Theatre fire in 1951.

*

However, for costumes which would fit his poetic drama, Yeats turned away from Craig and sought the help of Charles Ricketts, whose work he had admired for many years and who had designed costumes for Synge's *The Well of the Saints* for the Abbey Theatre in 1908. As early as January 1904 Yeats had suggested to Lady Gregory that they should, as soon as they were in a position to pay him, approach Ricketts to work for the Irish theatre. Early in November, Yeats 'went out to Ricketts on Friday evening as he offered to do scenery for a play.'[47] And by 12 November Ricketts could write in his Journal, 'In evening to Lady Gregory to discuss scenery, etc.'[48] and by December Yeats had commissioned him to design a 'Black Jester' costume for the prologue he had planned for *The Shadowy Waters*. At the end of 1905 Yeats brought Synge to meet Ricketts and eventually, on 14 May 1908, *The Well of the Saints* was staged at the Abbey with scenery and costumes designed by Ricketts.

Craig and Ricketts met in 1903. This confrontation gave Ricketts an occasion to confide to his Journal an opinion that reveals the basic difference in their approach to stage design.

Dec 29. Gordon Craig. Intelligent but diffuse. He could not understand my advocacy of arbitrary colouring in scenery, absence of coloured lighting effects, and general decorative treatment.[49]

Yeats's reaction to the costumes Craig had designed for *The Hour-Glass* was to seek out Ricketts to design others of his plays. This resulted in a magnificent series of costume designs for *The King's Threshold* which Yeats commissioned on 1 May 1914 for a revival of the play during the Abbey Theatre season at the Royal Court Theatre, London, in July 1914. On 6 June Ricketts recorded that Lady Gregory 'called, a little cowed, I think, by the splendour of the dresses designed for Yeats' *King's Threshold*.'[50] During the rehearsals before the opening on 2 July, Yeats wrote,

I think the costumes are the best dramatic costumes I have ever seen. They are full of dramatic invention, and yet nothing starts out, or seems eccentric. The Company never did the play so well, and such is the effect of costume that whole scenes got a new intensity, and passages or actions that had seemed commonplace became powerful and moving.[51]

Lady Gregory's response was as enthusiastic. She wrote,

I really felt quite overcome when I saw both the beauty and carefulness of your designs. I have had a copy of *Deirdre* sent for your acceptance. We shall be very grateful for any suggestions about shuffling the costumes. . . . I feel you are giving us a new start in life. Yeats will enjoy seeing his plays, which he hasn't done for some years.[52]

Ricketts created costumes for Yeats's Irish Heroic Age — with a richness of abstract designs, ample sweeping cloaks. His designs for Yeats plays, as well as those for *The King's Threshold*, include costumes for *Deirdre* and for *On Baile's Strand*, which was revived in the London season of the Abbey Company in June 1915. By the following summer Yeats hoped to have *The Player Queen* designed by Ricketts for a season at the Aldwych Theatre in London, but this project, the final one in which Ricketts was considered as designer for a Yeats play, was not realised.

The drawings made by Ricketts for Yeats reveal the designer's concern with purpose as well as with colour and form. His notes on the drawings suggest that elements of the designs are interchangeable between all the plays set in the 'Heroic Age' — a concept very much in accord with Yeats's ideas. The abstract patterns painted or embroidered on the garments, and the overall design which was not pinned to any specific country or period, allowed a flexibility in use while creating a rich effect that must have done much to enhance the visual impact of the imaginative poetic plays on the audience. These costume designs, in concept, are close in feeling to the costumes of the Japanese Nō theatre, and thus herald the next phase of Yeats's theatrical adventure.

*

Yeats conceived the idea of *The Player Queen* sometime in 1908 — perhaps an extension of the thought of a play about the capture of a blind Unicorn he had mentioned in a letter to Florence Farr in 1906. Work on *Deirdre* in the last months of 1906 and on *The Unicorn from the Stars* with Lady Gregory during 1907 delayed the drafting of the scenario until 1908 but, at the same time, his involvement with these tragic and abstract themes may have guided his concept of the new play. He worked on the scenario in October 1908, while rehearsals for *Deirdre* with Mrs. Patrick Campbell were in progress. He hoped that Mrs. Campbell would act in the play and during 1909 worked on a prose version to show her. In November 1909 he attempted to read the play, by then named *The Player Queen*, to her, but this proved abortive. Nevertheless, he hoped for some weeks to rekindle her interest in the play, but finally realised that she was not interested at that time and the work was laid aside, although he still hoped that she would eventually play it.

His thinking about the play was tempered by the other influences and interests in his life—the fantastic Venetian costumes and Serlio's treatise on Italian stage design of the sixteenth century which Gordon Craig reprinted in *The Mask*. And his work with the screens and the problems of practical staging at the Abbey from 1910 to 1913 may have given him an environment in which to visualise the action. He was trying to embody the elements of his private life and thought in a text which would succeed on the public stage before an audience who could never be expected to comprehend the private motivation of the apparent plot.

During the summer months of 1914, spent at Coole Park, he returned to work on the play, moving away from his original idea of a tragic piece to a high comedy, as he wrote to his father on 12 September,

I shall have almost finished my new play, to be called perhaps *The Woman born to be Queen*. It is a wild comedy, almost a farce, with a tragic background — a study of a fantastic woman.[53]

The creation of a new style of drama, influenced by the Japanese Nō theatre, occupied Yeats during 1915 and the first half of 1916. He does not seem to have resumed work on *The Player Queen* until the summer of that year. On 11 May he wrote to Lady Gregory that he had been able to do little work lately and that chiefly on *The Player Queen*, specifically the first part of the second act, which needed new touches. By May 1917 he had completed a revision of the text and had revived Mrs. Campbell's interest in the play. He hoped that she would play it for the Stage Society. Eventually, in January 1919, he accepted the fact that Mrs. Campbell would not appear in the play, and he wrote to the Honorary Treasurer of the Incorporated Stage Society, Mr. W. S. Kennedy,

Mrs. Campbell has wired to me that she sees no "present" likelihood of a performance at a London theatre such as she wants of my play, and that she cannot play it for you. I still don't know what she means by that word present; perhaps she thinks that I should leave her the play, and will think that I am treating her ungraciously if I take it from her. However I don't know what I can do except consent to your performance. If I could go to London now I would go and talk it over with her, but I can't. If she had any desire to keep the play I would leave it with her, but it is impossible to find that out. I cannot go to London till May 15 at the earliest and I must be there for the rehearsals; so I am afraid March is an impossible date. Don't commit yourself to Miss O'Neill about the part till we have had time to think. She may be the best possible, but I have been much out of London in recent years, and in any case I don't know what London actresses you can get. Miss O'Neill is an exquisite actress in dialect. I have never yet seen her equally good out of it. In dialect she is the one poetical actress our movement has produced. Of course if I had produced the play here there was no one else possible for heroine, and she may be the best one can get. Everything depends upon the actress. It wants a dominating personality with very varied powers, a woman full of animal force. It might be better to put the play off till your next season. We might persuade Mrs. Campbell to play it; at least if she saw her way to playing it occasionally on some tour afterwards.[54]

*

The Stage Society production opened on 25 May 1919* with Máire O'Neill in the leading part, Decima. On 9 December the Abbey Theatre production, billed as 'first production' on the programme, opened. (See facing page.) 'Though its purport is wrapt in mystery,' wrote Holloway, 'its beauty won home.' [55]

---

*   THE PLAYER QUEEN

Presented by the Incorporated Stage Society
at the King's Hall, Covent Garden, London
on 25 and 27 May 1919

First Old Man	Brember Wills
Second Old Man	Orlando Barnett
Septimus	Nicholas Hannen
Tom of the Hundred Tales	Cyril Wilson
Peter of the Purple Pelican	Ernest Warburton
First Countryman	J. Adrian Byrne
Second Countryman	Frederick Harker
The Tapster	Ernest Meads
A Big Countryman	Eric Barber
The Old Beggar	Brember Wills
The Prime Minister	Hubert Carter
Nona	Edith Evans
The Queen	Gwen Richardson
Decima	Maire O'Neill
Stage Manager	J. Leslie Frith
Players	Cyril Wilson, Ernest Warburton, Ernest Meads, Eric Barber, J. Adrian Byrne, Frederick Harker
A Bishop	Orlando Barnett

Produced and designed by Archibald Welland

Yeats did not publish *The Player Queen* until 1922, when it was printed in the November issue of *The Dial* and also included in *Plays in Prose and Verse*, with notes which reveal how the collaboration with Craig affected the final form of the play.

I began in, I think, 1907, a verse tragedy, but at that time the thought I have set forth in *Per Amica Silentia Lunae* was coming into my head, and I found examples of it everywhere. I wasted the best working months of several years in an attempt to write a poetical play where every character became an example of the finding or not finding of what I have called the Antithetical Self; and because passion and not thought makes tragedy, what I made had neither simplicity nor life. I knew precisely what was wrong and yet could neither escape from thought nor give up my play. At last it came into my head all of a sudden that I could get rid of the play if I turned it into a farce; and never did I do anything so easily, for I think that I wrote the present play in about a month; and when it was performed at the Stage Society in 1919 I forgot that it was my own work, so completely that I discovered from the surprise of a neighbour, that, indignant with a house that seemed cold to my

---

THE PLAYER QUEEN

First production by the Irish National Theatre Society Limited
at the Abbey Theatre, Dublin
on Tuesday 9 December 1919

First Old Man	Barry Fitzgerald
Second Old Man	Philip Guiry
Septimus	Arthur Shields
Third Old Man	R. C. Murray
Old Woman	Maureen Delany
Happy Tom	Peter Nolan
Peter of the Purple Pelican	T. Quinn
Citizens	Brian Herbert, J. J. Lynch, R. C. Murray, Philip Guiry
Tapster	F. J. McCormick
Countrymen	Hugh Nagle, J. G. St. John, P. J. McDonnell
Big Countryman	Ambrose Power
Old Beggar	Michael J. Dolan
Prime Minister	Eric Gorman
Nona	May Craig
Players	Margaret Nicholls, Barry Fitzgerald, B. Herbert, J. J. Lynch, P. J. McDonnell
Queen	Shena Tyrconnell
Decima	Christine Hayden
Stage Manager	Philip Guiry
Bishop	Peter Nolan

The Play produced by Lennox Robinson
The Scene designed by Lennox Robinson and painted by Seaghan Barlow

second act (since much reformed), I was applauding. If it could only have come into my head three years earlier. Since then the play has been revived twice at the Abbey Theatre.

It is the only play of mine which has not its scene laid in Ireland. While at work at the Abbey Theatre I had made many experiments with Mr. Gordon Craig's screens (see The Tragic Theatre in *The Cutting of an Agate*), and both the tragedy I first planned, and the farce I wrote, were intended to be played in front of those screens. My *dramatis personae* have no nationality because Mr. Craig's screens, where every line must suggest some mathematical proportion, where all is phantastic, incredible, and luminous, have no nationality.[56]

In the Preface to *Plays in Prose and Verse*, Yeats is even more definite about the play's indebtedness to Craig,

I wrote it, my head full of fantastic architecture invented by myself upon a miniature stage, which corresponds to that of the Abbey in the proportion of one inch to a foot with a miniature set of Gordon Craig screens and a candle; and if it is gayer than my wont it is that I tried to find words and events that would seem well placed under a beam of light reflected from the ivory-coloured surface of the screens.[57]

52. The Comic Scene of Serlio from *The Mask*, Vol. I, No. 1, 1908.

The fantastic architecture, indeed the final form of the play, may have been suggested by the Comic Scene of Serlio which Craig reproduced in the first issue of *The Mask* in 1908 with its accompanying essay partly translated into English,

The Comic Scene shall represent the exterior of the dwellings of private persons such as citizens, lawyers, merchants, parasites and other like men.
The house of the Procuress must not be lacking nor must the Scene be without a tavern. A Church is also very necessary. The method for setting these buildings in position I have already given.[58]

This has a close relationship to Yeats's stage direction for Act I of *The Player Queen* which calls for

An open place at the meeting of three streets. One can see for some way down one of these streets, and at some little distance it turns, showing a bare piece of wall lighted by a hanging lamp.

This is the permanent setting of the Commedia dell'Arte, the Italian comedy, and conforms to the classic arrangement of the theatres in which this drama was played. The second act setting, the Throne-Room, was one of those worked on by Yeats in his notebook of 1910 when he was plotting arrangements of the screens. Yeats's sketch on page 27 of the notebook shows such an arrangement with extensive notes on lighting (see above, p. 159). The printed stage direction reads:

The Throne-Room in the Castle. Between the pillars are gilded openwork doors, except at one side, where there is a large window. The morning light is slanting through the window, making dark shadows among the pillars. As the scene goes on the light, at first feeble, becomes strong and suffused, and the shadows disappear. Through the openwork doors one can see down long passages and one of these passages plainly leads into the open air. One can see daylight at the end of it. There is a throne in the centre of the room and a flight of steps that leads to it.

*

With, as its producer, Lennox Robinson described it, this 'most delightful, most annoying and most unsatisfactory play,'[59] the active Craig-Yeats collaboration came to an end, and Yeats took his next model from a different theatrical idiom which depended neither on scenery nor on lighting for its effect. Not until the nineteen thirties did he come to marry these styles in his pursuit of 'the condition of tragic pleasure.'

EXHIBITION OF DRAWINGS
AND MODELS FOR HAMLET:
MACBETH:THE VIKINGS:AND
OTHER PLAYS:BY EDWARD

GORDON CRAIG: ARRANGED
BY THE UNITED ARTS CLUB
44 SAINT STEPHEN'S GREEN
DUBLIN :: MCMXIII.

53. Edward Gordon Craig. Dublin Exhibition, 1913.
Catalogue cover (reduced).

Ezra Pound was approached by Mrs. Mary Fenollosa in the autumn of 1913 and asked if he would arrange and edit for publication her late husband's papers on Japanese literature. These deal with a culture on which very little had been published at that time in the western world. The selection of Pound as editor of the Fenollosa papers coincided with an invitation that he should act as part-time secretary to Yeats, which position he accepted because, outside the firm friendship he had formed with the Irish poet, he could at the same time pursue his own writing career which, on his acceptance of Mrs. Fenollosa's offer, included his arranging and editing of her husband's notebooks.

Ernest Fenollosa, who was born in America in 1853, had gone to Japan after graduation from Harvard University and taught at the University of Tokyo from 1878 to 1886. During these years he had developed such a profound knowledge and appreciation of traditional Japanese culture that, in 1888, he was appointed as manager of the Tokyo Fine Arts Academy. He became a practising Buddhist and his services to culture were rewarded by his being decorated by the Emperor.

Fenollosa was given an official appointment as Imperial Commissioner for Fine Arts with a brief to travel abroad and enlighten the western world about Japan's cultural heritage. In 1890 he became curator of the department of Oriental Art at the Boston Museum of Fine Arts, a post he occupied until 1897 when he returned to Tokyo. There he was made a Professor at the Imperial Normal School where he remained until his retirement in 1900. He went to live in London, and died there in 1908.

After Fenollosa's death his widow edited some of his papers for publication, notably the two-volume edition of *Epochs of Japanese and Chinese Art*, published in 1911. She then began to seek a suitable editor of the remainder of her husband's literary notebooks, which included his work on the classical Nō theatre — an editor whose concern would be with the literary quality of the work rather than one whose approach would be conditioned by academic practice. Her choice of Ezra Pound may have been prompted by such of his works as *The Spirit of Romance*, which he had published in 1910, and by the versions of Chinese poetry which were occupying him in 1913, some of which appeared in the April issue of *Poetry* (Chicago). Her agreement with Pound gave him a free hand to edit and publish the material and, late in the autumn of 1913, she handed over the bulk of the unpublished notebooks. The remainder of the material was despatched by post to Pound after she had returned to live in America.

In November 1913 Yeats and Pound moved from London to Stone
Cottage at Coleman's Hatch in Sussex for a three-month period, as
Yeats had arranged to go to give a lecture tour in America at the end
of January 1914. He spent much of this period completing two long
essays, 'Witches and Wizards and Irish Folk-Lore' and 'Swedenborg,
Mediums and the Desolate Places,' which were later published as
introductions to the two volumes of *Visions and Beliefs in the West
of Ireland* by Lady Gregory in 1920. During the same time, Pound
began his investigation, editing and 'finishing' of Fenollosa's notebooks on the Nō theatre and from these materials he chose as his first
task a version of the Nō play *Nishikigi*, which he had edited and
'completed' early in 1914 and which was published in the May issue
of *Poetry* (Chicago). The publication of this text was the first step
towards the book published in 1917 in London and New York under
the title *'Noh' or Accomplishment, A Study of the Classical Stage of
Japan* by Ernest Fenollosa and Ezra Pound.

So, in the late autumn of 1913, Yeats was introduced to the Nō
theatre of Japan, and felt that he had discovered a formula through
which he could channel into one direction the diverse theories and
explorations of dramatic practice which had occupied his work in
the theatre for over a quarter of a century. This contact, made
through Ezra Pound, provided him with the model on which he based
the style of his later dramatic works.

For centuries, the stage practice of the Nō drama had embodied
many of the concepts which Yeats had tried to define in his theatrical
writings and which, with varying degrees of success, he had attempted to have realised in productions of his own plays and those of
other playwrights through productions by the Irish National Theatre
and by the other theatrical companies with which he had worked.

During the two succeeding winters the poets spent periods together
at Stone Cottage and, as Yeats became more aware of the contents
of the Fenollosa notebook materials, he perceived the parallel relationship with his own dramatic theories. He suggested that, before
the larger work was completed, some of the Nō texts in these versions might be assembled to make a small book for the Cuala Press,

54. *Certain Noble Plays of Japan*. The Cuala Press, Dublin, 1916. Title page.
The device, 'bell, waterfall and fish,' by Robert Gregory, was first used on the
title page of *A Book of Saints and Wonders* by Lady Gregory, printed at the
Dun Emer Press in 1906 and was possibly chosen by Yeats for *Certain Noble
Plays* as being symbolic of the source material from which he might, after the
model of the Nō, create an Irish drama which would 'bring again to certain
places, their old sanctity or their romance.' [See facing page.]

CERTAIN NOBLE PLAYS OF JAPAN:
FROM THE MANUSCRIPTS OF ERNEST
FENOLLOSA, CHOSEN AND FINISHED
BY EZRA POUND, WITH AN INTRODUC-
TION BY WILLIAM BUTLER YEATS.

THE CUALA PRESS
CHURCHTOWN
DUNDRUM
MCMXVI

the handpress directed by his sister Elizabeth in Dublin. This book, *Certain Noble Plays of Japan : from the manuscripts of Ernest Fenollosa, chosen and finished by Ezra Pound* contains Pound's edited versions of four plays, *Nishikigi, Hagoromo, Kumasaka* and *Kagekiyo* and an Introduction by Yeats, dated April 1916, a lengthy essay in which he reveals the impact that his discovery of Nō had made on his own approach to theatrical practice. The Cuala edition of this book, which was limited to three hundred and fifty copies, was finished on 20 July, 'in the year of the Sinn Fein Rising,' as the colophon puts it, and published on 16 September in the same year.

This contact with Nō revealed to Yeats the possibility of devising a form for his own theatrical work with a discipline which could possibly accommodate, without using the devices and trappings of the conventional stage, the ideas he had been trying to express in dramatic form ever since he had begun to write for the stage thirty years before. Therefore, rather than coming unprepared to the idiom of Nō, he welcomed the contents of Fenollosa's notebooks as a manual from which he might develop some rules which could guide the development of a form for his own dramatic work, through which he had been seeking to proclaim the validity of the continuing presence of myth and its relevance to history in the world.

While the Introduction to *Certain Noble Plays of Japan* expresses Yeats's first impressions of the form of the classical drama of Japan, this essay also constitutes the first declaration of the principles which were, with very few exceptions, to decide the direction his own dramatic writing was to take from 1916 until his death in 1939. He found in Nō a form, however 'unpopular,' which could accommodate the elements he had learned during an apprenticeship in drama which had lasted over a quarter of a century and he was, in his dramatic writing during the remaining twenty-three years of his life, to elaborate variations within that framework which would allow him the freedom he sought to express his ideas.

During the same period in which he studied the Japanese texts and Fenollosa's notes, and wrote his Introduction, Yeats applied himself to the composition, revision and rehearsal of the first of his own plays in this new form, which, originally entitled *The Waters of Immortality*, was produced and published under the title *At the Hawk's Well*.

Although he had at last found and adapted, perhaps even invented, a dramatic form which could project his vision of the eternal truths underlying the histories, myths and legends of his native land, he felt that Dublin was not yet ready for the realisation of his dream, so he remained at work in London to experience and learn the disciplines and techniques vital to the presentation of his chosen form because, as he said in his Introduction to *Certain Noble Plays*, there alone :

I can find the help I need, Mr. Dulac's mastery of design and Mr. Ito's genius of movement; yet it pleases me to think that I am working for my own country. Perhaps some day a play in the form I am adapting for European purposes shall awake once more, whether in Gaelic or in English, under the slope of Slieve-na-Mon or Croagh Patrick ancient memories; for this form has no need of scenery that runs away with money nor of a theatre-building. Yet I know that I only amuse myself with a fancy; for my writings if they be sea-worthy must put to sea, I cannot tell where they may be carried by the wind. Are not the fairy-stories of Oscar Wilde, which were written for Mr. Ricketts and Mr. Shannon and for a few ladies, very popular in Arabia?[1]

*

'Nō begins with a mask, and within the mask the presence of a god'[2] is the opening sentence of Donald Keene's comprehensive book on the classical theatre of Japan and in this statement Professor Keene defines an essential quality of the model which inspired most of Yeats's dramatic writing after his discovery of that theatre. Therefore any consideration of the apprenticeship served by Yeats to this is best pursued in relation to certain of the basic elements which make up the stage idiom of the Nō.

The Nō theatre of Japan is a sophisticated, aristocratic and ritualistic art form which had achieved its final shape by the end of the sixteenth century, the Age of Shakespeare in Europe. In each of its elements, and in its total presentation, the purpose of Nō is the achievement of beauty, and the poetic texts, the acting, the music, the singing, the choreographic movement, the masks, the costumes and the stage properties, presented in the rigidly ordered atmosphere of the theatre, are all dedicated to this purpose, defined by Fenollosa in his essay which, as edited by Pound, forms the third section of *The Classic Noh Theatre of Japan*.

The beauty and power of Noh lie in the concentration. All elements — costume, motion, verse and music — unite to produce a single clarified impression. Each drama embodies some primary human relation or emotion; and the poetic sweetness or poignancy of this is carried to its highest degree by carefully excluding all obtrusive elements as a mimetic realism or vulgar sensation might demand. The emotion is always fixed upon idea, not upon personality.[3]

In this essay, Fenollosa sets out the parallels between the Nō theatre and the archetypal drama of the western world, that of classical Greece. He found that in the Japanese classical drama :

A form of drama, as primitive, as intense, and almost as beautiful as the ancient Greek drama at Athens, still exists in the world. Yet few care for it, or see it. In the fifth century before Christ the Greek drama arose out of the religious rites practised in the festivals of the God of Wine. In the fifteenth century after Christ, the Japanese drama arose out of religious rites practised in the festivals of the Shinto gods, chiefly the Shinto god of the Kasuga temple at Nara. Both began by a sacred dance, and both added a sacred chorus sung by priests. The transition from a dance chorus to drama proper consisted, in both cases, in the evolving of a solo part, the words of which alternate in dialogue with the chorus. In both the final form of drama consists of a few short scenes, wherein two or three soloists enact a main theme, whose deeper meaning is interpreted by the poetical comment of the chorus. In both the speech was metrical, and involved a clear organic structure of separate lyrical units. In both music played an important part. In both action was a modi-fication of the dance. In both rich costumes were worn; in both, masks. The form and tradition of the Athenian drama passed over into the tradition of the ancient Roman stage, and died away in the early middle ages fourteen centuries ago. It is dead, and we can study it from scant records only. But the Japanese poetic drama is alive today, having been transmitted almost unchanged from one perfected form reached in Kioto in the fifteenth century.[4]

Arthur Waley, in his book *The Nō Plays of Japan*, published in 1922, describes this concept of beauty, or *Yugen*, in the language of the Nō, as 'what lies beneath the surface.'[5] It is a dark concept of beauty as we would understand it, but also a noble concept — sen-suous, elegant and mysterious. It is a thing we seek in all great art which can arouse a 'stirring in the bones.' And it is by this quality that we are repaid for our attention to the form. The word Nō can be translated as 'talent' — talent displayed in performance, or, as Pound translates it, 'accomplishment.' In Nō this 'accomplishment' is achieved by the combination in performance of all the elements that constitute the form, so that it becomes, in the definition of Zeami, one of the greatest masters of the classical Japanese theatre, the art of elegant imitation.

Yeats saw in the Nō a concept of absolute beauty presented in an inflexibly ordered and symbolic framework, symbolic in all its elements both oral and visual. In this concept he saw a possible framework on which to build his own ideal form of theatre which would present pieces that were noble in their subject matter, but could also lend its form to comedy as well as tragedy. From an unpublished dialogue which Yeats composed in 1916, the year he began writing his 'Plays for Dancers,' and which he called 'The Poet and the Actress,' the following passage is quoted by Curtis Bradford in his study of *At the Hawk's Well*:

Is not all comedy a battle — a sham fight often — but still a battle? Now the art I long for is also a battle but it takes place in the depths of the soul, and one of the antagonists does not wear a shape known to the world or speak a mortal tongue. It is the struggle of a dream with the world. It is only possible when we transcend circumstances and ourselves, and the greater the contest the greater the art.[6]

*

The written texts of Nō are designed deliberately as part only of the total theatrical experience and must be combined with chant, music and movement to achieve completeness. In Fenollosa's description:

> The plays are written in a mixture of prose and verse. The finest parts are in verse; ordinary conversation lapses into prose; the choruses are always in verse.[7]

The language used in Nō is derived from the archaic Court language of fourteenth-century Japan and the formality of this language, combined with the manner of its recitation, establishes character and situation. The situations portrayed can cover a wide range, from the heroic to the farcical, but whatever the theme, as Pound states, 'The Noh, the symbolic and ritual stage is a place of honour to actor and audience alike.'[8] That this distinction was understood by Yeats can be seen by looking at the themes of the pieces he modelled on Nō in which can be found heroic, historical and comical subjects, all treated within the framework of the 'Plays for Dancers.'

One must also be aware of the distinction between the pure, noble, lyric drama which is Nō and the *Kabuki*, the popular drama of Japan which, although it is itself a theatrical form of high accomplishment, rich in colour and tradition which achieves its own unity of dance, music and acting, is more closely related to the stage arts of the West, using lavish settings and stage make-up rather than masks. All female roles in both Nō and *Kabuki* are portrayed by actors, a tradition akin to that followed in the English theatre of the time of Shakespeare, which is the approximate period at which *Kabuki* developed. In fact, some *Kabuki* plays derive from Nō originals and some of these, such as *Dojoji* are played today in the differing techniques of both traditions of Japanese theatre.

The construction of the text of a Nō play invariably follows an ordered pattern, within which further developments of theme or plot similarly obey the organisation of the principal action of the piece which forms the central part of the play. The three principal sections of a Nō text are:

1 The Introduction, *Jo* (the ideogram means 'beginning'), which introduces the plot or theme and in which the setting and the characters are in their 'time' and in 'location' often introduced

by a 'traveller' whose narrative is chanted against an accompaniment from the chorus and the musicians.

2 The 'Development,' which is the central action of the play and includes a dance or dances which comment on and extend the action by means of stylised movement, again accompanied by the chorus and the musicians. This central part of the play is known as *Ha*, for which the ideogram means 'breaking.'

3 The final part of the play is *Kyū* or Conclusion. Here, the ideogram means 'rapidity,' and this section of the play is often devised and played at a more rapid pace than the preceding sections. In this final part the plot is resolved, perhaps with a climactic dance and usually with a concluding chorus after which the actors, chorus, musicians and attendants leave the stage.

In addition, if the realisation of the theme of the play demands it, the central action, *Ha*, can itself be subdivided after the manner of the overall *Jo, Ha, Kyū* rule described above and this process of subdivision of the central action can be repeated as far as the requirements of the plot demand for the realisation of the theme. Thus, the construction of a musical composition is more closely allied to the structure of a Nō play text than is western dramatic style.

The excitement Yeats must have felt on seeing the Fenollosa notebooks, together with the play texts as 'finished' by Pound, and his awareness of the possibilities of devising a parallel form for the realisation of his own dramatic themes is evident in his Introduction to *Certain Noble Plays of Japan*, in which he stated:

These Japanese poets too feel for tomb and wood the emotion, the sense of awe that our Gaelic speaking country people will sometimes show when you speak to them of Castle Hackett or of some Holy Well; and that is why perhaps it pleases them to begin so many plays by a Traveller asking his way with many questions, a convention agreeable to me; for when I first began to write poetical plays for an Irish theatre I had to put away an ambition of helping to bring again to certain places, their old sanctity or their romance. I could lay the scene of a play on Baile's Strand, but I found no pause in the hurried action for descriptions of strand or sea or the great yew tree that once stood there; and I could not in "The King's Threshold" find room, before I began the ancient story, to call up the shallow river and the few trees and rocky fields of modern Gort.[9]

Working so closely with Yeats at this time may also have had an effect on Pound's versions of the Nō texts which seem to me, in some instances, to echo the kind of formalised Irish dialect that the Irish playwrights had created in their plays for the Abbey Theatre. Such passages as Synge's

Let you wait to hear me talking till we're astray in Erris when Good Friday's
by, drinking a sup from a well, and making mighty kisses with our wetted
mouths, or gaming in a gap of sunshine with yourself stretched back into
your necklace in the flowers of the earth[10]

from the love scene in *The Playboy of the Western World* seem to
me to have a similar ordering and cadence to certain texts as rendered
from the Nō by Pound, who had in fact published an essay on Synge
in *The Egoist* on 2 February 1914. Compare the opening chorus of
Nishikigi, as rendered by Pound:

Times out of mind I am here setting up this bright branch, this silky wood
with the charms painted on it as fine as the web you'd get in the grass-cloth
of Shinobu, that they'd be still selling you in this mountain.[11]

However different the situations that these speeches convey, the
language has a common quality which would make for a similarity
of rendering by actors cast in the Irish mode — the actors with whose
work and style Yeats was most familiar. But, in the writing of his
'Plays for Dancers,' however his thinking about the form might have
been prompted by such echoes, his texts have a character or flavour
which, whether in verse or in prose, is uniquely part of his personal
style, and his purpose in writing in his new form was very different
from that of the other dramatists who wrote for the Irish National
Theatre.

*

In performance, the order in which Nō plays are given is governed
by the category into which each piece falls. These categories are
determined by the plot and central character types of each piece.
The *Kadensho*, or secret book of *Nō*, defines the main categories of
plays and the order in which they should be played, and this source
book is quoted by both Fenollosa and Waley. These are:

1 *Shūgen* or 'God plays,' which are congratulatory pieces cele-
brating the Divine Age.

2 *Shura* or 'Battle plays,' in which the ghost of a warrior plays
the principal role.

3 *Kazura* or *Onna-mono*, 'wig-pieces,' in which the principal
character is a woman.

4 *Oni-Nō* or 'The Nō of spirits.' According to Fenollosa, 'Here
are shown the struggles and the sins of mortals, and the
audience, even while they sit for pleasure, will begin to think
about Buddha and the coming world.'

5 Plays which deal with the moral duties of man, the virtues
of benevolence, justice, politeness and wisdom.

6 Another *Shūgen*, a congratulatory piece — 'The Nō of happy wishes.' [12]

In addition to these main categories, *Kyogen* or farces, Invocations and Interludes are included in the repertoire. In a full Nō performance, plays in the six main categories are performed in the order determined above and separated by *Kyogen* and Interludes and, given thus, the whole performance is regarded as a single aesthetic experience.

The ordered manner of this classification both of play types and of the approach to the total performance as a single artistic unit must have held a strong appeal for Yeats who, for almost two decades had been seeking such an order for his presentation of ancient Irish texts, like those given in English versions by Lady Gregory in her books derived from Irish epic sources, *Gods and Fighting Men* and her retelling of the material of the *Táin Bó Cuailgne* under the title *Cuchulain of Muirthemne*, which book was the principal source for the series of plays Yeats constructed with Cuchulain as the central character.

Many of the difficulties he had faced even earlier in his playwriting career such as those encountered in writing *The Shadowy Waters* might have been solved through the medium of this style of theatre which could accommodate in one piece the range of characters he sought — the supernatural characters 'with eagles' faces,' the mortal heroes and heroine and the common sailors as well. It would also have allowed the pacing of the dramatic poem as spoken in a manner which avoided the 'stage business' and movement thought necessary in a theatre which served a so-called 'realism.' His work could have been directed in a form, as he described it in his Introduction to *Certain Noble Plays of Japan* :

Where a ship is represented by a mere skeleton of willows or osiers painted green, or a fruit tree by a bush in a pot, and where actors have tied on their masks with ribbons that are gathered into a bunch behind the head. It is a child's game become the most noble poetry, and there is no observation of life, because the poet would set before us all those things which we feel and imagine in silence.[13]

*

In 1904, when Yeats predicted in his essay, 'The Play, the Player and the Scene,' in *Samhain*, that 'the hour of convention and decoration and ceremony is coming again,' [14] he was not aware that, on the other side of the world, a theatre form which embodied these qualities had existed for centuries and that he would come, a decade later, to discover and adapt the form to his own purpose. Nor, in coming to the Fenollosa papers, does any detailed picture of the formally organised playhouses dedicated to the classical Japanese drama emerge. Pound's concern in editing Fenollosa's work was principally with the literature of the Nō, and he gives, in 'Noh' or Accomplishment, but a brief outline of the structure within which these dramas were performed:

I think I can now give a couple of texts without much more preface than saying that the stage is visible from three sides. It is reached by a bridge which is divided into three sections by three real pine trees which are small and in pots. There is one scene painted on the background. It is a pine tree, the symbol of the unchanging. It is painted right on the back of the stage, and, as this cannot be shifted, it remains the same for all plays.[15]

However, one can see that this description, though it is very brief and elementary, suggested to Yeats the arrangement of the stage elements for the 'Plays for Dancers' and as, during the nineteen-twenties he had a small theatre designed for poetic and experimental drama, the Peacock, built as part of the Abbey Theatre in Dublin, the elements of the Nō stage should be looked at in more detail.

Although the plays of the Nō theatre can be performed in any theatre, or in an open space indoors or outdoors, theatres which are specially built for the performance of Nō are entirely created for their purpose. Donald Keene describes such a theatre in his Nō, the Classical Theatre of Japan as

. . . unlike any other in the world. It is dominated by the large, gleaming stage projecting into the auditorium, a stage which by its size and majesty seems to assert that even without actors it would have sufficient reason to exist. Its ornate curved roof confirms this impression of independence : the stage . . . was formerly a separate building, and at the very beginning of its history may have served as the scene of ritual observances before the gods. . . .

The absence of a curtain, the unvarying light before and during a performance, the great pine painted on the back wall, all suggest less a Western stage — shabby and bare until it takes on life from a play — than a church, itself an architectural masterpiece but ready for the drama of the mass.[16]

The actual playing area is about eighteen feet square, with a space on the spectators' right for the chorus which is about three feet wide and the atoza or 'back space' which is occupied by the musicians and stage attendants and adds about nine feet to the depth of the stage. Entrances and exits are made along a bridge from the left, the hashi-gakari, which can vary from six to nine feet in width and in front of which stand three small pine trees. The end of the bridge is closed by a brocade curtain, behind which are the dressing rooms, and which is lifted to allow entrances and exits. The audience are seated to the

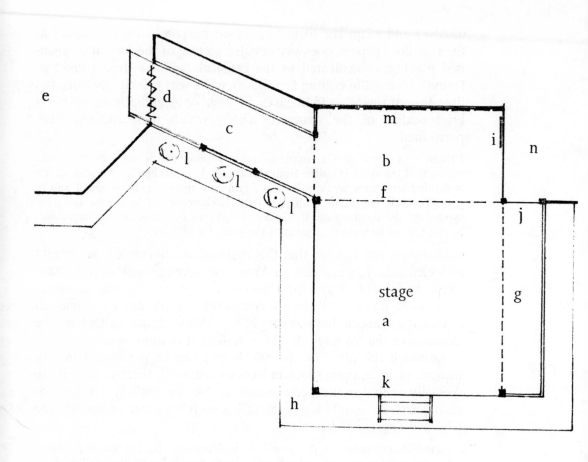

a   stage
b   *Atoza*, 'behind space'
c   *Hashigakari*, entrance passage
d   curtain
e   dressing room
f   musicians
g   chorus
h   *Shwasu*, the white gravel path
i   *Kindo*, 'hurry door'
j   the nobles' door
k   *Kizahachi*, steps to auditorium
l   the three pine trees
m   *Kagami ita*, the back wall
n   musicians' room
o   audience

o

auditorium

55. Outline plan of the Japanese No stage.

left and in front of the stage, and the auditorium is separated from the stage area by a path of white gravel, the *shirasu*.

The Nō stage is dominated by its permanent background, the *Kagami-ita*, literally 'mirror boards,' which is the back wall of the stage, usually made of vertical boarding on which is a painted representation of a huge pine tree, the *Yogo* pine, in commemoration of the birth of Nō. This symbolises the traditional descent of Nō from the world of the gods when, at the *Kasuga* shrine in Nara, the god of the shrine, in the form of an old man, danced beneath this tree, and annually at the festival of this shrine, a great Nō actor stands beneath this tree so that the god may make of him his reflection.

The presence of this symbolic and unchanging background made a considerable impact on Yeats in his approach to the Nō, so that we find him, after the performance of his first play in the mode, *At the Hawk's Well*, contributing a note to the version of the play as printed at the Cuala Press :

It has been a great gain to get rid of scenery and substitute for a crude landscape painted upon canvas three performers who, sitting against a screen covered with some one unchangeable pattern, or against the wall of a room, describe landscape or event. . . .[17]

In the stage direction to *The Dreaming of the Bones*, the second of his 'Plays for Dancers,' written in 1917 and printed at the Cuala Press in *Two Plays for Dancers*, 1919, he wrote :

A screen with a pattern of mountain and sky can stand against the wall, or a curtain with a like pattern hang upon it, but the pattern must only symbolise or suggest. One musician enters and then two others, the first stands singing while the others take their places. Then all three sit down by the wall with their instruments, which are already there — a drum, a zither and a flute. Or they unfold a cloth as in "The Hawk's Well," while the instruments are carried in.

Again, in *The Cat and the Moon*, written in 1917, but not printed until 1924, he directed that

The scene is any bare place before a wall against which stands a patterned screen or hangs a patterned curtain suggesting Saint Colman's Well. Three musicians are sitting close to the wall, with zither, drum and flute. Their faces are made up to represent masks.

In the later 'Plays for Dancers' which gradually departed further from the pure disciplines of Nō, Yeats moved away from the concept of the symbolic screen so that in *Fighting the Waves*, the version, revised for performance on the 'public' stage, of *The Only Jealousy of Emer*, which was performed at the Abbey Theatre in 1929, there is a front curtain 'with a wave pattern,' and in *The King of the Great*

Clock Tower, first performed at the Abbey on 30 June 1934, there is also an inner front curtain which 'may have a stencilled pattern of dancers.'

After the Peacock Theatre had been opened in 1927, his stage directions were often written with that particular stage in mind, but, as with his earlier experiences of stagecraft, however he adapted the idiom and practices he learned about, the main course of his writing for the stage, whether in 'public' or 'private' theatres was always dedicated to the purpose he had declared in 1891 of creating for Ireland 'a fine native drama of our own.'[18]

*

As early as 1904, in his essay, 'The Play, the Player and the Scene' which he published in that year's issue of *Samhain*, Yeats looked forward to forming a stage company which, with an enduring discipline pursued within the framework of the Irish National Theatre Company, would practise and develop their art. Some passages from the section marked '(2nd.)' in the essay, which deals with this, 'the Player,' show the validity his early principles retained when he came to relate them to Nō. He wrote:

If we are to make a drama of energy, of extravagance, of fantasy, of musical and noble speech, we shall need an appropriate stage management. Up to a generation or two ago, and to our own generation, here and there, lingered a method of acting and of stage management, which had come down, losing much of its beauty and meaning on the way, from the days of Shakespeare. . . .

Everybody who has spoken to large audiences knows that he must speak difficult passages, in which there is some delicacy of sound or thought upon one or two notes. The larger his audience, the more he must get away, except in trivial passages, from the methods of conversation. Where one requires the full attention of the mind, one must not weary it with any but the most needful changes of pitch and note, or by an irrelevant or obtrusive gesture. As long as drama was full of poetical beauty, full of description, full of philosophy, as long as its words were the very vesture of sorrow and laughter, the players understood that their art was essentially conventional, artificial, ceremonious.[19]

Even as early as this, in his capacity of theatre manager, Yeats was evidently seeking the qualities that he eventually found in the Japanese classical dramatic mode and he acknowledged, in the essay quoted above, that he would have to try to create what he sought in opposition to the thinking of the time. As he defines it:

An Irish critic has told us to study the stage management of Antoine, but that is like telling a good Catholic to take his theology from Luther. Antoine, who described poetry as a way of saying nothing, has preferred naturalistic acting and carried the spirit of science into the theatre. Were we to study his methods we might, indeed, have a far more perfect art than our own, a far more mature art, but it is better to fumble our way like children. We may grow up, for we have as good hopes as any other sturdy ragamuffin.

An actor must understand how to discriminate, cadence from cadence, and so cherish the musical lineaments of verse or prose that he delights the ear with a continually varied music. This one has to say over and over again, but one does not mean that his speaking should be a monotonous chant. Those who have heard Mr. Frank Fay speaking verse will understand me. That speech of his, so masculine and so musical, could only sound monotonous to an ear that was deaf to poetic rhythm, and one should never, as do London managers, stage a poetic drama according to the desire of those who are deaf to poetical rhythm. It is still possible, barely so, but still possible, that some day we may write musical notes, as did the Greeks, it seems, for a whole play, and make our actors speak upon them — not sing, but speak.[20]

In the Nō theatre the actor is trained from early childhood in the various disciplines which his chosen vocation in life demands. These include speech technique, as well as training in singing or chant and dance or choreographic and mimetic movement. An actor can make his debut in child roles as an accomplished performer as early in his life as at five years of age. By the time he is thirteen years old he may be given an adult supporting part, and by the time he is sixteen or so can become a leading player in his company. The continuity of each company or troupe as a closely allied community of players is a most important feature of the Nō theatre and, subject to the discipline imposed by his particular company, the actor's training and development continue throughout his life.

This rigidly ordered framework into which the actor's career, indeed, his whole life, is fitted, has been the major factor in the preservation, over a period lasting almost four centuries, of the texts of the plays, as well as the style of the performance as to speech, gesture and music in an unaltering tradition. When, at thirteen years of age, the novice actor is allowed for the first time to tie on his mask 'with ribbons that are gathered in a bunch behind his head,' he is initiated into a lifelong vocation dedicated towards the achievement of an immortal performance.

The stage company of Nō is made up of players, chorus, musicians and stage attendants. The parts portrayed by the players tend, by the nature of the style of drama, to fall into categories which are all, female parts included, played by male actors. Fenollosa defines the main categories of roles as follows:

Shite: The hero or chief character.
Tsure: The follower of the hero.
Waki: Guest, or guests, often a wandering priest.

Waki no tsure or *Wadzure*: Guest's attendant.
Tomo: An insignificant attendant.
Kogata: A very young boy.
Kiogenshi: A sailor or servant.
Hannya: An evil spirit.[21]

*

For Yeats, however, the decade that had passed since he had expressed his hopes of developing a disciplined and permanent theatre company in Dublin had been filled with troubles of many kinds — dissentions between the founders of the Irish theatre movement had led to the break-up of the managerial partnership and Edward Martyn's leaving the board. Further dissention led to a group of the players leaving in 1906 and, by 1909, the Fay brothers who between them had created the acting style which had won world fame for the Irish National Theatre had also left the company.

In November 1910, Miss Horniman withdrew her financial assistance from the Irish National Theatre and the company had to seek survival by finding for its repertoire more commercial successes, especially plays which could be toured in England and in the United States. Despite these setbacks at the Abbey Theatre, Yeats had continued to work towards his ideal and, during this difficult time went ahead with his experiments in staging with Gordon Craig, and installed Lennox Robinson as producer at the Abbey. He was continually hopeful that the type of company he sought could be brought together, but this hope had not been realised when the time came that he was ready to present his own adaptation of Nō in terms of practical staging. So, when he came to write his 'Introduction' to *Certain Noble Plays of Japan*, he had to confess that only in London could he find the help he needed. He continued to experiment with the form, and to seek out musicians, dancers and artists who could help him but the multiple skills he sought were never really co-ordinated at any time in the theatre he had founded, despite the addition of the School of Acting and the School of Ballet developed at the Abbey Theatre in the 1920's. The Irish National Theatre continued to rely on natural talent rather than on dedicated training.

Zeami, the great master whose writings define the basic artistic theories of Nō, stated of the the qualities of performance, that the essential *yūgen* or beauty is absolutely present in the acting when the performance of the Three Roles is beautiful. The Three Basic Roles were, in his definition, those of the old person, the woman and the warrior. Thus, the first play Yeats wrote in the manner he developed from the Nō conforms in its cast to these three Basic Roles — the Old Man, the Young Man (Cuchulain) and the Guardian of the Well, the Hawk-Goddess who is of the people of the Sidhe.

*

The spoken passages in Nō are declaimed in a very individual and accented style deriving from the form of the language in which they are written. This archaic form had originated in the formal language of the Japanese Court in the fourteenth century and had continued in use for formal correspondence down the centuries, in much the same way as legal terminology in English has retained its archaic forms down to the present day.

This formal language, in the performance of Nō, sounds extremely slow to Western ears, and also very strange because of its use of accentuated vowel sounds which, at moments of heightened significance in the plays are accompanied by improvisations from the musicians, which grow out of, or are inspired by, the emotion conveyed by the actors.

In addition to all this, the formal Nō stage has resonators, in the form of large earthenware jars, built into its substructure at significant places, and these can be used by the actors to place themselves during important moments so that the pitch or sound of the performance is controlled at will. In this respect, the sound of Nō in performance must, like other aspects of the style, be regarded as special to itself and not as having any direct bearing on the form which Yeats developed from his Japanese model.

The method of delivery of the lines of his poetic dramas had, however, been a major concern of Yeats for many years, in fact ever since his meeting with Florence Farr in the 1880's. His essay, 'Speaking to the Psaltery,' written with her assistance in 1902 and originally planned as a Dun Emer Press book, describes the early experiments originally made with his lyric poetry and assisted by Arnold Dolmetsch who

put us back to our first thought. He made us a beautiful instrument, half psaltery, half lyre, which contains all the chromatic intervals within the range of the speaking voice; and he taught us to regulate our speech by the ordinary musical notes.[22]

Although the experiments with the psaltery were originally directed towards the delivery of lyrical poetry, Yeats soon saw the possible application of such a system to the poetic drama he was trying to create and went on to observe that

Modern acting and recitation have taught us to fix on the gross effects until we think gesture, and the intonation that copies the accidental surface of life, more important than the rhythm; and yet we understand theoretically that it is precisely this rhythm that separates good writing from bad, that is the glimmer, the fragrance, the spirit of all intense literature.[23]

'Speaking to the Psaltery,' which has specimen settings in notation by Florence Farr appended, is a further confirmation that Yeats, in his thinking, had been pursuing a line parallel to the system of speech delivery he discovered in Nō — a parallel which had existed in the classical Japanese theatre for hundreds of years. And he also found that this 'noble' tradition had its origin in common forms which had developed from the vernacular, or, as he expressed it in his Introduction to *Certain Noble Plays of Japan* :

I love all the arts that can still remind me of their origin among the common people, and my ears are only comfortable when the singer sings as if mere speech had taken fire, when he appears to have passed into song almost imperceptibly. I am bored and wretched, a limitation I greatly regret, when he seems no longer a human being but an invention of science. To explain him to myself I say that he has become a wind instrument and sings no longer like active men, sailor or camel driver, because he has had to compete with an orchestra where the loudest instrument has always survived. The human voice can only become louder by becoming less articulate, by discovering some one musical sort of roar or scream. As poetry can do neither, the voice must be freed from this competition and find itself among little instruments, only heard at their best perhaps when we are close about them. It should be again possible for a few poets to write as all did once, not for the printed page but to be sung.[24]

This style of declamation with accompaniment is very difficult to achieve and, when he came to the realisation of the choruses in his plays, even before he became aware of Nō techniques, Yeats experienced great difficulties in having his intended effects achieved. But he continued in his attempts to have the dramatic effect of his work heightened by some form of musical delivery, as indicated in his notes to *Cathleen Ni Houlihan*, in the version which was printed in Volume IV of his *Collected Works*, 1908, where he directs that

The lines beginning "Do not make a great keening" and "They shall be remembered for ever" are said or sung to an air heard by one of the players in a dream.[25]

This seems to me to indicate Yeats's continuing search for a form of performance which, however alien and strange it might have appeared to an audience attuned to a 'naturalistic' theatre, would elevate the play and give it the quality of a ritual experience and which, granted the presence of the accomplished discipline in performance which he always sought, would enhance the dramatic moment, and so heighten the impact of the performed play on the audience.

But, as he indicated in the notes on the music for his plays which he printed in the various editions over the years, Yeats, with the exception of two performers he named, Sara Allgood and Florence Farr, rarely got from his players the effect he sought of a combination of speech and music, so that when he began to write his 'Plays for Dancers' he indicated in his directions which passages were to be sung, and embarked on a new series of adventures in search of composers who could set these plays.

*

The musicians, who are an integral part of the Nō ensemble, in fact constitute a small group of four players. One plays a flute made of bamboo (Nō-kan). The other three are percussion players, each playing a different kind of drum. These are the *Tsuzumi*, held at shoulder level by the musician and beaten by the fingers of the right hand, a very sensitive instrument on which the pitch can be altered by the player's manipulation of the tensioning strings; the *O-kawa*, a larger drum on which the skin is tightly tensioned, held on the lap and beaten by the fingers of the right hand to produce a high-pitched tone; and the *Taiko*, a drum of deep resonance which stands before the player and is beaten with wooden sticks.

The chorus in Nō consists of eight singers who perform the songs for which the basic pitch is set by the chorus leader and the *Kotoba* or narrative chants which describe and qualify the central action being performed by the players.

In his approach to musicians and chorus in the 'Plays for Dancers,' Yeats conceived a much simplified version of his Japanese model, where he combined chorus and musicians into three players who both played the instruments and spoke or chanted the choruses. He found, in Edmund Dulac, an artist who was prepared to compose the score for *At the Hawk's Well* along these lines, still closely following the model. Dulac's 'Note on the Instruments,' printed with his score in *Four Plays for Dancers*, illustrates this approach to the problem of realising Yeats's ideas:

A NOTE ON THE INSTRUMENTS

In order to apply to the music the idea of great simplicity of execution underlying the whole spirit of the performance, it was necessary to use instruments that any one with a fair idea of music could learn in a few days.

The following offer hardly any difficulty, while they provide a sufficient background of simple sounds which the performer can, after a very little amount of practice, elaborate at will.

A plain bamboo flute giving the appropriate scale.

A harp, a drum and a gong. For these last two, any instruments on oriental lines with a good shape and a deep mellow sound.

For the harp an ordinary zither, such as shown in the design of the musician, can be used. The strings, beginning by the lower ones, are grouped in nine or ten chords of four notes consisting of : the key-note, two strings in unison giving the fifth above, and the octave of the key-note.

Ex:

Beyond these chords there are seven double strings tuned to any pentatonic scale that suits the play.

The tuning of the chords and free strings would be altered according to the performance, and several flutes giving different scales would be required.

The same chords and scales should be used throughout any one play.

The instruments are distributed as follows : one musician plays the drum and gong, one the flute, the singer takes the harp.

The drum and the gong must be used at times during the performance to emphasize the spoken word; no definite notation of this can be given, and it is left to the imagination and taste of the musician.

SCALES FOR THE INSTRUMENTS

THE HARP.   *Free strings.*

Chords.

THE FLUTE.   etc. [26]

In 1917, a close friend of Ezra Pound's, Walter Morse Rummel, who had made musical settings for several of Pound's songs, composed the score for *The Dreaming of the Bones*, and the explanatory notes which accompany this score further illustrate how words and music are to be performed in relation to one another and give directions for the recital of Yeats's text against the background of the musical setting, emphasising the fact that the musical accompaniment must always be subordinate to the vocal parts. Rummel also suggests the addition of a bowed instrument to the flute and percussion arrangement mentioned by Dulac. These notes appear in *Four Plays for Dancers*, as a preface to Rummel's score for the play :

Music of tone and music of speech are distinct from each other.

Here my sole object has been to find some tone formula which will enhance and bring out a music underlying the words. The process is therefore directly opposed to that of tone-music creation, which from the formless directly creates the form, whereas I seek to derive a formless overflow from the already formed.

FIRST MUSICIAN : *A medium voice*, more chanting than singing, not letting the musical value of the sound predominate too greatly the spoken value.

The First Musician uses a *Plucked Instrument* (harp or zither) to reinforce the notes of his song in unison or in the octave. (It is advisable not to reinforce *each* note sung, but only each *beat*, unless certain difficulties of pitch would necessitate the reinforcing of such note.)

During the symphonic moments of the play the plucked instrument assumes a more individual part.

SECOND MUSICIAN : Using a *Flute*, of a soft and discrete quality.

THIRD MUSICIAN : Using a *Bowed Instrument*, one-stringed, more like a Hindu Sarinda, perhaps with a sympathetic vibrating string, giving a nasal sound. This part furnishes a bass, a sort of horizon to the song, and becomes more individual in the symphonic parts of the play.

FOURTH MUSICIAN : Using a Drum, preferably also an oriental model, played with the palm and the fingers of the hand. The drum part is indicated by — (long) and ᴗ (short). The numbers below these indications signify the fingers employed. The using of the palm of the hand is indicated by P.

In case there are only *Three Musicians*, the Second and Third Musicians can alternatively take the Drum part in places where they are unoccupied.

All instrumental music, especially during the speaking parts, must always leave the voice in the foreground.

W.M.R.[27]

In all these plays Yeats was conscious of the fact that the music should draw its inspiration from the Irish traditional ballad song and was, in this aspect, so far ahead of his time that only in the last two decades or so could he have readily found in Ireland traditional musicians who could have adapted their skills to the realisation of his plays on the stage. However, and principally with the assistance and advice of Ezra Pound, he continued his search outside Ireland to find composers who would set his plays, a pursuit which culminated in his most extravagant theatrical adventure, the re-writing of *The Only Jealousy of Emer* as a balletic drama, *Fighting the Waves*, with a score composed by George Antheil, to whom he was introduced by Pound during a stay at Rapallo in the Spring of 1929.

*

Masks in Nō are used for various categories of parts in the dramas — for women's parts, for warriors, for spirits both sacred and demoniac and for fantastic versions of characters from the animal world. But the true value of the mask is revealed only when worn by the player in performance. The mask, by cloaking the physical personality, allows the inner persona, the performed role, to inform the actor's presentation to his audience. But more than this, it is the supreme achievement of the masked player to convince the audience that the mask he wears has become part of his flesh. In a theatrical tradition where all female roles are played by male actors this is an immense challenge to the player, who has to convey by the manner both of the wearing of his mask and of his body movements, the essence of feminine beauty and must evoke the poetic feeling embodied in the role he portrays.

The making of a successful mask is, first, a challenge to the mask-maker, the creative artist who carves and paints the mask before the challenge of wearing it is presented to the actor. The actor then has to exploit a whole idiom in a special convention to convey the feeling and character of the role for which the mask is made. Nō masks are slightly smaller than life-size and are fixed with ribbons tied around the actor's head, a convention familiar to his audience, but one which presents a further challenge to the player who has to convince his audience of his performance despite the fact that a disillusioning border of his own face is visible around the edges of the mask. The mouthpiece of the Nō mask is designed to project the voice in a manner that is suitable to the specially modulated lines written for the parts which demand its wearing, and in this aspect it is important to consider that the parts requiring masks in Yeats's plays do not have this special quality in the lines written for them. Perhaps it might be worth considering the creation of a 'half mask' for texts in English. Yeats had come round to this belief by the time he wrote his later plays in this form, such as *The King of the Great Clock Tower* and its revised version entitled *A Full Moon in March*, written respectively in 1934 and 1935.

Something of the quality sought in the conventions of mask-wearing parts may be indicated by listing a group of mask types used to portray various female roles in the Nō. Youthful beauty in woman is depicted by the *Ko-omote*, which has full cheeks and a wide fore-head; the *Zo-onna*, with its classical perfection of features is some-times used for young woman parts, but also for angels and goddesses; the *Fukai*, literally 'deep' mask portrays older women, advanced not only in age but also in feeling and in experience; the *Rojo* mask represents an old woman who had once been beautiful; a deranged woman is depicted by the *Nasagami* mask, and, finally, the *Deigan* is the mask which represents a woman sworn, as a spirit, to fulfil a destiny or to exact a revenge; the name of the mask derives from the gold dust used to colour the eyes, which suggests a celestial spirit. The mask is never worn without a head-covering which may vary from a simple kerchief or hood to a most elaborate wig or headdress.

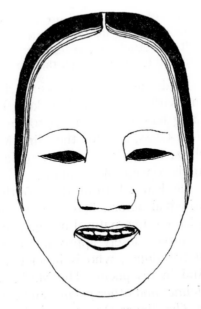

56. *Deigan*. Mask of the ghost of a beautiful woman whose destiny is unfulfilled. Compare Dervorgilla in *The Dreaming of the Bones*.

Long before Yeats discovered the Nō, Gordon Craig had introduced him to the possibilities of using masks for certain characters in his plays, as in the designs which Craig made in 1910 for *The Hour-Glass*, but in his discovery of Nō a new dimension was revealed to Yeats so that he felt:

It would be a stirring adventure for a poet and an artist, working together, to create once more heroic or grotesque types that, keeping always an appropriate distance from life, would seem images of those profound emotions that exist only in solitude and silence.[28]

This passage, written in 1917, after the performance of his first play in the form, is foreshadowed in a passage from his Introduction to *Certain Noble Plays of Japan*, written in the previous year:

A mask will enable me to substitute for the face of some common-place player, or for that face repainted to suit his own vulgar fancy, the fine invention of a sculptor, and to bring the audience close enough to the play to hear every inflection of the voice. A mask never seems but a dirty face, and no matter how close you go is still a work of art; nor shall we lose by staying the movement of the features, for deep feeling is expressed by a movement of the whole body. In poetical painting & in sculpture the face seems the nobler for lacking curiosity, alert attention, all that we sum up under the famous word of the realists "vitality." It is even possible that being is only possessed completely by the dead, and that it is some knowledge of this that makes us gaze with so much emotion upon the face of the Sphinx or Buddha.

Who can forget the face of Chaliapine as the Mogul King in *Prince Igor*, when a mask covering its upper portion made him seem like a Phoenix at the end of its thousand wise years, awaiting in condescension the burning nest and what did it not gain from that immobility in dignity and in power?[29]

In his later plays Yeats experimented with various forms of masks, and with various mask-makers, but I feel that the masks that Gordon Craig had designed in 1910 for the Wise Man and the Fool in *The Hour-Glass*, and for the Blind Man in the first of Yeats's Cuchulain plays, *On Baile's Strand*, remained always in his thoughts as central to his concept of the mask.

He learned from the Nō that masks should be used only by principal actors, heroic or tragic — Fool, Blind Man, King, Queen, spirit or supernatural being. The *Deigan* type of Nō mask would, for example, closely approximate to the woman part in *The Dreaming of the Bones*, who is in fact a tortured ghost seeking forgiveness. And in his poem, 'The Mask,' first printed in 1910 in *The Green Helmet and other poems*, and eventually included as one of the lyrics in *The Player Queen*, he indicates how the essence of this concept had been realised by him before his contact with the classical rules of the Japanese theatre :

THE MASK

"Put off that mask of burning gold
With emerald eyes."
"O no, my dear, you make so bold
To find if hearts be wild and wise,
And yet not cold."

"I would but find what's there to find,
Love or deceit."
"It was the mask engaged your mind,
And after set your heart to beat,
Not what's behind."

"But lest you are my enemy,
I must enquire."
"Oh no, my dear, let all that be;
What matter, so there is but fire
In you, in me?" [30]

In the stage directions to his 'Plays for Dancers' Yeats usually directs that the chorus have their faces made up to resemble masks, but the purpose of this direction is probably to assist the chorus to speak and sing their lines without emotive facial expressions or body movements.

*

Dance in Nō is not choreographic movement as understood in the ballet schools of the western world, but is a series of mimetic movements which derives from the text of the play and extends its communication to an audience which must be presumed to have an understanding of the significance of the various gestures and poses which make up the movements performed by the actor. Some of these movements may consist only of a simple circling of the stage by the actor, and some are so slow and grow so deliberately out of the speech that it is difficult to realise the point at which dance, or movement, begins or ends. But every movement, every gesture, in Nō has as its purpose the evocation of the central beauty, the ultimate 'deep' meaning of the play and the deeper this essential beauty or dignity, the fewer and simpler may be the gestures of the dance, in which every movement of head, body, arm or leg may comment upon and extend the text, without necessarily being a visual representation of the lines as would be the case in western mime. The Nō actor, too, has a most important accessory in the fan, which has, itself in use a second language or idiom of meaningful gesture combining with the actor's voice, body movement, mask and costume and the music and chanting of the chorus in the distillation of absolute beauty or 'accomplishment' which constitutes the performance. But this extra 'limb,' that fan, must be left to its Japanese context and cannot be considered in the context of Yeats's adaptation of the form.

However, rather than rhythmic dance, Yeats, in his 'Plays for Dancers,' demands from his actors a form of expressive movement which combines with his text and with the performance of chorus and music to round out the presentation of the play to the audience. From the beginning of his work in this form he realised the difficulties of finding actors who could both move and speak in accordance with his texts. For example, in the stage directions to *The Dreaming of the Bones* he states that the part of the Young Woman can be played by a dancer and her lines delivered by the actor who plays the Stranger.

In his search for a dancer for his plays he eventually discovered Ninette de Valois, an Irishwoman who had been trained by Diaghilev and founded her own school of dance in England in the 1920's. In a lecture given at the Yeats Summer School in Sligo on 21 August 1969, Ninette de Valois recalled:

The first time I met him was at the Festival Theatre in Cambridge where I had gone up to produce a play of Gordon Bottomley's. I put on some dances there and he happened to be in the audience and he asked the Director of the theatre could he meet me because he was very thrilled with the evening. I met him at the back of the theatre the next morning, or rather in the front, in the foyer, and it was terribly dark. I saw this great figure sitting in a chair there in profile, and he started a marvellous conversation with me. I was too terrified to notice anything really. The conversation was about the evening before and suddenly at the end he said to me, "I want you to come to Dublin and help me revise my plays for dancers which must be restaged and put back into the Dublin scene." [31]

This confrontation led to the public staging of the 'Plays for Dancers' in Dublin and to the founding of the Abbey School of Ballet under the direction of Ninette de Valois, and also led to Yeats's development of the later dance plays into forms which drew the inspiration for their movements from other sources than the rigid rules he had set himself on first coming into contact with Fenollosa's work. He also came to realise that the playing of a part which involved both dancing and speech could not necessarily be accomplished by one person, so that in the rewritten version of *The King of the Great Clock Tower* the part of the Queen has no lines to speak, and in the further development of the same plot, *A Full Moon in March*, the stage direction specifies that

when the inner curtain rises the player who has hitherto taken the part of the Queen is replaced by a dancer.

But, as the years passed, the form of dance movement indicated by Yeats for use in performances of his plays seemed to get further and further from the ideals he had originally developed from Nō and his final disillusionment with the various attempts to realise his ideal on the stage is reflected in the prologue to his last play, *The Death of Cuchulain*, which he finished on his deathbed in January 1939, where the Old Man who is the prologue to the play declaims:

I was at my wit's end to find a good dancer; I could have got such a dancer once, but she has gone; the tragi-comedian dancer, the tragic dancer, upon the same neck love and loathing, life and death. I spit three times. I spit upon the dancers painted by Degas. I spit upon their short bodices, their stiff stays, their toes whereon they spin like peg-tops, above all upon that chambermaid face. They might have looked timeless, Rameses the Great, but not the chambermaid, that old maid history. I spit! I spit! I spit!

*

In contrast to the ordered simplicity (almost barren in appearance) of the stage and the simple costumes of the chorus, musicians and stage attendants in the Nō, which are almost like uniforms identified with a particular 'school' or troupe of performers, the actors' costumes give a colourful magnificence which, combined with the music, speaking and chanting, and with the stylised movements adds enor-

mously to the mesmeric effect of the whole performance. The actors'
costumes, designed to reveal the function or status of the part played,
are constructed in a tradition in which make, pattern or style obser-
ves the same sense of order that governs every element of the Nō,
often in rich brocades and embroidered silks interwoven with gold
and silver threads. The design of the costumes assists rather than
hinders the stage movements and often a change in character or
personality, or a transformation from human to divine status in a
part is indicated by a costume change devised as part of the movement so that the whole concept of costume contributes to the
dramatic effect of the performance.

A similar approach to costume design for his plays had formed
part of Yeats's approach to his visualisation of his dramatic work
since the eighteen-nineties, particularly after he had made contact
with Craig and Ricketts in the first decade of this century. Ricketts
had designed for him costumes for 'types' rather than for individual
characters, so that such designs could, as could the masks designed
by Craig, be considered as becoming part of his new mode of drama,
particularly in his plays on heroic themes.

Another convention of the Nō which Yeats could accept and adapt
to his purpose without difficulty was that of stage properties. A
lacquered cask may be used to represent a great number of objects
and where specific properties are called for in the texts the audience
is expected to understand the conventional symbol. As Yeats put it,
'a ship is represented by a mere skeleton of willows or osiers painted
green.'[32] Thus, in At the Hawk's Well, the well is represented by a
square of blue cloth laid upon the playing space; and the painted
cubes of wood which represent the severed heads in The Death of
Cuchulain indicate Yeats's complete agreement with this convention
of the Nō theatre.

But, for his own dramatic purpose, Yeats created a unique and
special ritual which occurs in most of the 'Plays for Dancers.' This is
that of the 'unfolding and folding of the cloth' and is designed to
allow the chorus to partly conceal the playing area while this is being
set up and the actors are taking their places for the opening of the
main action of the piece, as the opening chorus is chanted. The ritual
is repeated during the closing chorus to cover the withdrawal of the
actors at the end of the play. Precise directions for this ritual occur
in the earlier 'Plays for Dancers' but not in the plays written after
the experimental annexe to the Abbey Theatre, the Peacock, had
been opened in November 1927, when Yeats had at his disposal a
stage which in size and arrangement he felt suitable for his verse

plays. This Yeatsian device might perhaps be considered as a link or 'bridge' between the Nō technique as adapted by him and the European conventional stage with its front or 'tableau' curtain.

*

When the first play he had derived from the Japanese Nō theatre had been performed and was first printed in *Harper's Bazaar* for March 1917, Yeats contributed a preface, which became his 'Note' on the play printed in later editions, in which he summed up his new-found approach to theatre. He wrote:

I need a theatre. I believe myself to be a dramatist; I desire to show events and not merely to tell of them; two of my best friends were won for me by my plays; and I seem to myself more alive at the moment when a roomful of people have the one lofty emotion. My blunder has been that I did not discover in my youth that my theatre must be the ancient theatre made by unrolling a carpet, or marking out a place with a stick, or setting a screen against a wall. Certainly those who care for my kind of poetry must be numerous enough, if I can bring them together, to pay half a dozen players who can bring all their properties in a cab and perform in their leisure moments.[33]

In the same essay, to which, in its second appearance, in *To-Day* (London), in May 1917, he gave the title, 'Instead of a Theatre,' he goes on to acknowledge the Nō, 'that most subtle stage,' as his first model, and this passage, parts of which have already been quoted in this present chapter, defines the idiom of the new directions which Yeats had given his plays:

I have found my first model — and in literature if we would not be parvenus we must have a model — in the "Noh" stage of aristocratic Japan. I have described in the introduction to Mr. Pound's "Certain Noble Plays of Japan" (Cuala Press) what had seemed to me important on that subtle stage. I do not think of my discovery as mere economy. It has been a great gain to get rid of scenery and substitute for a crude landscape painted upon canvas three performers who, sitting against a screen covered with some one unchangeable pattern, or against the wall of a room describe landscape or event, and accompany movement with drum or cymbal, or deepen the emotion of the words with zither and flute. Painted scenery, after all, is unnecessary to my friends and to myself, for our imagination, kept living by the arts, can imagine a mountain covered with thorn-trees, in a drawing-room without any great trouble, and we have many quarrels with even the best scene-painting. Then, too, the masks forced upon us by the absence of any special lighting and by the nearness of the audience who surround the players upon three sides, do not seem to us eccentric. We are accustomed to faces of bronze and of marble, and what could be more suitable than that Cuchulain, let us say, a half-supernatural legendary person, should show to us a face not made before the looking-glass by some leading player — there too, we have many quarrels — but moulded by some distinguished artist? We are a learned people, and we remember how the Roman Theatre, when it became more intellectual, abandoned "make-up" and used the mask instead, and that the most famous artists of Japan modelled masks that are still in use after hundreds of years. It would be a stirring adventure for a poet and an artist, working together, to create once more heroic or grotesque types that, keeping always an appropriate distance from life, would seem images of those profound emotions that exist only in solitude and in silence. Nor has any one told me after a performance that they have missed a changing facial expression, for the mask seems to change with the light that falls upon it, and besides, expression in poetical and tragic art, as every producer knows, is mainly in those movements that are of the entire body.[34]

Thus, even though Yeats's contact with Nō, by way of the Fenollosa/Pound versions, was several times removed from the original, it suggested to him the framework he had sought for his dramatic constructions and which he was to work over and develop for the remainder of his life. The plays which resulted from this influence are, only now, thirty years after his death, being recognised for their universal and enduring qualities.

Yeats did not attempt to write imitation Nō plays, but adapted the form to his own purposes and to embody not only his own themes but his philosophy. His actual contact with the Japanese form is defined by Hiro Ishibashi in her paper *Yeats and the Noh*, which she subtitled *Forms of Japanese Beauty and their Reflection in Yeats's Plays*:

Yeats recognised the Nō as a form of poetic drama and he created an entirely new form of his own. He discovered, as he said, that "the subtler forms of literature can be given dramatic expression." Yeats did what he did in this *genre* as early as 1915. It is not a great adventure in this decade for a composer or a poet to create a piece in the *genre* of the Nō, but it was then. He first imagined his own form of Nō when there were less than twenty pieces available in English translation out of about two hundred and forty extant Nō plays (which can be acted), after seeing only some fragmentary amateur performances of Nō, never having seen a complete stage production and never even having visited Japan. The discovery of a new form was the starting point of all his later plays. A creation, we thus see, can be born of a misunderstanding and a creative worker is free to turn misunderstanding into creation, if only his works have in themselves the power to exist as high art.[35]

AT THE HAWK'S WELL: A PLAY

Scene: The stage is any bare space in a room against a wall. Against the wall are placed before the play begins, a drum, cymbals, and a stringed instrument. The three Musicians enter slowly. One carries a black cloth. He stands in the middle of the space. The others stand one on either side and slowly unfold the cloth till a part of the stage is hidden. As they unfold it they move backward and outward so that the cloth makes an angle, with one Musician at the apex. Hid by the cloth a girl enters and crouches on the ground. The Musicians sing while the cloth is being unfolded.

I call to the eye of the mind
A well long choked up and dry,
And boughs long stripped by the wind,
And I call to the mind's eye
Pallor of an ivory face,
Its lofty dissolute air,
A man climbing up to a place
The salt sea wind has swept bare.

(They fold up the cloth singing)
I have dreamed of a life soon done,
Will he lose by that or win?
A mother that saw her son
Doubled over a speckled shin,

27

57. *At the Hawk's Well*. The opening page of the play as printed in *The Wild Swans at Coole, other verses and a play in verse*. Dublin, The Cuala Press. Edition limited to four hundred copies, finished in October 1917.

The first writing that Yeats attempted in the style that his new form
of drama would take, as he predicted in his Introduction to *Certain
Noble Plays of Japan*, was one of his series of plays which had as their
central character the Irish epic hero, Cuchulain. This play, entitled
The Waters of Immortality in its early versions, was finally produced
and published as *At the Hawk's Well*. It is the third of his plays
which has Cuchulain as the hero but, in the overall structure of the
epic, comes first in sequence. The theme of the play may have been
chosen by Yeats for his first attempt at a drama modelled on the Nō
because it offered the possibility of his using dramatic situations to
which he could find reasonably close parallels in his Japanese model.
The theme can be found as early as 1898 in a letter to Dorothea
Hunter in which Yeats wrote:

The souls of ordinary people remain after death in the waters and these waters
become an organized world if you gather up the flames that come from the
waters of the well when the berries fall upon it, and make them into a flaming
heart, and explore the waters with this as a lamp. They are the waters of
emotion and passion, in which all but purified souls are entangled, and have
the same relation to our plane of fixed material form as the Divine World of
fluid fire has to the heroic world of fixed intellectual form.[1]

The Young Man, later revealed as Cuchulain, is, in terms of the
Nō, really the *Waki* of the play, the wanderer who arrives on the
scene on his way to fulfil a destiny; a destiny which is not made fully
apparent to the audience unless the piece is played in its context in
the whole cycle, preceding *On Baile's Strand*. The Young Man's confrontation with the Guardian of the Well, who is revealed as the
bird-spirit, creates the occasion of the central dance movement in
which the hero is diverted by the spirit from his purpose, which is to
visit the well at the one moment when he may be granted the quality
of immortality. Just before the magic moment the Guardian of the
Well lures him away from the scene and towards a different destiny
and in doing so condemns the Old Man who has been waiting to
share the promised gift of immortality.

The emergence and development of the text through the several
extant drafts is traced in detail in *Yeats at Work* by Curtis B. Bradford, published by the Southern Illinois University Press in 1965.
Bradford's study reveals that many of the elements of the final text
are present even in the earliest prose draft, which indicates how
closely Yeats adhered to the rules he had formulated for himself
during his examination of the Nō plays and during his composition
of the Introduction to the Pound-Fenollosa book.

In its simplest outline, the structure of Yeats's first 'Play for

Dancers' consists of an opening chorus which sets scene and theme, followed by a narrative passage at the end of which the Guardian of the Well reveals herself as the bird-goddess and leads into the dance forming the climax of the piece during which the hero is deceived and strays from his purpose, only to be led on to a different destiny which is a confrontation with the warrior queen, Aoife. At this point the central action ends with the indication that the epic tale will be taken up again in some other aspect resulting from the changing of Cuchulain's destiny. The play ends with a final symbolic chorus.

As in the Nō, the chorus provides a commentary on the dance, the climax of which is described in Yeats's first prose draft of the play :

Chorus continues description of dance. How they go from rock to rock on the mountain side. Is it hate or is it love? Sometimes she leads him near the fountain, and then away. The fountain bubbles. At that moment the woman . . . breaks from him and runs out. He goes half way to the fountain, then hears the cry of the hawk and runs out after the woman. The Old Man gets up and goes to well.[2]

Even in this first attempt to create a new type of imaginative piece for the theatre, Yeats must have perceived that his audience would not feel, especially in a performance played outside a formal theatre, that they were present at anything other than a charade unless the performance was, in some manner, presented in a form heightened by ritual. Thus, while he derived from the Nō the general framework on which his play was constructed, and an approach to stage properties closely allied to that of his Japanese model, in that the well is to be represented by a square of cloth laid on the ground of the acting area — an extreme simplification of the elaborate and very beautiful stage property used to represent a well on the Nō stage — he created a ritual uniquely suited to his own form of drama. This detail, which did not occur in his Japanese model, but is, both in its concept and in its execution, an extremely effective theatrical device, is that of the 'unfolding and folding of the cloth' which accompanied the choruses that open and close the play. By its use he allowed his western audience the semi-deception of a device whereby the main characters took up their positions in the acting area while partly concealed by the spread cloth from the audience.

The 'cloth,' which, from the reproduction of Dulac's design for the original production of At the Hawk's Well, I would estimate to have been about eight feet wide and four feet high, was unfolded according to a ritual which is defined in the prompt book for the first production, and was therefore probably worked out in rehearsal. But the device of the cloth is present even in the earliest surviving draft

58. Cloth by Edmund Dulac. For the first production of
At the Hawk's Well, 1916.

for the play where the direction appears in its simplest form:

Chorus (2) spreads black cloth. When it is taken away Girl is sitting by square
cloth to show where well is.[3]

The development of the ritual of the cloth can be followed through
the various drafts of the play and by the time the text has proceeded
from manuscript to typescript it is suggested that the cloth have
'upon it the image of a hawk.'

The first printed version of the play, which appeared in the March
1917 issue of *Harper's Bazaar* under the title of *At the Hawk's Well
or Waters of Immortality*, may have been set up from the prompt
script of the production, with a Preface and reproductions from
Dulac's designs. The text of the play also appeared in the June 1917
issue of *To-Day* (London). In the play's first appearance in book form,
in the Cuala Press volume, *The Wild Swans at Coole, other verses
and a play in verse*, finished on 10 October 1917, the text of *At the
Hawk's Well* was set up from an earlier version of the script, but the
volume contains, at the end of the play, an amended version of the
Preface, now called 'A Note on "At the Hawk's Well"' and dated
December 1916.

The version printed in *Four Plays for Dancers*, London 1921, which
reverts to that derived from the prompt book, is accompanied by
Edmund Dulac's musical score and his designs for the cloth, masks
and costumes, 'A Note on the Instruments' and 'Scales for the Instruments.' There are also two photographs by Alvin Langdon Coburn
of the masks. In this version, in which the text is similar to that

printed in *Harper's Bazaar*, Yeats, in a lengthy opening stage direction, specifies the ritual of unfolding and folding the cloth, and also
indicates in some detail the approach adopted to the staging of the
first production of the play. This can be compared with the Cuala
Press printing of the scene direction which is reproduced on page 218.

The stage is any bare space before a wall against which stands a patterned
screen. A drum and a gong and a zither have been laid close to the screen
before the play begins. If necessary, they can be carried in, after the audience
is seated, by the First Musician, who also can attend to the lights if there is
any special lighting. We had two lanterns upon posts — designed by Mr.
Dulac — at the outer corners of the stage, but they did not give enough light,
and we found it better to play by the light of a large chandelier. Indeed, I
think, so far as my present experience goes, that the most effective lighting
is the lighting we are most accustomed to in our rooms. These masked players
seem stranger when there is no mechanical means of separating them from us.
The First Musician carries with him a folded black cloth and goes to the
centre of the stage towards the front and stands motionless, the folded cloth
hanging from between his hands. The two other Musicians enter and, after
standing a moment at either side of the stage, go towards him and slowly
unfold the cloth, singing as they do so :

> I call to the eye of the mind
> A well long choked up and dry
> And boughs long stripped by the wind,
> And I call to the mind's eye
> Pallor of an ivory face,
> Its lofty dissolute air,
> A man climbing up to a place
> The salt sea wind has swept bare.

As they unfold the cloth, they go backward a little so that the stretched cloth
and the wall make a triangle with the First Musician at the apex supporting
the centre of the cloth. On the black cloth is a gold pattern suggesting a hawk.
The Second and Third Musicians now slowly fold up the cloth again, pacing
with a rhythmic movement of the arms towards the First Musician and
singing.

At the end of the play this ritual is repeated to cover the exit of
the players while the closing chorus is being sung, and when the
chorus has ended the acting area is bare, as it was before the beginning of the play. The stage direction reads :

The Musicians stand up; one goes to centre with folded cloth. The others
unfold it. While they do so they sing. During the singing, and while hidden by
the cloth, the Old Man goes out. When the play is performed with Mr. Dulac's
music, the Musicians do not rise or unfold the cloth till after they have sung
the words "a bitter life."

This direction is followed by the texts of the 'Songs for the unfolding
and folding of the cloth,' with a further interpolated stage direction
as to the point in the text at which they fold up the cloth.

Later in his playwriting career Yeats was to provide other details of stage directions and alternative forms of this ritual, but it is his primary concession in adapting the Nō theatre to his own purpose.

Once more it was Ezra Pound who made available to Yeats the special talents he needed for the realisation of his newly developed dramatic form in performance. In London he could find skilled actors and fine musicians, but the presentation of *At the Hawk's Well* demanded, in addition, in its music, its movements and its visual appearance, knowledge of the art forms of the East, a quality not so easily found. Pound introduced Yeats to the two people whose understanding of his special requirements, however limited their real knowledge of his Japanese model, made a production possible. These were the Japanese dancer, Michio Ito, and the painter and musician, Edmund Dulac. Pound also introduced Yeats to the brilliant photographer, Alvin Langdon Coburn, who recorded the production in a series of fine photographs.

Edmund Dulac was born at Toulouse in France in 1882, and became a naturalised British citizen in 1912. Pound, in enlisting a faculty for his proposed College of Arts in London in 1914, had included him in its membership, which also included the photographer Coburn and an old acquaintance of Yeats's, Arnold Dolmetsch who had been for many years involved in Yeats's search for a manner of speaking or chanting his verse described in 'Speaking to the Psaltery' and who had, in fact, made the psaltery used by Florence Farr in her experiments and recitals of his poetry, both lyrical and dramatic, about the beginning of the century. At the time Yeats met him, Dulac was best known as a book illustrator and had decorated a number of editions of classics such as *The Arabian Nights*, 1907, and *The Rubiayat of Omar Khayyam*, 1909, in a highly decorative formalised style which is echoed in the masks and costumes he designed for *At the Hawk's Well*.

The lighter side of Dulac's relationship with Yeats is reflected in the amusing drawing, dated 1915, now in the collection of the Abbey Theatre, which depicts Yeats as an enormous puppet, leaning on a harp, and attached to strings manipulated by characters in Irish 'peasant' costumes, within a proscenium arch decorated by a shamrock. This, perhaps, symbolises Yeats's divided loyalties of the time— drawn in one direction by his managerial problems in the Irish National Theatre where popular 'peasant' dramas occupied most of the company's time and endeavours, and in the other by his vision of his newly discovered, and necessarily unpopular form.

Dulac designed the woodcut decorations to *A Vision*, 1926, and composed musical settings for several of the ballads Yeats wrote in the 1930's. He died in 1953.

Michio Ito (1893-1961) came from a wealthy Japanese family and after a period spent in the study of the traditional dance forms of his native country at the Mizuki Dancing School, where he graduated in 1911, he travelled to Europe to study European forms of dance and spent the following three years in Paris at the Dalcroze School. From Paris he went to London where he became a protégé of Ezra Pound's, and assisted Pound with his work of deciphering and editing the Fenollosa papers. Ito's study of Japanese dance forms was not related to the forms used in the Nō theatre, but he became interested in Nō forms when he came into contact with Pound in 1915, and in October of that year gave some performances of Nō dancing for Pound and a group of friends in a costume specially reconstructed by Dulac and Charles Ricketts.

In *W. B. Yeats and Japan*, Professor Shotaro Oshima quotes the following account of Ito's meeting with Yeats from reminiscences contributed by Ito to *Hikaku-bunka, Dai-ni shū (Comparative Studies of Culture)*, No. 2, Tokyo, 1956:

At the age of 23 or 24, I was chosen as a chief dancer at the Coliseum Theatre. In those days Pound told me he was editing a book of Noh plays which had been translated by Fenollosa. One of my uncles Matsuura had a passion for the Noh performance and had a Noh theatre in his own house, at Honjo in Tokyo. I was too accustomed to attending Noh plays with this uncle. I gained the idea that Noh was extremely dull, and in fact told Pound that it was very uninteresting. However, together with my friends Nijūichi Kayano, dramatist, and Taminosuke Kumé, painter, I visited Pound and Yeats. Both poets still wanted to hear a Noh recitation. And so Kayano and Kumé gave a recitation of Noh. To Yeats the feeling association between Noh and the new symbolic drama was exceedingly strong.[4]

As Ito was, by 1916, an accomplished mimetic dancer both in Eastern and Western modes, and had performed Japanese character dances in several London theatres, the adaptation of his skill to the dance element required by Yeats in *At the Hawk's Well* cannot have been too difficult, particularly as the form of dance movement peculiar to the Nō would have been at that time totally unfamiliar to any London audience.

The development of the dance element from its first concept to its performance in *At the Hawk's Well* can also be followed in Curtis Bradford's book which reveals through the drafts and preliminary scripts Yeats's increasing obsession with the technical details of the play. By the time the text has progressed from holograph to typescript Yeats has defined the dance movements of the Guardian of the

Well as consisting of three movements, each of two minutes' duration. By the time the play was printed in *Harper's Bazaar* in March 1917, in a version which was probably set up from the prompt book, the dance consists of four movements, not defined as to their duration, interpolated with an antiphonal commentary conducted between the Chorus and the Young Man. This text also indicates that all the movements of the characters of the play should be stylised, or, as Yeats expresses it, in his first stage direction to the central action of the play, following the entrance of the Old Man:

The Old Man stands for a moment motionless by the side of the stage with bowed head. He lifts his head at the sound of a drum-tap. He goes towards the front of the stage moving to the taps of the drum. He crouches and moves his hands as if making a fire. His movements, like those of the other persons in the play, suggest a marionette.

During the action, the Guardian of the Well utters the cry of a hawk, and to discover this sound and the movements of the bird, Yeats, Dulac and Ito visited the London Zoo to study the hawks there. The results were, however, disappointing, but Dulac, as Ito recalled in later years, asked what the Japanese word for hawk was, and this word, *taka*, was used in the performance as it produced a much more theatrically effective sound.

Yeats involved himself intensely in the preparations for the first production of his play. Ezra Pound was even persuaded to stand in at rehearsals when the actors were not available. But the realisation of a completely new form of theatre was not easily accomplished and dissentions with the musicians and the actors are reflected in a letter to Lady Gregory which he commenced on 28 March 1916, but did not complete until after the first performance had been given:

March 28 [1916]   *18 Woburn Buildings*

The play goes well but the musicians give more and more trouble and will have to be eliminated when we are through our first performances. The masks have the most wonderful effect. They keep their power when you are quite close.

Monday [*Postmark* 10 *April* 1916]

I think *At the Hawk's Well* was a real success though a charity audience is a bad one. We refused to admit the press as we considered it an experiment and in any case have no need of press in work intended for a few. We shall not do it again until June in order to get rid of Ainley and the musicians. The music Beecham says is good but one cannot discuss anything with a feud between Dulac and a stupid musician at every rehearsal. It seems better to get very simple music that can be kept under control. I may even repeat the lyrics myself and have no singing and no music but gong and drum played by Dulac and perhaps a dulcimer or flute.[5]

It is evident that Yeats realised the difficulties created and the limitations imposed by the special nature of the new theatre form he was attempting, and saw that he had to go outside the professional theatre to seek the helpers he needed. In his essay, 'A People's Theatre,' published in 1919, looking back on the experience, he concluded:

. . . who but the leisured will welcome an elaborate art or pay for its first experiments? In one thing the luck might be upon our side. A man who loves verse and the visible arts has, in a work such as I imagined, the advantage of the professional player. The professional player becomes the amateur, the other has been preparing all his life, and certainly I shall not soon forget the rehearsal of At the Hawk's Well, when Mr. Ezra Pound, who had never acted on any stage, in the absence of our chief player rehearsed for half an hour. Even the forms of subjective acting that were natural to the professional stage have ceased. Where all now is sympathy and observation no Irving can carry himself with intellectual pride, nor any Salvini in half-animal nobility, both wrapped in solitude.[6]

The excitement Yeats felt about realising his new form of drama is reflected in his letters of the time by passages such as the following, from a letter written on the morning of 2 April 1916, the day of the first performance, to his friend and patron in New York, John Quinn:

I am tired out with the excitement of rehearsing my new play — The Hawk's Well in which masks are being used for the first time in serious drama in the modern world. Ainley, who is the hero, wears a mask like an archaic Greek statue. I enclose a paragraph from the Observer. The play can be played in the middle of a room. It is quite short — 30 or 40 minutes. I am not satisfied with the production and shall withdraw it after Tuesday and start afresh. I hope to create a form of drama which may delight the best minds of my time, and all the more because it can pay its expenses without the others. If when the play is perfectly performed (musicians are the devil) Balfour and Sargent and Ricketts and Sturge Moore and John and the Prime Minister and a few pretty ladies will come to see it, I shall have a success that would have pleased Sophocles. I shall be as lucky as a Japanese dramatic poet at the Court of the Shogun.

My dress rehearsal, or really first performance, is given at Lady Cunard's today at 3-40, and I am to be there at 3. I shall go to lunch and then lie down for a little and after that I may be able to face the musicians. One of them insists on a guitar, and the scene of the play is laid in Ireland in the heroic age! His instrument is to appear to-day disguised by Dulac in cardboard, but the musician will struggle for the familiar shape. Beecham is coming to support me.[7]

Even the prospect of performing outside of 'theatrical' environment with a formal stage, proscenium, lighting and scenery was no new concept to Yeats. In the early days of the Irish National Theatre Society before Miss Horniman's bounty had made the creation of the

Abbey Theatre in Dublin possible, and when productions of the Society did, in many cases, require the formal trappings of the conventional stage, he had, as he expressed it in his essay "The Dramatic Movement' in *Samhain 1904*:

. . . been forced to perform in Halls without proper lighting for the stage, and almost without dressing rooms, and with level floors in the Auditorium that prevented all but the people in the front row from seeing properly. These Halls are expensive too and the players of poetical drama in an age of musical comedy have light pockets.[8]

With such experiences in the background of that part of his career which was occupied by the practical details of stage management and production, Yeats cannot have had any difficulty in adapting the performance details of *At the Hawk's Well* to its presentation in a large London drawing-room.*

In his sustained enthusiasm, continuing (on 10 April) his letter of 28 March, Yeats wrote to Lady Gregory about the first 'public' performance of the play given on 4 April, in aid of the Social Institute Union at 8 Chesterfield Gardens and preceded by a concert arranged and conducted by Sir Thomas Beecham:

The form is a discovery and the dancing and masks wonderful. Nobody seemed to know who was masked and who was not on Tuesday. Those who were not masked were made up to look as if they were. It was all very strange. Two press people got in, a wretched woman who came to describe the clothes of the fine ladies, and an American who paid a guinea for his ticket and who wants pictures from Dulac of masks and costumes for some American magazine. We turned a most obstinate photographer out of the dressing rooms. Coburn is to photograph us. It amuses me defying the press.[9]

The total effect of the performance, text, masks, costumes, music, dancing and the symbolic ritual of the unfolding and folding of the cloth must have seemed strange to its audience. However prepared

---

*   AT THE HAWK'S WELL

Produced privately in the drawing-room
of Lady Cunard's house, Cavendish Square, London,
on 2 April 1916

The Young Man	Henry Ainley
The Old Man	Allan Wade
The Guardian of the Well	Michio Ito
The three Musicians	Mr. Dulac, Mrs. Mann, Mr. Foulds

Directed by Edmund Dulac under the supervision of W. B. Yeats
Designed by Edmund Dulac
Music by Edmund Dulac
Choreography by Michio Ito

they were for the new form, they were still, in the London of 1916, conditioned by a realistic theatre which, although artificial or 'theatrical' in its style of presentation, was more nearly a reflection of the taste of the age than was Yeats's involved investigation of a deep and exotic inner concept of beauty which had little, if any, relationship to everyday life. Yeats, however, firmly believed that, with his new dramatic form, he had stirred the imagination of the discerning few, all that he had hoped, and was encouraged to continue writing plays in his new mode.

The practical realisation of the production can hardly have come up to Yeats's ideal. As the letter quoted above indicates, the stringed instrument was a guitar disguised with cardboard. In his paper, *Yeats and Music*, Edward Malins describes Dulac's score as 'tedious' and 'sometimes . . . insensitive to the rhythm of the words which are strait-jacketed against their natural accents.' [10]

Dulac's masks for the Young Cuchulain and for the Old Man, although they are fine examples of the maskmaker's art, must, by covering the entire faces of the players, have to some extent obscured the voices in rendering the blank verse of the text. But they did fulfil Yeats's purpose in creating images of 'half-supernatural legendary beings' and, in Alvin Langdon Coburn's photographs of the first London production, give an impression of how noble the characters of the drama seemed. Surprisingly, the Dancer, the Guardian of the Well, wore a headdress to suggest the hawk but, according to the stage direction, had his 'face made up to resemble a mask.'

The costumes, as reproduced in *Four Plays for Dancers* have, I think, less feeling of splendour than those designed by Charles Ricketts for the earlier Cuchulain plays at the Abbey and, in this aspect, Ricketts would perhaps have been a better costume designer for the noble and heroic types sought by Yeats. Ricketts' Cuchulain costume, designed for the Abbey revival of *On Baile's Strand* in 1915 would, combined with Dulac's mask, have created a figure more completely in keeping with the presentation of the Nō. Dulac's costume design for the musicians owes much to their Japanese originals.

Had Yeats in 1916 been as deeply under the influence of the Irish tradition in music as he was in his last years, his 'Plays for Dancers' might have developed in a direction that would have had a more direct impact in his own country and been presented regularly on the stage of the National Theatre of which he had been the chief begetter.

Yeats, however, extended the canon of his new theatrical idiom by his piece, variously headed 'Preface' or 'Note,' which accompanied

To be sung without accompaniment as they unfold the curtain.

I call to the eye of the mind A well long choked up and dry And boughs long stripped by the wind, And I call to the mind's eye Pall-or of an ivory face Its lofty dis-so-lute air, A man climbing up to a place The salt sea wind has swept bare. I have dreamed of a life soon done, Will he lose by that or win? A mo-ther that saw her son Dou-bled o-ver a speckled shin Cross-grained with nine-ty years Would cry, "How little worth Were all my hopes and fears And the hard pain of his birth!"

59. *At the Hawk's Well.* Opening chorus as set by Edmund Dulac, 1916.
Reproduced in *Four Plays for Dancers,* 1921.

the early printed texts of *At the Hawk's Well.* In the *Harper's Bazaar* version, the earliest printed, March 1917, this appears as a 'Preface.' The same piece with minor alterations appeared as an essay entitled 'Instead of a Theatre' in the May 1917 issue of *To-Day,* with a notice that the text of the play would appear in the next issue of the journal. In the Cuala Press volume, *The Wild Swans at Coole, other verses and a play in verse,* finished in October 1917, it appears as 'A Note on "At the Hawk's Well"' and is dated December 1916. It was reprinted in America in *Theatre Arts Magazine* in Detroit in January 1919, with the elimination of the cast list, and appeared as a 'Note on the First Performance of "At the Hawk's Well,"' dated 1916, in *Four Plays for Dancers,* 1921, which volume includes Dulac's score. It also appears, again with the music, in *Plays and Controversies,* 1923, the third volume in Macmillan's projected uniform edition of the *Works,* but does not appear in any other edition of the *Plays* issued during Yeats's lifetime.

The loss of his dancer so soon after the London production in 1916 must have been a severe setback to Yeats, which is reflected in the final passage of his 'Note' on *At the Hawk's Well*, in which he wrote:

Perhaps I shall turn to something else now that our Japanese dancer, Mr. Itow, whose minute intensity of movement in the dance of the hawk so well suited our small room and private art, has been hired by a New York theatre, or perhaps I shall find another dancer. I am certain, however, that whether I grow tired or not — and one does grow tired of always quarrying the stone for one's statue — I have found out the only way the subtler forms of literature can find dramatic expression.[11]

In the third edition of *A Bibliography of the Writings of W. B. Yeats* by Allan Wade, as revised by Russell K. Alspach, 1968, General Alspach identifies a hitherto unrecorded printing of the play as a twelve-page pamphlet, perhaps a rehearsal copy printed for a performance given in New York during November 1916, when the masks made by Dulac for the London production were shown at the gallery of Messrs. Scott and Fowles during an exhibition of the artist's work. Edmund Dulac told General Alspach that a performance, arranged by Mr. Martin Birnbaum, a partner in the gallery, was given at this time at the Greenwich Village Theatre, using his masks and that he played the Chorus and Michio Ito played the Guardian of the Well. This would appear to have been the first American production of the play.

Michio Ito's New York career as a dramatic dancer was a success and he was able to present a further production of *At the Hawk's Well* at the Greenwich Village Theatre there in 1918 using Dulac's masks, but with a new score by a Japanese composer, Kōsaku Yamada. In a letter dated 23 July 1918 to John Quinn, Yeats asked

if you saw the New York performance of my *Hawk's Well* I would be glad for some news of it. Fate has been against me. I meant these 'Noh' plays never to be played in a theatre, and now one has been done without leave; and circumstances have arisen which would make it ungracious to forbid Ito to play *The Hawk* as he will. I had thought to escape the press, and people digesting their dinners, and to write for my friends. However, Ito and his Japanese players should be interesting.[12]

A letter, dated 22 March 1920, from Yeats, then in New York, to Dulac, asks for authority to recover the masks from Martin Birnbaum who still had them in New York. Eventually, in 1924, Yeats recovered the masks, which are still in the possession of his family. As he wrote to Dulac on 28 January 1924:

It would be very kind of you, if, when the railway strike is over, you would get some picture packer at, of course, my expense, to pack up the masks, etc. and make the necessary Customs declaration, and send them to me here. I want to begin arranging performances. The psychological moment has come, for Dublin is reviving after the Civil War, and self-government is creating a little stir of excitement. People are trying to found a new society. Politicians want to be artistic, and artistic people to meet politicians, and so on. It seems to be the very moment for a form of drama to be played in a drawing-room.[13]

*

At the Hawk's Well was first seen in Dublin in a performance arranged as an 'At Home' for the members of the Dublin Drama League at Yeats's house on 23 March 1924, with the assistance of the Abbey players and using Dulac's music, and the costumes and masks which Yeats had just recovered from New York.

The formation of the Dublin Drama League may have been prompted by Edward Martyn's continuing attempts to bring the Irish National Theatre, through his Theatre of Ireland, back to a realisation of its original aims as expressed in *Samhain 1901* (see pp. 55-56 above). The purpose of the League is described thus in its programmes of the 1920's:

The Dublin Drama League was formed in 1918 to secure the production in Dublin of plays which would be unlikely to appear at any of the other theatres. The Committee of the League arranges five public performances a year and a number of private At Homes at which plays are read or acted. It is the only Society which attempts to keep Dublin in touch with the contemporary drama of the world and it has won a reputation for the high quality of the plays chosen for production and for the care with which they are presented.[14]

The Drama League was founded by Lennox Robinson, who, having been manager of the National Theatre Company since 1910, saw that the original purpose of the founders of the Company to include international masterpieces in its repertoire could not be pursued in the style in which the Abbey Company had developed. The venture was enthusiastically supported by Yeats who served as its President from its formation in 1918 until 1926, with Lennox Robinson as Vice-President, while Mrs. Yeats acted as Honorary Secretary.

Sean O'Casey, who attended the 'At Home' performance of *At the Hawk's Well*, 'candidly confessed' to Joseph Holloway that he could not understand it and, in describing the performance in his autobiographical *Inishfallen, Fare Thee Well*, 1949, revealed the extent of the gap between the concept of theatre at which Yeats had arrived and the style of theatre which the Abbey had developed.

He remembered once when he went to the house of Yeats, in Merrion Square, to see *The Hawk's Well* played in the drawing-room. The room was full of them, dressed in their evening best, the men immaculate in shiny sober black, the women gay and glittering in silk sonorous, and brilliant brocade, all talking animatedly and affectionately together, like teachers and children waiting for trams to come to bring them away on a Sunday school excursion. Sean tried to attach himself to the conversation by listening, but there was nothing to hear. No-one spoke to him, and, right or wrong, he felt that they were uncomfortable with a tenement-dweller in their midst. Yeats suddenly caught sight of him, came quick to him, and guided Sean to the front, where he wheeled over a deep and downy armchair as a seat for Sean.

— You'll be able to see well here, he said.

Yeats had read in a big book all about the Noh Plays, had spoken about them to others, and had seized on the idea that he could do in an hour what had taken a thousand years to create. And so with the folding and unfolding of a cloth, music from a zither and flute, and taps from a drum, Yeats's idea of a Noh Play blossomed for a brief moment, then the artificial petals faded and dropped lonely to the floor, because a Japanese spirit had failed to climb into the soul of a Kelt.

Passively funny was the sight of Mr. Robinson doing a musician, and Mick Dolan, the Abbey actor, acting Cuchullain, so serious, so solemn, his right hand, extended, holding a spear, saying so surlily-amiable, I am named Cuchullain; I am Sualtam's sin. No; charming and amiable as it all was, it wasn't a Noh Play. Poet and all as he was, Yeats wasn't able to grasp a convention, grown through a thousand years, and give it an Irish birth in an hour. Zither and flute and drum, with Dulac's masks, too full of detail for such an eyeless play, couldn't pour the imagination into the mind of those who listened and saw. The unfolding and folding of the fanciful cloth couldn't carry the stage to the drawing-room. No, the people's theatre can never be successfully turned into a poetical conventicle. A play poetical to be worthy of the theatre must be able to withstand the terror of Ta-Ra-Ra-Boom-Dee-Ay, as a blue sky, or an apple tree in bloom, withstands any ugliness around or beneath them.

There was a buzz of Beautiful when the cloth had been folded, and the musicians had taken their slow way from the room; and Sean wisting not what to say himself, added Very. There was grace and a slender charm in what had been done, now that he had had a long time to look back at it; but it wasn't even the ghost of the theatre.[15]

At the Hawk's Well was also presented in Dublin by the students of the Abbey School of Acting, again using Dulac's music and costumes, to a very small audience which included Yeats, at the Peacock Theatre on 18 November 1930. This student performance rekindled in Yeats the enthusiasm which he had felt when the play had been first performed in 1916, and inspired him to dedicate his next publicly issued collection of poems, *The Winding Stair and other poems*, 1933, to the artist in these terms:

Dear Dulac,
I saw my *Hawk's Well* played by students of our Schools of Dancing and of Acting a couple of years ago in a beautiful little theatre called "The Peacock," which shares a roof with the Abbey Theatre. Watching Cuchulain in his

lovely mask and costume, that old masked man who seems hundreds of years old, that Guardian of the Well, with your great golden wings and dancing to your music, I had one of those moments of excitement that are the dramatist's reward and decided there and then to dedicate to you my next book of verse.[16]

The play was produced by the Irish National Theatre Society on 25 July 1933, at the Abbey Theatre,* in a programme of one-act plays and ballets, due, perhaps to the revival of Yeats's enthusiasm, as the dedication to *The Winding Stair*, which was published in September, indicates.

*

In contrast to O'Casey's dismissal of the play and its almost total neglect in Ireland, Professor Shotaro Oshima in his book, *W. B. Yeats and Japan*, Tokyo 1965, concluded that,

In Japanese classic dramas Yeats discovered something in common with the imaginative and artistic temperament of the Celtic people. He was delighted with the Nō, which expresses reality on the stage, imposing it on a symbolic world tinged with joy, fears and sorrows. We may say that it was an analogy between the characteristics of the Celtic people and those of the Japanese, that made Yeats admire the Nō and found his new literature on that model. Yeats's never-abandoned interest in the tradition of his native country drove him to identify himself with the heroic and high-minded characters, such as Cuchulain, Usheen, the blind Raftery, or Cathleen Ni Houlihan. The dramatic characters of heroic manhood and womanhood in the Nō plays were as stimulating to his imagination as the legendary heroes of his motherland.[17]

At the Hawk's Well was not presented in Japan until December 1939, almost a year after Yeats had died, when Michio Ito, himself in retirement, again produced the play with Kōsaku Yamada's score which Professor Oshima describes as having

---

*   AT THE HAWK'S WELL

A Play for Dancers by W. B. Yeats
Produced by the Irish National Theatre Society
at the Abbey Theatre, Dublin
on Tuesday 25 July 1933

Singer	Joseph O'Neill
Musicians	J. V. Wynburne, Cepta Cullen, Julia Grey, Doreen Cuthbert
Guardian of the Well	Ninette de Valois
An Old Man	Michael J. Dolan
A Young Man	W. O'Gorman

Music and costumes by Edmund Dulac
Programme produced under the direction of Arthur Shields

the solemnity of tone and swelling rhythm of Japanese music throughout. From start to finish the tempo is slow, like that of Nō recitation, and in some passages old Japanese folk songs are suggested.[18]

At the Hawk's Well, translated into Japanese with notes by Tokuboku Hirata, was printed in *Eigo bungaku*, Tokyo, in the issues for February, March and April 1920. A further Japanese translation, by Jiro Nane, accompanied by a translation of *The Only Jealousy of Emer* appeared as *Two Plays for Dancers*, Tokyo 1928, and yet another, by Saisuke Nagasawa, appeared in 1932.

Kōsaku Yamada's settings of five pieces for *At the Hawk's Well* were published in Tokyo in 1930, with Japanese translations of the texts which he set, and part of the opening chorus in this setting is reproduced by Professor Oshima in his book, *W. B. Yeats and Japan*.

Finally, on 20 October 1949, *At the Hawk's Well* was adapted into a complete Nō form, with the title *Taka no izumi* by Mario Yoko-michi, which was published in October 1950 in *No-gaku no nūbe* and presented in December of the same year at the inaugural performance of the Society for the Nō Revival in Tokyo. A further Japanese adaptation, made by Hideo Audō with a score by Suguru Kawasaki, as a musical play, was selected by the Social Education Bureau of the Ministry of Education, and performed and published in 1961.

The acknowledgement of Yeats's sincerity in his attempt to adapt a Japanese form to Western use and the fact that there have been several Japanese versions of the play show how seriously the work has been accepted in Japan despite the lack of appreciation of these works by the National Theatre Yeats created for his own country — all of which adds weight to the claim made by Curtis Bradford that, in creating the 'Plays for Dancers,' Yeats had written 'the first success-ful poetic drama since the seventeenth century.'[19]

*

In the last week of the month during which *At the Hawk's Well* was performed in London, an event occurred in Dublin which changed the course of Irish history, and which affected much of Yeats's creative thought during the remainder of his life. On 24 April 1916, several of the Irish revolutionary groups rose together in arms against the seven-centuries-old occupation of Ireland by England and pro-claimed an independent Irish Republic. Within a week the armed rebellion was overthrown by the British forces, and in the week following 3 May, sixteen of the leaders of the Rising were executed in Dublin, among them the seven signatories of the *Proclamation of the Irish Republic* in which they had stated:

We declare the right of the people of Ireland to the ownership of Ireland, and to the unfettered control of Irish destinies, to be sovereign and indefeasible. The long usurpation of that right by a foreign people and government has not extinguished the right, nor can it ever be extinguished except by the destruction of the Irish people. In every generation the Irish people have asserted their right to national freedom and sovereignty; six times during the past three hundred years they have asserted it in arms. Standing on that fundamental right and again asserting it in arms, we hereby proclaim the Irish Republic as a Sovereign Independent State, and we pledge our lives and the lives of our comrades-in-arms to the cause of its freedom, of its welfare, and of its exaltation among the nations.

Yeats wrote to John Quinn on 23 May: 'I keep going over the past in my mind and wondering if I could have done anything to turn those young men in some other direction.'[20] In one of his last poems, 'The Man and the Echo,' printed in the month of his death, January 1939, he thought back to the excitement generated by the production in 1902 of his patriotic play *Cathleen Ni Houlihan* and wondered

> Did that play of mine send out
> Certain men the English shot?[21]

But, from the date of the Easter Rising onward, the event permeated his work and his famous poem, 'Easter 1916,' appeared in a privately printed edition in September of the same year. The application of the event to his new form of drama was inevitable and, within a year, he had postponed work on his new play, *The Only Jealousy of Emer* and conceived a play 'in the manner of *The Hawk's Well*,'[22] as he wrote to Olivia Shakespear on 15 May 1917. The writing of this play, which was inspired by the tragic course of Irish history, *The Dreaming of the Bones*, progressed rapidly and on 12 June he wrote to Lady Gregory:

I have almost finished my Dervorgilla play, I think the best play I have written for years. It has grown greatly since you saw it and is I am afraid only too powerful politically. I have nothing now to write but the lyrics and must leave London for that.[23]

The death of Florence Farr in Ceylon in June 1917 was also reflected by Yeats in the closing lyric to the play, with its images of strings, hands and voice. Her death at this time when he had adopted a totally new approach in his playwriting may also have seemed to him symbolic. On 6 July Yeats read *The Dreaming of the Bones* at Gogarty's house to a group of friends which included James Stephens, who found it 'marvellous.' Despite this loss of a valued friend and colleague and the severe emotional crises in his personal life during these months, he continued to revise his new play and could write to Lady Gregory on 12 August from Passy, in France, where he was resolving his personal relationships with Maud Gonne and her daughter Iseult:

I have finished my play. I think of calling it *The Dreaming of the Bones*. I have greatly improved it since you saw it — improving and adding to the lyrics and strengthening the atmosphere. Here they say it is my best play. It has evidently some popular quality. Rummel has consented to write the music and that was Dulac's wish. I read him the play in Paris where I was delayed one day by passport difficulties.[24]

On 8 September he wrote again from Passy, to Lady Gregory, to announce his return to London on 14 September when he expected to

carry back to London with me part at least of the music to my Noh play *The Dreaming of the Bones*. Sooner or later I shall want to get it up in Dublin but not yet.[25]

The text of the play, but without Rummel's music, was printed together with that of *The Only Jealousy of Emer* at the Cuala Press in a volume entitled *Two Plays for Dancers*, finished in January 1919 in an edition of four hundred copies. This book contains a very brief Preface which indicates that Yeats was firm in his resolution to pursue the new form he had chosen for his plays. The preface reads:

In a note at the end of my last book "The Wild Swans at Coole" (Cuala Press) I explained why I preferred this kind of drama, and where I had found my models, and where and how my first play after this kind was performed, and when and how I would have it performed in the future. I can but refer the reader to the note or to the long introduction to "Certain Noble Plays of Japan" (Cuala Press).

W. B. Yeats. October 11th. 1918

P.S.   That I might write "The Dreaming of the Bones," Mr. W. A. Henderson with great kindness wrote out for me all historical allusions to Dervorgilla.[26]

The Dreaming of the Bones, the second play which Yeats completed in his new form, corresponds closely to the Nō play *Nishikigi*, which Yeats knew from Pound's version, and about which he wrote in his 'Introduction' to *Certain Noble Plays of Japan*:

The ghost lovers in *Nishikigi* remind me of the Aran boy and girl who in Lady Gregory's story come to the priest after death to be married. These Japanese poets too feel for tomb and wood, the emotion, the sense of awe that our Gaelic speaking country people will sometimes show when you speak to them of Castle Hackett or of some Holy Well; and that is why perhaps it pleases them to begin so many plays by a Traveller asking his way with many questions, a convention agreeable to me; for when I first began to write poetical plays for an Irish Theatre I had to put away an ambition to bring again to certain places their old sanctity or their romance.[27]

The final chorus of *Nishikigi* is very close in spirit to the 'scene' of *The Dreaming of the Bones*, and also expresses the mood of the play. Pound renders this chorus as:

> We ask you do not awake,
> We will all wither away,
> The wands and the cloth of a dream.
> Now you will come out of sleep,
> You tread the border and nothing
> Awaits you; no, all this will wither away.
> There is nothing here but this cave in the field's midst.
> To-day's wind moves in the pines;
> A wild place, unlit and unfilled.[28]

In this type of atmosphere the theme of the seven-centuries-long betrayal which pervades *The Dreaming of the Bones* is well set. The actual, or historical locale in which Yeats chose to set *The Dreaming of the Bones* is the neighbourhood of the ruined Cistercian Abbey of Corcomroe in County Clare, a barren rock-strewn peninsula, near the Atlantic coastline. This enormous monastic ruin, sacked during the 'Protestant' Reformation, with the hills rising behind it out of the stony landscape and the tombs in the ruined Abbey, including that of Conall O'Brien, King of Thomond, surely suggests the sense of 'dreaming back' into the historic past with which the play is concerned. Even the Latin title of the abbey, *Sancta Maria in Petra Fertilis*, which might almost become in English 'Our Lady of the Fertile Rock' suggests the sense of miracle, of the supernatural which is, for many visitors, present there. Here, Yeats has fulfilled his ambition of helping to 'bring again to certain places their old sanctity or their romance.'[29]

The plot of the play springs from that moment in our country's history, which, as narrated in the Irish volume of Holinshed's *Chronicle*, 1577, reads

Dermucius or Dermote MacMurche King of Leinster and governor of the fifth part of Ireland, possessed all the East parts of the Isle alongst by the sea coast, an oppressor of the nobility, using much cruelty towards the lords and the great men of his country. To serve his lecherous lust, he secretly made suit in dishonest wise unto the Queen of Meath.[30]

This act of private lust, which led to public treachery, determined the whole course of Irish history. Yeats has, in *The Dreaming of the Bones*, taken Dermot and Dervorgilla, Holinshed's 'Queen of Meath,' as his wandering ghosts who seek forgiveness for bringing the Normans into Ireland and set the guilty pair forever present to each other at their moment of betrayal, but condemned to wander down the centuries unable to touch limb or lip. These troubled spirits should

TWO PLAYS FOR DANCERS
BY W. B. YEATS

THE CUALA PRESS
MCMXIX

60. *Two Plays for Dancers*. The Cuala Press, Dublin. Finished in January 1919 in an edition limited to four hundred copies. The volume contains *The Dreaming of the Bones* and *The Only Jealousy of Emer*. Title page.

have masks which echo certain features from the Japanese Nō, the woman's mask type being the *Deigan*, the mask of a female spirit sworn to fulfil a destiny. Yeats, however, was so impressed by the masks Dulac had created for *At the Hawk's Well*, that in the Preface to *Four Plays for Dancers* he says, reflecting on similar lines to his thoughts on Ricketts' costume designs created for 'heroic' parts years before:

The beautiful mask of Cuchulain may, I think, serve for Dervorgilla, and if I write plays and organize performances with any system, I shall hope for a small number of typical masks, each capable of use in several plays. The face of the speaker should be as much a work of art as the lines that he speaks or the costume that he wears, that all may be as artificial as possible. Perhaps in the end one would write plays for certain masks.[31]

In the stage direction to *The Dreaming of the Bones* Yeats has developed further his description of the screen before which the piece is played:

a screen, with a pattern of mountain and sky can stand against the wall, or a curtain with a like pattern hang on it, but the pattern must only symbolise and suggest.

Such a screen, painted on a surface of natural wood and displaying mountain and sky, might suggest, perhaps, the shapes of the two mountains which form a frame to Sligo Bay and which occupy a mystic place in Yeats's life and work — Knocknarea, where under a gigantic cairn, 'passionate Maeve lies stony, still,' and Ben Bulben where the tragic story of Diarmuid and Grainne ended, and under whose shadow Yeats himself rests for ever. The thorn tree, which begets so many images in Yeats's work, might be the immediate symbol on the screen.

The *Waki*, or Traveller, who sets the central plot in motion and within whose power it is to free the troubled spirits from their curse, is a young man who has fled from Dublin after fighting to free Ireland in the Easter Rising and is seeking a boat to take him to a safe refuge on one of the islands off the western coast. His confrontation with the ghosts of Diarmuid and Dervorgilla leads to the choreographic climax of the play, the climbing of the mountain, from the top of which the Traveller can describe for the audience the desolation of his native land:

> So here we're on the summit. I can see
> The Aran Islands, Connemara Hills,
> And Galway in the breaking light; there too
> The enemy has toppled roof and gable,
> And torn the panelling from ancient rooms;
> What generations of old men had known

> Like their own hands and children wondered at,
> Has boiled a trooper's porridge. That town had lain,
> But for the pair that you would have me pardon,
> Amid its gables and its battlements
> Like any old admired Italian town;
> For though we have neither coal, nor iron ore,
> To make us wealthy and corrupt the air,
> Our country, if that crime were uncommitted,
> Had been most beautiful.

The 'dreaming back' into history, in which Yeats here closely follows his Japanese model, conjures up the tormented ghosts, and, in his 'Notes' on the play, as printed in *Four Plays for Dancers*, 1921, he indicates his increased awareness of the practical limitations attending the performance of his new dramatic form:

Dervorgilla's few lines can be given, if need be, to Dermot, and Dervorgilla's part taken by a dancer who has the training of a dancer alone; nor need that masked dancer be a woman.[32]

In the same note, which is mainly concerned with the theme of 'dreaming back' he indicates that this play has preceded his working out of the system displayed in *A Vision*, the work around which his philosophical thought centred after his marriage in the autumn of 1917:

I wrote my play before the Robartes papers came into my hands, and in making the penance of Dermot and Dervorgilla last so many centuries I have done something for which I had no warrant in these papers, but warrant there certainly is in the folk-lore of all countries.[33]

Yeats also acknowledges his debt to W. A. Henderson in providing him with all the historical allusions to Dervorgilla, but, probably because he chooses to leave his ghost-figures unforgiven in *The Dreaming of the Bones*, he makes no allusion to Lady Gregory's play *Dervorgilla*, 1911, which portrays, with greater historical accuracy, the lady 'who brought the strangers in' working out, in old age, her penance at the Abbey of Mellifont in her native kingdom of Meath.

The play, which is the one in which Yeats most closely approaches a Nō original (*Nishikigi*), had political overtones which precluded its production in Dublin for fourteen years, and Walter Rummel's score was not used because, as Yeats expressed it in his Preface to *Four Plays for Dancers*:

At the end of this book there is some music by Mr. Rummell, which my friends tell me is both difficult and beautiful for *The Dreaming of the Bones*. It will require, I am told, either a number of flutes of which the flute-player will pick now one, now another, or an elaborate modern flute which would not look in keeping. I prefer the first suggestion. I notice that Mr. Rummell has written no music for the dance, and I have some vague memory that when we talked it over in Paris he felt that he could not without the dancer's help.[34]

This perhaps also indicates that by 1921 Yeats had developed reservations about Rummel's score, which he had described as 'very fine'[35] to John Quinn in a letter of 8 February 1918.

In October 1918 he offered *The Dreaming of the Bones* in London to Stephen Gwynn for publication in *Everyman*. Gwynn did not publish it, but Yeats's offer of the play to *The Little Review* in America resulted in its publication in the issue of January 1919. In his letter offering the play to Gwynn he described it as

one of my best things but may be thought dangerous by your editor because of its relation to rising of 1916. My own thought is that it might be published with editorial note either repudiating its apparent point of view or stressing the point of view. England once, the point of view is, treated Ireland as Germany treated Belgium. I doubt if a long poem or verse play is worth anything to a popular paper unless they make a feature of it and relate it to current interests.[36]

After the neglect of his original work by the National Theatre during the 1920's Yeats had scored popular successes at the Abbey Theatre, in 1929 with *Fighting the Waves* and in 1930 with *The Words upon the Window-Pane*, both texts designed for, as he described it, the 'public' stage, and *The Dreaming of the Bones* was finally staged at the National Theatre in 1931.* The production was one of a series called 'Mainly Ballet: the Abbey Directors' Sunday Entertainments,' organised to keep the theatre open while the main company was on an American tour. Rummel's score was abandoned as too difficult. But the production was a success and on 15 December Yeats wrote to Olivia Shakespear that

---

*   THE DREAMING OF THE BONES

Presented by the Irish National Theatre Society Limited
at the Abbey Theatre, Dublin
on Sunday 6 December 1931

Young Man	W. O'Gorman
Stranger	J. Stephenson
Girl	Nesta Brooking
Singer	Joseph O'Neill
Flautist	T. Browne
Zither	Julia Gray
Drum	Doreen Cuthbert

Produced by U. Wright
Music by J. F. Larchet

The play as put on the stage with its ceremonial movements (half round the stage meant a mountain climbed) seemed to me very beautiful. It was enthusiastically received.[37]

Joseph Holloway recorded in his diary that the 'imitation Japanese Noh play . . . was a complete success . . . but Dr. Gogarty afterwards said (of W. O'Gorman as the Young Man), "He was too common to represent those who occupied the G.P.O. in Easter Week." . . .'[38]

*

Yeats planned to follow *At the Hawk's Well* with another play derived from the Cuchulain epic, a treatment in his new form of drama of the consequences of the plot of *On Baile's Strand*. His letter of 10 April 1916 to Lady Gregory, from which his impressions of the first production of *At the Hawk's Well* have already been quoted, announces, in its postscript, his choice of this theme:

I want to follow *The Hawk's Well* with a play on *The Only Jealousy of Emer* but I cannot think who should be the changeling put in Cuchulain's place when he is taken to the other world. There would be two masks, changed upon the stage. Who should it be — Cuchulain's grandfather, or some god or devil or woman?[39]

The specific theme of the play may have been in Yeats's mind since his first winter at Stone Cottage with Pound, during which, on 18 January 1914, the two poets had been among a gathering of admirers who visited Wilfrid Scawen Blunt to pay homage to him in his seventy-fifth year. When Yeats had, in the first decade of the century, first conceived a cycle of poetic dramas based on the Cuchulain theme, he had, with Lady Gregory's help, persuaded Blunt to contribute the unsuccessful *Fand*, which was produced at the Abbey Theatre on 20 April 1907 and which derived from the same tale, *The Sickbed of Cuchulain*, to which Lady Gregory had given the title of 'The Only Jealousy of Emer' in her *Cuchulain of Muirtheimne*.

The tribute to Blunt, which Pound reported in the March issue of *Poetry* (Chicago) and which Yeats commemorated with his poem, 'The Peacock,' in the May issue of the same journal, possibly set Yeats to thinking of a re-working of the theme of *Fand* as a 'Play for Dancers' which might make the stage presentation of the other-world characters of the epic more dramatically effective. By the time he began to deal with this plot as a draft for a play, the philosophical theorising which was leading him towards writing the first version of *A Vision* gave a greater relevance to the particular theme in the overall context of his work.

The plot of *The Only Jealousy of Emer* may be taken as starting from the point in the epic which formed the situation at the end of

On Baile's Strand, where Cuchulain, in his anguished frenzy at killing his own son by Aoife — the son he had been led to beget as a distraction from his quest for immortality at the end of *At the Hawk's Well* — fights with and 'dies' in the waves.

In the play, in which the 'senseless image' of Cuchulain which has been washed up by the waves is laid on a bier in a fisherman's hut, it is joined on stage by an *alter ego*, the Figure of Cuchulain who is really the malevolent Bricriu, the Celtic spirit of discord, the agent who sets in motion the conflict between Cuchulain's women — wife, mistress and spirit — which forms the central action of the play. The technical scheme of the play follows closely that of *At the Hawk's Well*, but in his Note on the play, printed in *Four Plays for Dancers*, Yeats explains how his organisation of the material is linked with his other great preoccupation at the time, the writing of the first version of *A Vision*:

While writing these plays, intended for some fifty people in a drawing-room or a studio, I have so rejoiced in my freedom from the stupidity of an ordinary audience that I have filled "The Only Jealousy of Emer" with those little known convictions about the nature and history of a woman's beauty, which Robartes found in the *Speculum* of Gyraldus and in Arabia Deserta among the Judwalis. The soul through each cycle of its development is held to incarnate through twenty-eight typical incarnations, corresponding to the phases of the moon, the light part of the moon's disc symbolizing the subjective and the dark part the objective nature, the wholly dark moon (called Phase 1) and the wholly light (called Phase 15) symbolizing complete objectivity and complete subjectivity respectively. . . . The invisible fifteenth incarnation is that of the greatest possible bodily beauty, and the fourteenth and sixteenth those of the greatest beauty visible to human eyes. Much that Robartes has written might be a commentary on Castiglione's saying that the physical beauty of woman is the spoil or monument of the victory of the soul, for physical beauty, only possible to subjective natures, is described as the result of emotional toil in past lives.[40]

With this play Yeats shows the confidence he has gained in handling his new form but, to present the more involved details of the action he has, in his stage directions, increased the complexities facing the performers. The play opens with the directions to the chorus for the unfolding and folding of the cloth, which are almost identical with those in *At the Hawk's Well*. As given in the text printed at the Cuala Press in 1919 these read:

(*The fifteenth phase*)

ROBARTES   All thought becomes an image and the soul
Becomes a body : that body and that soul
Too perfect at the full to lie in a cradle,
Too lonely for the traffic of the world :
Body and soul cast out and cast away
Beyond the visible world.

AHERNE   All dreams of the soul
End in a beautiful man's or woman's body.

ROBARTES   Have you not always known it?

AHERNE   The song will have it
That those that we have loved got their long fingers
From death, and wounds, or on Sinai's top,
Or from some bloody whip in their own hands.
They ran from cradle to cradle till at last
Their beauty dropped out of the loneliness
Of body and soul.

ROBARTES   The lover's heart knows that.

AHERNE   It must be that the terror in their eyes
Is memory or foreknowledge of the hour
When all is fed with light and heaven is bare.

ROBARTES   When the moon's full those creatures of the full
Are met on the waste hills by countrymen
Who shudder and hurry by : body and soul
Estranged amid the strangeness of themselves,
Caught up in contemplation, the mind's eye
Fixed upon images that once were thought;
For separate, perfect, and immovable
Images can break the solitude
Of lovely, satisfied, indifferent eyes.

61. W. B. Yeats. Lines 58-83 from 'The Phases of the Moon' in *The Wild Swans at Coole*, London, 1919. Woodcut 'The Great Wheel,' by Edmund Dulac, from *A Vision*, 1926.

THE ONLY JEALOUSY OF EMER

Enter Musicians, who are dressed as in the earlier play.* They have the same musical instruments, which can either be already upon the stage or be brought in by the First Musician before he stands in the centre with the cloth between his hands, or by a player when the cloth is unfolded. The stage as before can be against the wall of any room.

All the characters are masked, although the two 'real' women, Emer and Eithne Inguba, may have 'their faces made up to resemble masks.' The masks worn by the Ghost of Cuchulain at the beginning of the action and by the Figure of Cuchulain were identical 'heroic' masks, but just before the Figure of Cuchulain (Bricriu) enters the action, the curtains of the bed or litter on which the sick Cuchulain lies are drawn 'so that the actor may change his mask unseen' to one showing a distorted face which is changed again to the 'heroic mask' at the end of the action when Cuchulain has returned to the 'real' world. This implies a Nō-style stage property, the bier which is carried onstage during the chorus, with curtains built onto its frame to conceal the changing of the masks.

The central dance of *The Only Jealousy of Emer* is the wooing of Cuchulain by the Woman of the Sidhe (Fand), and is described in the text thus:

The Woman of the Sidhe moves round the crouching Ghost of Cuchulain at front of stage in a dance that grows gradually quicker, as he slowly awakes. At moments she may drop her hair upon his head but she does not kiss him. She is accompanied by string and flute and drum. Her mask and clothes must suggest gold or bronze or brass or silver, so that she seems more an idol than a human being. This suggestion may be repeated in her movements. Her hair, too, must keep the metallic suggestion.

At the close of the play, when Cuchulain has returned to the 'real' world and calls on his mistress Eithne Inguba, leaving his wife Emer to grieve, the chorus repeats the ritual of the cloth while the acting area is being cleared.

Perhaps because Yeats had not yet found another dancer, or a composer to write a score for the lyrics and the dance in the play, *The Only Jealousy of Emer* did not achieve even a drawing-room performance. His Note on the text, as printed in *Four Plays for Dancers*, 1921, ends on this disillusioned note:

In writing these little plays I knew that I was creating something which could only fully succeed in a civilization very unlike ours. I think they should be written for some country where all classes share in a half-mythological, half-philosophical folk-belief which the writer and his small audience lift into a

---

*The Dreaming of the Bones.

new subtlety. All my life I have longed for such a country, and always found
it quite impossible to write without having as much belief in its real existence
as a child has in that of the wooden birds, beasts, and persons of his toy
Noah's Ark. I have now found all the mythology and philosophy I need in the
papers of my old friend and rival, Robartes.[41]

Yeats's original text of *The Only Jealousy of Emer* was not performed in Ireland or England until 1926, although the play was
successfully staged in a Dutch translation in Amsterdam in 1922, a
production of which Yeats did not apparently become aware until
after the Dublin Drama League premiere in 1926 of the play in its
original English text. The Drama League had, in 1924, presented the
first Dublin production of *At the Hawk's Well* in the poet's drawing-
room in Merrion Square as an 'At Home' for its members. The League
staged its productions at the Abbey Theatre on Sunday and Monday
nights during its occasional seasons and, although its work was not
primarily concerned with Irish plays, it presented the Irish premieres
of three of Yeats's 'Plays for Dancers.' *

Another 'Play for Dancers,' which Yeats had witheld from publication in *Four Plays for Dancers* was included in the same programme. This was *The Cat and The Moon*, which Yeats had
conceived as a *Kyogen*, or farce, in the mode of the Nō and written
in 1917. At this first public presentation in Ireland of his 'Plays for
Dancers' Yeats spoke from the stage before the performance and
availed of the opportunity to define the principles on which he had
modelled the plays.

Joseph Holloway recorded the occasion in his diary :

---

*   THE ONLY JEALOUSY OF EMER

Presented by the Dublin Drama League
at the Abbey Theatre, Dublin,
on Sunday and Monday, 9 and 10 May 1926,
in a double bill with the first production of *The Cat and the Moon*.
The programme was introduced by W. B. Yeats.

The Ghost of Cuchulain	F. J. McCormick
The Figure of Cuchulain	Arthur Shields
Emer	Eileen Crowe
Eithne Inguba	Shelah Richards
Woman of the Sidhe	Norah McGuinness
Three Musicians	John Stephenson, T. Moran,
	E. Leeming

Directed by Lennox Robinson under the supervision of W. B. Yeats
Costumes and masks by Norah McGuinness
Choreography by Ninette de Valois

Yeats made a speech of explanation before the Noh Plays or Plays for Dancers were played. The first, *The Only Jealousy of Emer*, in which "Cuchulain" is saved from the waves and his soul fled and replaced by a changeling from the Sidhe until the love of "Emer" calls it back again from . . . "The Woman of the Sidhe" . . . had J. Stephenson as the spokesman and chanter of the three "Musicians." Tom Moran and E. Leeming were the other two, the former playing a small drum and gong, and the latter the flute. Their getup was weirdly Japanese. Two carried in the bier on which the figure of "Cuchulain" lay, and the three drew a dark cloth with a strange device in gold across the stage, and when it was withdrawn the figures of "Emer" and the ghost of "Cuchulain" were discovered, and "The First Musician" told their story up to a certain point, and then the players took it up. "Eithne Inguba" came on and afterwards "The Woman of the Sidhe" (who had already appeared in *At the Hawk's Well* — a Noh play given at Yeats's own house some time ago !) The two figures of "Cuchulain" wore masks, also "The Woman," whose hands, arms and legs, and mask were gold. She tried to fascinate "The Ghost," till "Emer" called him back into his body, and then "The Musicians" again put the cloth across the front of the stage, and the players moved off, and two of them carried away the empty bier.

Immediately after, *The Cat and the Moon* began by the three "Musicians" returning to the stage, Lennox Robinson replacing E. Leeming . . . and the "Blind Beggar" came on bearing the lame one on his back. In this latter play, Carolan as the former and Dolan as the latter both played very well indeed. I liked Eileen Crowe's "Emer" in the opening play. Norah McGuinness, who designed the costumes and masks, as well as playing "The Woman of the Sidhe," gave an interesting performance of a strange, uncanny character. The masking of the "Ghost" and the "Figure of Cuchulain" was not effective, and Shelah Richards's getup as "Eithne Inguba" was to my eyes ugly.[42]

Norah McGuinness, who designed the production and danced the part of the Woman of the Sidhe, recalled her experience in an article 'Young Painter and Elderly Genius,' published in 1965.

About this time he asked me to do masks and costumes for his play, "The Only Jealousy of Emer." Edmond Dulac had previously done some very beautiful masks for him, which he showed me. I then did my masks for his play — baking them in my gas oven. The play was to have two performances in the Abbey Theatre, produced by the Dublin Dramatic Society.

I can't remember now just why, but for some reason I was asked to take the part of the "Woman of the Sidhe." I hadn't to speak (I suppose the musicians or someone else spoke the words)—I was rehearsed to do a dance of seduction. F. J. MacCormick, who played the Ghost of Cuchullain, was my victim.

I had never been on a stage before, so I was extremely nervous, as I stood in the wings at the first performance. I had a gold and black mask — a very scanty gold and black costume (designed by me)—and my limbs were painted gold.

Suddenly W.B. was beside me. He looked me up and down with approval — but alas, then said : "There was a boy in the Middle Ages who was covered in gold — and he died !" At that moment I got my cue to go on the stage. F. J.

MacCormick was waiting — on his knees, back to the audience — to be seduced by my dance. Every step and every gesture of my dance was a cue to what he had to say or do. I could only think of the boy in the Middle Ages; every step was forgotten and I flopped meaninglessly around the stage, while MacCormick hissed expletives at me.

I spent the night at Lennox Robinson's house, and the hottest bath-water did not remove the gold. After a restless night a visit to the chemist reassured me.[43]

*

When Yeats published his essay 'A People's Theatre, a letter to Lady Gregory,' in the two issues of *The Irish Statesman* for 29 November and 6 December 1919, he re-defined his concept of the Irish theatre and examined the diverging paths along which the realisation of his ideas had strayed. Even by that date he had realised that his own chosen mode of drama did not easily accord with the talents and skills of the National Company he had done so much to create. But he looked ahead to developments which were not to be realised for decades yet in theatres outside Ireland, to a concept of theatre practice to which, only in very recent times, has the theatre in Ireland come, and in this generally by way of companies other than the Abbey's.

In this essay, as he revised it for inclusion in his book *Plays and Controversies*, 1923, Yeats called for a combining of skills and of disciplines and, reviewing the situation in theatre as he then saw it, he predicted what, he felt, should be the guiding principle of the new approach:

I want to create for myself an unpopular theatre and an audience like a secret society where admission is by favour and never to many. Perhaps I shall never create it, for you and I and Synge have had to dig the stone for our statue and I am aghast at the sight of a new quarry, and besides I want so much — an audience of fifty, a room worthy of it (some great dining-room or drawing-room), half a dozen young men and women who can dance and speak verse or play drum and flute and zither, and all the while, instead of a profession, I but offer them "an accomplishment." However, there are my *Four Plays for Dancers* as a beginning, some masks by Mr. Dulac, music by Mr. Dulac and by Mr. Rummell. In most towns one can find fifty people for whom one need not build all on observation and sympathy, because they read poetry for their pleasure and understand the traditional language of passion. I desire a mysterious art, always reminding and half-reminding those who understand it of dearly loved things, doing its work by suggestion, not by direct statement, a complexity of rhythm, colour, gesture, not space-pervading like the intellect, but a memory and a prophecy : a mode of drama Shelley and Keats could have used without ceasing to be themselves, and for which even Blake in the mood of *The Book of Thel* might not have been too obscure.[44]

The Abbey, he felt, had developed into a true 'People's Theatre' which had drawn the materials of its drama, its players and producers from the indigenous traditions and native talents of his own country and had presented these materials through its productions with an honesty and a simplicity which, in the earlier years of the venture had been internationally recognised for its quality and its style. But this style was self-limiting in its development and had drifted so far from the theatre he had set out to achieve that its very success had, for him, become 'a discouragement and a defeat.' Nor could he see where these diverging paths could join again : not only in Ireland, but in a much wider context the age was not right — the world was not ready for the change.

The two great energies of the world that in Shakespeare's day penetrated each other have fallen apart as speech and music fell apart at the Renaissance, and that has brought each to greater freedom, and we have to prepare a stage for the whole wealth of modern lyricism, for an art that is close to pure music, for those energies that would free the arts from imitation, that would ally acting to decoration and to the dance. We are not yet conscious, for as yet we have no philosophy, while the opposite energy is conscious. All visible history, the discoveries of science, the discussions of politics, are with it; but as I read the world, the sudden changes, or rather the sudden revelations of future changes, are not from visible history but from its anti-self. Blake says somewhere in a "Prophetic Book" that things must complete themselves before they pass away, and every new logical development of the objective energy intensifies in an exact correspondence a counter-energy, or rather adds to an always deepening unanalysable longing. That counter-longing, having no visible past, can only become a conscious energy suddenly, in those moments of revelation which are as a flash of lightning. Are we approaching a supreme moment of self-consciousness, the two halves of the soul separate and face to face?[45]

*

At the time of writing 'A People's Theatre,' Yeats had at least five 'Plays for Dancers' in progress, of which three had been published but only one had been performed. Of the other two, the opening and closing songs of *The Cat and The Moon* had been printed in the London edition of *The Wild Swans at Coole*, 1919, but he had some difficulty in resolving the details of the central action of the play, a difficulty which still existed when he allowed it to be printed with a group of new poems at the Cuala Press, where the book, *The Cat and the Moon and certain poems*, was finished on 1 May 1924. In his note on the play in this edition he stated :

I wrote this play with the intention of including it in "Four Plays for Dancers" but did not do so as it was in a different mood. I published the musicians' song however in "The Wild Swans at Coole." I have amused myself by imagining incidents and metaphors that are related to certain beliefs of mine as are the patterns upon a Persian carpet to some ancient faith or philosophy. It has pleased me to think that the half of me that feels can sometimes forget all that belongs to the more intellectual half but a few images.[46]

Although the philosophy underlying *The Cat and the Moon* has attracted much critical attention, I feel that in this play Yeats was attempting a link between his new form of drama and the 'popular' plays to which the Abbey Theatre had largely devoted its efforts, and possibly attempting a dance play which might succeed on the 'public' stage. In the dedicatory preface to the Cuala volume, addressed to Lady Gregory, he wrote:

I renew an impression, especially from "The Cat and the Moon," which I have received much more powerfully from your "Gaol Gate" and as powerfully from "The Grasshopper" by Mr. Padraic Colum, and from a play of Mr. Daniel Corkery's — an odour, a breath, that suggests to me Indian or Japanese poems and legends.[47]

His acquisition of Thoor Ballylee, on the border of the Burren district of County Clare, and his proximity to Lady Gregory's house at Coole, to Edward Martyn's at Tulyra, and to George Moore's Irish home may have contributed to an approach, through the technique he had developed from the Nō, of combining his avowed purpose 'to bring back to certain places their ancient sanctity or their romance' with the expression, in an ironic reference, of his quarrel with Moore and Martyn. He had also found a theme which allowed him to model a play on the *Kyogen* or comic interludes which the Nō repertory contained, and, although the verses for the chorus appear with the printed text of the play, he suggests that the ritual of the unfolding and folding of the cloth is not essential.

The final passage of his Note on *The Cat and the Moon* in the Cuala edition indicates the mood in which the text, which is there dated 1917, was composed:

The Well itself is within a couple of miles of my Galway house, Thoor Bally-lee, and is sacred to St. Colman, and began a few years ago to work miracles again, rejuvenated by a Gaelic League procession in its honour. There is some story, which I have half forgotten, of a lame man and a blind man's arrival at it, though not of their quarrel there. I intended my play to be what the Japanese call a "Kiogen," and to come as a relaxation of attention between, let us say, "The Hawk's Well" and "The Dreaming of the Bones," & as the Musicians would be already in their places, I have not written any verses to be sung at the unfolding and the folding of a cloth. It is all the slighter because probably unfinished, and must remain unfinished until it has been performed and I know how the Lame Man is to move. Is he to remain, after he comes from the other's back, upon one knee, or crouching till he can pick up, as I have no doubt he does, the Blind Man's stick? Or is he but to walk stiffly, or limp as if a leg were paralysed? Whatever his movements are they must be artificial and formal, like the movement upon a puppet stage, or in a dance, & I may have to give him more words here and there to explain these movements. But it may never be played, never seem worth the trouble of making those two masks, or of writing the music and so I let it go as it is.[48]

When *The Cat and the Moon* was publicly issued in *Wheels and Butterflies*, 1934, Yeats replaced his original dedication and note on the play with a lengthy philosophical essay which explained the deep mysteries contained in the simple plot, and, as both were then dead, Martyn having died in 1923, Moore in 1933, he could explain that

The holy man in the big house . . . and his friend from Mayo were meant for Edward Martyn and George Moore, both of whom were living when the play was written. I think the audience understood the reference. . . .[49]

In the stage directions to the play, which was produced by the Dublin Drama League in 1926,* Yeats specifies a painted screen :

The scene is any bare place before a wall against which stands a patterned screen, or hangs a patterned curtain suggesting Saint Colman's Well. Three Musicians are sitting close to the wall, with zither, drum, and flute. Their faces are made up to resemble masks.

The two characters in the *Kyogen* 'wear grotesque masks' and the definitive version of the play indicates that Yeats had resolved the doubts expressed in his earlier Note. The final version of the play contains three dance movements, one a circling of the stage with the Blind Beggar carrying the Lame Beggar on his back, accompanied by drum taps and a stanza of the musicians' song; a passage, accompanied by drum and flute, during which the Blind Beggar beats the Lame Beggar with his stick; and a final dance, after the 'miracle' where

The Lame Beggar begins to dance, at first clumsily, moving about with his stick, then he throws away the stick and dances more and more quickly. Whenever he strikes the ground strongly with his lame foot the cymbals clash. He goes out dancing, after which follows the First Musician's song.

---

*   THE CAT AND THE MOON

Presented by the Dublin Drama League
at the Abbey Theatre, Dublin,
on Sunday and Monday, 9 and 10 May 1926

A Blind Beggar	Michael J. Dolan
A Lame Beggar	P. J. Carolan
Three Musicians	John Stephenson, T. Moran,
	Lennox Robinson

Directed by Lennox Robinson, under the supervision of W. B. Yeats

Incidentally, there is no mention of cymbals in any printed text and these, therefore, must have been introduced as a detail of the first production of the play in 1926.

*

Some critics have suggested that *Waiting for Godot* by Samuel Beckett may have been, to some degree, inspired by *The Cat and the Moon*, and perhaps this is so, but Yeats, by suggesting in his Note in the Cuala Press edition, the correspondence of his thinking with that of other Abbey folk dramatists — Lady Gregory, Padraic Colum and Daniel Corkery — and casting a folk tale in the sophisticated form of his 'Plays for Dancers,' provides a clue to a lengthier lineage. In support of this I would add to the list in Yeats's Note his reaction, expressed in a letter written to his father on 29 April 1909, to Lord Dunsany's one-act play, *The Glittering Gate* :

Dunsany is a man of genius, I think. We are doing a little play of his about a burglar who when he gets to the next world burgles the door of Heaven and finds within "nothing but blooming great stars," and a burglar whose doom is to open beer bottles for ever and to find them empty and be too thirsty to stop opening them.[50]

*

The genesis of *Calvary*, which, with *At the Hawk's Well*, *The Only Jealousy of Emer* and *The Dreaming of the Bones*, makes up the content of *Four Plays for Dancers*, 1921, may possibly be indicated in an outline plot which Yeats included in a letter to Lady Gregory, dated 14 January 1918 :

To-day I finished my new Cuchulain play and am hesitating on a new one, where a Sinn Feiner will have a conversation with Judas in the streets of Dublin. Judas is looking for somebody to whom he may betray Christ in order that Christ may proclaim himself King of the Jews. The Sinn Feiner has just been persuading a young sculptor to leave his studio and shoulder a rifle.

Judas is a ghost, perhaps he is mistaken for the ghost of an old rag-picker by the neighbourhood. I will not know whether the idea is too theoretical and opinionated [?] till I have made prose draft. Before that I shall write a couple of lyrics. . . .[51]

The lyrics written at this time by Yeats embody the expansion of his philosophical thinking which was leading him towards the first version of *A Vision* and are reflected in the songs which the chorus are given in *Calvary*. His questioning of the nature of Christ's life, and his sacrifice for mankind prompted the refrain to the songs, 'God has not died for the birds,' and shows a preoccupation with the aspect of Christ as man, offering himself as sacrificial victim for the salvation of his fellows. The generally accepted source of the final plot of

Calvary is one of Oscar Wilde's *Poems in Prose*, 'The Doer of Good,' which was first published in *The Fortnightly Review* in July 1894, and which is given here in full as it can be seen how Yeats, in the discipline imposed by his new dramatic form, had become selective as to the episodes which he built into the script for *Calvary* :

THE DOER OF GOOD *by* Oscar Wilde

It was night-time and He was alone.

And He saw afar-off the walls of a round city and went towards the city.

And when He came near He heard within the city the tread of the feet of joy, and the laughter of the mouth of gladness and the loud noise of many lutes. And He knocked at the gate and certain of the gate-keepers opened to Him.

And He beheld a house that was of marble and had fair pillars of marble before it. The pillars were hung with garlands, and within and without there were torches of cedar. And He entered the house.

And when He had passed through the hall of chalcedony and the hall of jasper, and reached the long hall of feasting, He saw lying on a couch of sea-purple one whose hair was crowned with red roses and whose lips were red with wine.

And He went behind him and touched him on the shoulder and said to him, "Why do you live like this?"

And the young man turned round and recognised Him, and made answer and said, "But I was a leper once, and you healed me. How else should I live?"

And He passed out of the house and went again into the street.

And after a little while He saw one whose face and raiment were painted and whose feet were shod with pearls. And behind her came, slowly as a hunter, a young man who wore a cloak of two colours. Now the face of the woman was as the fair face of an idol, and the eyes of the young man were bright with lust.

And He followed swiftly and touched the hand of the young man and said to him, "Why do you look at this woman and in such wise?"

And the young man turned round and recognised Him and said, "But I was blind once, and you gave me sight. At what else should I look?"

And He ran forward and touched the painted raiment of the woman and said to her, "Is there no other way in which to walk save the way of sin?"

And the woman turned round and recognised Him, and laughed and said, "But you forgave me my sins, and the way is a pleasant way."

And He passed out of the city.

And when He had passed out of the city He saw seated by the roadside a young man who was weeping.

And He went towards him and touched the long locks of his hair and said to him, "Why are you weeping?"

And the young man looked up and recognised Him and made answer, "But I was dead once and you raised me from the dead. What else should I do but weep?"

As a piece for performance in the style of his 'Plays for Dancers,' *Calvary* closely resembles the other three plays in its organisation —

the songs for unfolding and folding the cloth which open and close the play, the commentary, also delivered by the chorus, on the main actions of the drama and during the passage which divides the two principal dialogues — that of Christ with Lazarus, which is closely derived from Wilde's story, and the dialogue between Christ and Judas, which ends with the rejection by Christ of Judas's plea for forgiveness for his betrayal — a rejection which may be equated with that rejection by the young Sinn Feiner which sets in motion the final dance of *The Dreaming of the Bones*, and which preserves something of the Judas/Sinn Feiner relationship Yeats proposed as a possible play theme in the letter quoted above.

While the rejected Judas is made to hold up the cross, the action of the play is taken up by the three Roman soldiers who cast dice to determine which of them shall have Christ's cloak — a dance ended by Christ's cry 'My Father, why hast Thou forsaken Me,' which leads into the final chorus.

This play is possibly the most universally powerful of the first group of dramas derived by Yeats from the Nō — and the most elemental in its imagery — as the 'Note' on the published play explained:

I use birds as symbols of subjective life, and my reason for this, and for certain other things, cannot be explained fully till I have published some part at any rate of those papers of Michael Robartes, over which I have now spent several years. . . . Certain birds, especially as I see things, such lonely birds as the heron, hawk, eagle, and swan, are the natural symbols of subjectivity, especially when floating upon the wind alone or alighting upon some pool or river, while the beasts that run upon the ground, especially those that run in packs, are the natural symbols of objective man.[52]

Thus, the bird-symbolism of the choruses presents a series of contrasting images which Yeats explains in the next paragraph of his Note:

I have used my bird-symbolism in these songs to increase the objective loneliness of Christ by contrasting it with a loneliness, opposite in kind, that unlike His can be, whether joyous or sorrowful, sufficient to itself. I have surrounded Him with the images of those He cannot save, not only with the birds, who have served neither God nor Caesar, and await for none or for a different saviour, but with Lazarus and Judas and the Roman soldiers for whom He has died in vain.[53]

Calvary did not achieve a stage presentation in Yeats's lifetime and was printed only in *Four Plays for Dancers* and the subsequent collected volumes which derived from that text. However, its first printing attracted a Japanese translation by Mineko Matsumura, published in 1922. I think Yeats, in completing the text, saw what might be considered the end of a phase in his playwriting which he set to complete by the compilation of his work in this form, with the exception of the *Kyogen* or farce, *The Cat and the Moon*, into one volume containing the play texts, his notes, the musical settings by Dulac and Rummel and Dulac's designs for the only play of the four performed at that time. He wrote a Preface to the four plays, dated July 1920, in which he stated:

Should I make a serious attempt, which I may not, being rather tired of the theatre, to arrange and supervise performances, the dancing will give me most trouble, for I know but vaguely what I want. I do not want any existing form of stage dancing, but something with a smaller gamut of expression, something more reserved, more self-controlled, as befits performers within arm's reach of their audience.[54]

Arising out of his only practical experience of staging one of the 'Plays for Dancers,' Yeats went on in his Preface to expand his thoughts on the mask:

The beautiful mask of Cuchulain may, I think, serve for Dervorgilla, and if I write plays and organize performances on any scale and with any system, I shall hope for a small number of typical masks, each capable of use in several plays. The face of the speaker should be as much a work of art as the lines that he speaks or the costume that he wears, that all may be as artificial as possible. Perhaps in the end one would write plays for certain masks. If some fine sculptor should create for my "Calvary," for instance, the masks of Judas, of Lazarus, and of Christ, would not this suggest other plays now, or many generations from now, and possess one cannot tell what philosophical virility?[55]

Yeats selected T. Sturge Moore to make the cover design for *Four Plays for Dancers*, the first draft of which he rejected in a letter dated 6 September 1921, saying

I am sorry for it would make a fine design, but don't nail the hawk on the board. The hawk is one of my symbols and you might rather crudely upset the subconsciousness. It might mean nightmare or something of the kind for some of us here. Life when one does my kind of work is rather strange. I wish I could suggest something but nothing occurs to me. My main symbols are Sun and Moon (in all phases), Tower, Mask, Tree (Tree with Mask hanging on the trunk).[56]

The final design was modified according to Yeats's desires and Sturge Moore wrote in reply:

Please don't worry about the crucified hawk, which was rather a pictorial than a decorative idea and went with the other rejected features.[57]

Four Plays for Dancers was issued by Macmillan simultaneously in London and New York on 28 October 1921, and on 7 November Yeats wrote to Sturge Moore:

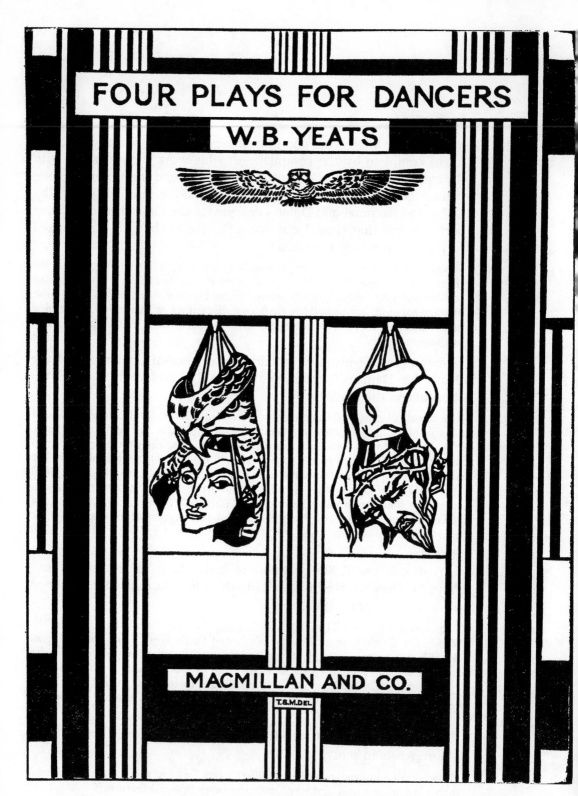

62. T. Sturge Moore. Binding design for *Four Plays for Dancers*, 1921.
The original drawing for this design is in the University of London Library.

I am delighted with your cover for *Four Plays* — it is particularly admirable as a black and white design. Hawk a little less good than the rest, but that is probably my fault for objecting to your crucified hawk. The design is however one of the best you have done, taken as a whole.[58]

The preoccupations of his life as a public figure in Ireland, the Irish Civil War, and the award of the Nobel Prize for Literature to Yeats in 1923, with the publication of several volumes of his works in a 'standard' edition, as well as the writing of his autobiographies and philosophical works occupied Yeats for the four years which followed the writing of his preface to *Four Plays for Dancers* in July 1920. Although he drafted a dance play, which Professor F. A. C. Wilson tentatively entitles *The Bridegroom*, in 1923, he did not proceed with this draft. He was probably influenced by the fact that his 'Plays for Dancers' had not, to his knowledge, achieved any productions other than those of *At the Hawk's Well* staged in London and by Michio Ito in New York and the private performance of the same play staged by the Dublin Drama League in his drawing-room in March 1924. The unfinished play can, in Professor Wilson's opinion, be related to the Nō play *Awoi No Uze*. *The Bridegroom* explores a theme, carried on from *Calvary*, which is an investigation of the differences between earthly and profane love, or between the sacred and the profane—making the assertion, in Professor Wilson's definition :

that the higher self in every man is identical with Christ; it is the Christ in man that a woman discerns and gives her love to; and this tremendous statement is meant in a quite literal sense. Yeats had read, in the Syriac Christian *Hymn of Bardestan*, that the higher self may be identified with Christ, and this is true, he says, even of a goat-girl and a young fisherman, even of adolescent passion and what the world calls illicit love.

The symbolism of bride and bridegroom is on one plane, and that a very relevant one, specifically Christian, and I think I detect an influence from the *Songs* of St. John of the Cross, where the symbols of tower, nightingale and divine horseman also appear.[59]

Arthur Waley's *The Nō Plays of Japan* was published in 1922, the year following the publication of *Four Plays for Dancers* and may have provided a spur to Yeats to attempt a further work in the form, as it contained a lengthy introduction which quoted extensively from the theoretical writings on the Nō, as well as providing a detailed annotation of the Buddhist 'Wheel of Life and Death' — a parallel with the construction of 'The Great Wheel' which Yeats had asked Dulac to realise as one of the illustrations to *A Vision*, and translations of *Awoi No Uze* occur in both the Pound/Fenollosa book and in Waley's.

63. Edward Calvert. 'The Chamber Idyll.'
Wood engraving, 1831.

Professor Wilson, too, seems very close to the matter of the projected play in naming it *The Bridegroom*. The title is closely connected with Yeats's preoccupations with the engravings of Edward Calvert, whose wood-engraving 'The Chamber Idyll' relates to the passage dealt with by Yeats in his essay 'Swedenborg, Mediums and the Desolate Places.' This formed the introduction to the second volume of *Visions and Beliefs in the West of Ireland*, written after his contact with the Nō, where he observed that

Swedenborg was but "the linen clothes folded up" or the angel sitting by the tomb, after Christ, the human imagination, had arisen. His own memory being full of images from painting and from poetry, he discovered more profound "correspondences," yet always in his boys and girls walking or dancing on smooth grass and in golden light, as in pastoral scenes cut upon wood or copper by his [Blake's] disciples Palmer and Calvert, one notices the peaceful Swedenborgian heaven. We come there, however, by no obedience but by the energy that "is eternal delight," for "the treasures of heaven are not negations of passion but realities of intellect from which the passions emanate uncurbed in their eternal glory." [60]

This unfinished piece represents the final work that Yeats attempted under the direct influence of the Nō. In May 1924, shortly after the Dublin performance of *At the Hawk's Well* in his Merrion Square drawing-room, the Cuala Press finished printing *The Cat and the Moon and certain poems*, in which edition his Note on the play ends thus, indicating his discouragement:

But it may never be played, never seem worth the trouble of making those two masks, or of writing the music and so I let it go as it is.[61]

*

Although the Nō influenced Yeats's dramatic work until the end of his life, his experience with the 'Plays for Dancers' must have been disappointing. He had adopted a form of theatre for which the Irish National Theatre Company did not have, or seek, the few resources necessary to present the plays and he was rarely, if ever, again to experience the excitement which the presentation of *At the Hawk's Well* gave him on its first production in Lady Cunard's London drawing-room on 2 April 1916.

8 *the symbol of a movement*

In *The Bounty of Sweden*, published in 1924 to celebrate his award
of the Nobel Prize for Literature in the previous winter, Yeats wrote

I think . . . of how deep down we have gone, below all that is individual,
modern and restless, seeking foundations for an Ireland that can only come
into existence in a Europe that is still but a dream.[1]

He had become a public figure in Ireland with his election to the
Senate of the Irish Free State in the previous year, and in the address
he delivered to the Royal Academy of Sweden on receiving his prize
he chose as topic 'The Irish Dramatic Movement' and he acknowledged, in that address, his realisation of the change in his position
in relation to the theatre in Ireland.

Perhaps the English committees would never have sent you my name if I had
written no plays, no dramatic criticism, if my lyric poetry had not a quality
of speech practised upon the stage, perhaps even — though this could be no
portion of their deliberate thought — if it were not in some degree the symbol
of a movement.[2]

The movement of which he had become a symbol, however, had
done nothing to promote the new dramatic form created by its
founder and Yeats had, in March 1924, to offer his Dublin drawing-
room for the first presentation in Ireland of one of the 'Plays for
Dancers,' *At the Hawk's Well*, the only one of these plays, as far as
he knew, to have achieved a performance at the time. With the exception of the first Abbey Theatre presentation of *The Land of
Heart's Desire* in 1911 and the Dublin premiere, in December 1919,
of *The Player Queen*, which had been first produced in London in
the preceding May, no new play by Yeats had been presented by the
Irish National Theatre Company since *The Golden Helmet* in 1908
and the re-written version of the same play, *The Green Helmet* in
1910.

Yeats approached the beginning of his sixtieth year under a cloud
of discouragement, and, seeing the theatre he had created devoted to
a 'realistic' style of presentation which could never be adapted to
the form of theatre in which his own work was developing, he allied
himself with the new 'revolutionary' movement which had grown
up in literary Dublin with among its leaders F. R. Higgins, Francis
Stuart and Cecil ffrench Salkeld. They proposed to publish a literary
paper, *To-Morrow*, for which Yeats drafted but did not add his name
to the manifesto, which was signed by H. Stuart and Cecil Salkeld.
This statement, which must be considered against *A Vision*, Yeats's
main preoccupation of the time, proclaimed

new form comes from new subject matter and new subject matter must flow
from the human soul restored to all its courage, to all its audacity. We dismiss

all demagogues and call back the soul to its ancient sovereignty, and declare that it can do whatever it please, being made, as antiquity affirmed, from the imperishable substance of the stars.[3]

But *To-Morrow* had to be withdrawn from circulation after two issues, Lennox Robinson suffered severe censure for a story he had contributed, and the brave attempt to re-direct Dublin's cultural outlook ended in a dismal notoriety. Yeats retreated into the completion of *A Vision*, and into writing the first of the powerful poems which characterised the final phase of his life.

Perhaps the most significant gesture to the younger generation made by Yeats at this time was his persuasion of Lady Gregory that the Abbey Theatre should be offered to the National Government, and on 27 June 1924 a letter signed by both Directors was addressed to President Cosgrave, offering the theatre, its entire contents, scenery, wardrobe and property to the Irish nation:

Dear President Cosgrave,

We have carried on our work at the Abbey Theatre for nearly twenty years and we may claim to have created a school of Irish dramatists and a school of Irish acting that has brought honour to our country. We have carried on our work in spite of the European War — which killed every repertory theatre in England save one — and in spite of the English war in Ireland. We do not claim to have done so unaided, at certain times we have had to appeal for help to friends in Ireland and England but always in times of stress we have said to our friends and to each other, "We must hold the Theatre together that we may offer it to the Irish Nation when Ireland achieves her independence." That, for many years, has been our determination. We believe that a Theatre which does not depend for its existence on the caprice of the public can play a great part in the education of a nation, can be — like the Comédie Française — one of the nation's glories, and we are aware that all civilised governments except those of the English-speaking nations and Venezuela — possess their State Theatre.

In that belief we now offer the Abbey Theatre, its entire contents, scenery and wardrobe and the property its owns to the Irish Nation.

We do not pretend that our gift is of great value counted as money. Like others in Ireland we, who were once rich, are now poor; nevertheless the value of the property is not inconsiderable and there is some value in a tradition of fine work finely done.

We offer the Theatre without conditions or restrictions. We resign our Directorship. It is for the Irish Government, should they accept our offer, to determine the method of carrying on our work — whether they will ask us to go on for a little longer or whether they will at once accept entire control. By tradition and accomplishment our Theatre has become the National Theatre of Ireland, it should no longer be in the possession of private individuals, it should belong to the State. Having created it and fostered it through twenty years we believe we can now confidently trust it to the Irish Nation.

(*signed*) AUGUSTA GREGORY
W. B. YEATS.[4]

Although President Cosgrave was not in any way interested in the theatre, his Minister for Finance, Ernest Blythe, to whom he referred the letter, was deeply interested and at the same time aware that the Theatre was in grave risk of bankruptcy. He succeeded in putting the case before the Government and having an annual subsidy voted, originally of £850, and so made the Irish National Theatre the first state-subsidised theatre in the English-speaking world.

Yeats spent the winter travelling in Sicily, where Ezra Pound was staying, and in Italy to aid his recovery from a period during which he must have been at times near to despair, and during this period he was deeply impressed by the two main streams of development in Christian art and iconography — the Byzantine mosaics and the Renaissance in Rome, where he spent considerable time pondering the Michelangelo frescoes in the Sistine chapel.

The 'sixty-year-old smiling public man' returned to Dublin in Spring 1925 and resumed his Irish life with renewed vigour. He made his presence felt in the Senate with speeches on divorce, in which he defended the Protestant minority view, and on censorship of books which he firmly opposed. With the backing of the Government subsidy he was in a position to think of developing a small theatre for poetry and experimental work as part of the Abbey Theatre, as well as facilities for schools of Acting and of Dancing.

*

The 'public' image of Yeats in 1925-26 is reflected in his renewed involvement in theatre affairs, particularly in his defence of the Abbey's presentation of *The Plough and the Stars* by Sean O'Casey, which opened on Monday 8 February 1926 and incited the Dublin audience to riotous protests on the succeeding nights so that by Friday of the week the theatre was 'detective lined.' Yeats addressed the protestors on several nights and, in a letter to H. J. C. Grierson, dated 21 February, he referred to the riots and concluded:

The theatre has now a great following. Indeed all things of the kind are going well with us — minds have been suddenly liberated from hereditary political passion and are looking for other interests. I feel constantly if I were but twenty years old and not over sixty all I ever wanted to do could be done easily.[5]

He had served his apprenticeship to the Nō theatre and published five 'Plays for Dancers' and now he resumed work on a project which he had commenced in 1908 and left aside after 1912 — his 'version for the modern stage' of Sophocles' *King Oedipus*. His dramatic work was once more directed at the 'public' audience and, even though he was to shape several more dramas in the mould he

had derived from the Nō, he never again approached his classical
model in the mood of reverent imitation in which he had conceived
his earlier works in that form.

By 22 April, despite a threat from the Republicans that they
would blow up the Abbey when *The Plough and the Stars* was revived, he could write to Olivia Shakespear that he must get to work
on an *Oedipus* chorus as the play was to be produced at the Abbey.
His approach to the Greek tragedy was direct and strong — some
of the choruses and the longer speeches were cut in order, Yeats
felt, to increase the dramatic impact of the whole piece, and, as his
version of *King Oedipus* progressed towards completion, he commenced a version of the sequel, *Oedipus at Colonus*.

In June Yeats was made Chairman of the Senate Committee to
supervise the design of the new Irish coinage, and his concern with
classical Greece led to his directive to the artists invited to submit
designs, here summarised in the report of the Committee, *Coinage of
Saorstát Eireann*, issued by the Irish Government in 1928:

As the most famous and beautiful coins are the coins of the Greek Colonies,
especially of those in Sicily, we decided to send photographs of some of these,
and one coin of Carthage, to our selected artists, and to ask them, as far as
possible, to take them as a model.[6]

During this year of great activity the various threads which made
up Yeats's creative life seemed woven together. Besides his Senate
work, his theatre activity and his supervision of the coinage project,
he saw through the press Lady Gregory's *Case for the Return of Sir
Hugh Lane's Pictures to Dublin*, and, during his time at Thoor Ballylee
in the summer, he planned 'a play about Christ meeting the worshippers of Dionysus on the mountain side'[7] — the first outline of
The Resurrection, a new 'Play for Dancers' which he completed
early in the following year.

Sophocles' King Oedipus opened at the Abbey Theatre on 7 December 1926 and, on the same date, Yeats wrote to Olivia Shakespear:

My version of *Oedipus* comes on to-night. I think my shaping of the speech
will prove powerful on the stage, for I have made it bare, hard and natural
like a saga, and that it will be well, though not greatly acted — it is all too
new to our people. I am more anxious about the audience, who will have to
sustain an hour and a half of tension. The actor who plays Oedipus felt the
strain at dress rehearsal so much that he could hardly act in the last great
moments — a good audience will give him life, but how will the Catholics
take it? In rehearsal I had but one overwhelming emotion, a sense as of the
actual presence in a terrible sacrament of the god. But I have got that always,
though never before so strongly, from Greek Drama.[8]

64. *Sophocles' King Oedipus.*
London, 1928. Cover (reduced)
Original $7\frac{1}{8} \times 5''$.

After the performance that evening,* Yeats wrote on the envelope of his letter '*Oedipus* great success. Critics and audience enthusiastic.' And, two years later, when the play was published, the front cover of the first edition bore extracts from the enthusiastic review which had appeared in *The New York Times*.

---

*   SOPHOCLES' KING OEDIPUS
               A version for the modern stage

Presented by the Irish National Theatre Society Limited
at the Abbey Theatre, Dublin
on Tuesday 7 December 1926

Oedipus	F. J. McCormick
Jocasta	Eileen Crowe
Creon	Barry Fitzgerald
Priest	Eric Gorman
Tiresias	Michael J. Dolan
Boy	D. Breen
First Messenger	Arthur Shields
Herdsman	Gabriel J. Fallon
Second Messenger	P. J. Carolan
Nurse	May Craig
Children	Raymond and Edna Fardy
Servants	Tony Quinn, Michael Scott, C. Haughton
Leader of the Chorus	J. Stevenson
Chorus	Peter Nolan, Walter Dillon, T. Moran, M. Finn, D. Williams

Produced by Lennox Robinson
The choruses set to music by Dr. J. F. Larchet
Set in an arrangement of Craig Screens

Yeats's Preface to the play, which, with the musical settings for the choruses, was printed only in the first edition, defines his approach to the staging of the play:

This version of Sophocles' play was written for Dublin players, for Dublin liturgical singers, for a small auditorium, for a chorus that must stand stock still where the orchestra are accustomed to put their chairs, for an audience where nobody comes for self-improvement or for anything but emotion. In other words, I put readers and scholars out of my mind and wrote to be sung and spoken. The one thing that I kept in mind was that a word unfitted for living speech, out of its natural order, or unnecessary to our modern technique, would check emotion and tire attention.

Years ago I persuaded Florence Farr to so train the chorus for a Greek play that the sung words were almost as intelligible and dramatic as the spoken; and I have commended that art of hers in Speaking to the Psaltery. I asked my Dublin producer Lennox Robinson to disregard that essay, partly because liturgical singers were there to his hand, but mainly because if a chorus stands stock still in half shadow music and singing should, perhaps, possess a variety of rhythm and pitch incompatible with dramatic intelligible words. The main purpose of the chorus is to preserve the mood while it rests the mind by change of attention. A producer who has a space below the level of the stage, where a chorus can move about an altar, may do well to experiment with that old thought of mine and keep his singers as much in the range of the speaking voice as if they sang "The west's awake" or sang round a binnacle. However, he has his own singers to think of and must be content with what comes to hand.

W. B. YEATS[9]

Lennox Robinson, the producer, contributed a note on the music which, added to the preceding quotation, extends Yeats's note and reveals some of the options which were open to the producer:

THE MUSIC FOR THE CHORUS

This music was used for the production of the play in the Abbey Theatre. It was written for a Leader and five others. The Leader's voice should be of tenor quality, the Second Voice a baritone, the Third Voice a bass, the other voices — and there can be as many as the producer likes — should be bass. The music should not be sung in strict time. If necessary, one of the Chorus can have a small flute or whistle and softly play a note or two before each chorus begins.

L.R.[10]

Joseph Holloway, the indefatigable chronicler of the Irish theatre, was enthusiastic about King Oedipus, but could not resist a typical ironic comment at the end of his diary entry for Tuesday, 7 December:

The word "great" would be fairly employed to describe the first performance at the Abbey of W. B. Yeats's prose version of Oedipus the King by Sophocles with F. J. McCormick as the king. All the Dublin literary folk were there. . . .

SECOND CHORUS.

65. *Sophocles' King Oedipus*. Setting of the second chorus.

The Greek play was simply and effectively set and dressed. The chorus sang or chanted too vocally, but, when J. Stephenson as "Leader of the Chorus" spoke, his words came very clearly. McCormick was very dignified in bearing and impressive of speech in the opening episodes; his sudden change when blind at the end might be considered too pronounced, and his voice too whiningly pitched, though his episode with the children was moving in the extreme; on the whole, however, his impersonation had the quality of greatness in it, and at the end of the tragedy he got four enthusiastic curtains; only once during the play did the audience break out into thoughtless applause, but it soon died down. . . .

Yeats's version of *Oedipus the King* was very clear in meaning and actable. . . .

On the bills the Greek play was announced as a "first production." I suppose that was why some called for "Author" at the end.[11]

*

The work on the final stages of *King Oedipus* excited Yeats so much that his version of the sequel, *Sophocles' Oedipus at Colonus* was almost complete before the first play was staged. On 6 December 1926 he wrote to Olivia Shakespear:

> My work on *Oedipus at Colonus* has made me bolder and when I look at *King Oedipus* I am shocked at my moderation. I want to be less literal and more idiomatic and modern. I shall finish tonight all the dialogue for *Oedipus at Colonus* and then will come six weeks' work at the lyrical choruses, two of which are very famous.[12]

On 13 March 1927 he sent her some lines from a chorus with the comment that 'the last line is very bad Grecian but very good Elizabethan and so it must stay.'[13] On 24 March he wrote that he was 'slowly revising' the play and reading Plato, and enclosed the first stanza of the chorus which he later published in *The Tower* as 'Colonus' Praise.' The completed text was ready for rehearsal during August and the play opened at the Abbey Theatre on 12 September.* Both of the Yeats versions of Sophocles were played during the season and, in a letter written early in October Yeats described some mysterious experiences which, he felt, accompanied the productions:

> *Oepidus* is haunted. Two typed copies sent to the publisher have [gone] astray in the post and that has held up publication for months. Then a couple of weeks ago Mrs. Phillimore (author of *Paul*) invited a woman to meet George who asked for the introduction because at the first performance of

---

*   SOPHOCLES' OEDIPUS AT COLONUS
                  A version for the modern stage

Presented by the Irish National Theatre Society Limited
at the Abbey Theatre, Dublin
on Monday 12 September 1927

Oedipus	F. J. McCormick
His daughters	
Antigone	Shelah Richards
Ismene	K. Curling
Polyneices, his son	Gabriel J. Fallon
Theseus, King of Athens	Michael J. Dolan
Creon, King of Thebes	
(brother-in-law of Oedipus)	Barry Fitzgerald
A Stranger	Arthur Shields
A Messenger	P. J. Carolan
Leader of the Chorus	J. Stephenson
Chorus	Peter Nolan, Walter Dillon, T. Moran, M. Finn, M. Scott
Servants and Soldiers	U. Wright, C. Culhane, G. Green, J. Breen, P. Raymond, W. J. Scott

Produced by Lennox Robinson

The King a year ago she had seen George, she said, first take me by the shoulders and shake me and then kiss me. I said nothing of the kind had happened but she insisted. Then George came into the room; upon which she said "But that was not the woman."

Then there is a phantom dog. During *Colonus* George and I were infuriated by the loud barking of a dog apparently in the gallery. We were surprised that nobody laughed. I went out after the play to find who had brought the dog. Person after person said they had heard no dog, then I met two people who had, but each heard it in a different place. It had barked, I heard, in the middle of a performance of *The King*, a week before. One chorus appeals to Cerberus not to disturb Oedipus with its barking. The company think it is a dog that starved to death in the theatre once, when it was closed for the summer. Poems seem to disturb the spirits — once at Gogarty's when I was reading out my *Calvary* and came to the description of the entrance of Lazarus, the door burst open as if by the blast of wind where there could be no wind, and the family ghost had a night of great activity. From all which you will see that I am still of opinion that only two topics can be of the least interest to a serious and studious mind — sex and the dead.[14]

Oedipus at Colonus was not printed until the issue of the *Collected Plays* in 1934, which included the text only, without commentaries or notes, but, in *On the Boiler*, 1939, Yeats wrote

when I prepared *Oedipus at Colonus* for the Abbey stage I saw that the wood of the Furies in the opening scene was any Irish haunted wood. No passing beggar or fiddler or benighted countryman has ever trembled or been awe-struck by nymph-haunted or Fury-haunted wood described in Roman poetry. Roman poetry is founded upon documents, not upon belief.[15]

*

Yeats, also in 1926, planned the stage for poetry and experiment which he felt that the Abbey Theatre needed, and, when the Mechanics' Institute decided to vacate the house which had served it as library and meeting place since its main building had been converted as part of the theatre in 1904, the Directors of the theatre acquired the house. Yeats commissioned Michael Scott, a young architect who had played with the company for several years, as his first independent job, to design the conversion. Michael Scott, who is today Ireland's most notable architect, undertook the conversion of the room which was the Institute's library on the first floor of the building into a tiny playhouse which was to prove itself, in the following decades, of great significance in the development of the Irish theatre.

This building, which had housed the pit entrance to the Abbey Theatre, was developed to contain a café on the ground floor with the little theatre on the first floor and with dressing rooms and rehearsal rooms on the top floor. Later the café was abandoned and the ground floor was used as the rehearsal room for the Abbey, and

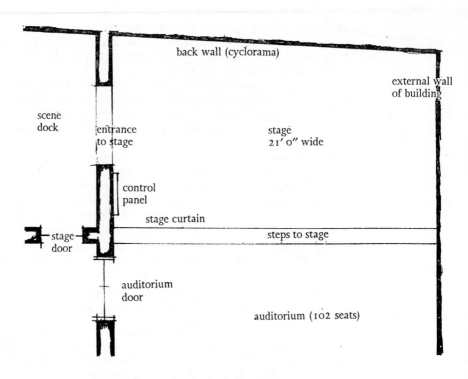

66. The Peacock Theatre, Dublin, 1927. Outline plan of stage.

home of the School of Acting under the direction of Lennox Robinson, while the top floor rehearsal room became the home of the Abbey School of Ballet, begun under the direction of Ninette de Valois.

The stage in the Peacock consisted of a platform at the end of a long Georgian room, some twenty feet wide, separated from the auditorium by two steps which were the full width of the stage and behind which ran the stage curtains. As the stage left wall was the external wall of the building and the back wall of the stage formed a permanent cyclorama, entrances onstage were made through an archway in the right wall of the stage which led to the scene dock and to the staircase to the dressing rooms. It was also possible to enter onto the forestage through the auditorium doors. As the room was not truly rectangular, the depth of the stage varied from side to side but its average depth was twelve feet. The auditorium, with a raked floor, had 102 seats.

Thus, the little theatre contained several aspects of Yeats's classic model — entrances from stage right and a similarity in the size of the playing area. And Yeats's close involvement in the creation of the Peacock is revealed in references to its stage and the front steps in the directions in several of his later 'Plays for Dancers,' written after the theatre was opened on 13 November 1927, such as in those to *The Resurrection*, published in the same year.

Joseph Holloway described the little theatre and its opening production in the 1927 section of his journal.

Friday, November 11. . . . A big room in the front building of the Abbey has been converted into a tiny theatre seating 100. It has been named The Peacock Theatre, and seats and decorations have all been carried out in peacock blue— even the front of the building facing Abbey Street has been painted a similar colour. A blue lookout truly, but I hope not for the little playhouse. A company calling themselves The New Players open the theatre for two nights on Sunday and Monday next with a play translated from the German of Georg Kaiser called *From Morn to Midnight*. 3/6 is the price charged for a seat. The Abbey is also starting a school for Ballet with one of the Russian Ballet for teacher. It has also a School for Acting as well — all finding a home in the Peacock Theatre. . . .

Sunday, November 13. The Peacock Theatre was opened by The New Players. Many not having seats sat in the passage. . . . I stood in the corner for the first scene of Georg Kaiser's play, *From Morn to Midnight*, and then left. The scenery was designed by Norah McGuinness, and the scenes used were of the weirdest kind. . . . The tip-up seats were peacock blue in shade and seemed comfortable. . . . The players, etc., were much about on the staircase — Kitty Curling, Denis Johnston (the producer), etc. U. Wright also came out from behind the curtain leading to the stage.

In the opening scene "The Cashier" (Laurence Elyan) absconded with money. "The Lady" in the scene was Meriel Moore who played so well in *The Constant Nymph*. Edith Dodd, May Carey, Irene Haugh, Kitty Curling, and other names I knew were in the long cast of 33 characters.

. . . Mrs E. S. Dodd is Hon. Secretary to The New Players. The company also intends to give performances in January, February, March, and April. The opening of the new tiny theatre was an interesting one.[16]

But the greatest contribution that the Peacock made to Irish theatre history was its use as the first home of the Dublin Gate Theatre Company, founded by Hilton Edwards and Micheál MacLiammóir, which opened its career on that stage with its production of *Peer Gynt* on 14 October 1928 and played its first two seasons there until the Gate Theatre was ready for occupation in Spring 1930.

Although few of its founder's plays were acted on the Peacock stage, Yeats, for the remainder of his life, was happy and proud that he had created the little theatre. In a letter to Edith Shackleton Heald on 2 August 1937, describing the work of Diana Murphy the embroidress, he wrote:

I have the same pleasure that I felt when I turned a great waste room full of cobwebs and dust at the Abbey Theatre into a beautiful little experimental theatre called The Peacock.[17]

The little theatre remained in use until after the fire which destroyed the Abbey Theatre on 17 July 1951. The Craig screens, built in 1911 for the Abbey, were reduced in height and served to mount productions of poetic plays, including those presented by Austin Clarke during the 1940's. So, although the service provided by the Peacock to Yeats's own drama was not all he had hoped of it, in creating a 'stage for poetry' he enriched the Dublin theatrical scene for several decades.

*

The 'play about Christ meeting the worshippers of Dionysus on the mountain side' was completed during the winter of 1926-27. This is the first version of *The Resurrection*, in which Yeats tried to follow the rules he had defined in the 'Plays for Dancers,' but, with the exception of the opening and closing songs, this first version has almost no dramatic action and is an argument, based on the philosophy expressed in *A Vision*, about the nature of Christ.

The decision to attempt *The Resurrection* as a 'Play for Dancers' may have been prompted by the Dublin Drama League production of *The Only Jealousy of Emer* and *The Cat and the Moon* at the Abbey Theatre on 9 May 1926. Lady Gregory's journal entries for 23 and 24 May indicate that *The Resurrection* had been drafted and that the second stanza of the opening song, commencing 'Another Troy must rise and set —', was almost in its final form.

Although this version of the play was published in the June 1927 issue of *The Adelphi*, Yeats realised that he had not solved the dramatic problems posed by the theme, and he put the piece aside for three years. The scenarios, which have been printed in *Yeats at Work* by Curtis Bradford, reveal the conflict about dramatic techniques which accompanied the development of the plot and the second scenario, plotted as 'a dance play for ordinary theatre' indicates the influence of Expressionism on Yeats's approach:

RESURRECTION (*cancelled*)

DANCE PLAY

Musician comes [in] as in my dance plays. Curtained place. Enter two men. The men go through movement of rolling back stone, which a musician describes. Figure of Christ enters in long spiral garment and stands in middle. Women enter and go through movements of unwinding grave clothes. Probably they sing while rolling back stone and when unwinding. Christ stands motionless. Song in which one voice says "Saul said why have you troubled me" and the other speaks "Coming forth from the tomb." Christ does not at first remember who or where he is. He vaguely remembers the crucifixion. Then they say "Yes, you died for men," and so on. This recalls all. Question and answer are in such form as to bring out the essential facts. Then Christ says, "I have taken away the sins of men," and asks who they are. They tell their deaths. Each has died for man. When he questions, Buddha says "No, I died of eating too much pork." Other interrupts. His sacrifice was the worst of all — he was not put to death. He renounced heaven to be always with mankind. Christ [cries] out in agony again, "The endless sin and misery of men, for whom the gods die in vain." All the others steal away except three women who kneel at his feet and Buddha who says, "This is your mother and two friends." The three Maries. And Christ hesitates and then says, "I am the way and the life."

Or musicians could be left out — orchestra takes their place. In which case the two figures who roll away stone should describe scene instead of musicians doing so.

Or it could be made a dance play for ordinary theatre as follows : Two black-clothed men. Hats to suggest fairly modern tall hats. They look at the heavens and say, "The moment has come to roll back the stone, the constellations are rightly placed." They roll away stone which is represented, not suggested merely. They discuss and describe. Christ comes from tomb still, except for feet, wrapped in grave clothes. Some women approach, friends of the god who has died, the men say. These women who wear clothes of no period with some tone to suggest the hospital nurse, dance, slowly unwinding the grave clothes. Christ when unwound does not know where he is. He has a vague memory, growing in intensity, of the crucifixion. The two men speak like doctors to a patient — all will be well in a moment, he should not think of such dreams, etc. Presently he bursts out that it was no dream, he remembers all now. He has taken away the sins of men. He speaks in exultation. He asks who these are who question. One is Dionysus, who describes his death; one is Buddha. There is perhaps a third. The son of the great Mother, perhaps, crucified in a pine tree. He asks Buddha, "Did you also die for the people?" Buddha says, "No, I died sitting under a tree from eating too much pork." The other says they never question him, his sacrifice was too great. He did not die, he refused heaven that he might be near mankind. "It is a tragedy to men to die, and to the gods to be born." Then Christ sees many persons coming. He asks "Who are these" and is told "Gods who have died for men." He is about to kneel, but Buddha stops him. He answers "I am still a man." Buddha says [?] "Only the god who suffers lives, or only the act is divine — in that we put on divinity; now one, now another as the turning heavens decree." They pass singing before him and bow as they pass. Their song is "Why have you troubled me said Saul" enlarged to a stanza or chorus, and verses about the risen Christ. They pass out and the women pass out, all but three. Christ bursts out about the eternal sins of man, his vain suffering. Buddha, who alone of the men remains, says, "Look, they kneel to you — Mary your mother, the other Maries, chief of all your worshippers." Christ spreads out his arms. "I am the life and the way." [18]

Although neither of these scenarios was developed into the first completed version of the play, the central idea was retained, and they reveal how the Nō-inspired elements from which the 'Plays for Dancers' had been constructed still obsessed Yeats — the 'dreaming back' and the women's dance. But the plot, when first worked up into a play text to express the philosophical idea behind it, became a conversation piece for three actors with the 'Songs for the Unfolding and Folding of the Cloth' at the beginning and at the end. The stage direction in the *Adelphi* printing, 1927, also reveals Yeats's hesitation as to whether the play should be performed on the 'public' or the 'private' stage :

THE RESURRECTION

Persons :
The Hebrew./The Egyptian./The Syrian./Christ.

If this play is performed upon an ordinary stage, the songs at the beginning and end should be omitted, and the noise of drum and rattle made behind the scene. When played, as it will be in Dublin at its first performance, near one end of an ordinary room, three musicians enter with drum and rattle which they place at one or both sides of the stage. They will probably have their faces made up to resemble masks, and Christ, when he appears towards the end, may wear a mask. One musician, singing and carrying a black cloth, goes to the centre of the stage towards the front and stands motionless, the folded cloth hanging between his hands. Two musicians, after standing for a moment at either side of the stage, go towards him, and then slowly unfold the cloth, singing as they do so. They unfold the cloth moving backward until the stage is shut off from the audience that an actor may take his place unseen; then they fold up the cloth once more, singing as they do so.[19]

*

While the 'Plays for Dancers' failed to arouse the enthusiasm or the interest of the Abbey Theatre directors, or of other theatrical managements either in Ireland or in England, one of these plays, *The Only Jealousy of Emer*, interested a leading Dutch actor-manager, Albert van Dalsum, who saw the possibilities of this new form of theatre as an extension of his own work. He had a Dutch translation of the play made by Hélène Swarth (1859-1941), an outstanding lyric poet who had written several verse-dramas. The sculptor Hildo Krop (1884-1972) was commissioned to make the masks for the production and the music was composed by Alex Voormolen (b. 1895), a leading composer who had studied in Paris and been influenced by Ravel.

Albert van Dalsum was born in Amsterdam in 1889. In his acting he sought a style which opposed naturalism and which could serve contemporary developments in playwriting. In his approach to theatrical production he was largely influenced by Gordon Craig's theories, especially in relation to the style of movement and acting imposed by the use of the mask. Craig's essay, *The Art of the Theatre*, had appeared in a Dutch translation in 1906, *De Kunst van het Theater*, and may well have influenced the young actor to strive for the development of the acting style with which he later became identified.

As a student of Craig's work, he may well have known Yeats's essay, 'The Tragic Theatre,' which Craig published in the October 1910 issue of *The Mask* and which Yeats later developed as the Preface to *Plays for an Irish Theatre* in 1911. Between 1919 and 1922, Craig published several essays in the Dutch periodical *Wendingen*, of which the most important was 'The Living Scene' which was printed in a special issue in January 1922, devoted to the International Theatre Exhibition in Amsterdam at which a selection of Craig's theatre designs were shown.

The Only Jealousy of Emer, translated by Hélène Swarth as *Vrouwe Emer's Groote Strijd*, was first presented by Albert van Dalsum in Amsterdam on 2 April 1922, preceded by a programme of dances presented by the choreographer Lili Green, who also arranged the dancing in Yeats's play.* The production was extensively noticed in the Dutch papers and was generally described as an interesting experiment which one reviewer saw as an attempt to point out in which direction the theatre itself might develop: 'More style, more severity and lack of freedom, less action, fewer unimportant details.' [20] Another wrote that

---

*   VROUWE EMER'S GROOTE STRIJD
(The Only Jealousy of Emer)

Maskerspel in een bedrijf van W. B. Yeats (vert. van Hélène Swarth)
Hollandsche Schouwburg, Amsterdam, 2 April 1922

PERSONEN
De Geest van Cuchulain	Albert v. Dalsum
Het Lichaam v. Cuchulain	Hans v. Meerten
Emer	Louise Kooiman
Eithne Inguba	Sara Heyblom
De Sidhe-vrouw	Lili Green
Koor	Mary Kool, Han Muller v. Gijen,
	B. de Roos

De handeling is ontleend aan de Iersche sagen.

Maskers van Hildo Krop
Muziek van Alex Voormolen
Regie Albert van Dalsum in samenwerking met Lili Green en Frans Huysmans

(De costuums werden naar ontwerp van Frans Huysmans vervaardigd op het atelier van Mej. Lancee — Den Haag)

Yeats's play, a work of divine and human life, a play in which the grief of life lasts as a profound echo, has qualities which are to be felt by being gleaned from what is hidden in the performance. This is, above all, Yeats's sphere, in which a darker nature breathes.[21]

The same critic felt that the audience,

however well-educated and appreciative of art it may have been, is unfamiliar with Yeats's work, and will perhaps seldom come closer to an understanding of it than to feel wonder, which is the beginning of emotion.[22]

The music of Alex Voormolen came off worst in the reviews. This was arranged for piano, and one paper pointed out that in *Four Plays for Dancers*, Yeats specified flute, drum and gong. The choreography, too, aroused some criticism, but the outstanding success of the presentation was the design, by Hildo Krop, of the masks.

The masks which Hildo Krop made for the play were modelled in papier maché, cast over plaster originals, from which he later had bronze replicas cast. These bronzes today occupy an honoured position on the grand staircase of the Stadsschouwburg in Amsterdam, and were shown in the Yeats exhibition, *Images of a Poet*, organised by D. J. Gordon and Ian Fletcher and mounted in Manchester and Dublin in 1961. For this exhibition, Mr. Krop made a replica of the Cuchulain mask, which is now in the University of Reading collection. This is made in the same manner as those used in the original production and is of papier maché, painted ivory with the shadows in deeper tones. There is a wig of thick woollen yarn attached to the mask.

*

Albert van Dalsum revived his production of *Vrouwe Emer's Groote Strijd* at The Hague in 1923 and at Utrecht in 1924. Obviously, Yeats did not know, at this time, either of Hélène Swarth's translation of his play or of van Dalsum's production. I have failed to locate a copy of the translated text, as no copy exists in the Nederlands Letterkundig Museum en Documentatiecentrum, which possesses the greater part of the literary inheritance of the poetess. Nor is there a copy of the script in the archives of the theatre, so that one must rely on the considerable reaction to the production both in the public press and in the various journals dedicated to the arts to assess today the impact made by this one play on a public without any predetermined bias either in favour of or against Yeats.

Vrouwe Emer's Groote Strijd, retitled *Maskerspel Vrouwe Emer*, was revived at the Stadsschouwburg in Amsterdam on 27 November 1926. In this performance, Albert van Dalsum and Hans van Meerten reversed the roles they had played in the first production. Louise Kooiman repeated her performance as Emer, Eithne Inguba was played by Willy Haak, and the Woman of the Sidhe by Sara Hey-blom, who had played Eithne Inguba in 1922. The members of the Chorus were different and there was a new musical score, composed by Alex de Jong. This performance, like that of 1922, was introduced by a selection of dances which were, on this occasion, all presented in masks. For two out of the four items in the dance programme, the masks were made by Hildo Krop.

The programme of the 1926 revival carries an extensive note, probably written by Albert van Dalsum, which explains the mytho-logical basis of the plot and concludes with the following paragraph:

So much is Celtic legend, but there is also the mask-play in which the poet Yeats revives the content of these legends for us in a new light. For him this legend is the eternal great conflict between *Man* and *Woman*. He sees here in its clearest form the enigma of sex, which is the great problem in modern life as in previous times. Cuchulain is for him no longer the prehistoric Irish hero and a suitable subject for philological study; instead, Cuchulain is *alive* again for him and has become so for us. We see the *Man* in him. And opposite to the Man : the Woman, present in two people; Emer who has mental life and Eithne Inguba who has sensual life. What binds man eternally to, and what alienates him eternally from woman, Yeats has brought to life in this mask-play.* [23]

*

Yeats did not become aware of the Dutch production of *The Only Jealousy of Emer* until after the 1926 revival at the Stadsschouwburg in Amsterdam of Albert van Dalsum's 1922 presentation. A friend sent him some photographs of the production and of the bronzes which Hildo Krop had cast from the masks. The impression these pictures made on Yeats was a significant factor in the next develop-ment of his dramatic work. The disillusioned tone of the Preface to

---

*Tot zoover de Keltische sage, nu het maskerspel waarin de dichter Yeats den inhoud van deze sage voor ons in een nieuw licht doet herleven. Voor hem is deze sage de eeuwige groote strijd tusschen *Man* en *Vrouw*. Het raadsel der sekse, dat groote probleem ook van ons moderne leven, wat ten allen tijde het groote probleem is geweest, hij ziet het hier in zijn duidelijkste voor-stelling belichaamd. Cuchulain is voor hem niet meer de voor-historische Iersche held en een schoon onderwerp voor philologische studie, maar Cu-chulain is weer *levend* voor hem en voor ons geworden. Wij zien in hem de Man. En tegenover den Man : de *Vrouw*, belichaamd in twee wezens : Emer, de geestelijk-liefhebbende en Eithne Inguba, de zinnelijk-liefhebbende vrouw. Dat wat de man eeuwig bindt aan de vrouw, en dat wat de man eeuwig van de vrouw vervreemdt heeft hij in dit maskerspel laten leven.

Four Plays for Dancers revealed that his first group of dramatic writings in the manner of the Nō had not attracted the attention he sought and the further works he attempted in the genre were, to a large extent, still unresolved drafts. But he had had a considerable success in the theatre with his versions of the two Sophoclean tragedies, produced at the Abbey in 1926 and 1927.

In Ninette de Valois he had, however, found a fine dancer willing to devote her talents to developing a School of Dancing for the Irish National Theatre. New and exciting actors had joined the Company which, with the assistance of a State subsidy since 1924, was in a position to pay its actors regularly, if not well, and to spend a little on the dressing of the productions. Popular success had come to the Abbey through the works of Seán O'Casey and such new dramatists as T. C. Murray, George Shiels and Brinsley MacNamara and, in addition to Yeats's versions of the Greek tragedies, the theatre had staged Eugene O'Neill's *The Emperor Jones*, Shaw's *Caesar and Cleopatra*, both designed by Lennox Robinson's talented wife, D. Travers Smith, and a fine *King Lear*, directed by Denis Johnston with F. J. McCormick in the title role.

The two-night season in which the Dublin Drama League had staged *The Only Jealousy of Emer* in its original text, together with the first production of *The Cat and the Moon*, in 1926, may have prompted Yeats to finish the first version of *The Resurrection* and give it to the Cuala Press to publish in the following year. In February 1927 Terence Gray presented *On Baile's Strand* at the Festival Theatre in Cambridge under the direction of Norman Marshall with choreography by Ninette de Valois and masks by Hedley Briggs. And in November the Peacock Theatre opened in Dublin.

By the Summer of 1927, Yeats was planning a season of Dance Plays at the Peacock, and he wrote to T. Sturge Moore, who was then designing the binding for *The Tower*,

I have got two fine Japanese Noh Masks and am trying to get some magnificent masks made by the Dutch Sculptor Van Krop for my *Only Jealousy of Emer*. With these masks I shall be able to give a series of Dance Plays here, as we have just added to the Abbey Theatre a small perfectly equipped theatre which holds a hundred people. I am hoping henceforth with the assistance of the Abbey School of Acting to make experiments for which the popular audience of a larger theatre is not ready. As the Young Players of the school will be comparatively inexperienced there will be some advantage to letting them appear before the public in a strange dramatic form, related rather to ritual than to the ordinary form of drama.[24]

There are three Nō masks in Yeats's collection, of the types known as *Joh*, *Heida*, and *Sumioshi-Otoko*, but it was Hildo Krop's masks that inspired him towards a new development in his 'Plays for Dancers.' The projected Peacock season did not occur in 1927, but Yeats came to think of *The Only Jealousy of Emer* in the context of the larger, 'public' stage, in a production in which Krop's masks would be used and appreciated by a wider public than he had so far envisaged for the play. He set to writing a version for 'the public stage' to which he gave the title of *Fighting the Waves*. When it was published in *Wheels and Butterflies* in 1934, he dedicated this to 'Hildo van Krop who made the masks.'

In Krop he had found his mask-maker, in Ninette de Valois his dancer and, during his stay at Rapallo in the Spring of 1929, appropriately through an introduction given by Ezra Pound, he discovered his composer. His letters written from Rapallo to various friends at this time convey the rapidity with which the play was changed from its original form in *Four Plays for Dancers* into a 'public' piece in a period which cannot have exceeded five or six weeks:

to Olivia Shakespear, 2 March
To-night we dine with Ezra — the first dinner-coated meal since I got here — to meet Hauptmann who does not know a word of English but is fine to look at — after the fashion of William Morris. Auntille — how do you spell him? — and his lady will be there and probably a certain Basil Bunting, one of Ezra's more savage disciples. He got into jail as a pacifist and then for assaulting the police and carrying concealed weapons and he is now writing up Antille's music. George and I keep him at a distance and yet I have no doubt that just such as he surrounded Shakespeare's theatre, when it was denounced by the first puritans.[25]

to Lady Gregory, 9 March
The getting away from all distractions has enriched my imagination. I wish I had done it years ago. Antheil is here and has started on a musical setting for a trilogy consisting of *The Hawk's Well*, *On Baile's Strand* and the new version of *The Only Jealousy* which I call *Fighting the Waves*. If he persists, and he is at present enthusiastic, it means a performance in Vienna in the autumn. He has a great name there since his setting of *Oedipus* a few months ago. He is a revolutionary musician — there was a riot of almost Abbey intensity over some music of his in America. There will be masks and all singing within the range of the speaking voice — for my old theories are dogmas it seems of the new school. His setting of *Fighting the Waves* should be ready for Miss de Valois to do in Dublin in May. He is about 28 and looks 18 and has a face of indescribable innocence. His wife, a first violinist from somewhere or other, looks equally young and innocent. Both are persons of impulse and he may or he may not get through his month of toil upon the three plays. He promises to keep the instruments required for *The Fighting of the Waves* within the range of the Abbey. During the fight in *Oedipus at Colonus* (he did both plays) there were twelve pianos played at once.[26]

to Shotaro Oshima, 24 March
... the date of my arrival in Dublin depends upon the date of a dance play

of mine. If our present plans are carried out the first performance will be on the 29th of April, but if it is put off, I shall get there two weeks later. The play is a new version of my *Only Jealousy of Emer* arranged for the ordinary stage, greatly simplified and with much more dancing. The music is being written by a young musician of the most advanced European school. His name is George Antheil and he has just had a great success in Vienna with a musical setting of Oedipus. His theories about the relation between music and speech very closely resemble my own.[27]

to Lady Gregory, 10 April
I heard some of George Antheil's music for *The Only Jealousy* the other day and it seemed to me the only dramatic music I ever heard — a very strong beat, something heroic and barbaric and strange.[28]

George Antheil (1900-1959) had been born in Trenton, New Jersey, and had come to Europe to pursue his career as a pianist and composer. He met Pound in Paris in 1923 and so impressed Pound that he wrote extensively in defence of Antheil's musical theories in which he saw in Antheil the musical exponent of futurism. Pound's *Antheil and the Treatise on Harmony*, published in Paris in 1924, did much to establish the composer's European reputation. In his autobiography, *Bad Boy of Music*, Antheil published his account of these weeks with Yeats at Rapallo from which derived the scheme to produce scores for three plays, all with Cuchulain as the central character — *On Baile's Strand*, and two of the 'Plays for Dancers,' *At the Hawk's Well* and *The Only Jealousy of Emer*. Of these, only one, that for *The Only Jealousy*, retitled *Fighting the Waves*, was completed:

Ezra now introduced me to a number of persons who habitually sat at the only free table of Rapallo's only decent restaurant, the Hotel Rapallo café. Two of them were Nobel Prize winners, William Butler Yeats and Gerhart Hauptmann. I had never even so much as met a Nobel Prize winner before, and now, every day, I could sit down with two of them and question them on all kinds of little mundane matters, such as what they were feeding their dogs on, had they read any good detective stories lately. etc. . . .
Yeats was always getting messages from spirits. He was also a veritable expert on seeing ghosts in broad daylight — a rather difficult feat, as I am told by those who are authorities on this subject.
I saw quite a bit of Yeats now, because when he discovered that I was a composer whom Ezra had once written a book about, he conceived the gay idea of my writing incidental music to three of his thoroughly Irish plays. (I did, finally, write music to one, *Fighting the Waves*, which he subsequently produced at the Abbey Theatre, Dublin.)
We would often sit together discussing our project, when suddenly he'd say : "Hello, William," and he'd tip his soft felt sombrero.
I'd follow his look and, seeing nobody within fifty feet of our table, I'd ask him, not without astonishment, where William was.

"Right in the chair alongside of you; he's the ghost of my indigestion," Yeats would say.

Yeats would sometimes talk quite a bit to William, and also other Irish spirits who had been kind enough to come all the way from Dublin to see him. Previously I had often visited Yeats at night, but now I developed the habit of seeing him exclusively in the daytime. Not being on such friendly relations with the spirits as Yeats, I hated the idea of walking home alone at night.

But I think I wrote him a good enough background score for his play. He seemed well enough pleased with it, at least in the introduction to his group of plays, Wheels and Butterflies, published by the Macmillan Company. Fighting the Waves was played in Dublin with notable success, and raving Dublin critics from then on decided that I was really an Irishman because the score (so they said) was so thoroughly Irish.

As a matter of fact, the secret of my success in writing such true Irish music is contained in the fact that Yeats's play is entirely about Irish ghosts. With "William" sitting there alongside of me at the café every day, what else could have happened but that William soon became quite visible and even audible, giving me not only most valuable tips on ancient Irish music, but also singing old Irish melodies (in a rather cracked voice, I admit) while I hastily wrote them down in my notebook.[29]

Yeats returned to Dublin early in May with Antheil's score, and set about having the revised play presented at the Abbey, using Krop's masks and a curtain and costumes designed by Lennox Robinson's wife, D. Travers Smith. He described the project in a letter of 31 July to Olivia Shakespear as 'The birth of a new art — if one does not make these announcements one looks so old fashioned.'[30] He described his purpose in restyling his play in his Introduction to the rewritten text, published in Wheels and Butterflies, 1934:

I wrote The Only Jealousy of Emer for performance in a private house or studio, considering it, for reasons which I have explained, unsuited to a public stage. Then somebody put it on a public stage in Holland and Hildo van Krop made his powerful masks. Because the dramatist who can collaborate with a great sculptor is lucky, I rewrote the play not only to fit it for such a stage but to free it from abstraction and confusion. I have retold the story in prose which I have tried to make very simple, and left imaginative suggestion to dancers, singers, musicians. I have left the words of the opening and closing lyrics for sung to modern music in the modern way they suggest strange patterns to the ear without obtruding upon it their difficult, irrelevant words. The masks get much of their power from enclosing the whole head; this makes the head out of proportion to the body, and I found some difference of opinion as to whether this was a disadvantage or not in an art so distant from reality; that it was not a disadvantage in the case of the Woman of the Sidhe all were agreed. She was a strange, noble, unforgettable figure.

I do not say that it is always necessary when one writes for a general audience to make the words of the dialogue so simple and so matter-of-fact; but it is necessary where the appeal is mainly to the eye and to the ear through songs and music. Fighting the Waves is in itself nothing, a mere occasion for sculptor and dancer, for the exciting dramatic music of George Antheil.[31]

*

The text of *Fighting the Waves* is almost completely a reorganisation and rewriting of *The Only Jealousy of Emer*. The play opens with a balletic Prologue danced by Cuchulain and a group of dancers who represent the waves before a symbolic front curtain which also carries the motif of waves. The ritual of the unfolding and folding of the cloth is replaced by a 'blackout' of the stage which allows the dancers to exit unseen before the entry of the Musicians who, in this version, are singers only, because the score as composed by Antheil calls for an orchestra.

PROLOGUE

Musicians and speaker off stage. There is a curtain with a wave pattern. A man wearing the Cuchulain mask enters from one side with sword and shield. He dances a dance which represents a man fighting the waves. The waves may be represented by other dancers : in his frenzy he supposes the waves to be his enemies : gradually he sinks down as if overcome, then fixes his eyes with a cataleptic stare upon some imaginary distant object. The stage becomes dark, and when the light returns it is empty. The Musicians enter. Two stand one on either side of the curtain, singing.

With the exception of the Musicians' choruses which are retained with only minor alterations from the original play, the text of the play is in prose, and there are two extra dances. In the first of these, a dance of seduction involving Fand and the Ghost of Cuchulain, the directions read :

Fand, the Woman of the Sidhe, enters. Emer draws a dagger and moves as if to strike her.

FIGURE OF CUCHULAIN (*laughing*). You think to wound her with a knife ! She has an airy body, an invulnerable body. Remember that though your lamentations have dragged him hither, once he has left this shore, once he has passed the bitter sea, once he lands in Manannan's house, he will be as the gods who remember nothing.

The Woman of the Sidhe, Fand, moves round the crouching Ghost of Cuchulain at front of stage in a dance that grows gradually quicker as he awakes. At moments she may drop her hair upon his head, but she does not kiss him. She is accompanied by string and flute and drum. Her mask and clothes must suggest gold or bronze or brass and silver, so that she seems more an idol than a human being. This suggestion may be repeated in her movements. Her hair, too, must keep the metallic suggestion. The object of the dance is that having awakened Cuchulain he will follow Fand out; probably he will seek a kiss and the kiss will be withheld.

FIGURE OF CUCHULAIN. Cry out that you renounce his love, cry that you renounce his love for ever.

Fand and Cuchulain go out.

The final dance occurs in the Epilogue, a slightly revised version of the 'Song for the unfolding and folding of the cloth' in *The Only Jealousy of Emer*, and echoes the opening of the play:

The Musicians return to their places. Fand, the Woman of the Sidhe, enters and dances a dance which expresses her despair for the loss of Cuchulain. As before there may be other dancers who represent the waves. It is called, in order to balance the first dance, "Fand mourns among the waves." It is essentially a dance which symbolises, like water in the fortune-telling books, bitterness. As she takes her final pose of despair the Curtain falls.

*

The reorganisation of *The Only Jealousy of Emer* into its 'public' form, *Fighting the Waves*, was perhaps also prompted by Arthur Waley's version of the Nō play *Atsumori* in his book, *The Nō Plays of Japan* (1921). This piece from the Nō of ghosts has many parallels with the plot of the Yeats play. The warrior hero, Atsumori, met his first death fighting in waves; he reappears in the play and mimes his death battle:

> Then Atsumori turns his horse
> Knee-deep in the lashing waves,
> And draws his sword.
> Twice, three times he strikes; then still saddled
> In close fight they twine; roll headlong together
> Among the surf of the shore.[32]

Antheil's music for the play, of which the vocal and piano parts were printed in *Wheels and Butterflies*, 1934, consists of an Overture to which the opening dance was performed, leading directly into the setting of the opening chorus and continuing into a brief movement to accompany the opening of the 'wave' curtain which reveals the tableau on stage. There is a setting of the First Musician's brief lyric, 'White shell, white wing!' and one of Fand's dance. The final chorus and Fand's last dance complete the score. The instrumentation, as described in a letter to me from Mrs. Antheil, dated 3 September 1974, is for 'small chamber orchestra: flute, clarinet, trumpet, trombone, bass drum, piano, first and second violin, cello and contrabass.' Mrs. Antheil has kindly allowed me to examine the manuscript of the score for *Fighting the Waves* and this reveals the complexity presented to the Abbey and the challenge to the resources of the theatre. In the setting for Fand's dance, Antheil makes such demands as

†Trombone should fit into its bell an enormous extension cardboard megaphone extending at least one yard from the end of the instrument.
*Actors on or behind scenes simply wail along with the marked downward chromatic passage.[33]

67. George Antheil. MS. orchestral score for *Fighting the Waves*, 1929.
Fand's dance.

The first, and only, production of *Fighting the Waves* opened at the Abbey Theatre on 13 August 1929,* to an audience that included many of Dublin's leading literary and artistic figures. When the text was published in *Wheels and Butterflies*, Yeats wrote that, although the production attracted large audiences, it had not been revived

because Mr. George Antheil's most strange dramatic music requires a large expensive orchestra. A memory of that orchestra has indeed roused a distinguished Irish lyric poet† to begin a dance play which he assures me requires but a tin whistle and a large expensive concertina.[34]

The production, with Krop's masks, the fine front curtain and the costumes designed by D. Travers Smith and the choreography of Ninette de Valois, must have been visually the most satisfying of the productions of Yeats's plays staged in his lifetime. The play was described on the programme as a 'Ballet-Play' and Yeats contributed a programme note which reveals how anxious he was to find a popular audience for the play.

NOTE. — In this dance play I have brought together "The Only Jealousy of Emer" and another Irish story. At the opening Cuchullain is shown fighting the waves in a frenzy of grief for he has killed his son. Then we see him lying in a bed, a seemingly drowned man, attended by his wife Emer and another. He is not dead but entranced. The Goddess Fand who loves him comes seeking to entice him away; she is defeated by the love of Emer and Cuchullain awakes. The play closes with Fand's dance among the waves, the dance of her despair. — W.B.Y.[35]

---

*   FIGHTING THE WAVES

Presented by the Irish National Theatre Society Limited
at the Abbey Theatre, Dublin
on Tuesday 13 August 1929

Cuchullain	Michael J. Dolan
Emer (his wife)	Meriel Moore
Eithne Inguba	Shelah Richards
Fand	Ninette de Valois
Singer	J. Stevenson
Ghost of Cuchullain	Hedley Briggs
Waves	Chris Sheehan, Mai Kiernan,
	Cepta Cullen, Doreen Cuthbert,
	Margaret Horgan, Thelma Murphy

Music by George Antheil
Costumes and Curtain designed by D. Travers Smith
Masks designed by Hildo Krop
Choreography by Ninette de Valois
Conducted by J. F. Larchet
The play produced by Lennox Robinson

†Probably F. R. Higgins, whose play *A Deuce of Jacks* was produced in 1935.

This concern is further reflected in his preface to the play, written for the published version in *Wheels and Butterflies*, but first printed in *The Dublin Magazine*.

But, although Yeats claimed in his letters that '*Fighting the Waves* has been my greatest success on the stage since *Kathleen-ni-Houlihan*,' [36] the view of the Dublin 'popular' audience he sought is probably more accurately expressed by Holloway to his journal:

I met F. J. McCormick and Eileen Crowe as I came out of the Abbey at 11 o'clock after the ballet, *Fighting the Waves*, and Mac said to me, "I see you have survived it. Oh, what noise!"

It is the first time I ever heard Stephenson sing that I didn't enjoy his lovely, clear, carrying voice. Oh, the harsh, discordant notes he had to sing. I said when I heard that Yeats liked the music that was enough for me — as he has no ear for sound! Those on the stage worked wonders against the braying. . . . There was an augmented orchestra to interpret the noisy discords — drums, flute, cornets, etc., and Miss Grey was at the piano. Dr. Larchet conducted and couldn't extract head or tail out of the score. The principals wore masks and also some of the dancers. It was a pity to waste such talent on such strange materials. . . .

Well, of all the noisy noise I ever heard George Antheil's music to *Fighting the Waves* capped it all, and, oh, to hear poor J. Stephenson as "singer" try to get music out of the discordant notes he had to vocalize, and also try to convey the poet's words he sang, was to hear a sweet clear voiced singer at times howl out notes that seemed out of tune. It was only when he was let declaim his lines unaccompanied that his words rang out with clarion clearness. . . .

The masked figures seemed strange to the eye, but there was a certain weirdness in that worn by the demon of the sea who replaces "Cuchullain" in the bed. . . . Those masks suggested the big-head of my early pantomime days, and conveyed nothing to me save a more or less obstruction to the spoken words. . . . The opening ballet of "Cuchullain" fighting the waves was decorative and beautiful to the eye, but the music that accompanied it was like the falling of a tin tray on the flags.

It took as many to concoct this ballet as go to make a musical comedy. . . . Fancy having to engage a full orchestra of musicians to try to play such stuff that could be as well interpreted by children on tin cans! . . . It was a really typical Abbey first night. [37]

*

Fighting the Waves marked the end of Yeats's attempt to write in a form very closely modelled on the Nō. In his plays of the next ten years, the final decade of his life, his 'accomplishment' was to develop in a more individual direction and, although always informed by the disciplines he had acquired from his classical Japanese model, was to flourish in a group of plays in various modes structured on facets of his 'private philosophy.'

9 *a bell with many echoes*

In the final decade of his life Yeats's theatrical adventure changed direction. With the production of *Fighting the Waves* at the Abbey Theatre in August 1929 he had reclaimed the public stage for poetry, and with considerable, but unrepeatable success. And this success, I feel, prompted the form which his next dramatic writing was to take — a form which would accommodate the ideas and themes of his Noble Drama to the technique that the Irish National Theatre Company had developed. The Abbey Theatre style had originally been conceived as 'realistic' but a generation of playwrights and of players who had grown up in the service of that theatre had generated a mannered style both of writing and of acting which was in its own way as individual, and as removed from its mundane models as the work of the Impressionist painters. The dramas of the 'Cork Realists', Lennox Robinson and T. C. Murray which, in the first decades of the century, had seemed very remote from the imaginative and fantastic approach of Synge and Fitzmaurice, developed during the 1920's into a manner which was a theatrical echo stylised from events and characters in real life, and to this O'Casey added the Dublin dimension with his masterpieces, *The Shadow of a Gunman*, *Juno and the Paycock* and *The Plough and the Stars*.

During the 1920's, too, the Abbey Theatre had achieved a stability which contributed significantly to its development. Lennox Robinson, who directed *The Player Queen* in 1919, had emerged as an accomplished producer and, between 1920 and 1929, he directed almost fifty Abbey premieres, among them *The Plough and the Stars*, both of Yeats's Oedipus plays and *Fighting the Waves*. The company included a group of leading players who had developed in the Theatre such as F. J. McCormick, Barry Fitzgerald, Arthur Shields, Maureen Delaney, Eileen Crowe and May Craig who played all through this period, which also saw the emergence of young players such as Shelah Richards and Ria Mooney. The government subsidy, small as it was, contributed to this stable development as did the political security implied by the establishment of the Irish Free State in 1922.

Yeats had become an important public figure in Ireland and his concerns, and perhaps a hint of the direction he felt his dramatic writing would take, can be found in the Commentary on *The Words Upon the Window Pane*, which he published in *The Dublin Magazine* in 1931:

Somebody said the other night that Dublin was full of clubs that met in cellars and garrets, he himself knew four, and had for their object our general improvement. He was scornful, said that they had all begun by drawing up a programme and passing a resolution against the censorship and would never do anything else. When I began my public life Dublin was full of such clubs that passed resolutions and drew up programmes and though the majority stopped there some did much to find an audience for a school of writers. The fall of Parnell had freed imagination from practical politics, from agrarian grievance and political enmity and turned it to imaginative nationalism, to Gaelic, to the ancient stories, and at last to lyrical poetry and to drama. Political failure and political success have had the same result except that to-day imagination is turning full of uncertainty to something it thinks European, and whether that something will be "arty" and provincial, or a form of life, is as yet undiscoverable. Hitherto we have walked the road, but now we have shut the door and turned up the lamp. What shall occupy our imagination? We must, I think, decide among these three ideas of national life; that of Swift; that of a great Italian of his day; that of modern England. If the Garrets and the Cellars listen I may throw light upon the matter, and I hope if all the time I seem thinking of something else I should be forgiven. I must speak of things that come out of the common consciousness where every thought is like a bell with many echoes.[1]

'My little play . . . came to me amidst considerations such as these,'[2] the Commentary continues, reflecting the concerns in Yeats's mind during the period in which he wrote *The Words Upon the Window Pane*. He visited Lady Gregory at Coole in September 1930 and found her in failing health. He could see the coming end of Coole Park and all it had represented both as haven and as symbol, and he predicted its fate in 'Coole Park 1929':

> Here, traveller, scholar, poet, take your stand
> When all those rooms and passages are gone,
> When nettles wave upon a shapeless mound
> And saplings root among the broken stone,
> And dedicate — eyes bent upon the ground,
> Back turned upon the brightness of the sun
> And all the sensuality of the shade —
> A moment's memory to that laurelled head.[3]

He returned to Dublin and set out to spend the winter months again working at Rapallo from mid-November. He caught cold in London on the way and on his arrival at Rapallo he became gravely ill with Malta fever and was unable to work until late in March 1930. By 7 April he could write to Lady Gregory,

When I am not reading detective stories I am reading Swift, the *Diary to Stella* and his correspondence with Pope and Bolingbroke; these men fascinate me, in Bolingbroke the last pose and in Swift the last passion of the Renaissance, in Pope, whom I dislike, an imitation both of pose and passion.[4]

In June he wrote to Olivia Shakespear that he was still reading Swift constantly[5] and before his return to Dublin in July he had written two scenarios, the first entitled 'Jonathan Swift,' and listed the persons in the play. He finished *The Words Upon the Window Pane* at Coole Park between August and October.

In *The Words Upon the Window Pane* Yeats organises themes closely parallel to those of his Nō-inspired plays into the framework of a realistic piece for 'the public stage.' The central action is a 'dreaming back,' akin to the central action of *The Dreaming of the Bones* in which the shades of Diarmuid and Dervorgilla are evoked or summoned by a 'traveller,' the young refugee from the Easter 1916 Rising. In *The Words Upon the Window Pane* the agent is the medium, Mrs. Henderson, who summons the voices of Swift, Stella and Vanessa to re-enact, in the context of a spiritualist seance, the tangled and enigmatic interweaving of their lives. The exposition of the play is cast into the dialogue of the participants arriving for the seance and the final resolution of the play is a solo piece by the actress who plays the medium. The earliest draft contains a passage which relates the theme to the stories of J. Sheridan leFanu, particularly to the collection entitled *In a Glass Darkly*, but this theme was abandoned as the plot developed.

By 23 October Yeats could inform Olivia Shakespear in a letter that he had finished the play[6] and on 29 October he wrote to Lady Gregory, '*Swift* is in rehearsal — I shall dedicate it to you.'[7] In the same letter he criticised a revival of the Abbey production of *King Lear* with F. J. McCormick in the title role, and concluded, 'an elaborate verse play is beyond our people.'[8] *The Words Upon the Window Pane* was produced at the Abbey Theatre on 17 November.* The play 'was a much greater success than I had ever hoped and beautifully acted,'[9] he reported to Olivia Shakespear, and he set about drafting a Commentary to define the reasoning behind the piece. To the original version of this Commentary, published in 1931

---

* THE WORDS UPON THE WINDOW PANE

Presented by the Irish National Theatre Society Limited
at the Abbey Theatre, Dublin
on Monday 17 November 1930

Miss McKenna	Shelah Richards
Dr. Trench	P. J. Carolan
John Corbet	Arthur Shields
Cornelius Pattison	Michael J. Dolan
Abraham Johnson	F. J. McCormick
Mrs. Mallet	Eileen Crowe
Mrs. Henderson.	May Craig

Produced by Lennox Robinson

in *The Dublin Magazine*, he added a second part which appeared in the Cuala Press edition and reveals his continuing involvement with the performance of his plays,

When I went into the theatre café after the performance a woman asked a question and I replied with some spiritualistic anecdote. "Did that happen with the medium we have seen to-night?" she said : and yet May Craig who played the part had never seen a séance. I had however assisted her by self-denial. No character upon the stage spoke my thoughts. All were people I had met or might have met in just such a séance. . . . If I had not denied myself, if I had allowed some character to speak my thoughts what would he have said? It seems to me that after reading many books and meeting many phenomena, some in my own house, some of it when alone in my room, I can see clearly at last. I consider it certain that every voice that speaks, every form that appears, whether to the medium's eyes and ears alone or to some one or two others or to all present, whether it remains a sight or sound or affects the sense of touch, whether it is confined to the room or can make itself apparent at some distant place, whether it can or cannot alter the position of material objects, is first of all a secondary personality or dramatisation of the medium's. Perhaps May Craig, when alone in her room after the play, went, without knowing what she was doing, through some detail of her performance.[10]

Holloway found the play 'practically a recitation for the medium — a part splendidly played by May Craig.'[11] May Craig had been coached in her role as Mrs. Henderson by Yeats himself and her performance was one of the most individual and accomplished of all Abbey characterisations. She continued to play the part in Abbey revivals until the 1960's.

Yeats's excitement at the success of the play prompted him to write the Commentary, an extremely important statement which examines the convictions underlying the play and relates his dramatic approach to the other elements of his creative and public life. In the letter of 2 December in which he communicated his excitement at the production to Olivia Shakespear, he continued

I want to bring out a book of four plays called *My Wheels and Butterflies* — the wheels are the four introductions. Dublin is said to be full of little societies meeting in cellars and garrets so I shall put this rhyme on a fly-leaf

> To cellar and garret
> A wheel I send
> But every butterfly
> To a friend.

The "wheels" are addressed to Ireland mainly — a scheme of intellectual nationalism.[12]

Yeats's 'intellectual nationalism' is perhaps best expressed in his choice of an eighteenth-century theme for a 'public play' in prose, written at this precise time of his life, after years spent as a senator attempting to give an individual dimension to Irish life. He wrote in the Commentary,

I collect materials for my thought and work, for some identification of my beliefs with the nation itself, I seek an image of the modern mind's discovery of itself, of its own permanent form, in that one Irish century that escaped from darkness and confusion. I would that our fifteenth, sixteenth, or even our seventeenth century had been the clear mirror, but fate decided against us.[13]

And he carried this theme into the text of his play, into John Corbet's contribution to the dialogue,

I hope to prove that in Swift's day men of intellect reached the height of their power — the greatest position they ever attained in society and the State, that everything great in Ireland and in our character, in what remains of our architecture, comes from that day; that we have kept its seal longer than England.

Conscious that, if he cast it in his own individual mode, his Swift play would not make the impact he desired, Yeats took the technique of the realistic theatre as developed at the Abbey and adapted it completely to his own purpose. He wrote to Joseph Hone on 20 November 1930 about Hone's book on Bishop Berkeley,

You have set Berkeley in his Irish world, and made him amusing, animated and intelligible. He is of the utmost importance to the Ireland that is coming into existence. . . . I want Protestant Ireland to base some vital part of its culture on Burke, Swift and Berkeley.[14]

The Words Upon the Window Pane is the complete justification of Yeats as a master craftsman of the theatre.

*

By the end of 1930, Yeats had found a place for *Wheels and Butterflies*, the book of new plays he had mentioned to Olivia Shakespear in his letter of 2 December, in the scheme of the 'Edition de Luxe of all my work published and unpublished'[15] which Macmillan proposed to publish (but which, in fact, never appeared) and was busy planning 'Months of re-writing. What happiness!'[16] which would include a reworking of *A Vision* and a completely new version of *The Resurrection* —

young men talking, the apostles in the next room overwhelmed by the crucifixion. Christ newly arisen passes silently through. I wrote a chaotic dialogue on this theme some years ago. But now I have dramatic tension throughout.[17]

The first version of *The Resurrection* (see above, pp. 270-72) which was printed in *The Adelphi* in June 1927, had lacked this quality of dramatic tension and had never been attempted in the theatre, but Yeats included songs from the play in his Cuala Press collection of poems, *October Blast*, in 1927 — the songs which the stage directions to the original version stated should be omitted if the piece were played on 'an ordinary stage.' This first version failed, I believe, because Yeats could not adapt the form he had developed from Nō in the 'Plays for Dancers' to accommodate an argument about the nature of Christ which was more proper to his 'private philosophy' as set out in *A Vision*. The experience of *Fighting the Waves* which broadened the stage concept of the 'Plays for Dancers,' followed by the discipline of writing *The Words Upon the Window Pane* as a piece for the 'public' stage, both contribute to the emergence of a new and specially Yeatsian form of play in the rewritten text of *The Resurrection*, which is modified by the ironic view of temporal life typical of all his writings of the 'thirties.

The challenge of the projected Edition de Luxe gave an urgency to the rewriting and the typescript, dated March 1931, formed the basis of the first printing of the new text, completed at the Cuala Press in October 1931, in *Stories of Michael Robartes and his Friends*, a book which, with the exception of *The Resurrection*, was made up of material for the rewritten version of *A Vision*. In this version of *The Resurrection*, Yeats had clearly made up his mind that it was a play for his small audience, and the opening stage direction reads:

Before I had finished this play I saw that its subject matter made it unsuited for the public Stage in England or in Ireland. I had begun it with an ordinary stage seen in the mind's eye, curtained walls, a window and door at back, a curtained door at left. I now changed the stage directions and wrote songs for the unfolding and folding of the curtain that it might be played like my dance plays, in a studio or a drawing-room or at the Peacock Theatre and before a specially chosen audience. If it is played at the Peacock Theatre the musicians may sing the opening and closing songs, each perhaps shortened by a verse, as they pull apart or pull together the proscenium curtain, the whole stage may be hung with curtains with an opening at the left. The song in the middle may be either spoken or sung, but must be accompanied by drum taps. If sung it may be shortened by a couple of verses. While the play is in progress if played at the Peacock, the musicians will sit towards the right of the proscenium on the steps which separate the stage from the audience.

For the later printing of the play in *Wheels and Butterflies*, 1934, Yeats wrote a Commentary or Introduction in which he links the play with his cyclical theory of world history and with the personal philosophy which he embodied in *A Vision* — the confrontation of the human with the phantom or supernatural world — a theme which extends and qualifies that of *The Words Upon the Window*

Pane. But even this rewritten version does not succeed in getting its meaning across in theatrical idiom, and its depends too much on expository dialogue with a lack of action to retain the interest of even the private audience of devotees to which it is addressed.

The Resurrection was not performed until 30 July 1934* when it shared the bill on the 'public' Abbey stage with the first produced version of *The King of the Great Clock Tower*. In a letter to Olivia Shakespear, Yeats linked the philosophical structure of both plays to his system.

Man becomes rational, no longer driven from below or above. My two plays ... both deal with that moment — the slain god, the risen god.[18]

But Holloway, the diligent recorder, was not impressed and his diary entry indicates that his dissatisfaction was shared by the Company,

When I asked Denis Johnston on his return after the interval following *The Resurrection*, "Well, what are people saying about it?", he replied that, "Robinson is in a terrible state over its production. Yeats came down to rehearsal yesterday and altered his grey curtains and platform on the stage, and Robinson is thinking of having omitted his name as producer on the programme."
I said, "As the characters have only to stand around and talk, there is nothing to produce about the piece." [19]

*

The founding figures of the Theatre were beginning to depart. Frank Fay died in Dublin on 2 January 1931. He had developed a throat ailment which destroyed his fine speaking voice and ended his career as an actor. He spent his last years as a teacher of elocution. Later in the year Lady Gregory became ill and was to pass her final year dying slowly at Coole. Yeats spent the greater part of his time there,

---

*   THE RESURRECTION

Presented by the Irish National Theatre Society Limited
at the Abbey Theatre, Dublin
on Monday 30 July 1934

The Hebrew	A. J. Leventhal
The Greek	Denis Carey
The Syrian	J. Winter
The Christ	Liam Gaffney
Musicians	Michael J. Dolan and
	Robert Irwin

Produced by Lennox Robinson
Masks by George Atkinson
Music by Arthur Duff

and worked slowly towards the new version of *A Vision*. He completed there his Commentary on *The Words Upon the Window Pane* and the Introduction to *Fighting the Waves*, both of which were printed in *The Dublin Magazine*. Charles Ricketts died in London in October — another link broken.

During this year Yeats's theatrical involvement was mainly with management of the Abbey — two- or three-day visits to Dublin to supervise the new School of Dancing. But he did travel to Belfast for his first broadcast, where he read some poems in a programme on 8 September. As Lady Gregory's condition worsened, there was some thought of transferring her to a Dublin nursing home, but Yeats was among those who felt she would be happier to end her days at Coole.

The principal Abbey company went on another American tour in October and the theatre was let to various Dublin companies during their absence, with occasional experimental productions mounted by the younger Abbey players and dancers. Among these was a series dubbed 'Mainly Ballet: the Abbey Directors' Sunday Entertainments' in which, on Sunday 6 December, *The Dreaming of the Bones* had its first production (see above, p. 241).

Lady Gregory died at Coole on 23 May 1932. Yeats was in Dublin when she died, looking after affairs in the Theatre. 'I have lost one who has been to me for nearly forty years my strength and my conscience,'[20] he wrote to Mario Rossi. He took on the responsibility for her papers and the editing of her unpublished memoirs, but his link with Coole was broken. He decided to find a permanent home for himself in Dublin and purchased Riversdale House in Rathfarnham. At the Abbey, he was occupied with management, principally with planning a further American tour during which he would accompany the players and deliver some lectures to fund his proposed Irish Academy of Letters, an institution which Yeats felt would consolidate the image of a cultured Ireland which he had striven for years to establish. The Academy was formally inaugurated at a meeting in Dublin on 14 September and elected Bernard Shaw as President, Yeats as Vice-President and Æ as Secretary and Treasurer. The Academy was to elect twenty-five members who had done creative writing important to Ireland and would, among its objects, engage the government in a battle against the censorship of literature which had been introduced in the previous year. Among the founder Academicians were Lennox Robinson, Frank O'Connor who later became a Director of the Abbey, F. R. Higgins, Brinsley McNamara, St. John Ervine, T. C. Murray, Austin Clarke and Padraic Colum. Including the officers, this meant that about half the membership of the Academy had devoted a large part of their creative lives to the Irish theatre. Sean O'Casey was invited to become a founder member, but declined.

Yeats felt it was doubtful if George Moore would accept membership and he does not seem to have been invited. Moore was, in fact, on his death-bed and died in London on 21 January 1933.

Among the awards and enterprises of the Academy was the Casement Award for poetry and drama, for which plays by Brinsley McNamara, Rutherford Mayne and Paul Vincent Carroll qualified between 1934 and 1939. The premier award of the Academy was the Gregory Medal, awarded to Yeats, Æ and Shaw as founders and subsequently to Douglas Hyde, Padraic Colum, Micheal MacLiammoir and Austin Clarke.

*

After his lecture tour in America, Yeats spent much of 1933 in Ireland. His health was failing and his blood-pressure was causing concern. He involved himself in party politics and allied himself with the right-wing 'Blueshirt' movement. He also resumed work on his memoirs, perhaps prompted by the challenge presented by Lady Gregory's papers. In April 1934 he decided to undergo the Steinach rejuvenation operation and afterwards went with his wife to Rapallo to rest and recuperate. However, in a letter to Olivia Shakespear in August 1933 he says, 'I think of interpolating a little dance play in between the essay and my book about Lady Gregory.'[21] The book on Lady Gregory became *Dramatis Personae*, and the essay was 'Initiation on a Mountain, An Introduction to *The Holy Mountain* by Shri Purohit Swami,' 1934. By November he had completed a first draft for the opening chorus of the play, which was eventually entitled *The King of the Great Clock Tower*, and he embodied this draft in a letter to Olivia Shakespear on 11 November:

First musician (singing)

> I wait until the tower gives forth the chime,
> And dream of ghosts that have the speech of birds;
> Because they have no thoughts they have no words;
> No thought because no past or future; Time
> Comes from the torture of our flesh, and these,
> Cast out by death and tethered there by love,
> Touch nerve to nerve, throughout the sacred grove
> And seem a single creature when they please.

Second musician (singing)

I call to mind the iron of the bell
And get from that my harsher imagery,
All love is shackled to mortality,
Love's image is a man-at-arms in steel;
Love's image is a woman made of stone;
It dreams of the unborn; all else is nought;
To-morrow and to-morrow fills its thought;
All tenderness reserves for that alone.[22]

The form of the play was a return to the style he had developed from the Japanese Nō, with choruses to open and close the play and a climax expressed in dance. At the same time, he was composing national ballads which he hoped might be sung from the stage of the Abbey Theatre. By January 1934 the play was in draft and formed a discipline to pace out his life which was otherwise concerned with work on *A Vision* and on *Dramatis Personae*, whenever his health allowed. At the end of May he went to Italy and stayed about a month to recover from his operation. While there, he showed *The King of the Great Clock Tower* to Ezra Pound whose disapproval of the piece is reflected in the preface to the Cuala Press edition which was finished in October 1934:

I wrote the prose dialogue of *The King of The Great Clock Tower* that I might be forced to make lyrics for its imaginary people. When I had written all but the last lyric I went a considerable journey partly to get the advice of a poet not of my school who would, as he did some years ago, say what he thought. I asked him to dine, tried to get his attention. "I am in my sixty ninth year" I said, "probably I should stop writing verse, I want your opinion upon some verse I have written lately." I had hoped he would ask me to read it but he would not speak of art, or of literature, or of anything related to them. . . . He took my manuscript and went away denouncing Dublin as "a reactionary hole" because I had said that I was re-reading Shakespeare, would go on to Chaucer, and found all that I wanted of modern life in "detection and the wild west." Next day his judgement came and that in a single word "Putrid".

Then I took my verses to a friend of my own school, and this friend said "go on just like that. Plays like *The Great Clock Tower* always seem unfinished but that is no matter. Begin plays without knowing how to end them for the sake of the lyrics. I once wrote a play and after I had filled it with lyrics abolished the play." Then I brought my work to two painters and a poet until I was like Panurge consulting oracles as to whether he should get married and rejecting all that did not confirm his own desire.[23]

Yeats was back in Dublin in July with the first version of *The King of the Great Clock Tower* in prose, ready for rehearsals at the Abbey Theatre. This version was performed on 30 July 1934. Ninette de Valois arranged the choreography and danced the non-speaking part of the Queen and F. J. McCormick, probably the finest actor ever to develop in the Abbey tradition, played the King. Arthur Duff's music was based on Irish ballad rhythms.

THE WICKED HAWTHORN TREE.

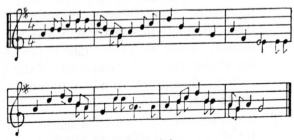

O, but I saw a solemn sight;
Said the rambling, shambling travelling-man;
Castle Dargan's ruin all lit,
Lovely ladies dancing in it.

68. Part of the final song from *The King of the Great Clock Tower* with music by Arthur Duff, drawing by Victor Brown. *A Broadside,* new series, No. 2, February 1935. The Cuala Press, Dublin (reduced).

Yeats described the theme of his play in a programme note:

I have used in "The King of the Great Clock Tower" the symbol used by Wilde in his "Salome." He had found in Heine a description of Salome dancing in Hell, throwing up into the air the head of John the Baptist. Heine may have found her in some Jewish legend, for her dance with the head is from the old ritual of the seasons, a celebration of the Mother godess and her slain god, enacted probably at a full moon in March at the opening of the new year. In an Irish form of perhaps the same symbol there is no dance, but the head of a slain lover singing to his mistress. I have combined dance and song.[24]

Yeats built a lot of his own symbolism into the play and, besides the source he quotes in Wilde's *Salome*, the play draws on an early Yeats folk-tale, 'The Binding of the Hair,' which was printed in the first edition of *The Secret Rose* (1897) and omitted from subsequent editions. In this tale, the Queen is enchanted by the bard Aodh who is, in turn, enchanted by her. After the battle in which the bard falls, his severed head chants to the Queen :

> Fasten your hair with a golden pin,
>   And bind up every wandering tress;
>   I bade my heart build these poor rhymes :
> It worked at them, day out, day in,
>   Building a sorrowful loveliness
>   Out of the battles of old times.
>
> You need but lift a pearl-pale hand,
>   And bind up your long hair and sigh;
>   And all men's hearts must burn and beat;
> And candle-like foam on the dim sand,
>   And stars climbing the dew-dropping sky,
>   Live but to light your passing feet.[25]

*The King of the Great Clock Tower** shared a bill with the first production of *The Resurrection* (see above, p. 291), but Holloway preferred the dance play, which is by far a better piece in performance. Ninette de Valois' dancing did not impress Holloway and he found that the music overpowered the voices of the chorus.

Yeats thought the production 'most effective' and wrote to Olivia Shakespear

it was magnificently acted and danced. It is more original than I thought it, for when I looked up *Salome* I found that Wilde's dancer never danced with the head in her hands — her dance came before the decapitation of the saint and is a mere uncovering of nakedness. My dance is a long expression of

---

*   THE KING OF THE GREAT CLOCK TOWER

Presented by the Irish National Theatre Society Limited
at the Abbey Theatre, Dublin
on Monday 30 July 1934

The King	F. J. McCormick
The Queen	Ninette de Valois
The Stranger	Denis O'Dea
First Musician	Robert Irwin
Second Musician	Joseph O'Neill

Produced by Lennox Robinson
Costumes by D. Travers Smith
Masks by George Atkinson
Music by Arthur Duff

horror and fascination. She first bows before the head (it is on a seat,) then in her dance lays it on the ground and dances before it, then holds it in her hands. Send the enclosed cutting to Dorothy to show to Ezra that I may confound him. He may have been right to condemn it as poetry but he condemned it as drama. It has turned out the most popular of my dance plays.[26]

*

In September Yeats received an invitation to meet Margot Ruddock, an actress who, with her husband, Raymond Lovell, was trying to create a poet's theatre in London. Yeats was attracted by the idea which offered him an outlet for his poetical and dance plays more accessible than the Abbey Theatre which was predominantly devoted to realistic drama. When he met Margot Ruddock in London early in October he realised that she might have the accomplishment to perform his own dramatic verse, and suggested that she might rehearse with Edmund Dulac.

From London, Yeats travelled to Rome as a guest of the Royal Academy of Italy to speak at the Congress on Dramatic Theatre held under the auspices of the Alessandro Volta Foundation, from 8 to 14 October. The President of the Congress was Luigi Pirandello, Italy's premier dramatist who was that year's Nobel Prize winner in Literature, and the attendance included delegates from theatres all over Europe. The Congress discussed the Theatre in relation to other media, to architecture, to stage design. Yeats was Chairman of the fourth session of the Congress, on 12 October, which had as theme 'Lo Spectaculo nella vita morale dei popoli' and received an ovation from the delegates at the beginning of the session.

The fifth, and final, session of the Congress, on 12 and 13 October, was devoted to the topic of state support for the Theatre and during it Yeats addressed the Congress on 'The Irish National Theatre.' In his lecture he surveyed the course of a movement from which his own work had diverged but of which he was the original inspirer. He began,

I am about to describe the rise and achievement of a small, dingy, impecunious theatre, known to Irishmen all over the world because of the fame of its dramatists and its actors, because of the riots that have accompanied certain of its performances, because of its effect upon the imagination of Ireland.

He described the disillusionment that followed the betrayal of Parnell forty years previously, and continued,

In the midst of that disillusionment, of that bitterness, the Irish imaginative movement began. Everywhere men and women turned from politics in despair. Four or five years after the beginning of this movement I was sitting in a garden off the Galway coast talking to my friend Lady Gregory. I told of an old ambition to found an Irish National Theatre. Her friend Dr. Douglas Hyde had founded the Gaelic League which had for its object the substitution of Gaelic, the ancient language of the country, for the English in which we had all come to write and think, but that if it were indeed possible, would take many years. We must put Irish emotion into the English language if we were to reach our own generation. The people, after generations of politics, read nothing but the newspapers, but they could listen (to what interminable speeches had they listened) and they would listen to plays.

The work of Lady Gregory, and that of Synge were described, and Yeats then spoke of himself,

During its first years our Theatre received its character from Lady Gregory's comedies, always gracious and indulgent in their attitude to life, from the bitter-sweet of Synge's tragic comedies, and from the work of a third writer who wrote in verse and chose his themes from ancient Irish legends. I was that third writer, and who am I, how shall I characterise myself? I also come of a Protestant family. My father was an artist, his work is in public galleries, but in his life he had little fame and a hard struggle to live. His small Kildare estate had vanished in the land war. Lady Gregory, John Synge and I were in some sense typical of an Ireland that was passing away, the Ireland of what the historians call "The Protestant Ascendancy", and it was right that we should give to the new Catholic Ireland that was about to take its place, a parting gift, the Irish National Theatre.

And after a commemoration of the players, of Miss Horniman's generosity in making the Abbey Theatre possible and of the rise of new writers in the theatre, especially O'Casey, he concluded,

For a few years the theatre had a great prosperity, but now the tide has sunk again, and it must every two or three years tour the United States. It is a repertory theatre, changing its bill every week, and the repertory is now immense, but the whole repertory seems to rise or sink in popular favour according to that granted to or witheld from some one dramatist. I await with confidence our next popular dramatist. Ireland has won its political freedom; the struggle for intellectual or imaginative freedom, for an escape from the tyranny of the second-rate, whether it comes from the commercialised art of the contemporary stage, or from the nightmare in our own souls, must, in some measure, be fought out upon the stage.[27]

Craig, too, had been invited to attend the Congress in Rome. However, he refused to deliver a formal address and went on condition that he represented only himself. On 10 October, Yeats asked his old friend to lunch and Craig expressed his willingness to work again for Yeats.

Craig did contribute to several of the discussions during the Congress — on the concept of a National Theatre, and on Theatre architecture and Yeats reported to Margot Ruddock on Craig's disagreement with the Bauhaus architect, Walter Gropius, who had delivered a paper on theatre design,

He [Craig] is the great man of the conference, all the young actors and producers gather round him. In the afternoon he started no end of a row. A famous German theatrical architect* had just described his latest invention, a stage that rolls and winds and turns in every possible way, when Craig rose : "A producer who works for that theatre must know all that so and so knows, and so and so, and when he knows all that his art will be dead, and when art is dead the passion is dead. I want men of 25 in the theatre", after that came uproar. Then Tairoff, a famous Russian producer, speaking with great passion said "it is time to get rid of machines". Then an Italian, Marinetti, defended them, an incredible orator. His hands went round and round in mid-air as though he were turning a wheel, and faster and faster as his passion demanded. Then another orator with equal passion denounced the machine, then everybody shouted, while the helpless chairman, Dukes, rang his bell. So on for an hour. When we were going home we had to stand in the hall waiting for taxis (it was raining) and there in the hall the row started again.[28]

In the discussion following three papers on new developments in stage design, Craig rose to the defence of his old friend,

The remarkable fervour shown by most of the speakers who have insisted on the prime importance of the Dramatic Poet, the written word, the part which lives when all else is forgotten, urges me to remind the delegates and all present, that we have had in our midst for three or four days a great Dramatic Poet and no one has till now even mentioned his name. . . . I refer to W. B. Yeats, of Ireland.[29]

And so Yeats and Craig, the poet and the stage manager, met for the last time. Each had contributed much to the other's life work and to the whole development of twentieth-century theatre.

*

During his visit to Rome, Yeats worked at a revision of *The King of the Great Clock Tower* and his letter to Margot Ruddock, quoted above, continues :

I am rewriting *The King of the Great Clock Tower* giving the Queen a speaking part, that you may act it. I have so arranged it that you can give place to a dancer (quite easy as you will both wear masks). The old version of the play is bad because abstract and incoherent. This version is poignant and simple — lyrical dialogue all simple. It takes years to get my plays right. . . .

O my dear, my mind is so busy with your future and perhaps you will reject all my plans — my calculation is that, as you are a trained actress, a lovely sense of rhythm will make you a noble speaker of verse — a singer and sayer. You will read certain poems to me, I have no doubt of the result, and October 19 I begin the practical work.[30]

He recast the dialogue into verse and by December was planning a programme for presentation in London in which the rewritten play

---

*Walter Gropius.

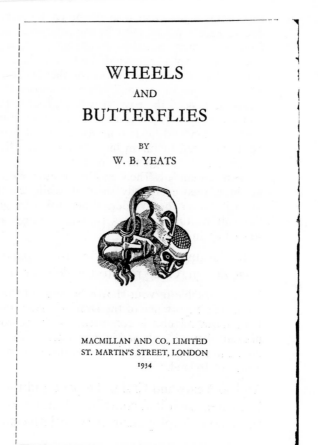

69. Title page of *Wheels and Butterflies*. London, 1934.

might appear under the title *A Full Moon in March*. The first version of the play, printed at the Cuala Press, is accompanied by a Commentary in which he relates his work with Florence Farr in the 1890's to his later involvement with the Nō theatre and with Antheil's work in *Fighting the Waves*.

In November, Macmillan published *Wheels and Butterflies*, containing, with their Commentaries, *The Words Upon the Window Pane*, *Fighting the Waves*, *The Resurrection* and *The Cat and the Moon*. *A Full Moon in March* which was called 'The Severed Head' in the manuscript drafts was finished about the end of the year and sent to *Poetry* (Chicago). This version was not performed in Yeats's lifetime, and the earliest record of performance I have located is one licensed by the Lord Chamberlain's Office to the Everyman Theatre, Hampstead, in June 1950. Yeats did not abandon the other version of the play and produced a separate text, a version in verse of *The King of the Great Clock Tower*. Both plays were printed together in *A Full Moon in March*, by Macmillan in London in November 1935. The title page of *Wheels and Butterflies* has a device which is based on an arrangement of the masks designed by Hildo Krop for the Dutch production of *Vrouwe Emer's Groote Strijd* and which Yeats had acquired for the Abbey Theatre production of *Fighting the Waves*.

In December 1934 the Abbey Theatre staged a production of Pirandello's *Six Characters in Search of an Author*, probably prompted by Yeats's meeting with the Italian playwright at the Rome Congress, and early in 1935 Yeats was planning a London production of *The Player Queen* to be presented by another participant in the Congress, the English playwright, Ashley Dukes, who was director of the Mercury Theatre in Notting Hill Gate. It was planned that Margot Ruddock would play Decima in this production and Tyrone Guthrie might produce it. This project came to nothing and by June, Yeats could refer to 'false, fleeting perjured Ashley'[31] in a letter to Olivia Shakespear.

The London programme became a 'Yeats Festival' at the Little Theatre from 28 to 31 October, in which *The Pot of Broth*, *The Hour-Glass* and *The Player Queen* were performed under the direction of Nancy Price. Margot Ruddock did not play the lead in *The Player Queen*, but did play the True Queen, a performance which Yeats liked.

Later, in 1937, Yeats made four broadcasts of poetry from London, in three of which Margot Ruddock read some of the poetry and this was the final occasion on which she performed his work.

Yeats did think she had 'the rudiments of a great actress' and she was in his mind during December 1935 when he was drafting *The Herne's Egg*:

I wish I could have seen more of your acting, it would have helped me to write the strange play I am now writing. My heroine, a holy woman, is raped by seven men and the next day calls upon the heavens to testify that she has never lain in any arms but those of her god. Heaven thunders three times, and the men who have raped her fall upon their knees. This is but one episode in a wild fantastic humorous, half-earnest play, my first full-length play.[32]

The idea of *The Herne's Egg* was first announced in a letter on 28 November to Dorothy Wellesley, 'as wild a play as *Player Queen*, as amusing but more tragedy and philosophic depth.'[33] Yeats arrived in Majorca on 13 December and on 19 December wrote to Ethel Mannin that he had finished 'the long detailed scenario of a play, the strangest wildest thing I have ever written.'[34] By 21 December he could write to Dorothy Wellesley, describing the metrical scheme and continuing

My play will, I think, be a full evening's entertainment, if it is ever played — my first full-length play. One of the characters is a donkey, represented by a toy donkey with wheels, but life-size. I am trusting to this play to give me a new mass of thought and feeling, overflowing into lyrics (these are now in play).[35]

The Herne's Egg is loosely founded on the old Irish tale of 'Congal,' probably in Sir Samuel Ferguson's rendering, but, like many of Yeats's works, draws both on his own private philosophy and on that of Shri Purohit Swami who was with him in Majorca. The play was written in between work on the Swami's edition of the *Upanishads.* As Yeats expressed it to Dorothy Wellesley, 'the play is his philosophy in a fable, or mine confirmed by him.'[36] Yeats chose a lively verse rhythm, allied to those he used in the ballad poetry of his last years, and a colloquial language for his text. The design of the play makes it necessary to understand something of its underlying mysticism to appreciate a performance. It is the most outspoken and erotic of all the plays, both in its language and its symbolism, and Yeats departs significantly from Ferguson's epic to adapt the tale to his own purposes. The themes of the hero's death, the violation of the heroine, and the animalism in the piece reflect earlier plays of Yeats's. Perhaps he is groping with the opposition of God to man, of the real to the phantom world which informed *The Resurrection.* His theory of the cycle of life, the Great Year of *A Vision,* is there too. But, as a piece of theatre, *The Herne's Egg* probably relates most closely to Yeats's attempt to write a piece of *Commedia dell'Arte* in *The Player Queen.*

The underlying theme of this play, as of all the last plays, is excellently surveyed in detail by Professor F. A. C. Wilson in *W. B. Yeats and Tradition* (1958).

Yeats offered the play to the Abbey Theatre and wrote to Dorothy Wellesley in November 1936

The Abbey announce that they will play *The Herne's Egg* in early spring — there will be uproar,[37]

but, eleven days later he wrote

The Abbey Theatre has decided not to do my new play. I am greatly relieved. I am no longer fit for riots and I thought a bad riot almost certain.[38]

The Herne's Egg was not staged until 29 October 1950 when it was presented by Austin Clarke's Lyric Theatre Company in a Sunday night production at the Abbey Theatre. The play was published in London in January 1938.

*

Purgatory, the last of Yeats's plays to be staged in his lifetime, returns for its theme to the Nō of ghosts which he had already explored in *The Dreaming of the Bones* and in *The Words Upon the Window Pane*. Although written with the Peacock stage in mind and although its scale is small — it is a short one-act play — *Purgatory* is the play which communicates its dark message to international theatre. As a piece of theatre, the play has a powerful intensity and is a challenge to producer and actor. The philosophical structure underlies the lines of the play, but never interferes with the theatrical validity of Yeats's text, which is spare and taut.

During the previous year the revised version of *A Vision* had been published and Yeats had written the Introduction designed for the abortive definitive edition. In 'An Introduction for My Plays' he revealed the underlying approach to writing *Purgatory*:

I have spent my life in clearing out of poetry every phrase written for the eye, and bringing all back to syntax that is for ear alone.[39]

Yeats announced his concept of the play in a letter to Edith Shackleton Heald on 15 March 1938, written from Cap Martin,

I have a one-act play in my head, a scene of tragic intensity, but I doubt if it will begin until I get to Steyning, or perhaps not till I get to Ireland.[40]

He commenced writing the play in England and completed the text in Ireland early in the summer. Completion of *Purgatory* must have been unusually easy for Yeats as the final text is arrived at from a scenario and two drafts. In a letter to Dorothy Wellesley, written after the first production, he corrects the Dublin misrepresentation of his curtain speech,

I have put nothing into the play because it seemed picturesque; I have put there my own conviction about this world and the next.[41]

The collapse of the Ireland of the Big House, with Yeats's fear that the weaker and more sinister traits of the old regime could be hereditary, is presented in an explicit and cruel plot in which the descendant of a once-noble family returns, a wandering tramp, to his old home and experiences the penitential revelations of the ghosts of his parents. He, the instrument of his father's death, becomes also that of his son's, and ends the play with a despairing call on God to 'appease the misery of the living and the remorse of the dead.'

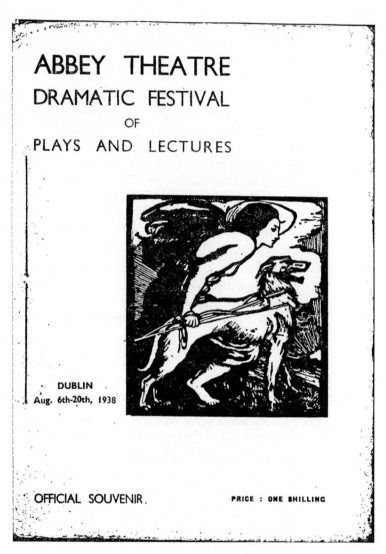

ABBEY THEATRE
DRAMATIC FESTIVAL
OF
PLAYS AND LECTURES

DUBLIN
Aug. 6th-20th, 1938

OFFICIAL SOUVENIR.   PRICE : ONE SHILLING

70. The Abbey Theatre Festival, 1938. Programme cover (reduced).

The play is almost a dramatic monologue delivered by the Old Man, for whom the boy, his illegitimate son, is a foil — and also the instrument of the perpetuation of the wrong already committed. The final cry is reminiscent of the powerful last line of *The Words Upon the Window Pane*. At the curtain of both pieces the principal remains the only living soul on the stage. Yeats's 'private philosophies' are very near the surface of the text, but the writing is so finely controlled that, as a piece of theatre, *Purgatory* succeeds magnificently.

Early in August 1938 Yeats returned to Dublin to see the final rehearsals of *Purgatory* which was in preparation for the Abbey Theatre Festival of Plays and Lectures. This Festival, under the general direction of Lennox Robinson, ran for two weeks commencing on 6 August and was the last time on which Yeats visited the theatre he had created. The occasion was a happy one for Yeats as his work for the theatre seemed to be fully acknowledged and, in addition to the first production of *Purgatory* and a lecture on his work, the programme included revivals of *Cathleen Ni Houlihan* and *On Baile's Strand*, all three plays designed by his daughter Anne, who had become Assistant Designer at the Abbey under Tanya Moiseiwitsch.

On 10 August, Yeats attended the first performance of *Purgatory*,* which scored a major public success with audience and critics alike. Despite his disapproval of Yeats's theme — 'a strange story of murder to rid the world of crime-makers,' [42] Holloway conveys something of the enthusiastic reception for *Purgatory* which was finely played by Michael J. Dolan and Liam Redmond in Hugh Hunt's production,

Michael J. Dolan rose to a great height of dramatic intensity in the role of "Old Man," and proclaimed the really fine actor he really is. From the moment of his entry to his final word, he had the house in the stillness of death, and real enthusiasm followed, and he was recalled over and over again. Liam Redmond played the part of the son effectively, and Anne Yeats's setting was in complete harmony with the dread story and aided the play immensely.

Holloway also pictures Yeats on his last visit to the Abbey,

Yeats was called, and on coming on the stage was loudly applauded. Then he put up his hand for silence and said, "I have embodied my thoughts about this life and the next in my play," and then retired. He walked feebly and nearsightedly off and on the stage. . . . W. B. Yeats seemed to me a "broken man." His upright bearing gone — a wreck of his former self. He was always an arresting figure, and in a crowd stood out as someone remarkable. It is a pity in his old age that sordidness of thought should have captured him, when one thinks of the lovely lyrics of his young days sparkling with lovely words strung to the most daintily expressed thoughts. Now the old poet's thoughts are turned to woe and desolation and the ugliness of life. Alas, Yeats has

---

* PURGATORY

Presented by the Irish National Theatre Society Limited
at the Abbey Theatre, Dublin
on Wednesday 10 August 1938

Boy	Liam Redmond
Old Man	Michael J. Dolan

Produced by Hugh Hunt
Setting by Anne Yeats

fallen into step with the modern worshippers of all that is ugly and foul, and sunshine is blotted out from his work.[43]

The designs made by Anne Yeats for *Purgatory* have not survived but she described the setting in an interview with John Unterecker in 1965:

MISS YEATS: Well I got into the theatre first, really, largely I think because Father was connected with the Abbey.

INTERVIEWER: Was that with the production of *Purgatory*? Or was it before then?

MISS YEATS: It was before that, actually. It was 1936. We went to Spain that year. Mother and Father were in Spain for some time and Michael and I went out for a couple of months and it was when I came back from Spain in the summer that I went in. I went in as a sort of head cook/bottle-washer, assistant to Tanya Moiseiwitsch.

INTERVIEWER: You were seventeen then, weren't you?

MISS YEATS: I was sixteen then. From 1936 to 1940 I was her assistant with a break of four months when I went to Paris and then in 1940 I became designer but I think it was in 1938 and 1939 that I had a couple of trial runs.

INTERVIEWER: What did you do?

MISS YEATS: I did *Purgatory* and I did — oh, some sort of non — but I'd better not say nondescript plays! Rather some class of play that was not of any great interest to anybody. I think probably I designed a kitchen or something like that.

INTERVIEWER: While you were doing *Purgatory* did you have much talk about the designs? Did you talk with your father about the designs before you worked on them, or did you just sit down with the manuscript?

MISS YEATS: No, I more or less sat down with the play and then did a sketch and showed it to him and talked about it. I knew the kind of thing that he'd want.

INTERVIEWER: How did you do it? What kind of a sketch was it?

MISS YEATS: It really could not have been simpler. It was just a bare whitish tree in the middle of the stage and a backcloth with the window cut out of it.

INTERVIEWER: Oh, you didn't try to build a solid set at all?

MISS YEATS: No, because you see the facilities were limited and it was only a "one-acter" and there were plays to follow. It would have cost them far more money than they would have been prepared to spend to build a whole solid set and there was very little light on the scene anyway, because the only light was on the tree and on the window and probably a stray bit of light on, you know. . . .

INTERVIEWER: On the actors?

MISS YEATS: Yes. But mainly it was the tree; and the backcloth, I remember, was black and the window was dark blue — exceptionally dark. The tree was sort of "whitey." It was very simple. I haven't the remotest idea what clothes they dressed in, but obviously they came out of the Abbey wardrobe.

INTERVIEWER: What about the figures in the window?

MISS YEATS : Well there was probably gauze in the window and they were probably very vague behind. I am sure there was gauze in the window. There would have had to be to keep it, you know, *straight*.

INTERVIEWER : Did you do designs for other plays by your father?

MISS YEATS : I did *Baile's Strand* but I think that's the only one.[44]

On the following day F. R. Higgins lectured on Yeats's work, under the title 'Yeats and Poetic Drama in Ireland.' In his lecture, Higgins paid tribute to Yeats's part in the management of the theatre's affairs as well as to his achievements in poetic drama.

. . . when the call was given he found an enthusiastic band of players willing to co-operate in the creation of his ideal — an Irish Theatre.

Yeats, the literary man of affairs with aims became then the literary man of affairs in action — the business man, the organiser, the lecturer, the controversialist; yet, overall, the towering personality of Yeats, the poet, remained in cautious aloofness. A profound sense of sincerity and reverence is most essential in the artist's approach to his craft — it makes him the servant of a sacred vocation, and incidentally it invokes obedience and energy in others. Yeats possessed the necessary sacerdotal air; and with his playwrights and players he did main work in planning the architecture of a National Theatre. Yes, his dignity of physique, his ceremonial manner, his haughtiness, all added to the legend of a mysterious personality—the occupant of a priestly office—impressing his early associates in the Theatre as blessed partakers in poetic rites. There was much more in Yeats than artistic mystery. The abilities of organisation are generally attributed to the most intelligent men of affairs. I have seen such men at work; I have seen Yeats at work in the same capacity, and indeed Yeats, without much ado, equals the best of those with ideas for organisation. Yeats, however, beats the best in organising his own life and purpose. The discipline he imposed on himself or the enthusiasm he awakened was expected and encouraged in others. He knew the art of management, and managed to find others to do the work. And so began the early Irish Theatre, that curious mixture of mystery, national enthusiasm, and non-professional energy. By precept and example he carved the outlines of great dramatic art in writing and acting. The Irish, by ear, have a natural gift for literary style — inherited maybe from Gaelic precision in speech. The new Irish writers could therefore learn their own style without the guidance of a penman. He believed that they could make the poetic play a living dramatic form again. The production of players, however, was a necessity; Yeats had his ideas on such mechanics; and his ideas are as essential today in our Irish Theatre as when he primarily explained them.[45]

This acknowledgement from his chosen successor in the management of the Theatre was confirmed by Lennox Robinson, who wrote in the Souvenir Programme of the Festival,

When in 1897, two or three people talked of forming an Irish National Theatre, they talked of something, the materials of which existed only in their imagination.

For the Irish National Theatre's beginning was as ridiculous as that — almost. Our Theatre began without a building, without a repertory of plays, without a company of players. True, one play did exist, an unacted Irish poetical play, *The Countess Cathleen*; and it would be picturesque and nearly true to say that the Irish National Theatre was created because Mr. W. B. Yeats had written a play which he could not get produced in England.[46]

These weeks of the Abbey Theatre Festival were also accompanied by controversy in Dublin about *Purgatory*. The controversy arose after Higgins' lecture on Yeats's work when an Irish-American priest, a professor at Boston, asked the lecturer to explain *Purgatory* and both Higgins and Lennox Robinson, who was chairman of the session, declined to enter into the matter. Yeats wrote to Dorothy Wellesley that his opening night curtain speech was misreported, and, to Edith Shackleton Heald,

My play has been a sensational success as far as the audience went. I have never seen a more excited house. . . . But I have had this before. The trouble is outside. The press or the clerics get to work — the tribal dance and the drums. This time the trouble is theological. As always I have to remain silent and see my work travestied because I will not use up my fragile energies on impermanent writing. The night after *Purgatory* my *Baile's Strand* was revived with a magnificent Cuchulain. I have not seen it for years and it seemed to me exactly right — ornate, elaborate, like a Crivelli painting. My daughter's designs for it and *Purgatory* — especially for this — were greatly admired. *Purgatory* perfectly acted. House crowded.[47]

But, conscious that his end was approaching, Yeats set about ordering his affairs. Under the title 'My Convictions,' he drafted his epitaph and perhaps the revival of his first Cuchulain play set him thinking how he might complete the sequence begun at the opening performance in the Abbey in 1904, and bow out of the Theatre.

During the Autumn of 1938 W. B. Yeats set about composing the play which was to embody his dramatic testament. A little earlier in that year, prompted by reading a book of essays about Rilke, he had composed his epitaph and chosen Drumcliff Churchyard in County Sligo as his burial place, beside the church where his great-grand-father had served as rector. A definitive collected edition of his work was planned by Macmillan and Company Limited, his London pub-lishers, to be called 'The Coole Edition', as a tribute to the memory of Lady Gregory, and during 1937 and 1938 he wrote introductions to the several volumes of this projected edition. Because of the Second World War, this collected edition never appeared and only the two-volume edition of the *Collected Poems* survived, to be issued in a signed limited edition in 1949, ten years after Yeats had died.

'An Introduction for My Plays,' written in 1937 for the 'Coole' edition, was not printed until 1961, when it was included in *Essays and Introductions*. In this, Yeats paid tribute to those who had shared in the making of 'The theatre for which these plays were written,' to

four players, Sara Allgood, her sister Maire O'Neill, girls in a blind factory who joined a patriotic society; William Fay, Frank Fay, an electric light fitter and an accountant's clerk who got up plays at a coffee house; three writers, Lady Gregory, John Synge and I. If we all told the story we would all tell it differently.[1]

'But I am old, I must have many false memories,' he continued and, having stated that the tradition of the style developed in the Irish National Theatre had its origins in the school of Talma, 'which permits an actor, as Gordon Craig has said, to throw up an arm calling down the thunderbolts of heaven, instead of seeming to pick up pins from the floor,' he surveyed his own discoveries in the theatre :

I wanted all my poetry to be spoken on a stage or sung, and because I did not understand my own instincts, gave half a dozen wrong or secondary reasons; but a month ago I understood my reasons. I have spent my life in clearing out of poetry every phrase written for the eye, and bringing all back to syntax that is for ear alone. Let the eye take delight in the form of the singer and in the panorama of the stage and be content with that. Charles Ricketts once designed for me a black jester costume for the singer, and both he and Craig helped with the panorama, but my audience was for comedy — for Synge, for Lady Gregory, for O'Casey — not for me. I was content, for I know that comedy was the modern art.

As I altered my syntax I altered my intellect. Browning said that he could not write a successful play because interested not in character in action but in action in character. I had begun to get rid of everything that is not, whether in lyric or dramatic poetry, in some sense character in action; a pause in the midst of action perhaps, but action always its end and theme. "Write for the

ear," I thought, so that you may be instantly understood as when actor or
folk singer stands before an audience. I delight in active men, taking the same
delight in soldier and craftsman; I would have poetry turn its back upon all
that modish curiosity, psychology—the poetic theme has always been present.
I recall an Indian tale : certain men said to the greatest of the sages, "Who
are your Masters?" And he replied, "The wind and the harlot, the virgin and
the child, the lion and the eagle." [2]

In the poems of these last years, Yeats returned again and again
to recall, to acknowledge 'all the Olympians,' [3] prompted, perhaps,
by 'the images of thirty years' [4] pictured on the walls of the Dublin
Municipal Gallery which he had helped to establish.

> You that would judge me, do not judge alone
> This book or that, come to this hallowed place
> Where my friends' portraits hang and look thereon;
> Ireland's history in their lineaments trace;
> Think where man's glory most begins and ends,
> And say my glory was I had such friends. [5]

And Ireland's history and its National Theatre movement share a
common theme in the third of his 'Three Songs to the One Burden' :

> Come gather round me players all :
> Come praise Nineteen-Sixteen,
> Those from the pit and gallery
> Or from the painted scene
> That fought in the Post Office
> Or round the City Hall,
> Praise every man that came again,
> Praise every man that fell.
> *From mountain to mountain ride the fierce horsemen.*
> Who was the first man shot that day?
> The player Connolly,
> Close to the City Hall he died;
> Carriage and voice had he;
> He lacked those years that go with skill,
> But later might have been
> A famous, a brilliant figure
> Before the painted scene.
> *From mountain to mountain ride the fierce horsemen.*
> Some had no thought of victory
> But had gone out to die
> That Ireland's mind be greater,
> Her heart mount up on high;
> And yet who knows what's yet to come?
> For Patrick Pearse had said
> That in every generation
> Must Ireland's blood be shed.
> *From mountain to mountain ride the fierce horsemen.* [6]

*

Oliver Sheppard, his sculptor friend from the early days spent at the Dublin Municipal Art School, was chosen by the Irish Government to design the memorial in the General Post Office in Dublin, commemorating the Easter Rising of 1916. Sheppard produced several designs for the bronze statue, among them a 'Boyhood of Cuchulain' and a 'Death of Cuchulain.' The chosen statue, 'The Death of Cuchulain,' showing the dead hero tied to a pillar stone with a raven perched on his shoulder, was erected in the central hall of the Post Office. This choice was very much in accordance with Yeats's philosophy concerning the recurring cycles of historical time which he expressed in *A Vision* and which is reflected in his poem, 'The Statues,' written on 9 April 1938,

> When Pearse summoned Cuchulain to his side,
> What stalked through the Post Office? What intellect,
> What calculation, number, measurement, replied?
> We Irish, born into that ancient sect
> But thrown upon this filthy modern tide
> And by its formless spawning fury wrecked,
> Climb to our proper dark, that we may trace
> The lineaments of a plummet-measured face.[7]

He sent this poem to Edith Shackleton Heald on 28 June and provided a gloss in his letter:

I enclose the poem you asked for. In reading the third stanza remember the influence on modern sculpture and on the great seated Buddha of the sculptors who followed Alexander. Cuchulain is in the last stanza because Pearse and some of his followers had a cult of him. The Government has put a statue of Cuchulain in the rebuilt Post Office to commemorate this.[8]

As his time ran out, all the images of a lifetime crowded in — pictures and bronzes, symbols and memories. He became 'Malachi Stilt-Jack,' an image from the circus pictures drawn and painted by his brother, Jack B. Yeats, 'All metaphor . . . stilts and all,'[9] and he summoned up his theatre ghosts among the symbols and images contained in the finest of his poetic commemorations, 'The Circus Animals' Desertion.'

> I
>
> I sought a theme and sought for it in vain,
> I sought it daily for six weeks or so.
> Maybe at last, being but a broken man,
> I must be satisfied with my heart, although
> Winter and summer till old age began
> My circus animals were all on show,
> Those stilted boys, that burnished chariot,
> Lion and woman and the Lord knows what.

II

What can I but enumerate old themes?
First that sea-rider Oisin led by the nose
Through three enchanted islands, allegorical dreams,
Vain gaiety, vain battle, vain repose,
Themes of the embittered heart, or so it seems,
That might adorn old songs or courtly shows;
But what cared I that set him on to ride,
I, starved for the bosom of his faery bride?

And then a counter-truth filled out its play,
The Countess Cathleen was the name I gave it;
She, pity-crazed, had given her soul away,
But masterful heaven had intervened to save it.
I thought my dear must her own soul destroy,
So did fanaticism and hate enslave it,
And this brought forth a dream and soon enough
This dream itself had all my thought and love.

And when the Fool and Blind Man stole the bread
Cuchulain fought the ungovernable sea;
Heart-mysteries there, and yet when all is said
It was the dream itself enchanted me :
Character isolated by a deed
To engross the present and dominate memory.
Players and painted stage took all my love
And not those things that they were emblems of.

III

Those masterful images because complete
Grew in pure mind, but out of what began?
A mound of refuse or the sweepings of a street,
Old kettles, old bottles and a broken can,
Old iron, old bones, old rags, that raving slut
Who keeps the till. Now that my ladder's gone,
I must lie down where all the ladders start
In the foul rag-and-bone shop of the heart.[10]

And, nearer his end, in 'The Man and the Echo,' he pondered, remembering the national impact of the early seasons of the Irish theatre, particularly the Spring season of 1902 when Frank Fay directed *Cathleen ni Houlihan* and Maud Gonne played the title role 'with weird power.' [11]

All that I have said and done,
Now that I am old and ill,
Turns into a question till
I lie awake night after night
And never get the answers right.
Did that play of mine send out
Certain men the English shot?[12]

*

Yet, in his last year, but perhaps with one eye on the possibility that he might survive to influence a further Irish generation, he set about putting together a new occasional review which he described, in a letter dated 11 November 1937, to Dorothy Wellesley, as 'a *Fors Clavigera* of sorts — my advice to the youthful mind on all manner of things, and poems.' [13] (Ruskin, the apostle of Pre-Raphaelitism, had called his journal *Fors Clavigera*, and addressed himself in its pages to offering advice on all manner of things.) In his review, Yeats proposed 'to write out a policy for young Ireland.' [14] On 16 June 1938 he wrote to Maud Gonne, giving her permission to say what she liked about him in her autobiography, *A Servant of the Queen*, and described the review.

On the Boiler is an occasional publication like my old *Samhain* which I am about to bring out. The first number will be published in about a month. Perhaps you will hate me for it. For the first time I am saying what I believe about Irish and European politics. I wonder how many friends I will have left. Some of it may amuse you. [15]

By 13 July he had finished assembling the copy for the first (and only) number of *On the Boiler*, in which he planned to include the first printing of *Purgatory*, and had given the material to F. R. Higgins who was to see it through the press. The first printing, however, proved unacceptable and was rejected by the Cuala Press with the result that publication of *On the Boiler* was delayed until the autumn of 1939, after the issue of the posthumous *Last Poems and Two Plays* which the Cuala Press published in July.

The Preface to *On the Boiler*, dated October 1938, states its policy and relates it to the earlier publications in which Yeats and his associates had defined the aims of the Irish National Theatre movement and, at the same time affirms the continuity of the ideal.

Many years ago I brought out an occasional publication called, according to the season, *Beltaine* or *Samhain*; it contained my defence of the Abbey Theatre, its actors and its plays. Though I wrote most of it, Synge's *Riders to the Sea*, some of Lady Gregory's little comedies, as well as my *Cathleen Ni Houlihan*, appeared first in its pages. In this new publication I shall write whatever interests me at the moment, trying, however, to keep some kind of unity, and only including poem or play that has something to do with my main theme. [16]

And, in the section headed 'Preliminaries' he returned to his commemoration of those who had helped him to realise a lifetime's work in the theatre.

The attitude towards life of Irish writers and dramatists at this moment will have historical importance. The success of the Abbey Theatre has grown out of a single conviction of its founders : I was the spokesman because I was born

ON THE BOILER

By

W. B. YEATS

THE CUALA PRESS · DUBLIN

PRICE: THREE SHILLINGS AND SIXPENCE

71. *On the Boiler*, Dublin 1939. Front cover (reduced). Original 9¾ × 7½″.

arrogant and had learnt an artist's arrogance — "Not what you want but what we want" — and we were the first modern theatre that said it. I did not speak for John Synge, Augusta Gregory and myself alone, but for all the dramatists of the theatre.

He echoed the *Advice to Playwrights who are sending Plays to the Abbey Theatre Dublin*, which he had drafted some thirty years before.

Again and again somebody speaking for our audience, for an influential newspaper or political organisation, has demanded more of this kind of play or less, or none, of that. They have not understood that we cannot, and if we could would not comply; the moment any dramatist has some dramatic sense and applies it to our Irish theme he is played. We may help him with his technique or to clear his mind of the second-hand or the second-rate in their cruder forms, but beyond that we can do nothing. He must find himself and mould his dramatic form to his nature after his own fashion, and that is why we have produced some of the best plays of modern times, and a far greater number of the worst. And what I have said of the dramatists is true of the actors, though there the bad comedians do not reach our principal company. I have seen English producers turn their players into mimics; but all our producers do for theirs, or so it was in my day and I suppose it is still the same, is to help them to understand the play and their own natures.

And he went on to conclude this section of On the Boiler with a celebration, a thanksgiving for what his involvement in 'a fine native drama of our own' [17] had given him.

Yet the theatre has not, apart from this one quality, gone my way or in any way I wanted it to go, and often looking back I have wondered if I did right in giving so much of my life to the expression of other men's genius. According to the Indians a man may do much good yet lose his own soul. Then I say to myself, I have had greater luck than any other modern English-speaking dramatist; I have aimed at tragic ecstasy and here and there in my own work and in the work of my friends I have seen it greatly played. What does it matter that it belongs to a dead art and to a time when a man spoke out of an experience and a culture that were not of his time alone, but held his time, as it were, at arms length, that he might be a spectator of the ages. I am haunted by certain moments : Miss O'Neill in the last act of Synge's *Deirdre* "Stand a little further off with the quarrelling of fools"; Kerrigan and Miss O'Neill playing in a private house that scene in Augusta Gregory's *Full Moon* where the young mad people in their helpless joy sing "The boys of Queen Anne"; Frank Fay's entrance in the last act of *The Well of the Saints*; William Fay at the end of *On Baile's Strand*; Mrs. Patrick Campbell in my *Deirdre*, passionate and solitary; and in later years that great artist Ninette de Valois in *Fighting the Waves*. These things will, it may be, haunt me on my deathbed; what matter if the people prefer another art, I have had my fill. [18]

*

By mid-October, Yeats had drafted his last play, *The Death of Cuchulain*, and on the twentieth of that month he wrote to Ethel Mannin, explaining his approach in the work and linking its structure to the cones or gyres on which the framework of his philosophical system is based in *A Vision*.

Goethe said the poet needs all philosophy but must keep it out of his work. I am writing a play on the death of Cuchulain, an episode or two from the old epic. My "private philosophy" is there but there must be no sign of it; all must be like an old faery tale. It guides me to certain conclusions and

LAST POEMS AND TWO PLAYS
BY WILLIAM BUTLER YEATS.

THE CUALA PRESS
DUBLIN IRELAND
MCMXXXIX

72. *Last Poems and Two Plays.* The Cuala Press, 1939. Title page.

gives me precision but I do not write it. To me all things are made of the conflict of two states of consciousness, beings or persons which die each other's life, live each other's death. That is true of life and death themselves. Two cones (or whirls), the apex of each in the other's base.[19]

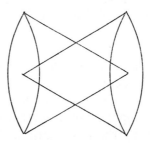

And, old and tired and waiting for the end, he went on to clothe and hide the skeleton of his 'private philosophy' with layers of deep mystery and so to round off the epic which had occupied him for over half a century. By mid-December, at Cap Martin in the south of France, he had tired himself finishing the play, but, at the same time, was making notes for a second issue of *On the Boiler*.[20] With V. C. Clinton-Baddeley he was also planning 'a small book dealing with the relations between speech and song'[21] and writing a lyric that had 'risen out of' the play.[22]

Dorothy Wellesley and some other friends came to be near the dying poet and she recollected his reading *The Death of Cuchulain* to them.

The first evening I went to see him I was astounded at what seemed a miraculous return to health. He looked healthier, and his brain was more active than ever, if such a thing could be possible. Almost his first words were: "I want to read you my new play." And this he did. In spite of the confusion of a much corrected manuscript, he read with great fire. It was *The Death of Cuchulain*. I was much moved, half aware that it was in some sense a premonition of his own death, though I did not know it was to come so soon.[23]

On the first day of his final month, January 1939, Yeats was well enough to write to Edith Shackleton Heald that too much excitement at finishing his play and reading it out had tired him, but that he thought,

my play is strange and the most moving that I have written for some years. I am making a prose sketch for a poem — a kind of sequel — strange too, something new.[24]

The 'kind of sequel' was the poem 'Cuchulain Comforted' which he finished on 13 January and which was the second last poem written by him. He continued to make corrections to *The Death of Cuchulain* until 27 January, the day before he died. And, in these final days, he also drafted a manuscript order of contents for *Last Poems and Two Plays* which included the play under the title 'Cuchulain's Death.' [25] The book was printed by his sister Elizabeth at the Cuala Press in Dublin and finished in the second week in June.

*

The Death of Cuchulain was not produced until ten years after Yeats's death, when it was presented by Austin Clarke's Lyric Theatre Company at the Abbey Theatre on 2 December 1949.* Thirty-eight years after his death Yeats's last play has not yet been staged by the Irish National Theatre which he founded.

*

---

* THE DEATH OF CUCHULAIN

Presented by the Lyric Theatre Company
at the Abbey Theatre, Dublin
on Sundays 2 and 9 December 1949

An Old Man	Art O'Murnaghan
Cuchulain	Enda McGarry
Eithne Inguba	Ronnie Masterson
Aoife	Marjorie Williams
Emer	Christine Kane
The Morrigu, Goddess of War	Mairead Connaughton
A Blind Man	Oliver Bradley
A Servant	John O'Riordan
A Street Singer	Edward Farrell
Flautist	Hilda Layng
A Piper and a Drummer	

Produced by Evelyn MacNeice
Settings and costumes by Anne Yeats
Lighting devised by Dorothy Day
Dance of Emer produced by Eveline Burchill
Music for the dance composed by Brian Boydell
Air for street ballad in the play by Arthur Duff

An acknowledgement on the programme reads:
> The Lyric Theatre Company wishes to thank the Directors of the Abbey Theatre for the special Grant kindly given to help this performance.

A programme note, probably compiled by Austin Clarke, reads:
> This is the first production of the poet's last play. According to the ancient stories, Maeve of Connaught had recourse to druidic craft when her armies were defeated by Cuchulain. The hero retired to a remote stronghold, where he remained a prey to melancholy, suspicion and strange foreboding.

While, in its general organisation, *The Death of Cuchulain* follows the form of the 'Plays for Dancers,' Yeats widened the scope of his 'accomplishment' in his final play to accommodate the idiom of the other forms of theatre in which he had worked. Like much of the writing of his last years, the play is set from the viewpoint of 'an old man looking back on life' and is, both in its spoken text and in its stage directions, full of echoes which prompt recollection or pay tribute to elements of his whole lifetime in the theatre. Most of the critical writing that the play has attracted concentrates on laying bare the 'private philosophy' which forms the framework on which the piece is constructed. Of this, however, Yeats said there must be no sign, and so I feel it might be a good approach to the play as theatre if, as Yeats suggested, the presence of the philosophy is accepted and, in its light, we examine the 'tragic ecstasies' of the piece, the echoes and commemorations of his life in the theatre which might strike his 'audience of fifty or a hundred,' made up of people who 'must know the old epics and Mr. Yeats's plays about them.'

The Death of Cuchulain is organised according to a scheme which closely reflects that of the 'Plays for Dancers' in that it has

An Opening Section, or Prologue, which here is a monologue delivered by the Old Man rather than a song.

The central action, in four 'movements' with a dance as climax.

    1   Cuchulain and Eithne (the 'traveller')
    2   Cuchulain and Aoife
    3   Cuchulain and the Blind Man
    4   The Morrigu introducing Emer's dance

The closing song, here a street ballad.

No Dramatis Personae are listed in the Cuala Press printing of the play, but the list is given here in the order of that printed in the later trade edition published by Macmillan. The 'Persons in the Play' are:

Cuchulain, the hero of all five plays in the 'series.'

Eithne Inguba, his mistress, who also appeared in *The Only Jealousy of Emer* and in the rewritten version of the same play, *Fighting the Waves*.

Aoife, mother of Cuchulain's only son. This was the son he killed in *On Baile's Strand*. Aoife was the leader of

the fierce women of the hills,
Aoife and all her troop

in the offstage action in *At the Hawk's Well*.

Emer, Cuchulain's wife, who appeared in *The Green Helmet* and *The Only Jealousy of Emer* (*Fighting the Waves*). In *The Death of Cuchulain* Emer is the dancer and does not speak.

The Morrigu, Goddess of War, a spirit who can change her form and who may, in Yeats's mythology, be equated with The Guardian of the Well in *At the Hawk's Well* and The Woman of the Sidhe in *The Only Jealousy of Emer* (*Fighting the Waves*). Both of these are dancing parts and, in *The Death of Cuchulain*, in which the Morrigu has one speech, a choreographic movement is implied.

An Old Man, 'looking like something out of mythology.'

A Blind Man, 'the Blind Man of *On Baile's Strand*.'

A Servant.

A Singer, a Piper and a Drummer, the musicians common to all the 'Plays for Dancers.' In *The Death of Cuchulain* there is no opening song and the singer is specified as a 'Street Singer' in the stage direction which precedes the closing lyric.

*

A bare stage of any period is presented to the audience. The removal of the inessential for which Yeats had striven all his life is complete. The piece could be performed 'in a studio or a drawing-room like my dance plays, or at the Peacock Theatre before a specially chosen audience.'[26] Nor does the entrance of the Prologue, 'a very old man looking like something out of mythology,' who enters alone and without music on to the bare stage, provide any clue to the nature of the drama, but with his entrance the echoes begin. The never-played Prologue written in 1903 for *The King's Threshold* (not used 'as, owing to the smallness of the company, nobody could be spared to speak it,'[27]), also designed for an Old Man, is the model for this text, and its reflection here perhaps recalls the hardships and makeshifts of the early days in the Irish National Theatre.

The Old Man speaks:

I have been asked to produce a play called *The Death of Cuchulain*.

He defines himself as the producer. And, although most critics equate this character with Yeats, I believe that, looking back on life, Yeats would not have taken the full credit due to the producer himself and that here he acknowledged the work of the Fays, Frank and Willie, in the early days, and most of all, that of his master in stage technique, Edward Gordon Craig.

'I have been selected,' the Old Man says,

because I am out of fashion and out of date like the antiquated romantic stuff the thing is made of. I am so old that I have forgotten the name of my father and mother, unless indeed I am, as I affirm, the son of Talma.

Nor do I believe that Yeats would fully so introduce himself. But Craig, the illegitimate son of Ellen Terry and of Edward Godwin, the architect, designer, producer for John Todhunter's experimental theatre in Bedford Park in the 1880's, was born into a lineage that was of the theatre. He, the revolutionary reformer who wrote *On the Art of the Theatre*, might well be called 'the son of Talma' and, in this guise be a direct link with the writer, theatre reformer Yeats who, in his poem, 'A Nativity,' written in 1936, had, among the riddles of which the poem is composed, named Delacroix and Irving, Ellen Terry's stage partner, and celebrated Talma in the couplet,

> What hurries out the knave and dolt?
> Talma and his thunderbolt.[28]

François-Joseph Talma (1763-1826), supporter of the French Revolution, opened the Théâtre de la République on the site of the present Comédie Française and played there until the French National Theatre was reconstituted under Napoleon. He reformed theatrical speech by 'suppressing the declamations of the tragic declamatory style and allowing the sense rather than the metre to determine the pauses.'[29] He was also a reformer of stage costume, and had many designs made after classical models by his friend the painter J. L. David. Delacroix painted a commemorative portrait of Talma which is in the collection of the Comédie Française and Yeats may have seen this — a parallel with the series of portraits, many painted by Yeats's father, which are in the Abbey Theatre.

Remembering these things, Talma the revolutionary, the reformer of speech, of costume, of acting style, may have been added to the amalgam of attributes of Yeats and Craig which can be found in the Old Man. Perhaps, too, there is something there of the Old Man Yeats as disguised by Edmund Dulac in the woodcut frontispiece to *A Vision*. But, principally, there are Yeats and Craig.

Both 'wrote certain guiding principles on a bit of newspaper' — Craig in the lavish programme booklets of his early productions such as that for *Dido and Aeneas* which Yeats saw in London in 1900, in *On the Art of the Theatre* published in its first form in 1905 ('A drama is not to be read, but to be seen upon the stage'[30]), his several later books and in his journal of the art, *The Mask*, to which Yeats contributed some of his own 'guiding principles'; Yeats in his essays on the theatre, in his introductions and commentaries written to accompany the texts of his plays and in his Journals, *Beltaine*,

Samhain, The Arrow and finally in *On the Boiler* where he offered his 'advice to the youthful mind on all manner of things.' [31]

The Old Man seeks 'an audience of fifty or a hundred,' and both Craig and Yeats offered their advice to limited numbers. The Peacock Theatre seated a hundred and two — not more in number 'than those who listened to the first performance of Milton's *Comus.' Comus,* Milton's masque, was 'done privately and probably so labelled to distinguish it from the plays of the public stage.' [32]

The mention of Milton leads to the matter of the play. The literary heritage of the epic is stated — Virgil, Homer, Milton, all lead to the particular, to 'the old Irish epics and Mr. Yeats's plays about them.' And such people as make up the small audience, 'however poor, have libraries of their own' and so will have had access to 'the old epics' in Lady Gregory's versions and are equipped to fill in the gaps in the sequence. For *The Death of Cuchulain* is not described as part of the epic cycle originally planned in the closing year of the last century. It is 'the last of a series,' the early plan finally abandoned.

Here Yeats acknowledges that the five Cuchulain plays cannot, without extreme manipulation, both of style and of mood, be made to fit together as a cycle. In the order of the epic plot, the plays should be placed

1   *At the Hawk's Well* in which the young Cuchulain is introduced as The Young Man and is not named until the closing action of the play, leading to his begetting his only son by Aoife. This is a 'Play for Dancers,' written in 1916.

2   *The Golden Helmet (The Green Helmet)* an heroic farce, written under Lady Gregory's influence, which has no direct connection in plot or style with the other plays about Cuchulain. Prose version, 1907, *The Golden Helmet*, re-written in verse as *The Green Helmet*, 1909.

3   *On Baile's Strand*, written in 1903 in Shakespearian blank verse, is in its action a 'sequel' to *At the Hawk's Well* and deals with the death, at Cuchulain's hand, of his only son.

4   *The Only Jealousy of Emer (Fighting the Waves).* In this the action is a direct consequence of *On Baile's Strand*, Cuchulain's sickbed following his remorse at the death of his son. *The Only Jealousy of Emer*, one of the first group of 'Plays for Dancers,' was written in 1917-1919 and rewritten for the 'public stage' as *Fighting the Waves* in 1928.

5   *The Death of Cuchulain.* 1938-1939.

The Death of Cuchulain, Yeats's resolution of his epic theme is addressed to friends who will understand. It is a 'butterfly,' not a 'wheel' spun towards the 'Cellars and Garrets,' those superficial pretenders to knowledge, 'people who are educating themselves out of the Book Societies and the like, sciolists all, pickpockets and opinionated bitches.' We are left with the mystery of the 'pick-pockets' as the Old Man's excitement builds with the rhythm of the speech to such a pitch that, offstage, the musicians sound their instruments to interrupt and the audience is made aware of a further dimension of the 'accomplishment.'

'Musicians are the devil,' Yeats wrote of the rehearsals for *At the Hawk's Well* in London in 1916. Here, at last, he has clarified his approach to the music for his plays. He had returned to his indigenous tradition in his last years and had discovered, as he wrote to Edith Shackleton Heald on 6 August 1937, that

The Irish race — our scattered 20 millions — is held together by songs.[33]

and he wrote the ballads of these years that they might be sung between the acts at the Abbey Theatre and feed into that tradition. On 11 February 1937 he wrote to Ethel Mannin,

These ballads of mine though not supremely good are not ephemeral. The young will sing them now and after I am dead.[34]

This is 'the music of the beggar-man, Homer's music.' He had found at last in Ireland the music he had sought all his life. He wrote to Edmund Dulac, who had composed the score for *At the Hawk's Well* in 1916 and had also set some of the late ballads,

I want to get back to simplicity and can best do it — I believe — by writing for our Irish unaccompanied singing. Every change I make to help the singer seems to improve the poems. A man of my ignorance learns from action.[35]

No Dulac, no Rummel, no Antheil is called for here. This last solution was perhaps foretold by the 'distinguished Irish lyric poet' who, recoiling from the impact of the 'large expensive orchestra' necessary to perform Antheil's score for *Fighting the Waves*, was 'roused to begin a dance-play which,' he assured Yeats, 'required but a tin-whistle and a large expensive concertina.'[36] This is 'the music of the beggar-man,' perhaps that of 'The Last Gleeman,' Dublin's Michael Moran, *alias* Zozimus, who had been celebrated by Yeats a half-century before in his essay published in *The National Observer* of 6 May 1893.[37]

And in introducing the musicians, the Old Man suggests the oral transmission of epic literature through the ages before the written or the printed word was readily at hand and the epic heritage was preserved in 'Homer's music.'

Before the night ends you will meet the music. There is a singer, a piper, and a drummer. I have picked them up here and there about the streets, and I will teach them, if I live, the music of the beggar-man, Homer's music.

'I promise a dance,' the Old Man continues. 'The father of the dramatist was the dancer,' Craig wrote in *On the Art of the Theatre*,

The first dramatist understood what the modern dramatist does not yet understand. He knew that when he and his fellows appeared in front of them the audience would be more eager to *see* what he would do than to *hear* what he might *say*. He knew that the eye is more swiftly and powerfully appealed to than any other sense; that it is without question the keenest sense of the body of man.[38]

The dance springs from the music. 'There must be severed heads,' announces the theme of the dance, echoing the obsession with *Salome* which had inspired *The King of the Great Clock Tower* and *A Full Moon in March*. Emer, Cuchulain's grieving queen, is the part to be danced, and the severed heads of Cuchulain and his enemies, her stage props, have been simplified from the cubist masks created by Hildo Krop for *Vrouwe Emer's Groote Strijd* in 1922 in Amsterdam and later acquired by Yeats for the Abbey's production of *Fighting the Waves*, and have here become 'parallelograms of painted wood.' (These same masks had inspired the symbolic, almost heraldic device which adorned the title page of *Wheels and Butterflies* in 1934.) And with these elementary and abstract properties, the dancer must realise Emer for the audience and transmit to them a part of the epic history.

The dancer of the promised dance is therefore one of special qualities. And the Old Man goes on to give a clue to the identity of the dancer. He 'could have got such a dancer once but she has gone.' He does not say that he *had* such a dancer once and, if we accept the spare precision of Yeats's writing in his last play, we can follow this lead. The Yeats persona embodied in the Old Man refers to Ninette de Valois, whom Yeats had 'discovered' at Terence Gray's theatre in Cambridge in 1925 and had persuaded to come to Dublin and work at the Abbey to create the School of Ballet there, but who had, by 1938, founded the Sadlers Wells Ballet in London and moved into the very world of 'the dancers painted by Degas.' But if the Old Man's character is read as an amalgam of Yeats and Craig, the intended dancer of the Craig persona might be Isadora Duncan — Isadora, who had been introduced into Europe in Loie Fuller's company.

When Loie Fuller's Chinese Dancers unwound
A shining web, a floating ribbon of cloth,
It seemed that a dragon of air
Had fallen among dancers, had whirled them round
Or hurried them off on its own furious path;[39]

Isadora, Loie Fuller's protégée, Gordon Craig's mistress, had been drawn by Craig in Berlin in 1905, dancing, with 'floating ribbons of cloth.' John Butler Yeats had written enthusiastically about her from New York in 1908. She had toured in 1919 with Walter Rummel, composer of the score for *The Dreaming of the Bones*, as her accompanist and she may have in her essay, 'The Dance and Nature', suggested the theme for the opening dance in *Fighting the Waves*. ('I see waves rising through all things.'[40]) She based her own dance movements on Classical Greek sculpture. Yeats wrote in *A Vision*:

Those riders upon the Parthenon had all the world's power in their moving bodies, and in a moment that seemed, so were the hearts of man and beast set upon it, that of a dance : but presently all would change and measurement succeed to pleasure, the dancing-master outlive the dance.[41]

Isadora certainly spat 'upon the dancers painted by Degas' while Ninette de Valois had, by 1939, become one with them. And Isadora died violently and tragically, her own scarf, caught in the wheel of a moving car, strangling her ('a floating ribbon of cloth'). As the Old Man says,

I could have got such a dancer once, but she has gone; the tragi-comedian dancer, the tragic dancer, upon the same neck love and loathing, life and death.

And here he forewarns his audience of one of the tragic ecstasies in the play to come, the moment when Aoife will enshroud the dying Cuchulain in her veil ('a floating ribbon of cloth') — a hint of the poem that is 'a kind of sequel,' 'Cuchulain Comforted' with its imagery of throats and shrouds and singing head. The depths of the mystery almost surface — the imagery of William Blake and of the harlot's song which ends the play. The themes of the drama are announced and the Old Man bursts into a tirade against the 'dancers painted by Degas' and, with an interpolated invocation to the timeless, 'Rameses the Great,' (mummies and mummy-cloths), he ends the Prologue, spitting.

The stage is darkened, the curtain falls.

*

The music (pipe and drum) introduces the play proper and, when the curtain rises, a bare stage is revealed — a half minute is specified to allow the audience to feel this emptiness — no painted scenery gives a hint of place or time, nor is there an opening chorus to set the mood of the drama. But the direction for the 'Plays for Dancers,' 'The stage is any bare space before a wall' is reflected, and the entry of the first character also echoes the Nō, the model for the 'Plays for Dancers.' She is Eithne Inguba, the young mistress of Cuchulain who has figured in *The Only Jealousy of Emer* and, as in the Nō, she is a traveller, a messenger and, with her entrance, the action of the play commences. Her embassy, from Emer, Cuchulain's wife, reveals the sad state of an Ireland calling on its heroes to act — Emhain burns, Muirthemne burns and, though Cuchulain's death may come of it,

> The scene is set and you must out and fight.

A hint is here, perhaps, of the whole course of Ireland's tragic history — seven centuries in arms against the oppressor and, in Yeats's own lifetime, the 1916 Easter Rising, brought nearer the mind's surface in the first dialogue after the scene-setting intro- duction — the letter (from Emer) which 'tells a different story,' a postponement of action, such as that sent by Eoin MacNeill to delay the Rising on Easter Sunday 1916 — the theme of 'The Statues,'

> When Pearse summoned Cuchulain to his side,
> What stalked through the Post Office?

and Yeats's gloss on the poem, 'Cuchulain is in the last stanza because Pearse and some of his followers had a cult of him,'[42] comes to mind. And, with Cuchulain's decision to act, 'I am for the fight,' the Morrigu, the crow-headed war goddess, emanation of the Woman of the Sidhe, appears to Eithne and creates a change in the action which echoes the treachery with which the seven-hundred-year action of the Irish situation commenced — the betrayal of the country to the Normans by Diarmuid and Dervorgilla, the theme of *The Dreaming of the Bones*. The 'dreaming back' of the Nō play is here, but reversed, as Eithne offers herself to Cuchulain's 'cooks, scullions, armourers, bed-makers, and messengers' to be used and put to death

> By what foul way best please their fancy,
> So that my shade can stand among the shades
> And greet your shade and prove it is no traitor

while the traitors of *The Dreaming of the Bones* are condemned to wander through all eternity, their treachery unforgiven. Even as Cuchulain dismisses her argument as part of an intrigue, a servant announces that 'all wait the word' and Cuchulain answers, 'I come to give it.' He goes, having commanded that Eithne receive fair treatment, leaving her the last words of the scene, an affirmation of the truth of the oracle

> I might have peace that know
> The Morrigu, the woman like a crow,
> Stands to my defence and cannot lie,
> But that Cuchulain is about to die.

The pipe and drum again announce the change in the action as a blackout allows the stage attendants to set the pillar stone against which the mortally wounded Cuchulain tries to fasten himself with his belt. The next confrontation is with Aoife, who recalls the plot of the first 'Play for Dancers,' *At the Hawk's Well.* Aoife, now 'an erect white-haired woman,' takes up the story of the offstage action from the end of the earlier play when, crying

> He comes ! Cuchulain, son of Sualtime's comes !

he turned his back on the Waters of Immortality to confront 'the fierce women of the hills, Aoife and all her troop.' Aoife recalls this rejection —

> You asked their leave
> When certain that you had six mortal wounds,
> To drink out of the pool

and goes on, as she binds him to the stone, to prompt his memories of the begetting of his son 'At the Hawk's Well under the withered trees' and of the almost sacrificial death of that son, at his father's hand, on Baile's Strand. The sacrificial death of the god is imminent and yet another portent is revealed — the isolation of the dying hero from the battle all around :

> The grey of Macha, that great horse of yours
> Killed in the battle, came out of the pool
> As though it were alive, and went three times
> In a great circle round you and that stone,
> Then leaped into the pool.

We are very near the system of the 'private philosophy' as Aoife performs the next ritual action, the enshrouding of Cuchulain. Deliberately, in the calm, she winds her veil around him. Cuchulain is 'comforted.' The Nō ritual of costume change is performed, and the oblation to the gods is prepared, awaiting the sacrificial knife. The death of the only son, the Firstborn, is recalled, and his begetting — the action of 'beings or persons which die each other's life, live each other's death.' [43]

Somebody comes.

The Blind Man of 'On Baile's Strand' comes in.

The traitor priest is specified. Seumas O'Sullivan, poet and editor, created the part, Craig designed his mask. He celebrates the opening of the Abbey Theatre at which *On Baile's Strand* was first performed.

> I stood between a Fool and the sea at Baile's Strand
> When you went mad

and he produces the hand-props from *On Baile's Strand*, his bag, his knife (echoes of *Purgatory*). The stealing of the chicken is remembered, the treachery of Judas, payment in pennies. And Cuchulain utters a premonition, perhaps a realisation of his assumption into myth:

> There floats out there
> The shape that I shall take when I am dead,
> My soul's first shape, a soft feathery shape

and in these, his final moments, with absolute dramatic economy he announces the Morrigu's scene before his throat is slit.

The stage darkens. . . .

Music of pipe and drum, the curtain falls.

The Morrigu, the Woman of the Sidhe, Fand, takes the stage alone. In her epic manifestation, 'with a crow's head,' she is surrounded by severed heads — the *Salome* obsession of *The King of the Great Clock Tower* and *A Full Moon in March* is explored to the full. She invokes the dead and summons up, through the severed head of the warrior, the end of Irish hope. She arranged the dance for a mute Emer. She, the dancer in hawk's guise of *At the Hawk's Well*, the demon Fand of *The Only Jealousy of Emer*, who embodied the Beardsley Woman of the Sidhe, summons up the grieving Emer to round out the epic in mime:

Emer runs in and begins to dance. She so moves that she seems to rage against the heads of those that had wounded Cuchulain, perhaps makes movements as though to strike them, going three times round the circle of the heads. She then moves towards the head of Cuchulain; it may, if need be, be raised above the others on a pedestal. She moves as if in adoration or triumph. She is about to prostrate herself before it, perhaps does so, then rises, looking up as if listening; she seems to hesitate between the head and what she hears. Then she stands motionless.

And, before the final blackout, 'There is silence, and in the silence a few faint bird notes,' we are brought through the gyres from the still centre of the 'tragic ecstasy' to bird song — to another manifestation, to the world of the ballad-writer Zozimus, who in 'some Irish Fair of our day' has the last word:

Emer and the head are gone. . . . There is no one there but the three musicians. They are in ragged street-singers' clothes; two of them begin to pipe and drum. They cease. The Street-Singer begins to sing.

The ballad with which we end is, on the face of it, a good Irish ballad, but here, at the very last, Yeats still strikes the echoing gong. The 'harlot' who 'sang to the beggar-man' may well be Blake's, weaving Old England's winding-sheet. The Tarot is reflected in the great horses, the long pale faces, which may also reflect the monastic carvings on the high crosses of an Ireland unravaged by the Normans. The flesh is there, and the realisation that these heroes 'were living men.'

In the final stanza, we come back to our own time, back to the Art School companion, Oliver Sheppard, who created for a new Irish nation the Cuchulain statue in the General Post Office, typefying Pearse, of whom some men had a cult. And the final question is posed:

> An old man looking back on life
> Imagines it in scorn. . . .
> So ends the tale that the harlot
> Sang to the beggar-man.

In the Cuala printing, the final stage direction reads:

The curtain falls.

What is the right thing for me to do in regard to
the I. N. Th. now? Oct. 9th/03.

Some change is directed by the highest.
Irresolution as to the course of action.
Anger in the mind.
Most solid materiality needed.

19 cards bad.
5 Trumps - within my
own Will.
5 Energy must
prevail.

Three 3 o - deceit - I think something
now which is not fact.

I am in a happy friendly successful current, which
will carry me on if I decide with a certain amount of
self-assertion. That will restore peace & be well
for a youngish man. All will change for the
better & quarrels will pass away. Some gift will
cause quarrels & anger but it will bring good
fortune &. gain whilst away from home - self-assertion is absolutely necessary.

73. Enlargement of Miss Horniman's letter offering to subsidise
the Irish National Theatre.

Appendix A

MISS HORNIMAN'S LETTER TO W. B. YEATS OFFERING TO
SUBSIDISE THE ABBEY THEATRE. A NOTE BY KATHLEEN RAINE.
See p. 104.

Miss Horniman's reading of the Tarot cards is made in accordance with *The
secret workings of the Golden Dawn Book 'T'; The Tarot by S.R.M.D. and
others.* S.R.M.D. is MacGregor Mathers, and members of the Society would
have followed his method and interpretation of the Keys. Although in manuscripts, detailed descriptions of the symbols depicted on the cards are given,
no pack corresponding to Mathers' descriptions was ever printed. The Waite
pack was not available until 1907; and as Miss Horniman's consultation was
made in 1903 it is likely that she used the Marseilles pack. Yeats himself used
this pack, his copy being much worn and much annotated.

'The opening of the key' is made as follows. First, the Enquirer (in this
case Miss Horniman, who is also her own Diviner) shuffles the cards, at the
same time thinking 'earnestly' of the matter in hand. The cards are then
placed on the table in a single pack, face downwards. 'This represents the
Name YHVH, which is now to be separated into component letters. He therefore is to cut the pack, as nearly as possible in the middle as his eye can
direct, and to place the uppermost portion to the right of the lowermost; the
former will represent YH and the latter VH.' The pack is again cut into two
parts, placing the uppermost portion to the right and left respectively of their
lower halves. These four packets are now taken to represent the four letters
of the Divine Name. They are then turned upwards so that the bottom card
of each packet is seen. These four cards give a preliminary, overall indication
of how matters stand.

Miss Horniman has in every case but one indicated the twenty-two Trumps
or Key cards by their astrological equivalent as given in Mathers' *Book 'T'.*
The Moon (corresponding to the Tarot Key II, the High Priestess) is in the
position of Yod, which corresponds to the element of fire and the suit of
Wands, with all the symbolic attributes of the fiery element of creativity,
energy and acts of intuitive imagination. The High Priestess signifies 'feminine
power,' but also whatever belongs to the Moon and its instability. This card
could well be taken to indicate 'some change' — the sense in which Miss
Horniman has understood it.

The nine of Swords in the place of HE (signifying the element of water and
the suit of Cups) is also an ill-aspected card, described by S.R.M.D. as 'Lord
of Despair and Cruelty,' with added meanings of 'malice, suffering, want,
loss, misery, burden, oppression, labour, subtlety and craft, lying dishonesty
and slander.' Even with the added meanings of (when well-aspected) 'obedience, patience, faithfulness, unselfishness,' there seems little promise of good
in this card; which, together with the ten of Wands ('The Lord of Oppression')
in VAU, the place of the element of air, the suit of Swords and of mental
activity, justify Miss Horniman's reading, 'Anger in the mind.' The sign of
Capricorn in the fourth place corresponds to the Tarot Key XV, the Devil.
This is the place of HE, the element of earth, the suit of Pentacles, and
materiality. Her comment 'Most solid materiality needed' seems a strange one
in so inflammatory a context. A further comment on the ten of Wands reads
'Cruel and overbearing force and energy but applied only to selfish and

material ends. Sometimes shows failure in a matter, and the opposition too strong to be controlled arising from the person's too great selfishness in the beginning.' That this matter is on a mental level is of course indicated by the situation in VAU. This outcome could be seen as an accurate prediction of the final defeat and withdrawal of Miss Horniman from the affairs of the Abbey Theatre.

Each of the four packets is now examined in order to discover the querent's 'significator,' which has been chosen before the reading begins. Miss Horniman is represented by the Queen of Swords, and this card is in the third packet as indicated by the cross. 'Sickness and trouble' are associated with this packet.

The operation which follows is performed only with the packet which contains the enquirer's significator. The cards are laid out in a horse-shoe and note is taken of the position of the significator. If the horse-shoe is considered in terms of the Zodiac we see that the Queen of Swords is situated near the mid-heaven in the sign of Gemini (Cancer is shown in the adjoining decanate) and she is therefore in a strong position, being Queen of the airy suit of Swords in a sign of Air. It is also indicated by the arrow that the Queen looks to the left. It is important to note the direction in which the court-cards are 'looking.' (If such a card is upside-down, it will of course appear to be looking in the direction opposite from that of its upright position.)

Miss Horniman's comment '19 cards bad' is not reassuring. Her next comment '5 Trumps — within my own Will' is based on the statement in the Book 'T' that 'a preponderance of the Keys represents influences beyond the control of the Enquirer.' Presumably, therefore, as the Key Trumps do not here preponderate, the situation is within her own will.

A majority of Wands in this packet suggests that the matter in hand will be characterised by energy and creativity, but also by quarrelling and opposition. Miss Horniman reads this preponderance as 'Energy must prevail'; she dismisses S.R.M.D.'s reading of three 3's to mean 'deceit' as being 'now which is not a fact.' In all cases she tends to put a favourable interpretation on the warning signs, which suggests that she had in fact already made up her mind to give her support, no matter what the cards should advise.

The cards are now counted, according to certain rules, from the significator. Since the Queen of Swords faces to the left, the first count of four cards is to the left; which brings us to the King of Wands. From the King of Wands we again count four cards, to the two of Swords. The counts from the smaller cards are made according to their own number — two from the two of Swords to the four of Swords, four on to the four of Pentacles, and four again to the Trump Key, the Wheel of Fortune (position 6) which corresponds to Jupiter. This Key is one of the nine cards indicated by the double Hebrew letters, and the next count is therefore seven — to the three of Wands. Counting three on, we again come to Trump Key XI, Strength, which corresponds to Libra. It is one of the ten Keys indicated by the Hebrew single letters, followed by a count of twelve cards. This count of twelve cards brings us to the Princess of Wands, whose number (seven) brings us again to the three of Wands, which has already appeared in the reading; therefore, the counting stops at this point.

We pass on to the two of Swords which is described as 'The Lord of Peace

Restored.' Miss Horniman's conclusion that peace will be restored for 'a youngish man' (Yeats) is evidently drawn from this card, which is followed by the four of Swords, 'The Lord of Rest from Strife.'

The four of Pentacles follows; this is described as the 'Lord of Earthly Power,' and is 'assured material gain, success, rank, dominion, earthly power completed, but leading to nothing beyond. Prejudiced, covetous, suspicious, careful and orderly but discontented.' The Abbey Theatre, with Miss Horniman's financial help, did become a success; it is also true that for her there was 'nothing beyond' and ultimate discontent. Between the five and the ten of Wands ('Lord of Strife' and 'Lord of Oppression') Miss Horniman's power, represented by the material foundation of the financial support she is proposing to give the Theatre is (as regards herself) beset with difficulties, and doubtless will (as she herself reads the situation) be beset with 'quarrels and anger.' It will, however, lead to the 'Lord of Established Strength' (the three of Wands).

The Trump Key which corresponds to the sign of Libra in position 8 is Strength; and this card may well justify Miss Horniman's reading of 'a certain amount of self-assertion' being 'absolutely necessary.' In position 9 is the Princess of Wands who, between the eight and the three of Pentacles ('The Lord of Prudence' and 'The Lord of Material Works') is well-aspected. 'Building up, creation, realisation' and the like are here suggested. The Princess of every suit signifies the element of earth; in the case of the Princess of Wands, the Earth of Fire, the material aspect of a matter which is in its essential nature a matter of creative imagination and spiritual energy. If she represents Miss Horniman, the optimistic reading of the outcome of the venture would be very largely justified, for she has 'brilliance, courage, beauty, force, sudden in anger or love, desire of power, enthusiasm, revenge.' Ill-aspected, she is 'superficial, theatrical, cruel, unstable, domineering.' However, here she is well-aspected, and the succeeding and final card is, again, the three of Wands, Established Strength.

The cards so obtained are as follows :

> Queen of Swords
> King of Wands
> Two of Swords
> Four of Swords
> Five of Pentacles
> Wheel of Fortune (Jupiter)
> Three of Wands
> Strength (Libra)
> Princess of Wands
> Three of Wands

Let us see how Miss Horniman read this as a 'happy friendly successful current' in which 'all will change for the better and quarrels will pass away.' The meanings of the cards according to the book are as follows :

The Queen of Swords (Miss Horniman) is between the Tarot Key VII, the Chariot, (corresponding to the sign of Cancer), and the three of Cups, which is certainly a happy friendly card, the 'Lord of Abundance.' Extended meanings of this card give 'abundance, plenty, success, pleasure, sensuality, passive success, good luck and fortune, Love, gladness, kindness and bounty.' The

Chariot is a symbol of 'the spirit of man controlling the lower principles . . . rising above the clouds of illusion and penetrating the higher sphere.'

Passing to the King of Wands (presumably Yeats) who is the 'Prince of the Chariot of Fire,' we find that this person with whom the querent is dealing is characterised by the fiery creativity and imaginative energy of his suit and is described as 'swift, strong, hasty, rather violent, yet just and generous, noble and scorning meanness.' He looks to the left, away from the querent, and this, according to the Book 'T', signifies 'the departure of a person or the going off or wane of some event.' Yeats did in fact eventually 'depart' from Miss Horniman, whose relationship with the Abbey Theatre also 'waned.' The three of Wands ('The Lord of Established Strength') next to the King seems to signify the strength of Yeats's own position in the affair.

This seems to be as far as Miss Horniman carried her reading. The further operation of pairing the cards, beginning at the outer ends of the horseshoe and proceeding inwards, would give these further indications :

The Fool (Tarot Key o, corresponding to the Hebrew letter aleph), is paired with the ten of Wands. The Fool sometimes represents heedlessness, sometimes the 'divine folly'; in any event, a beginning of some kind. The ten of Wands is not a good card; it indicates overbearing force used for selfish ends and 'sometimes shows failure in a matter, and the opposition too strong to be controlled arising from a person's too great selfishness at the beginning.'

The four of Swords ('Lord of Rest from Strife') paired with the four of Pentacles ('Lord of Earthly Power') would seem to suggest that change for the better comes through money and practical aid.

The two of Swords ('Lord of Peace Restored') with the five of Wands ('Lord of Strife') signifies a quarrel made up, yet with some remaining tension.

The Prince of Cups with the two of Pentacles ('Lord of Harmonious Change') seems to augur well for Yeats, who in this context is likely to be the Prince of Cups, 'graceful, poetic, venusian, indolent, but enthusiastic if roused.'

Strength, paired with the Wheel of Fortune, would have encouraged Miss Horniman, again, in her belief that 'self-assertion' was needed to set the wheel in motion.

The King of Wands with the three of Pentacles again links Yeats with the 'Lord of Material Works.' Again a favourable aspect, especially in a commercial transaction.

The Princess of Wands with the three of Cups indicates for Miss Horniman an element of pleasure, friendship and enjoyment in the venture; and the Queen of Swords with the eight of Pentacles ('The Lord of Prudence'), counsels caution to the Queen.

The Tarot Key VII (the Chariot) with IV (the Emperor, corresponding to the sign of Aries), would seem a fortunate aspect. The Chariot is 'Lord of the Triumph of Light' and the Emperor is described as 'Son of the Morning, Chief among the Mighty.' It could be read as an indication that the energising force of the Emperor, who is the 'doer' among the Tarot Keys, will set the Chariot in motion; as Yeats did indeed set the Abbey Theatre successfully upon its way.

Appendix B

PROGRAMMES OF FIRST PRODUCTIONS OF YEATS'S PLAYS

The programmes which are transcribed in the text are those of all first pro-
ductions of the plays in Yeats's lifetime which I have been able to trace.
Calvary, A Full Moon in March, The Herne's Egg *and* The Death of Cuchulain
were produced posthumously. The programme of The Death of Cuchulain *is*
included in the text of the book.

Plates

It was in this house, then the property of Florimond Alfred Jacques, Comte de Basterot, that Augusta Lady Gregory of Coole Park, in the summer of 1898, met William Butler Yeats at the request of her neighbour Edward Martyn: & there began between them the conversations which led to the founding of the Abbey Theatre.

I Plaque in Dooras House commemorating the founding of the Irish National Theatre. The date should, of course, be 1897 but is taken from Lady Gregory's *Our Irish Theatre* where she gives it as 1898. See p. 27.

II Miss Horniman sewing costumes for the Irish National Theatre Company. She designed and made the costumes for *The King's Threshold* (1903) and *On Baile's Strand* (1904). Drawing by John Butler Yeats, 1903. Collection of Senator Michael Butler Yeats. See p. 88 ff.

III Frank Fay as Cuchulain in *On Baile's
Strand*. Frontispiece to *Samhain 1904*.
See p. 120.

IV Joseph Holloway by Lilian Davidson.
Oil on canvas. Collection of the Abbey
Theatre, Dublin.

v Lady Gregory by John Butler Yeats, 1903. Oil on canvas.
Collection of the National Gallery of Ireland.

VI Robert Gregory. Scene design for *Deirdre*, 1906. Watercolour.
Collection of Miss Anne Yeats. See p. 127.

VII Edward Gordon Craig. Design for *The Hour-Glass* in *Plays for an Irish Theatre*, 1911. See p. 161.

VIII Edward Gordon Craig. Design for *Deirdre* in *Plays for an Irish Theatre*, 1911. See pp. 173-74.

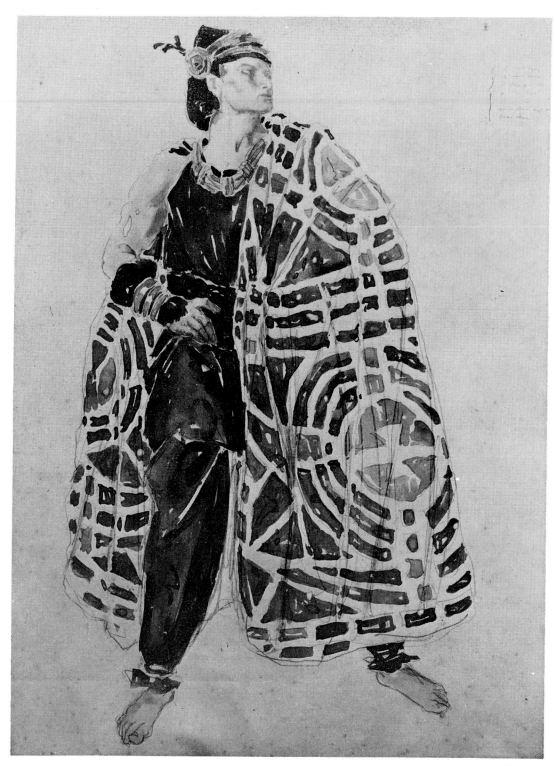

IX Charles Ricketts. Cuchulain. Costume design for *On Baile's Strand*, 1915.
Watercolour. Collection of Miss Anne Yeats. See pp. 181-82.

x Charles Ricketts. Blind Man
   and Fool. Costume designs
   for *On Baile's Strand*, 1915.
   Watercolour. Collection of
   Miss Anne Yeats.

xi Charles Ricketts. King.
    Costume design for *The
    King's Threshold*, 1915.
    Watercolour. Collection of
    Miss Anne Yeats.

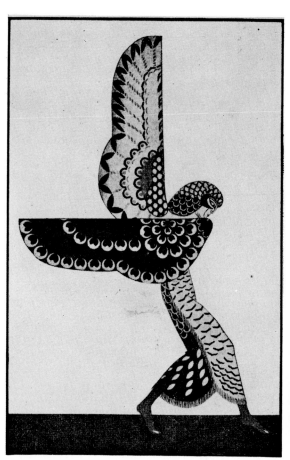

XII Edmund Dulac. The Guardian of the Well. Costume design for *At the Hawk's Well*, 1916, in *Four Plays for Dancers*, 1921. See p. 221 ff.

XIII Edmund Dulac. Cuchulain. Costume design for *At the Hawk's Well*, 1916, in *Four Plays for Dancers*, 1921.

XIV Edmund Dulac. The Old Man. Costume
design for *At the Hawk's Well*, 1916,
in *Four Plays for Dancers*, 1921.

XV Edmund Dulac. A Musician. Costume
design for *At the Hawk's Well*, 1916, in
Four Plays for Dancers, 1921.

XVI Edmund Dulac. Cartoon of W. B. Yeats as a puppet, manipulated
by the Abbey Players, 1915. Watercolour. Collection of the
Abbey Theatre, Dublin. See p. 223.

XVII Edmund Dulac. Cuchulain. Mask for *At the Hawk's Well*, 1916.
Collection of Senator Michael Butler Yeats. See p. 228 and p. 255.

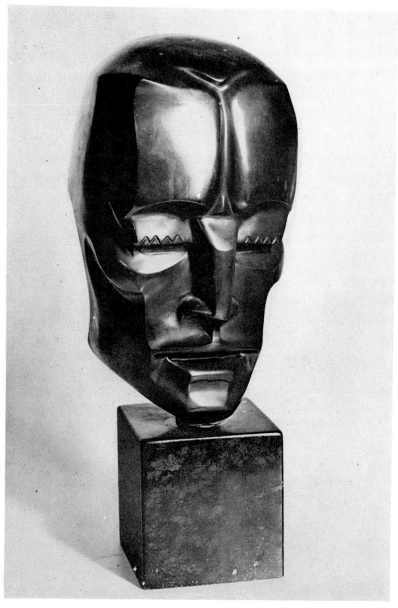

XVIII Hildo Krop. Cuchulain. Mask for *Vrouwe Emer's Groote Strijd*, 1922. Original in papier mâché, reproduced from a replica cast in bronze, in the collection of the Stadsschouwburg, Amsterdam. See p. 274.

XIX The Woman of the Sidhe.   XX Emer.

XXI Eithne Inguba.   XXII Bricriu (The Ghost of Cuchulain).

XIX-XXII Hildo Krop. Masks for *Vrouwe Emer's Groote Strijd*, 1922. Originals in papier mâché, reproduced from replicas cast in bronze, in the collection of the Stadsschouwburg, Amsterdam.

Woman·of·the·Sidhe·

XXIII Norah McGuinness. The Woman of the Sidhe. Costume design for
The Only Jealousy of Emer, 1926. Watercolour. Collection of the artist.
See pp. 246-48.

XXIV D. Travers Smith. *Fighting the Waves.* Design for curtain, 1929. Watercolour. Collection of the artist. See p. 283.

XXV D. Travers Smith. Cuchulain. Costume design for *Fighting the Waves,* 1929. This costume was designed for use with Hildo Krop's mask. Watercolour. Collection of the artist.

XXVI F. J. McCormick as Oedipus in *Sophocles' King Oedipus*. The Abbey Theatre, Dublin, 1926.

XXVII F. J. McCormick as the King in *The King of the Great Clock Tower*. The Abbey Theatre, Dublin, 1934.

Bibliography

Books by or with contributions by W. B. Yeats

STANDARD EDITIONS

The Collected Plays of W. B. Yeats. London 1952.

The Variorum Edition of the Plays of W. B. Yeats edited by Russell K. Alspach United States Military Academy assisted by Catherine C. Alspach. London 1966.

The Collected Poems of W. B. Yeats. London 1950.

The Variorum Edition of the Poems of W. B. Yeats edited by Peter Allt late of Trinity College, Dublin and Russell K. Alspach United States Military Academy. New York 1957.

Autobiographies. London 1955.
> This volume contains *Reveries over Childhood and Youth, The Trembling of the Veil, Dramatis Personae, Estrangement, The Death of Synge, The Bounty of Sweden.*

Mythologies. London 1959.

Essays and Introductions. London 1961.
> Among the contents are *Ideas of Good and Evil, The Cutting of an Agate,* 'A General Introduction for My Work,' and 'A General Introduction for My Plays.'

Explorations. London 1962.
> Among the contents are selections from *The Irish Dramatic Movement, Wheels and Butterflies* and *On the Boiler.*

Selected Prose. Edited by A. Norman Jeffares. London 1964.

The Letters of W. B. Yeats. Edited by Allan Wade. London 1954.

*

PUBLICATIONS ISSUED IN YEATS'S LIFETIME

Mosada. Dublin 1886.
The Wanderings of Oisin and other poems. London 1889.
The Countess Kathleen and Various Legends and Lyrics. London 1892.
The Land of Heart's Desire. London 1894.
——— London 1912.
The Secret Rose. London 1897.
The Shadowy Waters. London 1900.
——— London 1907. (Acting Version)
The Celtic Twilight. London 1902.
Cathleen Ni Hoolihan. London 1902.
——— London 1906. (Theatre Edition)
Where There is Nothing. Dublin 1902.
——— London 1903.
Ideas of Good and Evil. London 1903.
The Hour-Glass. London 1903.
——— London 1907. (Theatre Edition)

The Hour-Glass, Cathleen Ni Houlihan, The Pot of Broth. London 1904, Dublin 1905.
The King's Threshold and On Baile's Strand. London 1904.
—— The King's Threshold. Dublin 1905.
—— Stratford-upon-Avon 1911. (Theatre Edition)
—— On Baile's Strand. Dublin 1905.
—— London 1907. (Theatre Edition)
The Pot of Broth. London 1905. (Theatre Edition)
The Unicorn from the Stars and other plays. New York 1908.
The Collected Works in Verse and Prose. Volumes I - VIII. Stratford-upon-Avon 1908.
Advice to Playwrights. . . . Dublin c. 1908.
Deirdre. Stratford-upon-Avon 1911. (Theatre Edition)
The Green Helmet. Stratford-upon-Avon 1911. (Theatre Edition)
Plays for an Irish Theatre. London and Stratford-upon-Avon 1911.
The Countess Cathleen. London 1912. (Revised Version)
The Cutting of an Agate. London 1919.
Four Plays for Dancers. London 1921.
Plays in Prose and Verse. London 1922.
The Player Queen. London 1922.
Plays and Controversies. London 1923.
[Axel by Villiers de l'Isle Adam, trans. H. P. R. Finberg. Preface by W. B. Yeats. London 1925.]
Sophocles' King Oedipus. London 1928.
Letters to the New Island. Cambridge, Mass., 1934.
Wheels and Butterflies. London 1934.
A Full Moon in March. London 1935.
A Vision. London 1937.
The Herne's Egg. London 1938.

*

BOOKS PRINTED AT THE CUALA PRESS

In the Seven Woods. 1903.
Discoveries. 1907.
The Green Helmet and other poems. 1910.
The Hour Glass. 1914.
Responsibilities. 1914.
Reveries over Childhood and Youth. 1916.
Certain Noble Plays of Japan. 1916.
The Wild Swans at Coole. 1917.
Two Plays for Dancers. 1919.
Four Years. 1921.
The Cat and the Moon. 1924.
The Bounty of Sweden. 1925.
Estrangement. 1926.
October Blast. 1927.
Stories of Michael Robartes and his Friends. 1932.
The Words Upon the Window Pane. 1934.
The King of the Great Clock Tower. 1934.
Dramatis Personae. 1935.

Broadsides. 1935.
Last Poems and Two Plays. 1939.
On the Boiler. 1939.
Florence Farr, Bernard Shaw, W. B. Yeats. ed. Clifford Bax. 1941.
Mosada. 1943.

*

JOURNALS

Beltaine 1-3. Dublin and London 1899-1900.
Samhain (six issues). Dublin and London 1901-1908. (The complete series was reprinted in London in 1970.)
Paragraphs from 'Samhain.' Dublin 1909.
The Arrow 1-5. Dublin 1906-1909.
—— W. B. Yeats Commemoration Number. Dublin 1939.

*

POSTHUMOUS PUBLICATIONS

Letters on Poetry from W. B. Yeats to Dorothy Wellesley. London 1940.
J. B. Yeats. Letters to his son W. B. Yeats and others. ed. Oliver Elton. London 1944.
Letters to Katharine Tynan. ed. Roger McHugh. Dublin 1953.
W. B. Yeats and T. Sturge Moore. Their Correspondence. ed. Ursula Bridge. London 1953.
Irish Renaissance. ed. Robin Skelton and David R. Clark. Dublin 1965.
Yeats at Work by Curtis B. Bradford. Carbondale 1965.
A Tower of Polished Black Stones. ed. David R. Clark and George Mayhew. Dublin 1971.
Druid Craft. ed. Michael J. Sidnell, George P. Mayhew and David R. Clark. Dublin 1972.
Ah, Sweet Dancer. ed. Roger McHugh. London and Dublin 1970.
Uncollected Prose, Vol. I. ed. John P. Frayne. London 1970.

*

PERIODICALS

Irish : *United Ireland, The Freeman's Journal, The Evening Herald, The United Irishman, New Ireland, Sinn Fein, The Evening Telegraph, The Irish Times, The Dublin Magazine, To-Morrow, The Irish Statesman.*

Other : *The Bookman, The Dome, The Studio, The Times, The New York Times, The Saturday Review, A Review of English Literature, Shenandoah.*

The Mask.

*

THEATRE PROGRAMMES

The Abbey Theatre, Dublin; the Royal Court Theatre, London; the Incorporated Stage Society, London; the Lyric Theatre Company, Dublin; Stadsschouwburg, Amsterdam.

*

MANUSCRIPT SOURCES

Senator Michael B. Yeats.

Miss Anne Yeats.

The Abbey Theatre papers in the National Library of Ireland.

Joseph Holloway's 'Impressions of a Dublin Playgoer' in the National Library of Ireland.

The National Gallery of Ireland.

The Estate of Gordon Craig.

The Estate of George Antheil.

*

Other Works

Anon. *The Abbey Row*. Dublin 1907.

George Antheil. *Bad Boy of Music*. London 1947.

Denis Bablet. *Edward Gordon Craig*. London 1966.

Aubrey Beardsley. *Letters from Aubrey Beardsley to Leonard Smithers*. ed. R. A. Walker. London 1937.

F. R. Benson. *My Memoirs*. London 1930.

Eric Bentley ed. *The Theory of the Modern Stage*. London 1968.

Curtis B. Bradford. *Yeats at Work*. Carbondale 1965.

—— *Yeats's 'Last Poems' Again*. Dublin 1966.

David R. Clark. *W. B. Yeats and the Theatre of Desolate Reality*. Dublin 1965.

Convegno di Lettere 8-14 Octobre 1934 : Il Teatro Drammatico. Rome 1935.

Edward Gordon Craig. *On the Art of the Theatre*. London 1905.

—— *Index to the Story of My Days*. London 1957.

—— *Woodcuts and Some Words*. London 1924.

—— Patent Application. *Improvements in Stage Scenery*. Redhill 1910.

—— *Exhibition of Drawings and Models for Hamlet, Macbeth, The Vikings and Other Plays*. Dublin 1913.

—— *Gordon Craig et le Renouvellement du Théâtre*. Bibliothèque Nationale. Paris 1962.

—— Edward Gordon Craig. *Designs for the Theatre*. ed. Janet Leeper. London 1948.

—— *The Mask*. Florence 1908 et seq.

Edward Elgar. *Incidental Music and Funeral March from Grania and Diarmid*. London and New York 1902.

T. S. Eliot. 'The Poetry of W. B. Yeats.' In *The Permanence of Yeats*, ed. Hall and Steinmann. New York 1961.

Una Ellis-Fermor. *The Irish Dramatic Movement*. London 1939.

Frank J. Fay. *Towards a National Theatre*. ed. Hogan. Dublin 1970.

Gerard Fay. *The Abbey Theatre*. Dublin 1958.

James Flannery. *Miss Annie F. Horniman and the Abbey Theatre*. Dublin 1970.

Lady Gregory. *Our Irish Theatre*. London and New York 1913; ed. McHugh. Gerrards Cross 1972.

—— *Cuchulain of Muirthemne*. London 1902.

—— *Mirandolina*. London 1924.

Phyllis Hartnoll ed. *The Oxford Companion to the Theatre*. London 1957.
Joseph Holloway. *Joseph Holloway's Abbey Theatre*. ed. Hogan and O'Neill. Carbondale 1967.
—— *Joseph Holloway's Irish Theatre*, Vols. I-III. ed. Hogan and O'Neill. Dixon, California 1969-70.
Joseph Hone. *W. B. Yeats*. London 1943.

Hiro Ishibashi. *Yeats and the Noh*. ed. Kerrigan. Dublin 1966.

James Joyce. *The Day of the Rabblement*. Dublin 1901.

Donald Keene. *Nō, the Classical Theatre of Japan*. Tokyo 1966.

Edward Malins. *Yeats and Music*. Dublin 1968.
George Moore. *Hail and Farewell : Ave*. London 1911; *Salve*. London 1912; Collected edition, ed. Cave. Gerrards Cross 1976.

Sean O'Casey. *Autobiographies*. London 1963.
F. Hugh O'Donnell. *Souls for Gold*. London 1899.
Robert O'Driscoll. *Symbolism and Some Implications of the Symbolic Approach*. Dublin 1975.
Shotaro Oshima. *W. B. Yeats and Japan*. Tokyo 1965.

Ezra Pound and Ernest Fenollosa. *The Classic Noh Theatre of Japan*. New York 1959.

Patrick Rafroidi, Raymonde Popot, William Parker eds. *Aspects of the Irish Theatre*. Lille 1972.
Charles Ricketts. *Self Portrait* . . . ed. Lewis. London 1939.
Lennox Robinson. *Curtain Up*. London 1942.
—— *Ireland's Abbey Theatre, a History*. London 1951.
—— ed. *The Irish Theatre*. London 1939.

Francis Steegmuller. *Your Isadora*. London 1974.
J. M. Synge. *The Playboy of the Western World*. Dublin 1907.

Allan Wade. *A Bibliography of the Writings of W. B. Yeats*. Third edition, ed. Alspach. London 1968.
Arthur Waley. *The Noh Plays of Japan*. London 1922.
F. A. C. Wilson. *Yeats and Tradition*. London 1958.
—— *Yeats's Iconography*. London 1960.

Notes

Quotations from the printed texts and stage directions to Yeats's plays are not annotated as these may be found in context in *Collected Plays*, 1952, or in the *Variorum Edition of the Plays*, 1966. Neither are cast lists annotated. These are listed, with references to the text, in Appendix B.

Standard editions of Yeats's works are denoted by the following abbreviations:

Var. Pl. : *The Variorum Edition of the Plays.*
A. : *Autobiographies.*
E & I : *Essays and Introductions.*
L. : *The Letters of W. B. Yeats.*
UP : *Uncollected Prose.*

I   a fine native drama of our own

1   *Four Years II*, A. 115
2   *Reveries XXII*, A. 81
3   *Ibid.*
4   *Reveries XXII*, A. 82
5   *Reveries XXII*, A. 83
6   *Reveries XV*, A. 65
7   Quoted in Allan Wade : *A Bibliography of the Works of W. B. Yeats* (London 1951), 27
8   Joseph Hone: *W. B. Yeats 1865-1939* (London 1962), 26
9   Hone, 24
10   *Reveries XV*, A. 65
11   *Ibid.*
12   *Reveries XVI*, A. 66-67
13   *Reveries XXIV*, A. 87
14   *Reveries XXV*, A. 90
15   *Ibid.*
16   *Reveries XIV*, A. 62
17   *Reveries XVII*, A. 72
18   *Reveries XVII*, A. 73-74
19   *Reveries XVIII*, A. 74-75
20   *Reveries XX*, A. 76
21   L. 117
22   L. 117-18
23   *Reveries XXVI*, A. 92
24   *Selected Prose*, ed. A. Norman Jeffares (London 1964), 47
25   L. 43
26   *Four Years IV*, A. 119-20
27   *Four Years IV*, A. 121
28   *Florence Farr, Bernard Shaw and W. B. Yeats*, ed. Clifford Bax (Dublin 1941), xiii-xvi
29   *Four Years IV*, A. 121
30   *United Ireland*, 11 July 1891. *UP* I, 193-94
31   *Four Years XXIII*, A. 193-94
32   L. 108
33   L. 112
34   L. 114
35   L. 207
36   T. S. Eliot : 'The Poetry of W. B. Yeats.' A lecture delivered to the Friends of the Irish Academy of Letters at the Abbey Theatre, Dublin, June 1940
37   Owen Seaman : 'Ars Postera' in *Battle of the Bays*. London 1896
38   L. 230
39   *The Bookman*, April 1894. UP I, 322-25
40   W. B. Yeats : Preface, dated 20 September 1924, to *Axel*, translated by H. P. R. Finberg (London 1925), 11
41   L. 230-31
42   Hone, 108
43   *Farr, Shaw and Yeats*, 19-20
44   *The Land of Heart's Desire* (1912), 47
45   *Plays and Controversies* (1923), 299-300
46   Una Ellis-Fermor : *The Irish Dramatic Movement* (London 1939), 92
47   L. 232
48   L. 236
49   L. 237
50   *A Tower of Polished Black Stones*, Early versions of *The Shadowy Waters* by William Butler Yeats, arranged and edited by David Ridgley Clark and George Mayhew with five illustrations by Leonard Baskin and drawings by the poet. Dublin 1971
51   *Druid Craft*, the writing of *The Shadowy Waters*. Manuscripts of W. B. Yeats transcribed, edited and with a commentary

by Michael J. Sidnell, George P. Mayhew and David R. Clark. Amherst, Massachusetts; Dublin and London 1972

52 *Druid Craft*, 191
53 *Letters from Aubrey Beardsley to Leonard Smithers* edited with an introduction and notes by R. A. Walker (London 1937), letters LXXII, LXXXIII, LXXXVIII, LXXXIX
54 *Druid Craft*, 192
55 L. 278
56 L. 279-80
57 L. 280
58 'Mr. Robert Bridges,' *The Bookman*, June 1897. Reprinted as 'The Return of Ulysses' in *Ideas of Good and Evil*, 1903. E & I 199
59 *Ibid.*
60 L. 280
61 'A Symbolic Artist and the Coming of Symbolic Art,' *The Dome*, London, December 1898, 233-34

62 Lady Gregory: *Our Irish Theatre* (London and New York 1913) 3, 5-7; ed. McHugh (Gerrards Cross 1972) 19
63 *The Trembling of the Veil*, 'The Stirring of the Bones' VI, A. 381
64 *Our Irish Theatre*, 8-9; 1972 edn, 20
65 *Samhain 1901*, 3
66 *Dramatis Personae* VII, A. 401
67 George Moore : *Hail and Farewell : Ave* (London 1911), 45; ed. Cave (Gerrards Cross 1976), 78
68 *Ave*, 1; 1976 edn, 55
69 *Dramatis Personae* VII, A. 401-02
70 *Dramatis Personae* VII, A. 402
71 *Ave*, 40-41; 1976 edn, 75-76
72 *Ave*, 41-42; 1976 edn, 76
73 *Dramatis Personae* X, A. 413
74 Holloway : 'Impressions,' preface, 3
75 Holloway : 'Impressions,' preface, 4-5

2   to restore the theatre of Art

1 L. 308-10
2 L. 315
3 Moore : *Hail and Farewell: Ave*, 94-95; 1976 edn, 105-06
4 *Beltaine* 1, 7-8
5 E & I, 16
6 *Beltaine* 1, 23
7 *Beltaine* 1, 5
8 *Joseph Holloway's Abbey Theatre*, 6
9 *Ave*, 98-99; 1976 edn, 108
10 F. Hugh O'Donnell : *Souls for Gold*. London 1899
11 *Dramatis Personae* X. A. 415-16
12 *Dramatis Personae* X. A. 416-17
13 *Dramatis Personae* X. A. 417
14 *Ibid.*
15 Max Beerbohm : 'In Dublin.' *The Saturday Review*, 13 May 1899
16 L. 451
17 *Explorations*, 305-06
18 *The Countess Cathleen* (1912), 123

19 *Beltaine* 2, 4-5
20 *Beltaine* 2, 23
21 *Beltaine* 3, 4
22 L. 347
23 L. 348
24 Edward Gordon Craig : *Index to the Story of my Days* (London 1957), 239
25 Arthur Symons : 'A New Art of the Stage.' *The Theory of the Modern Stage*, ed. Eric Bentley (London 1968), 139-40
26 Haldane MacFall: 'Some Thoughts on the Art of Gordon Craig.' *The Studio*, No. 102, September 1901, 255
27 Beerbohm : 'In Dublin'
28 Craig : *Index*, 229
29 MacFall : 'Some Thoughts on the Art of Gordon Craig,' 256-57
30 E & I, 97
31 E & I, 101-02
32 E & I, 109

33 L. 351 (to Lady Gregory)
34 L. 351-52
35 L. 355-56 (to Lady Gregory?)
36 *Samhain 1901*, 14-15
37 *Samhain 1901*, 8. 4-5
38 George Moore : *Hail and Fare-well : Salve* (London 1912), 101; ed. Cave (Gerrards Cross 1976), 312
39 Moore : *Salve*, 102; 1976 edn, 313
40 Moore : *Salve*, 102-03; 1976 edn, 313
41 Moore : *Salve*, 105; 1976 edn, 314
42 Edward Elgar: *Incidental Music and Funeral March from Grania and Diarmid (sic)*, London and New York 1902

43 *The Freeman's Journal*, 22 October 1901
44 *The Evening Herald*, 22 October 1901
45 *Joseph Holloway's Abbey Theatre*, 15
46 James Joyce : 'The Day of the Rabblement.' Dublin 1901
47 Frank J. Fay: 'The Irish Literary Theatre.' *The United Irishman*, 26 October 1901
48 Frank J. Fay: 'The Irish Literary Theatre.' *The United Irishman*, 2 November 1901
49 *The Freeman's Journal*, 24 October 1901
50 F. R. Benson : *My Memoirs* (London 1930), 311
51 *Dramatis Personae* XVIII, A. 442-43

3   a return to the people

1   'Mr. Yeats and the Stage.' *The United Irishman*, 4 May 1901
2   *Ibid.*
3   'The Irish Literary Theatre.' *The United Irishman*, 4 May 1901
4   *Dramatis Personae* XXI, A. 449
5   *Ibid.*
6   Frank J. Fay (*attrib.*) : 'Some Account of the Early Days of the Irish National Dramatic Society.' See *Towards a National Theatre* by Frank J. Fay, ed. Robert Hogan (Dublin 1970), 101-07
7   Quoted in Lennox Robinson : *Ireland's Abbey Theatre, A History 1899-1951* (London 1951), 26-27
8   Quoted in Gerard Fay : *The Abbey Theatre* (London 1958), 37
9   L. 368 (to Lady Gregory, 3 April 1902)
10 'The Man and the Echo.' *Last Poems and Two Plays* (Dublin 1939), 27
11 *The United Irishman*, 5 May 1902
12 *Joseph Holloway's Abbey Theatre*, 17

13 *The Collected Works* (1908), Vol. IV. (*Var. Pl.* 233)
14 *The Unicorn from the Stars and other plays* (New York 1908) (*Var. Pl.* 1295)
15 *Plays in Prose and Verse* (London 1922), 433
16 *Samhain 1902*, 9
17 L. 367
18 L. 365-66
19 Quoted in Craig : *Index*, 242
20 L. 371
21 L. 373 (to Arnold Dolmetsch)
22 *In the Seven Woods* (Dublin 1903), 22
23 L. 375
24 *Ibid.*
25 L. 378
26 *Ibid.*
27 L. 385-86
28 *The Unicorn from the Stars and other plays* (1908), preface (*Var. Pl.* 1296)
29 L. 380
30 *Samhain 1902*, 3
31 L. 392
32 *W. B. Yeats and T. Sturge Moore. Their Correspondence 1901-1937* ed. Ursula Bridge (London 1953), 4-5

33 Drawing in the collection of Senator Michael Butler Yeats
34 L. 387-88
35 *The Collected Works IV.* (1908) (*Var. Pl.* 644)
36 *W. B. Yeats and T. Sturge Moore,* 5
37 *Joseph Holloway's Abbey Theatre,* 23-24
38 *Joseph Holloway's Abbey Theatre,* 21-22
39 Lady Gregory: *Our Irish Theatre,* 107; 1972 edn, 64
40 *Plays for an Irish Theatre* (1911) (*Var. Pl.* 645)
41 *Samhain* 1903, 9-10
42 *Plays in Prose and Verse* (1922), 420-21 (*Var. Pl.* 254)
43 *The Times,* 8 May 1903
44 L. 371
45 Quoted in James W. Flannery: *Miss Annie F. Horniman and the Abbey Theatre* (Dublin 1970), 8
46 *Ibid.,* 9
47 *Ibid.*
48 L. 409 (8 August 1903)
49 *The King's Threshold and On Baile's Strand* (1904) (*Var. Pl.* 314-15)
50 *Plays in Prose and Verse,* 423 (*Var. Pl.* 315)
51 *Joseph Holloway's Abbey Theatre,* 24
52 *Joseph Holloway's Abbey Theatre,* 25

53 MS. 13269, National Library of Ireland
54 *New Ireland,* 17 October 1903
55 L. 425 (20 January 1904)
56 *Samhain* 1903, 8
57 *Collected Works VIII* (1908), note to prologue (*Var. Pl.* 314)
58 *The United Irishman,* 9 September 1903 (*Var. Pl.* 313-14)
59 *Our Irish Theatre,* 3; 1972 edn, 18
60 *W. B. Yeats and T. Sturge Moore,* 5-7
61 *Druid Craft,* eds. Sidnell, Mayhew and Clark, 303-04
62 *The Shadowy Waters* (1900) (*Var. Poems* 746-47)
63 *Self Portrait taken from the Letters and Journals of Charles Ricketts R.A.* ed. Cecil Lewis (London 1939), 110
64 L. 455-56
65 *Poems 1899-1905* (1906) (*Var. Pl.* 340-41)
66 *The Arrow,* Vol. I, No. 2, 24 November 1906, 3-4
67 *The Shadowy Waters* (acting version) (1907) (*Var. Pl.* 317)
68 T. S. Eliot: 'The Poetry of W. B. Yeats.' The First Annual Yeats Lecture Delivered to the Friends of the Irish Academy at the Abbey Theatre Dublin, June 1940. Quoted in *The Permanence of Yeats,* eds. Hall and Steinmann (New York 1961)

4 a household of living art

1 *Joseph Holloway's Abbey Theatre,* 24-25
2 L. 371
3 MS. 13068, National Library of Ireland
4 *Joseph Holloway's Abbey Theatre,* 32
5 *Joseph Holloway's Abbey Theatre,* 38
6 *Joseph Holloway's Abbey Theatre,* 38-39
7 *Samhain* 1904, 53-54
8 *Joseph Holloway's Abbey Theatre,* 42, 44, 45, 46, 47

9 *The Irish Times,* 5 August 1904
10 *The Freeman's Journal,* 1 December 1904
11 *Samhain* 1904, 6
12 *Samhain* 1904, 15
13 The Abbey Theatre, Dublin: Special programme for the British Association Visit, September 1908
14 *Joseph Holloway's Abbey Theatre,* 50-51
15 Lady Gregory: *Cuchulain of Muirthemne* (London 1902), vii, xvii

16 L. 369 (to Lady Gregory, 5 April 1902)
17 L. 366
18 L. 376 (16 June 1902)
19 L. 391
20 L. 397
21 L. 424-25 (January 1904)
22 L. 427 (21 January 1904)
23 *Samhain 1904*, 24, 32
24 *Samhain 1904*, 33
25 L. 444-45
26 *Joseph Holloway's Abbey Theatre*, 48-50
27 *Poems 1899-1905* (Quoted in *Var. Pl.* 526)
28 *Plays in Prose and Verse*, 438
29 *Plays for an Irish Theatre*, 221
30 *Samhain 1905*, 3
31 L. 460
32 L. 458
33 L. 468
34 L. 471-72
35 *The Arrow*, Vol. I, No. 2, 24 November 1906, 2
36 L. 475-76 (21 July 1906)
37 L. 481-82
38 David R. Clark : *W. B. Yeats and the Theatre of Desolate Reality* (Dublin 1964), 40-41
39 *Joseph Holloway's Abbey Theatre*, 74-75
40 L. 482-83
41 *The Arrow*, Vol. I, No. 1, 20 October 1906
42 *Joseph Holloway's Abbey Theatre*, 77
43 *Joseph Holloway's Abbey Theatre*, 79
44 *The Freeman's Journal*, 30 January 1907
45 'The Playboy of the West.' *Sinn Féin*, 9 February 1907
46 *The Arrow*, Vol. I, No. 3, 23 February 1907
47 *The Abbey Row* (1907), 3

48 L. 501
49 Quoted in Hone : *W. B. Yeats*, 220-21
50 E & I, 260
51 E & I, 259
52 Copy in the Henderson Papers, National Library of Ireland
53 L. 484
54 *Plays in Prose and Verse*, 426
55 Programme, The Abbey Theatre, Dublin, 21 November 1907
56 Cf. *Var. Pl.* 454
57 E & I, 523-24
58 *The Green Helmet* (Dublin 1910), (13)
59 L. 512 (to John Quinn, 15 November 1908)
60 *Samhain 1908*, 1
61 *On the Boiler*, 14
62 'Estrangement,' XXIII-XXIV. A. 470-71
63 *The New York Times*, 15 January 1933. Quoted in L. 537 n
64 L. 537 (to H. J. C. Grierson, 12 October 1909)
65 *The Death of Synge* XXXVI, A. 522-23
66 L. 533 (to John B. Yeats, 7 August 1909)
67 L. 534
68 L. 538 (to Lady Gregory, 26 November 1909)
69 L. 539
70 *Ibid.*
71 L. 539-40 (29 November 1909)
72 L. 544 (to Lady Gregory, 10 December 1909)
73 L. 545 (to Lady Gregory, 26 December 1909)
74 W. B. Yeats and Lady Gregory: *Paragraphs written in Nov., 1909, with Supplement and Financial Statement* (Dublin 1909), 3-4

5 the condition of tragic pleasure

1 L. 545-46
2 L. 546
3 Programme, The Abbey Theatre, Dublin, 3 March 1910; *The Mask*, Vol. 2, No. (9), January 1910, 148. In the *Mask* printing, the piece is initialled J. S. (John Semar), a pseudonym used by Craig

4 *The Mask*, Vol. 2, No. (12), April 1910, 193

5   Edward Gordon Craig : (Patent Application) No. 1771, A.D. 1910. *Improvements in Stage Scenery*. (Redhill, His Majesty's Stationery Office, 1910) pp. 4, 4 plates

6   'The Tragic Theatre.' *The Mask*, Vol. 3, No. (4-6), October 1910

7   *The Evening Telegraph*, 9 January 1911. Quoted in Denis Bablet : *Edward Gordon Craig* (London 1966), 130

8   W. B. Yeats: Notebook of Scene Arrangements 1910. Collection of Senator Michael B. Yeats

9   Programme, The Abbey Theatre, Dublin, 24 February 1910

10 *Ibid.*

11 *Mirandolina*, translated and adapted from *La Locandiera* of Goldoni by Lady Gregory. London 1924

12 Quoted in Janet Leeper: *Edward Gordon Craig. Designs for the Theatre* (London 1948), 47

13 The costume designs by Edward Gordon Craig for *The Hour-Glass* (1910) are in the collection of Miss Anne Yeats

14 *Plays for an Irish Theatre*, 220-21

15 *Plays for an Irish Theatre*, xiii-xiv

16 Catalogue : *Exhibition of Drawings and Models for Hamlet, Macbeth, The Vikings and Other Plays by Edward Gordon Craig*. Dublin 1913

17 L. 554, 21 October 1910

18 L. 555, 24 November 1910

19 *Joseph Holloway's Abbey Theatre*, 140

20 *Joseph Holloway's Abbey Theatre*, 146

21 *The Evening Telegraph*, 26 November 1910

22 L. 555

23 Programme, The Abbey Theatre, Dublin, 12 January 1911

24 *The Irish Times*, 13 January 1911

25 *Joseph Holloway's Abbey Theatre*, 148

26 'The Tragic Theatre.' *The Mask*, Vol. 3, No. (4), October 1910, 79

27 *Var. Pl.* 577

28 *Var. Pl.* 583

29 *Var. Pl.* 597

30 *The Land of Heart's Desire* (London 1912), 47

31 Quoted in 'Some new letters from W. B. Yeats to Lady Gregory' by Donald T. Torchiana and Glenn O'Malley. *A Review of English Literature*, Vol. IV, No. 3 (London, July 1963), 11

32 *The Countess Cathleen* (London 1912), 123. The whole passage is quoted above, pp. 46-47

33 *The Land of Heart's Desire* (London 1912), 47

34 *Plays for an Irish Theatre*, xiii

35 *Plays for an Irish Theatre*, 215

36 L. 567 (5 March 1912)

37 *Plays for an Irish Theatre*, xii-xiii

38 L. 560 (to John B. Yeats, 17 July 1911)

39 Letter to Sydney Cockerell, 14 September 1911, in *Self Portrait taken from the Letters and Journals of Charles Ricketts R.A.*, ed. Cecil Lewis (London 1939), 166-67

40 Quoted in 'Some new letters from W. B. Yeats to Lady Gregory' by Donald T. Torchiana and Glenn O'Malley. *A Review of English Literature*, Vol. 4, No. 3 (London, July 1963), 13

41 L. 577 (5 March 1913)

42 Quoted in 'From One Theatrical Reformer to Another : W. B. Yeats's Unpublished Letters to Gordon Craig.' *Aspects of the Irish Theatre*, eds. Patrick Rafroidi, Raymonde Popot, William Parker (Lille 1972), 284

43 *The Freeman's Journal*, 19 March 1913

44 Programme, The Abbey Theatre, Dublin, 17 May 1913

45 29 July 1913, W. B. Yeats to Gordon Craig. Quoted in Bablet : *Edward Gordon Craig*, 130

46 *Joseph Holloway's Abbey Theatre*, 246

47 L. 442 (to Lady Gregory, 7 November 1904)
48 *Self Portrait* ed. Lewis, 112
49 *Self Portrait*, 100
50 *Self Portrait*, 196
51 L. 587 (to Charles Ricketts, 11 June 1914)
52 *Self Portrait*, 198
53 L. 588

54 L. 654-55 (21 January 1919)
55 *Joseph   Holloway's   Abbey Theatre*, 206
56 *Plays in Prose and Verse*, 428-29
57 *Plays in Prose and Verse*, vi-vii
58 *The Mask*, Vol. 1, No. (1), 16
59 Lennox Robinson : *Curtain Up. An   Autobiography.*   (London 1942), 63

6   ancient memories

1   *Certain Noble Plays of Japan* (Dublin 1916), xix
2   Donald Keene : *Nō, The Classical Theatre of Japan* (Tokyo 1966), 19
3   Ezra Pound and Ernest Fenollosa : *The Classic Noh Theatre of Japan* (New York 1959), 69
4   *The Classic Noh Theatre of Japan*, 59-60
5   Arthur Waley : *The Nō Plays of Japan* (London 1922), 21
6   Curtis Bradford : *Yeats at Work* (Carbondale 1965), 215
7   *The Classic Noh Theatre of Japan*, 67
8   *The Classic Noh Theatre of Japan*, 9
9   *Certain Noble Plays of Japan*, xiv-xv
10 J. M. Synge : *The Playboy of the Western World*, Act II
11 *Certain Noble Plays of Japan*, 1
12 Cf. Ezra Pound : Introduction to *The Classic Noh Theatre of Japan*, 9-10
13 *Certain Noble Plays of Japan*, xiii
14 'The Play, the Player and the Scene.' *Samhain 1904*, 33
15 Ezra Pound : Introduction to *The Classic Noh Theatre of Japan*, 12
16 *Nō, The Classical Theatre of Japan*, 83

17 *The Wild Swans at Coole, other verses and a play in verse* (Dublin 1917), 44
18 *United Ireland*, 11 July 1891. Reprinted in *Uncollected Prose*, I, 193
19 'The Play, the Player and the Scene.' *Samhain 1904*, 28-29
20 'The Play, the Player and the Scene,' 29-30
21 *The Classic Noh Theatre of Japan*, 15
22 'Speaking to the Psaltery.' *Ideas of Good and Evil*. E & I, 16
23 'Speaking to the Psaltery,' 18
24 *Certain Noble Plays of Japan*, iii-iv
25 *Cathleen Ni Houlihan. Collected Works IV*. 1908
26 *Four Plays for Dancers* (London 1921), 90
27 *Four Plays for Dancers*, 108
28 *The Wild Swans at Coole*, 45
29 *Certain Noble Plays of Japan*, vii-viii
30 *Collected Poems*, 106
31 Transcript by Niema Ash (1960)
32 *Certain Noble Plays of Japan*, xiii
33 *The Wild Swans at Coole*, 43
34 *The Wild Swans at Coole*, 43-44
35 Hiro Ishibashi : *Yeats and the Noh. The Dolmen Press Yeats Centenary Papers VI*, ed. Liam Miller (Dublin 1966), 151

7   I but offer them 'an accomplishment'

1   L. 293-94 (1 January 1898)
2   Curtis Bradford: *Yeats at Work*, 180

3   *Yeats at Work*, 176
4   Shotaro Oshima : *W. B. Yeats and Japan* (Tokyo 1965), 180

5 L. 611
6 *The Irish Statesman*, 6 December 1919. *Explorations*, 256
7 L. 610
8 *Samhain 1904*, 3
9 L. 611
10 Edward Malins : *Yeats and Music. The Dolmen Press Yeats Centenary Papers XII*, ed. Liam Miller (Dublin 1968), 503
11 *The Wild Swans at Coole*, 47
12 L. 651-52
13 L. 702
14 Dublin Drama League programme, 1926. *Coll.* Denis Johnston
15 Sean O'Casey : *Autobiographies II* (London 1963), 232-33
16 *The Winding Stair and other poems* (London 1933), v
17 *W. B. Yeats and Japan*, 51-52
18 *W. B. Yeats and Japan*, 172
19 *Yeats at Work*, 216
20 L. 614
21 *Collected Poems*, 393
22 L. 626
23 *Ibid.*
24 L. 629
25 L. 631
26 *Two Plays for Dancers* (Dublin 1919), vii
27 *Certain Noble Plays of Japan*, xiv-xv
28 *Certain Noble Plays of Japan*, 16
29 *Certain Noble Plays of Japan*, xv
30 Raphael Holinshed : *The Historie of Irelande . . .* (London 1577), II, 21
31 *Four Plays for Dancers*, vi
32 *Four Plays for Dancers*, 129
33 *Four Plays for Dancers*, 131

34 *Four Plays for Dancers*, vi
35 L. 645
36 L. 654 (18 October 1918)
37 L. 788
38 *Joseph Holloway's Irish Theatre*, I, 81
39 L. 612
40 *Four Plays for Dancers*, 105
41 *Four Plays for Dancers*, 106
42 *Joseph Holloway's Irish Theatre*, I, 13
43 *The Irish Times*, supplement for the Yeats Centenary. 10 June 1965
44 *The Irish Statesman*, 6 December 1919. *Explorations*, 254-55
45 *Explorations*, 258-59
46 *The Cat and the Moon and certain poems* (Dublin 1924), 39
47 *The Cat and the Moon*, xi
48 *The Cat and the Moon*, 40-41
49 *Wheels and Butterflies* (London 1934), 141
50 L. 529
51 L. 645
52 *Four Plays for Dancers*, 135-36
53 *Four Plays for Dancers*, 136
54 *Four Plays for Dancers*, v
55 *Four Plays for Dancers*, vi
56 *W. B. Yeats and T. Sturge Moore. Their Correspondence 1901-1937*, 38
57 *Ibid.*
58 *W. B. Yeats and T. Sturge Moore*, 40
59 F. A. C. Wilson : *Yeats's Iconography* (London 1960), 243-44
60 *Explorations*, 44
61 *The Cat and the Moon and certain poems*, 41

8   the symbol of a movement

1 *The Bounty of Sweden XII, A.* 554
2 'The Irish Dramatic Movement,' *A.* 559
3 *To-Morrow*, Vol. I, No. 1 (Dublin, August 1924), 4
4 To President Cosgrave. Quoted in Lennox Robinson : *Ireland's*

Abbey Theatre, A History 1899-1951, 125-26
5 L. 711
6 'What we did or tried to do,' I. *W. B. Yeats and the Designing of Ireland's Coinage*, ed. Brian Cleeve (Dublin 1972), 9-21

7   L. 715 (to Olivia Shakespear, 25 May 1926)
8   L. 720
9   Sophocles' King Oedipus (London 1928), v-vi
10 Sophocles' King Oedipus, 55
11 Joseph Holloway's Irish Theatre, I, 20
12 L. 721
13 L. 722
14 L. 729-30
15 On the Boiler (1939), 28
16 Joseph Holloway's Irish Theatre, I, 28-29
17 L. 894
18 Curtis Bradford: Yeats at Work, 239-41
19 Var. Pl., 900
20 Review by Cornelis Veth in Nieuws van den Dag, Amsterdam, 3 April 1922
21 Review, signed 'Ks.' in Algemeen Handelsblad, Amsterdam, 3 April 1922
22 Ibid.
23 Stadsschouwburg, Amsterdam, Programma Masker Matinee, 27 November 1926

24 W. B. Yeats and T. Sturge Moore. Their Correspondence 1901-1937, 110
25 L. 758-59
26 L. 760. Antheil's settings of Sophocles' plays were not made for Yeats's versions
27 Shotaro Oshima : W. B. Yeats and Japan, 8-9
28 L. 761-62
29 George Antheil: Bad Boy of Music (London 1947), 180-81
30 L. 765
31 Wheels and Butterflies (1934), 69-70
32 Arthur Waley : The Nō Plays of Japan, 73
33 George Antheil : Unpublished MS. score to Fighting the Waves, fol. 16
34 Wheels and Butterflies, vii
35 Programme, The Abbey Theatre, Dublin, 13 August 1929
36 Joseph Holloway's Irish Theatre, I, 50-51

9 a bell with many echoes

1   'The Words Upon the Window Pane. A Commentary.' The Dublin Magazine, Vol. VI (New Series), No. 4, October-December 1931. 5
2   Ibid.
3   Collected Poems, 274-75
4   L. 773
5   L. 776
6   L. 777
7   L. 778
8   Ibid.
9   L. 779 (2 December 1930)
10 The Words Upon the Window Pane (Dublin 1934), 25-27
11 Joseph Holloway's Irish Theatre, I, 69
12 L. 779
13 The Dublin Magazine, October-December 1931, 6
14 L. 779
15 L. 780 (to Olivia Shakespear, 27 December 1930)

16 Ibid.
17 Ibid.
18 L. 826 (to Olivia Shakespear, 7 August 1934)
19 Joseph Holloway's Irish Theatre, II, 35
20 L. 796 (6 June 1932)
21 L. 814
22 L. 817
23 The King of the Great Clock Tower (Dublin 1934), preface
24 Programme, The Abbey Theatre, Dublin, 30 July 1934
25 The Secret Rose (1897), 9. Quoted in Robert O'Driscoll : Symbolism and Some Implications of the Symbolic Approach : W. B. Yeats during the Eighteen-Nineties (Dublin 1975), 26-27
26 L. 826-27 (7 August 1934)

27 'The Irish National Theatre.' *Convegno di Lettere 8-14 Octobre 1934-XII. Tema : Il Teatro Drammatico* (Rome, Reale Accademia d'Italia, 1935), XIII. 386-392

28 *Ah, Sweet Dancer, W. B. Yeats and Margot Ruddock — Their Correspondence,* ed. Roger McHugh (London 1970), 22-23

29 *Convegno di Lettere,* 269

30 *Ah, Sweet Dancer,* 23

31 L. 835 (16 June)

32 *Ah, Sweet Dancer,* 64-65 (25 December 1935)

33 L. 843

34 L. 845

35 L. 846

36 *Letters on Poetry from W. B. Yeats to Dorothy Wellesley* (London 1940), 46

37 L. 868

38 L. 871

39 E & I, 529

40 L. 907

41 L. 913 (to Dorothy Wellesley, 13 August 1938)

42 *Joseph Holloway's Irish Theatre,* III, 12

43 *Ibid.*

44 *Shenandoah,* Vol. XVI, No. 4 (Summer 1965), 7-9

45 *The Irish Theatre.* Lectures delivered during the Abbey Theatre Festival held in Dublin in August 1938, ed. Lennox Robinson (London 1939), 74-75

46 Abbey Theatre, Dublin : Dramatic Festival Souvenir (Dublin 1938), 7

47 L. 913-14 (15 August 1938)

10   I have aimed at tragic ecstasy

1 E & I, 527

2 E & I, 529-30

3 'Beautiful Lofty Things.' *Collected Poems,* 348

4 'The Municipal Gallery Revisited.' *Collected Poems,* 368-70

5 *Ibid.*

6 'Three Songs to the One Burden,' III. *Collected Poems,* 373-74

7 *Collected Poems,* 375-76

8 L. 911

9 'High Talk.' *Collected Poems,* 385-86

10 *Collected Poems,* 391-92

11 L. 368 (to Lady Gregory, 3 April 1902)

12 'The Man and the Echo.' *Collected Poems,* 393

13 L. 900

14 L. 900-01 (to Edith Shackleton Heald, 28 November 1937)

15 L. 909-10

16 *On the Boiler,* (7)

17 'Plays by an Irish Poet.' *United Ireland,* 11 July 1891. Reprinted in *Uncollected Prose,* I, 190-94

18 *On the Boiler,* 13-14

19 L. 917-18

20 L. 921 (to Ethel Mannin, 23 December 1938)

21 L. 919 (to V. C. Clinton-Baddeley, 13 December 1938)

22 L. 921 (to Edith Shackleton Heald, December 1938). The lyric was the poem 'Cuchulain Comforted,' *Collected Poems,* 395-96

23 *Letters on Poetry from W. B. Yeats to Dorothy Wellesley,* 211

24 L. 922

25 See Curtis Bradford : 'Notes on the text and chronology of composition of Yeats's *Last Poems.' Yeats's 'Last Poems' Again. The Dolmen Press Yeats Centenary Papers VIII,* ed. Liam Miller (Dublin 1966), 283 ff.

26 Stage direction to *The Resurrection. Collected Plays,* 579

27 L. 409 n.

28 *Collected Poems,* 387-88

29 *The Oxford Companion to the Theatre,* 783

30 Edward Gordon Craig : *On the Art of the Theatre* (London 1905), 140

31 L. 900
32 *The Oxford Companion to the Theatre*, 518
33 L. 895
34 L. 881
35 L. 892-93 (15 July 1937)
36 *Wheels and Butterflies*, vii
37 *Mythologies*, 47-53
38 *On the Art of the Theatre*, 140-41

39 'Nineteen Hundred and Nineteen,' II. *Collected Poems*, 234
40 Isadora Duncan : *The Art of the Dance*. Quoted in Francis Steegmuller : *Your Isadora* (New York 1974), 91
41 *A Vision* (1937), 276
42 L. 911
43 L. 921

Index

In the index all page references are in arabic numerals (83, 125). References to text illustrations are in bold arabic numerals (**25**, **56**) and references to plates are in small roman numerals (xiv, xxv). Text illustrations may be located by reference to the list of illustrations, p. viii ff. All the plates follow p. 336.

Yeats's concepts of drama and of stagecraft (speech and music; design, scenery, costume, lighting; masks and dance and movement) are indexed under *Yeats, W. B.*, with separate headings.